LETTERS FROM ROUSSEAU

A volume in the series

Agora Editions

General Editor: Thomas L. Pangle

Founding Editor: Allan Bloom

A list of titles in this series is available at www.cornellpress.cornell.edu.

LETTERS FROM ROUSSEAU

SELECTED CORRESPONDENCE

EDITED BY EVE GRACE
AND CHRISTOPHER KELLY

CORNELL UNIVERSITY PRESS
Ithaca and London

First published 2025 by Cornell University Press

Library of Congress Cataloging-in-Publication Data

Names: Rousseau, Jean-Jacques, 1712–1778, author. | Grace, Eve, editor. | Kelly, Christopher, 1950– editor.
Title: Letters from Rousseau : selected correspondence / edited by Eve Grace and Christopher Kelly.
Description: Ithaca : Cornell University Press, 2025. | Series: Agora editions | Includes bibliographical references and index.
Identifiers: LCCN 2024049619 (print) | LCCN 2024049620 (ebook) | ISBN 9781501781933 (hardcover) | ISBN 9781501781940 (ebook) | ISBN 9781501781957 (pdf)
Subjects: LCSH: Rousseau, Jean-Jacques, 1712–1778—Correspondence. | Rousseau, Jean-Jacques, 1712–1778—Intellectual life.
Classification: LCC PQ2037 .A1 2025 (print) | LCC PQ2037 (ebook) | DDC 846/.5—dc23/eng/20250131
LC record available at https://lccn.loc.gov/2024049619
LC ebook record available at https://lccn.loc.gov/2024049620

Contents

Acknowledgments

We would like to thank Colorado College, the Boston College Association of Retired Faculty, and Tom Pangle for generous grants for assistance in the publication of this book. Their support has made it possible to include many more of Rousseau's letters than would have been possible otherwise.

LETTERS FROM ROUSSEAU

Introduction

The usefulness of an extensive correspondence for a biographer is obvious, but one may well ask how much it can add to the understanding of the thought of someone who published as many works as Rousseau did. He himself lamented the desire of one of his publishers to include correspondence in a collection of his works, saying, "What! they want to insert into my works the private letters that I write, and which ought to be seen only by those to whom they are addressed; if you were capable of that extravagance, I would send you the accounts of my laundress and butcher, in order to put them in as well."[1] In fact, his laundry and bakery accounts, along with some information about butchers, have been preserved, although they have not yet contributed much to scholarship about Rousseau's thought. While in this context Rousseau makes the sensible distinction between his public "works" and his private correspondence, this distinction is not always easy to maintain.

Rousseau was acutely aware of the advantages of the literary form of letters and the pleasures that readers find in perusing someone else's mail. Throughout his career he published "works" in the form of private

---

1. Letter to Duchesne, December 25, 1763.

letters addressed to particular individuals. At the beginning of his career as an author, he responded to numerous critics of his works with open letters.[2] The *Second Discourse* contains an important dedicatory epistle to the Republic of Geneva. At the height of his career, Rousseau wrote two important works in the same form: the *Letter to M. d'Alembert on the Theater* and the *Letter to Beaumont*. To these can be added the *Letters Written from the Mountain*, addressed to an anonymous Genevan. During his lifetime, his best-selling work was his epistolary novel, *Julie, or the New Heloise* (1761). This work bore the subtitle *Letters of Two Lovers Who Live in a Small Town at the Foot of the Alps*. Some of the success of this book was owed to the fact that Rousseau left open the question of whether it was fact or fiction. Many readers, in point of fact, assumed that he was one of the two lovers whose letters he was publishing.[3] None of these were works that ought to be seen only by those to whom they are addressed; they are public works in the form of private letters. They show Rousseau's proficiency at addressing a general audience through the medium of the direct address to a particular individual. In a study of responses to the *Letter to d'Alembert*, Bruno Bernardi hypothesizes that Rousseau used the device of the open letter as a way of educating his readers about how they should read his texts.[4] One can apply Bernardi's hypothesis to a work like the *Letter to Beaumont*, in which Rousseau constantly reminds the reader that he is addressing himself to the archbishop of Paris, even to the point of declaring what the archbishop and he would say to each other if they could meet in private.

---

2. Rousseau responded to critics of the *First Discourse* with the "Letter to M. the Abbé Raynal," in *Collected Writings of Rousseau*, ed. Roger D. Masters and Christopher Kelly (Hanover, NH: University Press of New England, 1991–2010) (hereafter *CW*), 2:23–24; the "Letter from J. J. Rousseau of Geneva to M. Grimm (*CW* 2:84–92); and the "Letter by Jean-Jacques Rousseau of Geneva about a New Refutation of His Discourse by a Member of the Academy of Dijon" (*CW* 2:175–79). He also began, but did not finish, a letter to Charles Bordes (*CW* 2:182–85). He wrote, but did not publish, the "Letter from Rousseau to M. Philopolis" (*CW* 3:127–32) in reply to a critic of the *Second Discourse*. To a pamphlet war over the relative merits of Italian and French music, he contributed the "Letter from a Symphonist of the Royal Academy of Music to His Comrades in the Orchestra" (*CW* 7:134–40) and the "Letter on French Music" (*CW* 7:141–74).

3. For a valuable account of the novel in eighteenth-century France and England that treats the epistolary novel, see William Ray, *Story and History: Narrative Authority and Social Identity in the Eighteenth-Century French and English Novel* (Oxford: Blackwell, 1990).

4. Bruno Bernardi, "Rousseau Lecteur de ses lecteurs: La controverse de 1758 sur les 'cercles,'" *Annales de la Société Jean-Jacques Rousseau* 47 (2007): 348. In the same collection of essays, Michèle Crogiez Labarthe applies the same principle of reading to the correspondence in general. See "L'Art poétique de Rousseau dans sa correspondence," *Annales de la Société Jean-Jacques Rousseau* 47 (2007): 429–51.

There is no question, then, that Rousseau was a master of the letter as a literary form. This mastery was maintained in his private correspondence. Indeed, many of the letters he wrote to private individuals were written with a view to possible publication, although Rousseau was almost always careful not to publish any of these without the permission of his correspondent. Among the most notable examples of such letters are the so-called "Moral Letters" to Sophie d'Houdetot, the letter to Voltaire on providence, the letters to Malesherbes, the letter to Franquières, and the botanical letters to Madeleine-Catherine Delessert. In each of these cases Rousseau did, in fact, intend the original letter for its addressee, but he also made it clear that he regarded it as suitable for later publication. All of these letters, as well as others, are cases in which Rousseau made a substantive statement about important issues at the core of his thought. While the original addressees should be kept in mind (as suggested by Bernardi's hypothetical rule for reading), these come very close to being open, rather than private, letters.

When Rousseau made preparations for publication of a complete edition of his works, he sent to his friend DuPeyrou, who was planning to take charge of the edition, a list of the works that should be included.[5] In doing so, he reconsidered his objections to including private correspondence. He declared that he would place in the sixth and final volume, along with various writings on music, "Letters and Memoranda on Various Subjects." This indicates that he regarded at least some of his correspondence as potentially belonging among his published "works." While this edition was not produced during Rousseau's lifetime, DuPeyrou did eventually publish a multivolume *Oeuvres* in 1782 (with a supplement in 1787), which contains 197 letters from Rousseau, along with several written to him, under the heading "Collection of Letters on Philosophy, Morality, and Politics." This title gives a good indication of the sort of topics that Rousseau addresses in his correspondence.

To be sure, Rousseau did not write all of his letters with the intention of seeing them published. Indeed, when he was a young man he would have had little hope of this. It is also true, however, that once he became famous, he wrote knowing that his letters could, or even certainly would, be read by many other people. He learned the hard facts of the matter when he wrote a reply to Voltaire's acknowledgment of the receipt of a copy of the *Second Discourse*, only to find it published

---

5. See letter 124.

a few months later without his permission.[6] A few years later, he withheld permission to publish another letter to Voltaire on the grounds that this would require Voltaire's permission as well as his own.[7] Rousseau's refusal did not prevent its eventual publication, again without his permission. In short, Rousseau quickly understood that even a private letter was likely to go into general circulation. Some correspondents, such as the marquis de Mirabeau, Marianne Alissan de La Tour de Franqueville, and Dom Deschamps, informed Rousseau that they wanted to publish his correspondence with them, and they no doubt were disappointed by his refusal to endorse their project. La Tour de Franqueville refrained from publication during her life but arranged for publication of two volumes of their correspondence after her death. Rousseau would not have been surprised.

There is another way in which even private correspondence was not completely private in eighteenth-century France: public authorities often intercepted correspondence. Even before Rousseau became famous, he had come to the attention of the authorities because of his associations. Although these early police reports did not present him as dangerous, saying only that he was a man of "eminent merit" but prickly,[8] the situation may have changed for the worse after the warrant was issued for his arrest in 1762. Rousseau certainly believed that his letters might be, and in some cases had been, opened, and at one point he instructed his friend DuPeyrou that they should communicate using an elaborate code. The possibility that his letters might be read by the police must have influenced Rousseau's manner of expressing himself, especially when he was writing to people whom he did not know and was discussing the issues that had landed him in trouble. At the very least, this means that he was careful about disclosing his most controversial thoughts in any letter.

All of the considerations given above indicate that Rousseau's correspondence should not be regarded simply as the casual and sincere expression of whatever was on his mind at the moment. Indeed, he indicates that he was constitutionally incapable of writing a casual letter. In a passage in the *Confessions* in which he discusses his painstaking

---

6. See letter 19.

7. See letter 52.

8. The police report was written between 1750 and 1753, well before the peak of Rousseau's fame. See Robert Darnton, "A Police Inspector Sorts His Files: The Anatomy of the Republic of Letters," in *The Great Cat Massacre and Other Episodes in French Cultural History* (New York: Basic Books, 1984), 181.

process of writing, he says that he was unable to adopt a less careful way of writing, even in informal correspondence: "Even writing letters on the most trivial subjects costs me hours of fatigue; or if I want to write successively what comes to me, I can neither begin nor end, my letter is a long and confused verbiage that is barely intelligible when it is read."[9] The cases in which multiple drafts of letters have been preserved confirm this remark. The letters in this book will clearly show the effort Rousseau put into writing them.

While Rousseau was acutely aware of audiences beyond the nominal addressees of his letters, this does not mean that he refrained from expressing personal matters when writing. When he wrote to Voltaire, he wrote as "a friend of the truth" writing to "a philosopher,"[10] but he was quite capable of adopting a more intimate tone when writing to his friends. He also wrote very differently to the men and women (often many years younger than he was) who wrote for his advice or approval. His letters show him in good and ill humor, in sickness and in health. Thus, even when he makes general statements about issues of philosophic importance, the reader must always consider the circumstances in which the letter was written and the particular correspondent to whom it was addressed.

Rousseau's correspondents included famous individuals such as Voltaire, Diderot, d'Alembert, Hume, Mirabeau, Frederick the Great, and Linnaeus, as well as prominent figures whose names are less well known today. No less interesting are letters written to people who are known mainly because they corresponded with Rousseau. For example, he engaged in discussion of theological, political, and philosophic issues with numerous Protestant clergymen and academics, many of whom were a generation younger than he. Not surprisingly, he received letters from aspiring writers who wanted his advice and, even more, his endorsement. Perhaps most significantly, he also exchanged letters with young people, men and women, whom he had never met but who wrote to him about moral dilemmas concerning how to live their lives or bring up their children. Such exchanges, most of which took place when he was a political outcast, show something about how readers reacted to Rousseau through his writings when government, ecclesiastical, and intellectual authorities were persecuting him.

---

9. *Confessions*, CW 5:96.
10. See letter 28.

The subjects of philosophy, politics (including the domestic politics of Geneva and Corsica), and morality are the most significant ones of the letters, but this list does not exhaust the issues Rousseau discusses in them. To those issues, in particular, should be added theological matters that increasingly troubled and inspired readers over the course of Rousseau's career. Young ministers worried over his orthodoxy, and other youthful readers were concerned that he seemed too orthodox. Rousseau also has much to say about friendship in both general reflections and reproaches to those who claimed to be his friends. He also engaged in disputes with publishers over the proper way to publish his books, and with censors who stood in the way of their publication. The detail into which Rousseau went with publishers, censors, and critics shows the seriousness with which he approached making his writings public. This, in turn, means that one should be wary about substituting the letters for the books. Rousseau knew very well what he wanted to say and how he wanted to say it. Nevertheless, he took unusual care to preserve some of his letters and thereby invites us to learn from them.

We have divided the letters into several periods, each section of which is provided with a biographical introduction. The first section covers more than half of Rousseau's life. The second covers the years of his first literary fame, his life in Paris, and his return to Geneva to recover his citizenship. The third covers the period of enormous literary productivity and personal turmoil after he left Paris to live in the country. The fourth covers the period of exile in which Rousseau, having been forced to leave France at a moment's notice, traveled from place to place. The final one covers the last years of his life, after he had returned to France from England.

We conclude this introduction with a few words about the editing and use of Rousseau's correspondence. The completion of R. A. Leigh's edition of the *Correspondance complète de Jean-Jacques Rousseau* in 1998 (thirty-four years after the publication of the first volume) prompted a renewed interest in Rousseau's letters.[11] Among the first to take advantage of this comprehensive edition were biographers of Rousseau. In English, the most notable biographies were the three-volume work by Maurice Cranston and the more recent single volume by Leo

---

11. Jean-Jacques Rousseau, *Correspondance complète de Jean-Jacques Rousseau: Édition critique*, ed. R. A. Leigh, 52 vols (Geneva: Institut et Musée Voltaire, 1965–98) (hereafter Leigh).

Damrosch.[12] Leigh's work has been supplemented by the more recent seven volumes of letters by Rousseau in the *Oeuvres complètes* published jointly by Éditions Slatkine and Éditions Champion (Geneva: Slatkine 2012). Collections of essays by scholars who consider the correspondence from a variety of perspectives have followed. There have also been single-volume French editions of letters to and from a particular correspondent or on philosophic subjects, as well as a monograph on one correspondent in particular.[13] The one significant predecessor of this book, in which a selection of letters is presented in English, is Charles W. Hendel's *Citizen of Geneva: Selections from the Letters of Jean-Jacques Rousseau* (New York: Oxford University Press, 1937). In many instances, however, Hendel provides only brief excerpts rather than entire letters. All of the letters we have selected are presented in their entirety.

This book aims to give a selection of Rousseau's letters, many never before translated into English, that are of particular importance for understanding his thought.

---

12. See Maurice Cranston, *Jean-Jacques: The Early Life and Work of Jean-Jacques Rousseau, 1712–1754* (Chicago: University of Chicago Press, 1982); Maurice Cranston, *The Noble Savage: Jean-Jacques Rousseau, 1754–1762* (Chicago: University of Chicago Press, 1991); and Maurice Cranston, *The Solitary Self: Jean-Jacques Rousseau in Exile and Adversity* (Chicago: University of Chicago Press, 1997); Leo Damrosch, *Jean-Jacques Rousseau: Restless Genius* (Boston: Mariner Books, 2007). Each volume of Cranston's biography appeared after the relevant volumes of Leigh's edition of the correspondence.

13. Chrétien-Guillaume de Lamoignon de Malesherbes and Jean-Jacques Rousseau, *Correspondance* (Paris: Flammarion, 1992); Jean-Jacques Rousseau and Marie-Anne Alisson de La Tour, *Jean-Jacques Rousseau/Madame de La Tour: Correspondance*, ed. Georges May (Arles: Actes Sud, 1998); Jean-Jacques Rousseau, *Lettres philosophiques: Anthologie*, ed. Jean-François Perrin (Paris: Le Livre de Poche, 2003); and Mary McAlpin, *Gender, Authenticity, and the Missive Letter in Eighteenth-Century France: Marie-Anne de La Tour, Rousseau's Real-Life Julie* (Lewisburg, PA: Bucknell University Press, 2006).

PART I

Rousseau before the First Discourse

1712–50

It is not very surprising that we have no letters from the first sixteen years of Rousseau's life, during which he lived in or near Geneva. His extant correspondence begins shortly after he ran away from Geneva on March 14, 1728, a date that he regarded as one of the decisive turning points of his life. Between this date and the "sudden illumination" in October 1749 that led to the composition of the *Discourse on the Sciences and the Arts*, the work that launched him to literary celebrity, there are seventy-seven extant letters. Of these we are presenting seven, as well as one written to Voltaire after the "illumination" but before the publication of the *First Discourse*.

This period of Rousseau's life can be divided into two parts. During the first (1728–42), Rousseau, in effect, educated himself, largely while living in Annecy and then Chambéry with Mme. de Warens. In the letters from this period, Rousseau shows himself to be searching for a career that will provide him with a livelihood while taking advantage of his talents. In addition to giving his thoughts about possible positions, he gives a clear indication of his devotion to intellectual life in a letter to his father, probably written in 1735 or 1736. The other letters from this period show the subject matter of his studies. In a letter to a bookseller, who later published some of his works, he placed an order for a diverse assortment of books, including works of mathematics, novels, and a collection of Cicero's works. His concern with the quarrels between Enlightenment skepticism and religious orthodoxy is shown by the inclusion of both Bayle's *Dictionary* (the masterpiece of skeptical learning) and Archbishop James Ussher's *Annals*, which piously traced the history of the world from creation. The depth of Rousseau's thought on one of the specific topics that guided his studies is indicated by a long letter on optimism, a subject to which he returned in 1756 with his letter to Voltaire on providence. Rousseau closes his early letter on optimism with an expression of dissatisfaction with the provincial environment in which he lived and where he had come to feel that his talents were unappreciated.

The aspiration to find a more suitable environment for his intellectual ambitions led to the second period of these early letters (1742–49), when Rousseau lived in Paris, with a short interlude in Venice. When he arrived in Paris, he had armed himself with a plan for a new system of musical notation and a play. He was convinced that either these accomplishments or others would quickly allow him to make his way. He was able to present his *Plan Regarding New Signs for Music* to the Academy of Sciences but without much success, either with the academy or with his additional efforts to promote his system. Eventually, Rousseau took a position with the Dupin family as a sort of secretary and research assistant. His activity in this position was impressive, although it was not lucrative. He took courses in chemistry, compiled several thousand pages of notes on the political and moral influence of women, and participated in composing a criticism of Montesquieu's economic thought. In his free time, he continued to work on music, composing an unsuccessful opera and even being recruited to work on redoing one cowritten by Rameau and Voltaire.

This last project led to the first of Rousseau's letters to Voltaire, explaining his participation in this labor. Eighteen years older than Rousseau, Voltaire was well established as a leading writer in a variety of genres, and Rousseau had been studying his works since his time at Chambéry. This letter of a young aspirant to his literary hero shows the younger man's admiration for Voltaire, and Voltaire's answer showed his willingness to encourage a novice who acknowledged his own status. There is no evidence that Rousseau and Voltaire ever met, although Voltaire frequented the Dupin family while Rousseau worked for them. Rousseau may have seen Voltaire at these dinners, along with Montesquieu, Buffon, Fontenelle, and the abbé de St. Pierre.[1]

---

1. *Confessions*, CW 5:245.

Rousseau also struck up friendships with men closer to his own age, such as the abbé de Condillac, d'Alembert, and—most significantly—Denis Diderot. He and Diderot formed a very close intellectual cooperation in which, initially, the younger Diderot acted as the senior partner. The two men planned to start a periodical modeled on the *Spectator*, and Diderot recruited Rousseau to contribute the articles on music for the *Encyclopedia*, which was just getting underway. Finally, it was on his way to visit Diderot, who had been imprisoned in the Chateau de Vincennes, that Rousseau read the proposal for the competition that led him to write the *First Discourse*. Rousseau presented the moment of reading the question posed by the Academy of Dijon as a "sudden illumination." The letters written in the years leading up to this turning point show that he had prepared for it with wide-ranging studies. The "illumination" was sudden only in that it brought these diverse strands into an organized system of thought.

Jacques Barillot

Summer–Autumn 1735
Rousseau frequently ordered books from Barillot and his son, particularly after he received the inheritance of a share of his mother's estate in 1737. In 1735 he moved with Mme. de Warens from Annecy to Chambéry.

Sir,

One must agree, sir, that you have a great deal of talent for obliging in a manner that doubles the value of the services you are rendering. I had genuinely expected an answer as polite and witty as could be, but I found in yours things that are for me of a completely different merit; sentiments of affection, of kindness, of an outpouring, if I dare to speak this way, characterized by sincerity and the voice of the heart. Mine is not mute about all that, but it would like to find energetic terms to its taste which, without wounding respect, could express friendship well enough. None of the expressions that present themselves satisfy me on that point. I do not, like you, have the happy talent of bringing together in a dignified way the language of the pen with that of the heart; but sir, continue to speak to me in that tone sometimes, and you will see that I will profit from your lessons.

I have chosen the books from the enclosed list. As for Bayle's *Dictionary*, I find it excessively expensive.[1] I will not hide from you that I am extremely passionate about having it, but I did not count on it amounting to more than 60 livres. If the one you are talking about that has things crossed out in the margins does not exceed this price by much, I will make the best of it. In this case, sir, some precautions must be taken in sending it, because it would be difficult for me to obtain permission to import it. If you judge it appropriate, you could make use of M. who could bring it in and would doubtless be willing to do so if you asked him to; I believe that it would be less suitable for me to propose it to him, as I do not have the honor of being well enough known to him for that. I leave everything to your judicious conduct.

It is the edition in quarto of Cicero that I am looking for. You must have it. If you do not have it, I will wait. I also thought that the *Geometry* by Manesson Mallet was in quarto.[2] If you have it in this form, I will take it. If not, I will do without it for a while longer, since moreover I do not yet have the necessary instruments, and you will send me in its place Ozanam's *Mathematical Recreations*.[3]

You know that we are lacking the 9th volume of *Ancient History* and the last one of *Cleveland*, that is to say, the one that has been added by another hand.[4] We also have only the first two parts of *Marianne*.[5] Please add all this to your shipment, so that our books do not remain imperfect.

Hoffmanni Lexicon;[6]
Newton Arithmetica;[7]
Ciceronis Opera Omnia Quarto;

---

1. The fifth edition of Pierre Bayle's *Historical and Critical Dictionary* had been published in 1734. This work was one of the most significant and radical works of the Enlightenment. Rousseau's remark about the difficulty of getting permission to import it shows how controversial the work was.

2. Alain Manesson-Mallet's *Practical Geometry* was a multivolume work first published in 1702.

3. Jacques Ozanam's work, originally published in 1684, was republished in 1735.

4. *Ancient History* was written by Charles Rollin. The abbé Prévost had published the first four volumes of *Cleveland* in 1731–32. His publisher paid an anonymous author to write a concluding volume. Prévost resumed the novel in 1738.

5. The first two volumes of Marivaux's *Life of Marianne* had appeared in 1728 and 1734, respectively. The rest of the novel appeared in stages from 1735 to 1741. Rousseau later sought out Marivaux in Paris and asked his advice about his play *Narcissus*. See *Confessions, CW* 5:241.

6. Johann Jacob Hoffman's *Universal Lexicon* was a sort of encyclopedia.

7. Isaac Newton's *Universal Arithmetic* was originally published in 1707.

Usserii Annales;[8]
Practical Geometry by Manesson Mallet;
Elements of Mathematics by P. Lami;[9]
Bayle's Dictionary.

If you judge that the *Works* of Despréaux in the edition in quarto can go through on top of all that, you will be kind enough to add it.[10]

Please send me the whole order as soon as possible and I will make my note out to Monsieur Conti for the total following the notice that you will give him or me.

---

8. James Ussher (or Usher) published his *Annals of the Old and New Testament* in 1673, and it was reedited in Geneva in 1722. Ussher's work concerned, among other things, the age of the world, which he estimated was created on October 23, 4004 BCE, at around six o'clock in the evening.

9. Rousseau read numerous works by Bernard Lamy. Lamy's *Elements of Mathematics* was published in 1680 and was frequently republished.

10. Barillot had published a two-volume edition of the *Works* of Nicholas Boileau-Despréaux in 1716.

CHAPTER 2

Isaac Rousseau

Autumn or winter 1735–36

Isaac Rousseau (1672–1747) was a watchmaker. After his wife died in 1712 shortly after giving birth to Jean-Jacques, he brought up his son until 1722, when, after a quarrel that led to legal action, he left Geneva.

Sir and very dear Father,

In the last letter which you had the goodness to write me the 5th of this month you exhort me to communicate my views on the subject of obtaining a post. I pray you excuse me if I took a long time in answering. The subject is important; I needed a few days to shape my reflections and to formulate them clearly in order to share them with you.

I agree with you, my very dear Father, on the necessity of making the choice of a post early on, and of occupying oneself in usefully tending to one's choice. I had already understood that, but until now I have always seen myself as excluded from the absolutely necessary presupposition in such a case, without which man cannot act, which is the possibility of doing so.

Let us suppose for example that my genius had naturally turned toward study, either for the Church or for the Bar; clearly, I would have needed the assistance of money, either for my food, or my clothing, or again to provide for the cost of the studies. Let us also set out the case that commerce had been my goal. In addition to my upkeep, it would have been necessary to pay for an apprenticeship, and finally to find adequate capital to establish myself respectably. The costs would not have been much less for the choice of an occupation. It is true that I already knew something about that of engraver, but besides the fact that it has never been to my taste, it is certain that I did not know anywhere near enough to be able to support myself and that no master would have taken me on without paying the costs of an apprenticeship.[1]

That, in my opinion,[2] is the case for all the different posts that I could reasonably have chosen. I will leave it to you to judge for yourself, my dear Father, whether it depended on me to fulfill the requirements.

What I have just said can only concern the past; at my age it is too late to think about all that, and my miserable condition is such that when I could have adopted a solid course of action I lacked all the necessary aids, and now that I have grounds to hope to see myself advance a little, the age of childhood, that precious time to learn, has passed forever.

Let us then see what would be suitable to do at present in the situation in which I find myself. In the first place, I can practice music, which I know passably well enough to do; secondly some talent I have for writing (I am talking of style) could help me to find employment as secretary at some great lord's; finally, I could in a few years and with a little more experience serve as governor of some young people of quality.

As to the first item, I have always rather congratulated myself on the good fortune that I have had of making some progress in music, for which I am flattered as having a rather delicate taste, and here my dear Father is how I reasoned.

Music is an art of little difficulty in practice; that is to say, in every country one easily finds whereby to exercise it. Men are made in such a way that they rather often prefer the agreeable to the useful; one must handle them by their weaknesses and profit from them when one can without injustice. Now what is more just than to derive a decent contribution from one's work? Music is therefore of all the talents that I may have, not perhaps in truth the one which most honors me, but at least the most certain as to its ease, for you will agree that one does not always easily find entry into eminent houses, and while one is

---

1. The word *assujettissement*, meaning "subjection," was used as a synonym for "apprenticeship" in Geneva.

2. Rousseau used *sentiment*.

seeking and taking action, one has to live, and music can always serve as grounds for expectation.

That is how I considered that music could be useful to me. Here is for the second item regarding the post of secretary.

As I have already found myself in the situation,[3] I know more or less the various talents which are necessary in this employment: a clear and very intelligible style, a great deal of exactitude and faithfulness; prudence in handling affairs that may be within one's jurisdiction; and above all inviolable secrecy. With these qualities, one can make a good secretary. I can flatter myself that I possess some of them; I work every day at acquiring the others, and I will spare nothing to succeed.

Finally, as to the post of governor of a young lord, I naturally confess that this is the condition for which I feel a little predilection. You will begin by being surprised. Please put off deciding for a moment.

You must not think, my dear Father, that I have given myself over so utterly to music that I have neglected every other kind of work. The goodness with which Madame de Warens granted me a refuge in her home has obtained for me the advantage of being able to make good use of my time, and that is what I have done with enough care until now.

First, I devised a system of study for myself that I have divided into two principal heads: the first comprehends everything which serves to enlighten the mind and to ornament it with useful and agreeable knowledge, and the other comprises the means of shaping the heart to wisdom and virtue. Madame de Warens has the goodness to supply me with books, and I have tried to make the most progress possible and to divide my time in such a way that none of it remained useless.

In addition, everyone can do me justice regarding my behavior. I cherish good morals and I do not believe that anyone has anything considerable to reproach me against their purity. I am religious, and I fear God; for that matter, subject to extreme weaknesses and full of defects more than any other man in the world, I feel how many vices there are to correct in me. But, after all, young people would be fortunate if they always fell into the hands of people who had as much hatred for vice and love for virtue as I do.

In this way, as to what concerns the sciences and literature, I believe that I know as much as is needed for the instruction of a young

---

3. Rousseau had worked as a sort of secretary when he was in Turin in 1728–29.

gentleman; besides, it is not precisely the office of a governor to give lessons, but only to take care that they are fruitful. And effectively, it is necessary that he knows on all the subjects more than his pupil must learn.

I have nothing to reply to the objection one could make, on the basis of the irregularity of my past behavior. As it is not excusable, I do not pretend to excuse it. Just so, my dear Father, I initially said to you that it would only be in a few years and with more experience that I would dare to undertake to put myself in charge of someone's conduct. I plan to correct myself entirely and I hope to succeed at it.

On the basis of everything that I have just said, you could still object that these are no solid posts, principally as to the first and third items, and on these points I pray you to consider that I do not propose them to you as such but only as the sole resources to which I could resort in the situation in which I find myself, in case present aid happened to fail me. But it is time to develop my real ideas and to conclude.

You are not unaware, my dear Father, of the infinite obligations I have to Madame de Warens. It is her charity which has several times delivered me from misery, and [she] who has for eight years constantly attached herself to provide for all my needs and even far beyond the necessary. The goodness she had to shelter me in her house, to furnish me with books, to pay teachers for me, and above all her excellent instructions and her edifying example have provided me the means to a fortunate education, and to turn to good my mores which were then still undecided. There is no need for me to emphasize here the greatness of all her benefactions. The bare exposition I am making of them is enough in your eyes to make you feel all their worth at first glance. Judge, my dear Father, all that must take place in a well-made heart in gratitude for all that. Mine is limitless, and see how far my happiness extends: I have no means of manifesting it save the sole one which can make me perfectly happy.

My plan therefore is to implore Madame de Warens to be so good as to allow me to spend the rest of my days near her, and to give back to her until the end of my life all the services which will be in my power. I want to make her taste, as much as will depend on me, by my attachment for her and by the soundness and the regularity of my behavior, the fruits of her cares and of the pains she has taken over me. This is not a frivolous way to testify to my gratitude. This wise and lovable lady has sentiments beautiful enough to find whereby to be paid for her good deeds by her good deeds themselves and by the continual homage of a heart full of zeal, esteem, attachment, and respect for her.

I have reason to hope, my dear Father, that you will approve of my resolution and that you will assist it with all your power. With that all difficulties will be lifted, the post is ready made and assuredly the most solid and the happiest which could be in the world, because in addition to the advantages which result from it in my favor, it is founded on one side and the other on goodness of the heart and on virtue.

What is more, by doing this I do not mean to find an honest pretext for living in laziness and idleness. It is true that the emptiness of my daily occupations is great; but I have entirely dedicated it to study, and Madame de Warens can attest that I have fairly regularly followed this plan, and until now she has only complained of excess. That my taste will change is not to be feared; study has such a charm that once one has once tasted it, one can no longer detach oneself from it; and, moreover, its object is so beautiful that there is no one who could blame those who are happy enough to find it to their taste and to occupy themselves with it.

That, my dear Father, is the exposition of my views. I beg you very humbly to approve of it, to write to Madame de Warens, and to exert yourself near her to make them succeed. I have reason to hope that the steps you take will not be fruitless, and that they will turn out to our common satisfaction.

I am, etc.

Chapter 3

Unknown Correspondent

[Possibly 1738]
It is not known who the twenty-two-year-old Savoyard is to whom Rousseau addressed this letter or whether it was ever sent. It is striking that the First Promenade of the Reveries, *written about forty years later, echoes the beginning of this letter.*

Behold you then, sir, deserter from the world and its pleasures; at your age and in your situation, it is a very surprising metamorphosis. When a man of 22, gallant, lovable, polite, witty as you are, and moreover not discouraged by fortune, makes up his mind to retire out of simple taste and without being stirred up to do so by some failure in his business or his pleasures, one can be assured that such a precious fruit of good sense and reflection will bring neither disgust nor repentance after it. Founded on that assurance, I dare pay you a compliment with regard to your reclusion that will not be repeated to you by many people; I congratulate you on it. Without wanting to highlight too much what there is that is great and perhaps heroic in your resolution, I will tell you frankly that I have often regretted that a mind as precise and a soul as fine as yours might have been made only for gallantry, card games, and champagne. You were born, my very dear sir, for a better occupation. The slightly passionate but delicate taste that drags you toward pleasures soon caused you to see through the insipidity of the most brilliant ones; with astonishment you will feel that the simplest and the most modest ones have neither less attraction nor less vivacity. Henceforth you know men, you no longer need to see them so much to learn to despise them; now it will be good for you to consult yourself a little to know in your turn what opinion you ought to have of yourself. Thus, while you are trying out a different sort of life, you will be making a little examination of your interior, the fruit of which will not be useless to your tranquility.

I would not, sir, like you to give yourself carelessly over to excess; doubtless you have not utterly renounced society, or relations with men. Since you decided by pure choice, and without any regrettable reverse having constrained you to it, you will take good care not to become wedded to the melancholic rages of misanthropes, mortal enemies of the human species. You are allowed to despise it; well and good, you will not be the only one; but you ought always to love it. Whatever they say, men are our brothers, despite us and them; very harsh brothers in truth, but with respect to them we are no less obliged to fulfill all the duties that are imposed on us. Having said that, it must be admitted that one cannot dispense oneself from carrying the lantern enough to establish relations and connections for oneself, and when, unfortunately, the lantern does not show anything, it is surely necessary to treat with oneself, and to take oneself as friend and as confidant for lack of anyone else.[1] But it is necessary to be acquainted with this confidant and this friend, and to know how and to what point one can trust him, for often appearance deceives us, even about ourselves. Now the tumult of cities and the fracas of society are hardly suited to this examination; the distractions of external objects are too lengthy and too frequent there. One cannot enjoy there a little solitude and tranquility. Let us flee to the country, let us go there to seek a repose and a contentment that we have not been able to find amid gatherings and entertainments. Let us try out this new sort of life; let us taste a little of these peaceful sweet things about which Horace, a fine connoisseur if there is one, made so much.

That, sir, is how I suspect that you reasoned.

---

1. Diogenes the Cynic carried a lantern even in the daylight, saying that he was looking for an honest man. In a famous engraving done after Rousseau died, Moreau le Jeune presents Diogenes as extinguishing his lantern upon seeing Rousseau arrive at the Elysian Fields.

CHAPTER 4

François-Joseph de Conzié

January 17, 1740

Rousseau regularly talked with Conzié about literature and philosophy and frequently borrowed books from him. Rousseau returned to the subject of optimism in his letter to Voltaire of August 18, 1756 (see below). Here he shows both his reservations about optimism and his willingness to attack poor arguments against it.

I am most obliged to you, sir, for your kindness in lending me Pope along with *Critical Sentiments*.[1] This paper contains some rather good things; nevertheless, by its neological style, I would take it as being from some member of the Academy, if two or three instances of incorrect language, such as, for example, sparkling ideas "of fire," and death "weighed" according to a certain *style*, did not make me doubt it.

What can one think of a critique which dares to praise the vivacity, the turns of phrase, and the power of expression of this anonymous translation, a contemptible copy of M. de Resnel's; and, everywhere that it deviates from his, loaded with forced turns of phrase and harsh expressions, without graces, without ornaments, and giving the impression rather of the dry recitation of a college professor than the smiling

---

1. The work or periodical to which Rousseau refers here is unknown.

depictions of a poet. The critic may be a very good philosopher, without being knowledgeable in poetry: but in such a case, one limits oneself to reasonings, and one does not meddle with things pertaining to taste.

There are many other reproaches to make to Mr. Pope than those contained in this paper, of which several even miss the target. It is not true, for example, that this author's work is only a tissue of ideas and imaginings, denuded of harmonies and solidity. It is a very absurd system, yet thoroughly linked, and whoever does not see the chain and its consequences should blame his own eyes.

Neither is it true, following Mr. Pope, that man in the general system is inferior to the beast, or even in equality with it. He teaches the contrary in very pompous words.

> What gradation do we find established
> From the vermicules with which the earth is filled
> To man, this chief, this king of the universe![2]

It is a sophism to suppose that man is equal to the beast because they need one another. Reciprocal needs link the master and the domestic, without making them equal for all that.

Everything is linked. Who knows where the chain comes to an end?[3]

The meaning of this verse is very obscure. M. de Crouzas himself declares that he does not understand it.[4] Our critic, who has not understood it at all, charges him because of it with impiety. That is commonplace. The cardinal de Retz was saying one day to Ménage, teach me a little to be knowledgeable about poetry. That would take too much time, says Ménage, but when someone shows you some verses, always say that they are worth nothing; you can hardly go wrong. One would say that most professors give a rather similar lesson to their pupils. When someone makes an argument of which you understand nothing, immediately cry out that it is impious: that will be so much gained.

"Ah! What impious uncertainty!" If the critic wanted to say something by this phrase, it is surely that one must not doubt that the

---

2. We have translated directly from the French version. Pope's original language from the *Essay on Man* is given in the notes. In the original this passage reads, "Far as creations' ample range extends, / The scale of sensual mental pow'rs ascends; / Mark how it mounts, to man's imperial race, / From the green myriads in the peopled grass" (1.199–202).

3. "The Chain holds on, & where it ends unknown" (Pope, *Essay on Man* 3.26).

4. Jean-Pierre de Crousaz (1663–1750) published a commentary on Pope's poem in 1738. In his letter to Voltaire on optimism, Rousseau says that he is unaware of Crousaz's argument, but this remark indicates that he had read it not long after it appeared.

chain of beings ends immediately in God. I dare to defy him to give another turn to his exclamation without falling into gibberish. Now, that being the case, I say that it is on himself that the reproach of impiety must fall.

This is the Gordian knot of Mr. Pope's system, and I flatter myself, sir, that you will not mind if I try to untie it, all the more since of all the critics of this poet, none seems to have paid enough attention to it.

Mr. Pope supposes

> That of the divine decrees wise profundity,
> To the most perfect plan giving preference,
> Must give birth to a world in which its power shines.[5]

This is the hypothesis of all possible worlds, a part of that famous system of Leibniz's which has caused so many disputes; disputes that besides are not about to end, because most of them are between theologians.

Mr. Pope continues and says that this preferred world, that is to say, the one God really created, must be constructed in such a way

> That, even though separated nothing there is disunited,
> That growing by degrees all the way to infinity
> The different beings, without leaving any interval,
> Keep in their progress a just equality.[6]

Here then is a chain composed of all the beings, in which each species occupies its rank in proportion to the degree of excellence and perfection with which it is endowed. For such is how Mr. Pope understands it:

> Roam through, gather all the diverse Beings,
> Begin with this God which gave them life.
> What an astonishing spectacle, what an infinite chain!
> Pure Spirits in the Heavens, men, fish,
> Birds, inhabitants of the earth, and the airs, and the waters,
> Different insects that the eye barely discovers.[7]

---

5. "Of systems possible, if 'tis confest / That wisdom infinite must form the best" (Pope, *Essay on Man* 1.43–45).

6. "Where all must full or not coherent be, / And all that rises, rise in due degree" (Pope, *Essay on Man* 1.45–46).

7. "Vast chain of Beings! which from God began, / Nature's aethereal, human, angel, man, / Beast, bird, fish, insect; what no eye can see / No glass can read" (Pope, *Essay on Man* 1.229–32).

Concerning the links of this chain, we can suspect only two or three of those closest to us still with enough difficulty. For, despite all the pains that Montaigne and Pope give themselves to ennoble instinct, there remains an enormous leap from there to reason, and I highly doubt that their paralogisms can have persuaded them. Nevertheless, we know of no being between the animals and us to fill that interval. From us to angelic natures, our enlightenment is no less limited, and if one agreed with Montaigne that there is more difference between one man and another man than between a man and a beast, that would still conclude nothing until we had also proved that there is more difference between one man and another man, than a man and an angel.

In truth, Cardan would have seen no great difficulty there, he who found within himself such high excellence that he suspected his soul of holding a middle position between human substances and the divine nature.[8] Which makes me also remember Galien, who used to compare himself to the Emperor Trajan, and Paracelsus, who affirmed that one of his hairs was much more learned than all the universities.[9] By the modesty of these three Gentlemen would you recognize them as doctors? But let us come back to our chain.

Let us accept, if one wishes, a proportional gradation from plants to insects, from insects to animals, from animals to man, from man to angels, and let us rise through imagination to the most sublime order of the angelic hierarchy. Do you not feel, sir, that there we are brought up short, and that after having tortured our mind to arrange a very small number of little links, we find ourselves invincibly ignorant about the extremities of this chain?

Everything is linked. Who knows where the chain ends?

Let us push conjectures and hypothesis as far as they can go and let us take as admitted that the vilest of insects, the least organized of all the plants, the most imperfect of all the minerals, and finally the least atom of matter is the inferior link of this chain. The issue is to discover the other extremity. Mr. Pope supposes that it ends with God and says so in categorical terms. He does not, however, suppose this without having sensed its consequences. At least one has grounds to infer this from this reversal of reflection, which in involuntary doubt makes him—or at least his translator, for actually that [phrase] is not

---

8. Girolamo Cardano (1501–76).

9. Galien was a doctor in the second century, and Paracelsus (1493–1541) was a Swiss doctor and alchemist.

in the English—recognize, as if trembling, that God alone knows where the chain ends.

> This chain follows in succession, answer, where does it end?
> Who can instruct you? The eternal power.[10]

This is how M. du Resnel has rendered the passage, based on which you will be warned that it is his translation I have before me while examining the paper in question—which is a matter of indifference here, since it is Pope himself who is being critiqued.

A few more clarifications on a matter that is so important. Could we occupy our minds with a more majestic subject, and one more worthy of all our attention?

To say that the chain of beings ends immediately with God is to uphold a sentiment condemned by religion as impious, and by reason as absurd.

You said (I am speaking to Mr. Pope),

> That growing by degrees all the way to infinity
> The different beings, without leaving any interval,
> Keep in their progress a just equality.[11]

And you say elsewhere that this chain begins where the supreme Being ends, for here it comes to the same thing. That is to say that all the intervals being proportional, there is no more distance between God and the species that immediately follows him than, for example, between the human species and that of the angels; that not only must one recognize a limited interval between a finite being and an infinite one, but also that this interval is no more considerable than that between saint Peter and the angel Gabriel. Either I understand nothing about reasoning, or that is your doctrine.

What will you think, sir, of a system which establishes a relation between things which cannot have any, and which even brings this relation closer so as to give us some idea of it?

You will note that all the reasons one could allege for acknowledging subordinate divinities, and Plato's other impertinent remarks, would never do away with the objection. For one would always press upon them this dilemma: either your subordinate divinities are infinite, or

---

10. "The Chain holds on, & where it ends, unknown" (Pope, *Essay on Man* 3.26).

11. "Where all must full or not coherent be, / And all that rises, rise in due degree" (Pope, *Essay on Man* 1.45–46).

they are not. If they are infinite, in order to link the chain we will have to acknowledge a relation between them and the inferior beings, that is to say, between the infinite and the finite. That is the case you wanted to avoid. If you acknowledge them to be finite, it is still the same case, because from these you still must arrive at God.

A mathematician might be surprised to hear me say that there is no relation between the finite and the infinite. I know that there is one, but this relation being infinite, having an infinite relation or not having any are synonymous terms regarding the question at issue.

Let us conclude that the chain of beings does not end with God, at least not by a proportional gradation. Reason will never find a relation between God and any other being whatsoever, between the creator and the work, between time and eternity, in a word, between the finite and the infinite. If therefore there is irreligion in Mr. Pope's thought, it is when he says that the chain of beings ends with God, instead of saying that the chain of created beings ends we know not where. And the critic, who has tranquilly let this proposition pass by so as to clamor about impiety when Mr. Pope repairs his impiety, shows that he does not conceive what he is saying, and that he judges things without understanding them.

I believe, at least, that it must appear this way. For it is impossible to guess the reasons of an imperious censor who contents himself with deciding without explaining why and who, furthermore, apparently wants that *sit pro ratione voluntas*.[12]

Are you not indignant to see Mr. Pope accused of epicureanism precisely where his morality rises to, and almost puts itself on the level of, that of the Gospel? It is certain that the first three letters contain the seeds of extremely dangerous errors for whoever would put them in the worst light. But as to the fourth, there is no man who is a little sensitive to the beautiful who does not feel his heart warmed by the sublime maxims scattered there. Compare the verses to which the critic attaches himself and which, in truth, are extremely badly done, with these by M. du Resnel which even convey much more precisely the sense of the English.

> Know that all the goods which wise nature
> In bringing us into the light of day, provides for our use,

---

12. "Let my will serve as an explanation" (Juvenal, *Satires*, 6.223).

> The seductive charm with which the senses intoxicate
>   themselves,
> The even more ravishing pleasures of the mind,
> The goods which bear the character of happiness
> Are, health, peace, the bare necessities.[13]

And tell me, sir, if you recognize there the lessons of Epicurus, such, at least, as they are ordinarily represented to us. There is more. The great defect of critics is to attach themselves to particular thoughts which, being susceptible to ambiguity when they are taken separately, cannot be determined according to their true meaning unless they are examined in their connection to the body of the work, and in the place where they ought to be. That is above all the ordinary abuse of all those who judge things superficially, and it is, without contradiction, that of our critic. In order fully to convince him, one would only have to analyze this fourth letter. What does Mr. Pope say there? That whoever is endowed with sound sense and a good heart has the source of happiness within his own means. That happiness does not consist in external goods. That this happiness cannot exist without virtue and without that sweet peace of heart which he calls the worthy daughter of heaven. That, in consequence, vice can never be happy. That virtue delivered to pain still tastes more contentment than vice amid pleasures, for he says so in express terms.

> Prey to pain, alone in its retreat,
> It still tastes a secret sweetness.
> Vice feels less amid pleasures
> Which without filling its heart, irritate its desires.[14]

All of this is repeated more than twenty times in this letter with a power, a vehemence, and a pathos which touches and delights. If those are the principles of Epicurus, every decent man must glory in being his sectarian.

It is true, for example, that Mr. Pope does not absolutely say that virtue alone can make a man happy, and who would dare say it? The

---

13. "Know, all the god that individuals fine, / Or God and Nature meant to meer mankind, / Reason's whole pleasures, all the joys of sense, / Lie in three words, *Health, Peace,* and *Competence*" (Pope, *Essay on Man* 4.75–78).

14. "Without satiety, tho' e'er so bless'd / And but more relished as the more distress'd" and "The broadest mirth unfeeling Folly wears / Less pleasing far than Virtue's very tears" (Pope, *Essay on Man* 4.307–8, 315–16).

Stoics pretended to believe it. When Posidonius was tormented by gout and shouted to his pain that he would never concede that it was an ill, perhaps he was foolish enough to imagine that he would persuade Pompey that his cries were cries of joy. But I am very sure that within himself he recognized himself most sincerely as a liar and a prattler. A Christian that one is tormenting because of his faith would really be very unhappy if the force of his mind and the aid of grace did not bring closer to him, as if they were present, the rewards which will be the prize for the pains he suffers. But what according to Mr. Pope is needed, along with virtue or the peace of heart which is its fruit, to bring to its height man's happiness? Only two things, health and the necessary. Happy the heart moderate enough to content itself with that! It is a sad sight to see men on this earth hasten after honors and chimerical goods and estrange themselves by so doing from the genuine sources of happiness to which Mr. Pope seeks to bring them back.

Regarding Mr. Pope's silence on religious matters, one would have a right to reproach him for it, if it were the case that he had promised a summary of theology. Philosophers are surely to be pitied: if they happen to speak on a few points about the faith, the Sorbonne rises up and asks them with what they are meddling? If they take the course of not breathing a word about it, they are unfailingly called atheists and deists. In truth, fools would be too happy with their lot if they knew what misery it is to possess some reason.

The critic finishes his examination with a sally which one must spare out of consideration for wit and gaiety. In general, one must read his observations with pleasure, almost as one takes pleasure in admiring the brilliance of the colors of the rainbow, even though one knows they have nothing solid about them.

I perceive, sir, that in wanting to write you a letter, I have nearly produced a dissertation. I ask your pardon for it, but in truth it is your fault. Why are you not like the others, and how did you take it into your head to want to be so reasonable? Is Chambéry the country of reason, and when it happens to a man who thinks to meet another one there, is it possible not to abuse such a rare advantage? Some time ago I was at a gathering at which M. Vaucanson happened to be.[15] His automaton flautist was much talked about, and with praises with which he must have been satisfied, if it is possible for amour-propre ever to be. You can

---

15. Jacques de Vaucanson (1709–82) invented a number of machine tools and automata. Voltaire calls him a rival of Prometheus in his *Discours en vers sur l'homme* (1734–37).

imagine that the fine wits who happened to be there did not spare him the comparison with Prometheus with which Voltaire had so pompously treated him. As for me, I said then, my admiration must be all the less suspect since I am accustomed to sights that I dare call even more marvelous. People looked at me with astonishment. I come, I added, from a country full of machines which are rather well made, which know how to play quadrille and faro, which swear, drink Champagne wine, and pass the day spouting lies to other quite pretty machines which give as good as they get. People began to laugh; and what would have amused you is that two or three machines which were there laughed even more than the others.

I hope, sir, that in taking my frankness in the sense in which I offer it, there will be nothing in it to displease you, and that you will pardon it in a man who speaks from experience, and who has several times had occasion to say, like Ovid among the Sarmatians,

> Barbarus hic ego sum, quia non intelligor illis:
> Et rident stolidi verba Latina Getae[16]

I have the honor of being, with a profound respect, sir,

Your very humble and very obedient servant.

---

16. "Here I am the barbarian because no one understands me / And Latin words are the laughingstock of the stupid Getae" (Ovid, *Tristia* 10.37). Rousseau later used the first of these lines as the epigraph of the *First Discourse*.

CHAPTER 5

Charles-Philippe Monthénault d'Égly

February 1743

This is the earliest surviving letter written after Rousseau arrived in Paris some-time in late 1741 or early 1742. In August 1742 he presented his Plan Regarding New Signs for Music *to the Academy of Sciences. After a lukewarm reception by the academy, he published a revised version titled* Dissertation on Modern Music, *intended for a less learned audience, in January 1743. This letter concerns Rousseau's efforts to publicize this work. Monthénault d'Égly was the first intellectual of any reputation to praise Rousseau in print.*

I was preparing, sir, to send you an extract of my work; but I have found one in the *Observations on Modern Writings,*[1] which will excuse me from that effort, and to which your readers will be able to have recourse. M.L.D.F. says that this extract is by one of his friends, who is very well versed in music. It is indeed written as by a man of the profession: I am sorry only that the author has not grasped my thought everywhere, nor even understood my work, all the more so since I had tried to put into it all the clarity of which my subject was susceptible. For example,

---

1. This journal published an extract from Rousseau's *Dissertation* at the beginning of February 1743. It was edited by the abbé Pierre-François Guyot Desfontaines, to whom Rousseau refers below as M.L.D.F. and M.D.F. He translated Swift and Pope.

the observer says (p. 272) that in my system the notes change name in accordance with the occasions; he makes me say it myself. Yet nothing is less true, since the same notes always and invariably bear the same names: 1 is always *do*, 2 always *re*, etc. He has also misunderstood the changes of tone, and for lack of having consulted the examples that I put in my work, he has confused the first note of the song that follows the change of tone, with the first note of the tone. Otherwise, aside from several slighter errors, I have nothing to set straight in that extract. One would wish that the reflections that the observer added to it were a little better informed. It matters little to my system that Aretino was the first to express the sounds of the octave by the commonly used syllables: on the authority of Dionysius of Halicarnassus,[2] I want the ancient Egyptians to be honored for that invention and even, if necessary, for the Hymn of Saint John.[3] I consent, if such is the observer's good pleasure, that all translations be cast into the fire, except perhaps that of his friend M. the abbé; that our numbers are only corruptions of Greek letters; but in the end I do not see how all these remarks bear on the system I have proposed. A witty woman can, even without being a great musician, say while bantering that, if I change the notes of music into numbers, perhaps on the contrary I will substitute notes for numbers in the accompaniment; but, as charming as it is, the witticism is not, I think, solid enough to engage a journalist to cite it apropos of nothing. However that may be, I declare to the observer that I do not intend to fall out with the ladies, and that from now on I condemn everything of which they will disapprove.

As to the incorrectness of my language, I readily agree. A Swiss would not, I believe, act properly in playing the purist; and on this point M.D.F., who is not unaware of my fatherland, could have engaged the gentleman his friend to have some indulgence for me as a foreigner. Even the Academy of Sciences gave the example and did not disdain to compliment me on my style. I know, nevertheless, how I ought to

---

2. Guido d'Arezzo, also known as Aretino (ca. 991/992–after 1033), was a monk and important music theorist who invented or perfected the musical staff. R. A. Leigh has suggested that "Dionysius of Halicarnassus" is a reference to Aelius Dionysius (second century CE), a rhetorician and writer on music, and not the historian known as Dionysius of Halicarnassus, who is thought to be his ancestor. Leigh 51: note h.

3. Aretino used the verses of the Hymn of St. John, written in the eighth or ninth century, to indicate the notes in the scale. Each of the first six phrases of each stanza begins on successively higher notes in Aretino's setting of the verses to music. The scale is drawn from the first syllable of each verse.

receive praises which honor my zeal rather than my talents, and I am really obliged to the observer for having visibly depicted by means of some italic characters the ridiculousness of one sentence the reading of which I myself cannot bear since then. I do not believe that it will ever occur to me to write a second of a similar construction, and such is the use that I claim to make of my faults, whenever anyone will be willing to make me take notice of them.

I do not believe, moreover, that this word *Academy* rouses the observer's criticism, and I am persuaded that the stroke that he added to it, after a rather natural reflection on my part, is only pure banter that he himself feels very well does not mean anything. To convince himself that it is often necessary to speak differently to the public than one does to an Academy, he has only to ask M.D.F. in conscience whether he would not make some changes to his writings, had he only academicians for readers.

Gratitude does not allow me to conclude this letter without thanking the observer for the praises with which he honors me. I believe they are sincere, without flattering myself that I deserve them; for, if on one hand he accompanies them with attenuations suited to making them less suspect, on the other he silently passes over numerous defects no less important than those he noticed. For example, by citing the passage from *Lucretius* that I put on the title page of my book, he copies the mistake that I made through inattentiveness, by writing the word *animus* instead of the word *sensus* of which the poet made use.[4] Now, since one could not suspect an observer who is so attentive about mistakes not to have noticed that one, it is very evident that it is only out of indulgence that he did not note it, not wanting, doubtless, entirely to strip me of the rank of man of letters with which he favors me in part. What seems strange to me is that he explains that epigraph in a sense which, he says, I did not consider, and which nonetheless I had considered so well, that it appears to me the only reasonable one that one can give it in the context.

---

4. Rousseau's epigraph was from *De rerum natura* 5.1412–13: "changes the sense toward what went before." Lucretius is discussing the effect of new discoveries.

Chapter 6

François-Marie Arouet, called Voltaire

December 11, 1745

Voltaire and Rameau had collaborated on The Princess of Navarre, *which was performed at the festivities surrounding the marriage of the dauphin (the future Louis XV) in January 1745. The work was recast and was to be performed under the title* Festivals of Ramiro. *Because both Voltaire and Rameau were occupied with other projects, Rousseau, who had recently written and composed his opera* The Gallant Muses, *was asked to make some changes in the libretto and the music. Voltaire's friendly, if condescending, response to this letter can be found in book 7 of the* Confessions *(CW 5:281–82).*

Sir,

For fifteen years I have been laboring to make myself worthy of your glances, and of the efforts with which you favor the young Muses in whom you discover some talent. For having composed the music of an opera, however, I find myself—I do not know how—metamorphosed into a musician. It is, sir, as being of that profession that M. the Duke of Richelieu has charged me with the scenes with which you linked your divertissements from the *Princess of Navarre*; he even demanded that I make the changes in the framework necessary to make them suitable to your new subject. I made my respectful representations. M. the Duke insisted, I obeyed. That is the only decision that suits the state of my fortune. M. Ballod has taken it upon himself to communicate these changes to you. I applied myself to reducing them to the smallest number of words possible. That is the only merit that I could give them. I beg you, sir, to be willing to examine them, or rather to substitute ones more worthy of the place they are supposed to occupy.

As for the recitatives, I also hope, sir, that you will be willing to judge them before the performance and indicate to me the places where I will have strayed from the beautiful and the true, that is to say your thought. Whatever success these feeble attempts might bring me, they will always be glorious for me, if they procure me the honor of being acquainted with you, and of showing you the admiration and the profound respect with which I have the honor of being, sir, your very humble and very obedient servant.

JJRousseau

CHAPTER 7

Françoise-Louise de La Tour, dame de Warens

January 27, 1749

In 1747 Diderot took over the editorship of the Encyclopedia, *along with Jean Le Rond d'Alembert (whom Diderot introduced to Rousseau at the time of the* Banterer *project). They quickly began recruiting writers for the enterprise, and, toward the end of 1748, Diderot commissioned Rousseau to write the articles on music. In the* Confessions, *Rousseau says that Diderot gave him only three months to finish the articles. Rousseau finished them on time, but publication of the* Encyclopedia *was delayed when Diderot was arrested after publishing the* Letter on the Blind. *The first volume did not appear until 1751. The articles that Rousseau had written during this period appeared in volumes 2 and 3.*

An extraordinary labor that has arisen for me and very bad health for bearing it have prevented me, my very good mama, from fulfilling my duty toward you for a month. I have taken on the responsibility for some articles for the great *Dictionary of the Arts and Sciences* that is going to be put into press. The job increases under my hand, and it is necessary to return it on the set day, so that, overburdened with this work and without prejudicing my ordinary occupations, I am constrained to take my time out of the hours when I sleep. I am exhausted: but I have promised, I must keep my word. Moreover, I am hitting some people who harmed me where it hurts,[1] and bile gives me strength as well as wit and knowledge.

Rage is enough and is worth an Apollo.[2]

I have my head buried in old books; I am learning Greek. Each has his own arms: instead of writing songs about my enemies, I write dictionary articles about them. I am counting on the one being worth at least as much as the other and on it lasting longer.

There, my dear mama, is what would be the excuse for my negligence, if I had one that was admissible with you, but I feel very well that to claim to justify myself would be a new wrong. I admit mine, while asking you to pardon me. If the ardor of hatred prevailed for a few moments in my occupations over that of friendship, believe that it is not made to have the preference for very long in a heart that belongs to you. I leave everything to write to you; that is genuinely my natural state.

In sending you in response to the last of your letters the one I received from Geneva, I added nothing to it of my hand. But I think that what I expressed to you was decisive and could have dispensed me from any other answer, especially since I would have had too much to say.[3]

I beg you to be willing to take charge of my tender thanks to the brother,[4] and to tell him that I enter perfectly into his intentions and his reasons, and that I lack only the means of contributing to them more genuinely. We must hope that a more favorable time will bring us closer to a stay, as the same manner of thinking brings us closer in sentiments.

Farewell, my good mama. Do not imitate my bad example, give me news of your health more often, and pity a man who is succumbing under an unrewarding labor.

---

1. The expression "tenir au cul et aux chausses" (to hold by the ass and the shorts) can mean either to hold someone tightly or to hit them on the point they value most. It is used by Molière in *The Miser*, act 3, scene 1. Rousseau is referring to the composer Jean-Philippe Rameau, who had damaged Rousseau's reputation as a composer. Diderot softened the articles in the *Encyclopedia*, but Rousseau later engaged in an exchange of pamphlets with Rameau.

2. Boileau, *Satires* 1.144.

3. There is no record of either of the letters referred to in this paragraph.

4. This is a reference to Jean-Samuel-Wintzenried de Courtilles, who was Rousseau's successor in Mme. de Warens's household. See *Confessions*, CW 5:219–27.

CHAPTER 8

Voltaire

January 30, 1750

Rousseau wrote this letter after a report had spread that a man named Rousseau had ostentatiously refused to applaud at a performance of Voltaire's play Orestes. The letter's conclusion may indicate that Voltaire had complained about this, thinking that Jean-Jacques Rousseau was the culprit. Voltaire replied that he understood that Rousseau was not capable of such an action. This is the first time Rousseau identifies himself as "citizen of Geneva" in something he wrote. He used this designation in most of his writings and acquired the nickname "Citizen." At this time, however, Rousseau's conversion to Catholicism after he had run away from Geneva had caused him to lose his citizenship, which he did not reacquire until 1755.

Sir,

In the past one Rousseau declared himself to be your enemy out of fear of acknowledging himself to be your inferior.[1] Not being able to approach the first in genius, a different Rousseau wants to imitate his bad behavior.[2] I bear the same name as them, but having neither

---

1. Jean-Baptiste Rousseau (1690–1741) had a notorious quarrel with Voltaire.
2. This is probably Pierre Rousseau (1716–85), who later was on good terms with Voltaire.

the talents of one nor the self-assurance of the other, I am even less capable of having their wrongs toward you. I willingly consent to living unknown, but not dishonored, and I would believe that I was if I had failed in the respect that all literary people owe you, and which all those who deserve it themselves have for you.

I do not want to expand on this subject, nor infringe, even with you, upon the law that I have imposed on myself never to praise anyone to his face. But sir, I will take the liberty of telling you that you have judged a good man badly by believing him capable of paying with ingratitude and arrogance the kindness and decency you showed him regarding the *Festivals of Ramiro.* I have not forgotten the letter with which you honored me on that occasion; it completely convinced me that, despite some vain calumnies, you are genuinely the protector of nascent talents that need it. It is in favor of those whose trial I was making that you deigned to promise me friendship. Their fate was unfortunate, and I should have expected it. A solitary man who does not know how to speak, a timid, discouraged man, did not dare to present himself to you. What would have been my title to do so? It was not zeal that I lacked, but pride; and not daring to offer myself to your eyes, I waited for some favorable occasion to bear witness to you of my respect and my gratitude.

Since that day I have renounced letters and the fantasy of acquiring some reputation, and despairing of attaining it by dint of genius as you have, I have disdained attempting like vulgar men to reach it by dint of intrigue; but I will never renounce my admiration for your works. You have depicted friendship and all the virtues as a man who knows them and loves them. I have heard envy murmur; I have despised its clamors and I have said without fear of deceiving myself: these writings that elevate my soul and inflame my courage are not the productions of a man indifferent to virtue.

Neither have you judged well about a republican, since I was known to you as such. I adore freedom; I equally detest domination and servitude, and do not want to impose them on anyone. Such sentiments are hardly in harmony with insolence. It is more suited to slaves or to even more vile men, to little authors jealous of the great.

I protest then, sir, that not only has Rousseau of Geneva not made the speeches that you have attributed to him, but that he is incapable of making similar ones. I do not flatter myself with deserving the honor of being known to you, but if ever that happiness comes to me, this will be only, I hope, through aspects worthy of your esteem.

I have the honor of being, with profound respect, sir, your very humble and very obedient servant.

JJRousseau
Citizen of Geneva

Part II

After the "Illumination"

1750–56

After the publication of the *First Discourse* in early 1751, Rousseau quickly became one of the leading men of letters in Europe. As Diderot said, the *Discourse* had immediate success "beyond the skies; there is no precedent for such a success."[1] Soon, writers from all over Europe defended learning against Rousseau's criticism. Over the next year and a half, Rousseau's responses to critics made him even more famous. His fame helped him to arrange for a performance, and then the publication, of his play *Narcissus*. In the midst of this controversy over the *Discourse*, his opera *The Village Soothsayer* enjoyed astonishing success. In 1753, Rousseau participated in a pamphlet war over the relative merits of French and Italian music and began work on the *Discourse on the Origin of Inequality*. There are about 130 extant letters from this period. Of these we are presenting 18.

The success of the *Discourse* and his enthusiasm for the principles expressed in it led Rousseau to leave his employment with the Dupin family and to try to live independently. Around this time he wrote a letter explaining why he had his newborn children brought to the newly constructed foundling hospital. Many of the letters from this

---

1. *CW* 5:304.

period, however, articulate Rousseau's responses to the reactions to his works. After responding vigorously to attacks on the *First Discourse*, he decided not to engage in print with those that also followed the *Second Discourse*. The publication of the latter work also corresponded to Rousseau's trip to Geneva to reacquire the citizenship he had lost when he converted to Catholicism in 1728. While he had become famous for identifying himself as a citizen of Geneva since his letter to Voltaire in 1750, he did not regain the legal status of Genevan citizen until 1754. His reintegration into Geneva was complicated by the boldness of the *Second Discourse* and especially by its dedication to Geneva (officially written before his arrival there and published after his departure). On that trip, he also established relations with a number of Genevans, with whom he began exchanges of letters that went on for years. Among the most important of these correspondents were three relatively young Genevan clergymen—Jacob Vernes, Paul Moultou, and Antoine-Jacques Roustan—as well as the older Jean Perdriau. At first, Rousseau's warmest relations were with Vernes, but the two ultimately broke over the religious sentiments expressed in *Julie* and especially in *Emile*.

Upon his return to Paris, Rousseau gave some thought to moving permanently to Geneva, but these plans were forestalled when his friend Mme. d'Épinay offered him residence in the Hermitage, a house she had constructed on her estate. In a letter to Malesherbes from 1762, Rousseau says that with this move to the country, "I began to live only on April 9, 1756" (letter 71). His rejection of the social world of Paris in favor of the country only served to add to Rousseau's notoriety.

Chapter 9

Academicians of Dijon

July 20, 1750

In October 1749, Rousseau read the announcement of the Academy of Dijon's contest on the question "Has the restoration of the sciences and arts tended to purify morals?" while he was on the way to visit Diderot, who was imprisoned in the Chateau de Vincennes. On July 9 of the following year, the academy announced that he had won the prize.

Gentlemen,

You honor me with a prize for which I competed without aspiring to it, and which is all the dearer to me since I expected it less. Preferring your esteem to your rewards, I dared to sustain before you against your own interests the stand that I believed to be that of truth, and your generosity in crowning my courage is crowned even more itself. Yes, Gentlemen, what you have done for glory is a laurel added to your own. Plenty of other judgments will honor your enlightenment; it is to this one that it belongs to honor your integrity.

I am, with profound respect, Gentlemen, your very humble and very obedient servant.

JJRousseau

CHAPTER 10

Suzanne Dupin de Francueil

April 20, 1751

Shortly after the publication of the First Discourse *at the beginning of 1751, Rousseau left his position as secretary and research assistant with the Dupin family. Rousseau wrote this letter to the wife of his employer's son the year after he had his third child (out of an eventual five) put into a foundling hospital. Rousseau kept a copy of this letter in his papers, rendered in a numerical code much simpler than ones he had used in Venice and was to use later.*

Yes, madam, I have put my children in the Foundling Hospital. I have entrusted the establishment made for that purpose with their support. If my poverty and my ills deprive me of the power of carrying out such a dear care, it is a misfortune for which I ought to be pitied, and not a crime with which to reproach me. I owe them sustenance; I have procured it for them better or at least more securely than I would have been able to do so myself. This point is above everything else. Next comes the consideration of their mother, who must not be dishonored.

You are acquainted with my situation; I earn my bread from day to day with difficulty enough. How would I feed a family in addition? And if I were constrained to have recourse to the profession of author, how would domestic cares and the bother of children leave me in my garret the tranquility of mind necessary to do lucrative work? Writings dictated by hunger hardly bring in anything and this resource is soon exhausted. Thus, it would be necessary to have recourse to protection, to intrigue, to tricks, to court some low employment, to turn it to account by the ordinary means; otherwise it will not feed me and will soon be taken away from me. In sum, to abandon myself to every infamy for which I am filled with such a just horror. To feed myself, my children, and their mother with the blood of the poor! No, madam, it would be better for them to be orphans than to have a rogue for a father.

Overwhelmed by a painful and mortal malady, I can no longer hope for a long life. Were I able to support these unfortunate people who are destined to suffer during my life, one day they would pay dearly for the advantage of having been kept up a little more delicately than they could be where they are. Their mother, victim of my indiscreet zeal, burdened by her own shame and her own needs, almost as much of a valetudinarian as I am and even less in a condition to feed them, will be forced to abandon them to themselves, and I do not see anything for them but the alternative of making themselves into bootblacks or bandits, which soon comes down to the same thing. At least if their status were legitimate, they could find resources more easily; but since they must carry the dishonor of their birth and that of their poverty at the same time, what will become of them?

Why did I not marry, you will say to me? Ask your unjust laws, madam. It did not suit me to enter into an eternal contract, and one will never prove to me that any duty obliges me to do so. What is certain is that I did nothing of the sort and that I do not want to do anything of the sort. One must not have children when one cannot feed them. Excuse me, madam, nature wants one to have them, since the earth produces enough to feed the whole world; but it is the social station of the rich, it is your station that steals from mine my children's bread. Nature also wants one to provide for their sustenance; this is what I have done. If a refuge for them did not exist, I would do my duty and resolve to die of hunger myself rather than not feed them.

Does this expression "Foundling Hospital" give you the impression that they found these children in the streets exposed to perish if chance does not save them? Rest assured that you would not have any more horror than I would for the unworthy father who could resolve upon that barbarism; it is too far from my heart for me to deign to justify myself for it. There are established rules. Inform yourself about what they are, and you will know that the children leave the hands of the midwife only to pass into those of a nurse. I know that these children are not brought up delicately; so much the better for them, they become more robust for it. They are not given anything superfluous, but they have what is necessary; they are not made into gentlemen, but peasants or workers. I do not see anything in this manner of bringing them up that I would not choose for my own, were I the master of doing so. I would not at all prepare them by means of softness for the maladies that fatigue and the inclemency of air give to those who are not made for them. They would not learn either how to dance or to get on a horse, but they would have good indefatigable legs. I would not make them into either authors or office workers. I would not train them to handle the pen, but the plough, the file, or the plane, instruments that make one lead a healthy, laborious, innocent life which one never abuses to do evil, and which does not attract enemies when one does good. That is what they are destined for by the rustic education they are being given. They will be happier than their father.

I am deprived of the pleasure of seeing them and have never savored the sweetness of paternal embraces. Alas. I have already told you; I do not see anything in this but something to feel sorry about, and I am delivering them from poverty at my expense. In his republic Plato wanted all the children to be brought up in such a way that each would remain unknown to his father and all would be children of the State. But this education appears low and base. There is the great crime, that is what impresses you as it does other people, and you do not see that by always following the prejudices of society you take for the dishonor of vice what is only that of poverty.

CHAPTER 11

Abbé Antoine Cordonnier de l'Étang

Spring 1752

At last, my dear abbé, behold you a curate: I rejoice for it with all my heart and am charmed at having been *vates* for you in every respect.[1] Please believe that my friendship can stand the test of fortune. Despite my disdain for all titles and for the fools who bear them, despite my hatred for everything that is called positions and for the rogues who occupy them, I believe that I could even see you become a bishop without ceasing to love you.

Enough others will pay you compliments, without caring about you. But as I am your friend, I want to give you advice. I believe that I am showing you my attachment better by that than by lavishing all the praises that flattery does not dare to refuse to those who are unworthy of it, but which propriety prohibits toward those who deserve them. I will be Gros Jean if you wish;[2] but unfortunately for the people, there are many fewer such Gros Jeans than curates who might need them.

Behold you free at last, that is to say, subject to a single master, although the most imperious of all, which is duty. For although the

---

1. *Vates* is Latin for "seer."
2. Gros Jean is an ignoramus who gives advice to, or censures, those who know things.

yoke of reason is less subject to caprice, it is no less harsh than the tyranny of men, and there is no slave who has more trouble satisfying his master than a decent man finds in satisfying himself. It is even worse when one has other people under one's supervision. Then the freedom is only apparent; it is enough for the free man to have to govern himself, but whoever commands others necessarily has engagements to fulfill, and is no less subject than those very people who obey him.

Of all the sad bonds that attach a man who is above others, yours appears to me to be the most bearable. You are going to be beneficent by station, a pacific magistrate, a father; you will have the right to do all the good you want without anyone daring to find it bad, and no one will have the power to constrain you to do evil.

These prerogatives, sir, are great, rare, and perhaps belong only to a country curate. For, aside from the fact that city curates appear to me already rather great lords to be decent people, they are too far from finding in their parishioners the simplicity, the docility necessary to be able to make them live wisely.

CHAPTER 12

Charles Borde

May 1753

Borde replied to the First Discourse *with the* Discourse on the Advantages of the Sciences and the Arts, *to which Rousseau responded with his* Final Reply. *Borde then returned to the attack with a* Second Discourse on the Benefits of the Sciences and Arts. *Rousseau began, but did not complete, a second response.*

I prefer, sir, to write you a short letter than to be in the wrong with you any longer. I am languishing, as you know; moreover, M. de Gauffe-court might have told you how lazy I am about writing to my friends, for I do not write at all to others. Thus, my temperament accuses me but my sentiments justify me. They have not changed about you. I have forgotten neither your kindnesses to me nor my attachment for you; and our literary dispute has not caused the slightest alteration in my heart. Our common friends may have spoken to you about how I think about this and besides, you ought to believe me, so I will no longer insist upon that.

I have heard about your last reply to M. Duclos who has read it, and who thinks very well of it.[1] I am grateful for the promise you made to send it to me. You are, of all those who have entered into the lists, the only adversary of whom I was afraid, or rather the only one from whom I hoped for new enlightenment. For despite the heat that I put into the dispute, I swear to you that I have no other genuine side than that of the truth, and that I am ready to abandon my own side as soon as anyone makes me see that I am wrong. But to conceal nothing from you, I have meditated upon my subject so much that I believe I have foreseen all the objections, and there is not one of them, according to me, that does not have an unanswerable solution. I therefore do not at all promise you not to respond, or to respond politely, but I do promise you very willingly, not to do so without informing the public about my feelings for an adversary whom I esteem and whom I love.

You congratulate me upon the choice of my friends, and you are right. Never has a man been luckier than I in that regard, and yet I would believe that I am more so, if you were to come to Paris to enlarge our little society. Good day, sir.

Rousseau

---

1. Charles Pinot Duclos (1704–72) had written *Considerations on the Morals of this Century* (1751). Rousseau dedicated his opera *The Village Soothsayer* to him.

Chapter 13

Élie-Catherine Fréron

[End of 1753]
Rousseau is replying to an article that Fréron had published in Letters on Some Writings of This Time, *in which he mentions the* Letter of a Hermit to J. J. Rousseau. *A part of the issue here concerns whether publishing anonymously allows one to write more frankly, as Fréron argues, or whether it encourages dishonesty, as Rousseau claims. Rousseau does not seem to have sent this letter.*

Since you judge it appropriate, sir, to make common cause with the Author of the *Letter of a Hermit to J. J. Rousseau*, you will find it very good that this response is also common to the two of you. As for him, if such an association offends him, he ought not to hold it against anyone but himself, and his hardly honest behavior has very well deserved this humiliation.

You are right to say that the false hermit has put on the mask. In fact, he has put it on in more than one manner, but I hardly conceive how this artifice has given him the right to speak to me with more frankness. For I admit to you that in my eyes that gives him much less the appearance of a frank man that that of a scoundrel and a coward who seeks to take cover so as to do harm with impunity; but he has deceived himself. Public disdain has sufficed as my vengeance, and from all that I have lost only a very sweet sentiment, which is the esteem that I believed I owed to an honest man.[1]

I do not intend to undertake the defense of the *Devin du Village* against him. More than anyone else, a Hermit ought to be allowed to speak badly about Opera, and I do not expect that you would be the one to disapprove of anyone arrogantly passing judgment about the things he knows the least.

The comparison of J. J. Rousseau with a pretty woman seems utterly amusing to me; it put me in such a good mood that I want, this time, to take the ladies' side. I would ask you, first, what gives you the right to conclude against her that allowing herself to be seen taking a walk constitutes proof that she desires to please, if she does not, for that matter, give any mark of this desire. The pretty woman would be even better justified if, with this supposed taste for taking delight in herself, it was impossible for her to see herself without showing herself, and the unique mirror was, for example, in the public square. For then it is evident that to satisfy her own curiosity it would be very necessary for her to reveal her face to that of others, without one being able to accuse her of having sought to please them, unless an air of coquetry and all the simpering of conceited women showed the design to do so. It therefore remains, for both the Hermit and you, sir, to tell us the steps that J. J. Rousseau has taken to captivate the benevolence of the Spectators, the cabals he has formed, his flatteries of the public, the court he has paid to grandees and women, the efforts he has given himself to gain advocates and partisans; or you will have to explain what means a private man could use to see his work at the theater without letting it be seen by the public at the same time. For I could not have the opera played for myself alone behind closed doors as Lully did.[2] I find this additional difference in the parallel, that one does not adorn oneself for oneself alone, and the most beautiful woman relegated forever alone in a desert would not even think there about grooming herself, while a lover of music could be alone in the world, and not leave off enjoying himself very much at the performance of an opera. That, sir, is my response, to you and your comrade, in the pretty woman's name and in my own. Moreover, a hermit who talks about nothing but women,

1. Rousseau's note: "The so-called hermit was a M. de Bonneval, a good enough man, and who did not lack erudition. I had had some relations with him and never any problems."

2. Rousseau's note: "This is how Lully had his opera *Armide* played once, seeing that it was not succeeding. He applauded himself loudly upon leaving; the place was full at the following performance."

about grooming, and about opera, hardly gives a better opinion of his virtue than the behavior of yours gives of his character and his letter gives of his intelligence.

You reproach me, sir, for a crime in which I glory and which I am seeking to aggravate day by day. It is not, doubtless, easy for you to conceive how one can enjoy one's own esteem. But so that you might not fail, either the Hermit or you, to give such a sentiment those qualifications that are so menacing that you do not even dare to name them, I declare to you once again very publicly that I esteem myself very much, and that I do not despair of managing to esteem myself even more. As for the praises that some would like to give me and which you in advance make into a crime for me, why would I not consent to them? I surely consent to your insults, and you see well enough that there is hardly more modesty in one of these consents than in the other. By reproaching me for my pride you force me to have some; for even if, by the way, one were the most modest of all men, how could one not presume a little too much on oneself upon receiving the same honors as the Voltaires, the Montesquieus, and all the illustrious men of the century, of whom your satires are the eulogy, almost as much as their own writings. So I believe I owe you thanks and not reproaches for having assented to my prayer, when, persuaded along with the whole public that your praises dishonor a man of letters, I had you asked by one of your friends to spare me on this point, leaving you all freedom with regard to insults. If, in accordance with your custom, you had limited yourself to that, I would never have responded to you. By repulsing the little and new attack that you made against the truths that I have demonstrated, however, one can charitably highlight your invectives, as one puts hay on the horn of a nasty bull.

The only thing that makes me angry about our petty entanglements is the harm they are going to do to my enemies. Young scribblers, who hope to make a name for yourselves only at the expense of mine, all your insults of me are forgotten in advance and I pardon them as the giddiness of your age; but the hermit's example assures me of my vengeance. It will be cruel without me getting mixed up in it, and I give you over to M. Fréron's praises.

I return to you, sir, and since you want me to, I am going to try to clarify with you some ideas relative to a question pending before the public for a long time. You complain that this question has become boring and too trite. You must believe it; for no one has labored more than you to cause that to be true.

As for me, without going back over demonstrated truths, I will content myself with examining the ingenious and new problem that you have imagined on this subject. That is, to engage some academy to propose this interesting question: "Whether daylight has contributed to purifying morals?" After which, taking the negative, you will say some extremely fine things in favor of darkness and blindness, you will praise the method of running with eyes closed in the most unknown country, of renouncing all light in order to consider objects, in a word, like the bobtailed Fox who wanted everyone else to cut off their tails, you will exhort everyone literally to deprive himself of the organ that you figuratively lack.[3]

Based on the tone that they tell me reigns in your little sheets, I judge that you must have applauded yourself very much for having been able to turn to ridicule one of the most serious questions that can be debated. But you have already given your proofs, and after having so agreeably joked about the *Spirit of the Laws*, it is not difficult to do as much about any subject whatsoever. On this occasion, I found your joke to be rather good and I think that, in general, if that is the only weapon you dare to handle, you sometimes make use of it with enough skill to wound merit and truth. But find it good that, while leaving the laughers to you, I claim the friends of reason; especially since, what would you do with those people on your side?

You find then, sir, that science is to the mind what light is to the body. Nevertheless, in taking these words in your own sense I see this difference, that without the use of eyes men could neither conduct themselves nor live. Whereas with the help of reason alone and the simplest observations of the senses, they can easily do without all study. The earth was peopled and the human species continued to exist before there was any question of any of these fine sorts of knowledge. Do you believe that it would continue to exist in an eternal darkness? It is reason, but not science, that is to the mind what sight is to the body.

Another no less important difference is that although light is a necessary condition without which the things about which you are speaking would not be done, one cannot say in any way that daylight is the cause of those things, whereas I have showed how the sciences are the cause of the ills that I attribute to them. Although fire burns a combustible body that it touches, it does not follow that light burns a combustible body that it illuminates. That, however, is the conclusion that you draw.

---

3. This example is from La Fontaine, *Fables*, 5.5.

If you had taken the trouble to read the writings that you do me the honor of despising and that you must at least hate extremely, for they are by an enemy of the wicked, you would have seen in them a constant distinction between the numerous stupidities that we honor with the name of Science—those, for example, with which your collections are full—and the real knowledge of the truth. You would have seen in them, from the enumeration of the evils caused by the former, how dangerous their cultivation is and, from the examination of the mind of man, how incapable it is of the second, unless it is in things immediately necessary to his preservation, about which the coarsest peasant knows at least as much as the best philosopher. So that in order to put some appearance of parity between the two questions, you ought to assume not only an illusory and deceitful daylight, which shows things only under a false appearance, but also a vice in the visual organ which alters the sensation of light, shapes, and colors; and then you would have found that in fact it would be better to remain in an eternal darkness than to see how to conduct oneself only in order to go break one's nose against rocks, or wallow in the mire, or bite and rend all the decent people one could reach. The comparison of daylight suits natural reason, whose pure and beneficent light illuminates and guides men; science can be better compared to those will-o'-the-wisps which, they say, seem to illuminate passersby only to lead them to precipices.

Filled with a sincere admiration for those rare geniuses whose immortal writings and pure and decent morals illuminate and instruct the universe, every day I notice more and more the danger there is in tolerating that heap of scribblers who do not dishonor literature any less by means of the praises they give it than by the manner in which they cultivate it. If all men were Montesquieus, Buffons, Ducloses, et al., I would ardently desire that they cultivate all the Sciences so that the human species would be only a society of wise Men. But you, sir, who doubtless are so modest since you reproach me so much for my pride, you will willingly agree, I am sure, that if all men were Frérons, their books would not offer extremely useful teachings, nor would their character offer a very amiable society.

Do not fail, sir, I beg you, when your Piece has won the prize, to enter these little clarifications into the Preface. In the meantime, I wish you many laurels. But if in the career you are going to follow, success does not live up to your expectation, refrain from deciding, as you say, to envelop yourself in your own esteem, for in it you would have a bad coat.

CHAPTER 14

Lancelot, comte de Turpin de Crissé

May 12, 1754

The comte had sent Rousseau a copy of Philosophic and Literary Amusements of Two Friends, *which he had written with Jean Castillon. The first piece in the collection was a letter in verse addressed to M.J.J.R.D.G (Monsieur Jean-Jacques Rousseau of Geneva). The letter urged Rousseau to renounce his misanthropy.*

In giving you my thanks, sir, for the collection that you sent me, I would add some for the epistle that is at its head and that it is claimed is addressed to me, if the lesson it contains were not spoiled by the praise that accompanies it and that I want to hasten to forget, in order to have no reproach to make to you.

As for the lesson, I find its maxims very sensible; they only lack, it seems to me, a more precise application. I would have to change mood and character strangely if the duties of humanity ever ceased to be dear to me, under the pretext that men are wicked. I punish neither myself nor anyone else by denying myself a too numerous society. I free the others of the sad spectacle of a man who suffers or of an importunate observer, and I free myself of the bother of relations with many people about whom happily I would know nothing but the names. I am not at all subject to the boredom with which you reproach me; and if I feel it sometimes, it is only in fine gatherings, where I have the honor of finding myself very out of place in every way. The only society that has appeared desirable to me is the one that one maintains with one's friends, and I enjoy it with too much happiness to regret that of high society. Moreover, if I did hate men as much as I love them and pity them, I am afraid that to see them more closely might be a bad way to patch things up with them; and, however happy I might be in my relations, it would be hard ever to find myself with anyone as well as I am with myself.

I thought that justifying myself before you was the best evidence I could give that your opinions have not displeased me, and that I set store by your esteem. Let us come to you, sir, by whom I should have begun. I have already read a part of your work and in it I see with pleasure the lovable and decent use that you and your friend make of your leisure and your talents. Your collection is not bad enough that it should discourage you from labor, or good enough to deprive you of the hope of making a better one afterward. Work, then, under your divine masters, to extend their rights and your glory. To conquer, as you have begun to do, the prejudices of your birth and your station, is to put yourself much above them both. But to join the example to lessons of virtue, that is what one has a right to expect from anyone who preaches it in his writings. Such is the honorable engagement that you have just undertaken and that you are working to fulfill.

I am with all my heart, sir etc.

CHAPTER 15

Georges-Louis Le Sage

July 1, 1754

Eaux-Vives

This letter was written during Rousseau's visit to Geneva to regain his citizenship. Eaux-Vives was, at that time, a separate community, but it is now part of Geneva.

Sumite materiam vestris qui scribitis aequam viribus[1]

1. The musician who in 1720 said that the simplest music was the most beautiful, made there, it seems to me, a strange remark. I would like it as much if he had said that the best Actor is the one who makes the fewest gestures and speaks the most calmly. As to Lully's rumblings, I agree that they are flat and in bad taste.

2. I am extremely surprised that they find in the *Devin du Village* the same rumblings as in the Opera *Roland.*[2] It must be that since I do not find there the slightest connection, I am strangely blind on this point. Moreover, it is not an easy thing to determine the cases in which music contains rumblings and those in which it

---

1. "Let those who write fix on a subject to which their strength is equal." Horace, *De arte poetica*, lines 38–39.

2. An opera by Lully from 1685.

does not. I have made some rules for myself to distinguish these cases, and I have carefully followed these rules in practice. *Rem a me saepe deliberatam et multum agitatam requiris.*[3]

3. If music consists only of simple songs and pleases only by means of physical sounds, it could happen that provincial tunes would please as much as or more than those of the court. But whenever music will be considered as an imitative art, like poetry and painting, it is in the city, it is at the court, it is wherever many men, gathered together, practice the pleasant arts, that one learns to cultivate them. In general, the best music is that which combines physical pleasure and moral pleasure, that is, which appeals to the ear and the interest of sentiment.

alterius sic
Altera poscit opem et conjurat amice.[4]

4. If Molière consulted his servant, it is doubtless about the *Médecin malgré lui*, Nicole's witticisms, and the quarrels of Sosie and Cléantis. But unless Molière's servant was a very extraordinary person, I would bet that this great man did not consult her about the *Misanthrope* or about *Tartuffe*, or about the fine scene of Alcmène and Amphitryon. Musicians must not consult the ignorant save with the same discernment, all the more so since musical imitation is more indirect, less immediate, and requires more subtlety of sentiment to be perceived than that of Comedy.

5. Although the principles of theatrical beauty have not been brought either by the moderns or even by Aristotle himself to the degree of clarity of which they are susceptible, they are easy to establish. These principles appear to me to be reduced to two, namely *imitation* and *interest*, which apply equally well to music. For fear of obscurity, I will not say that the beautiful consists in the imitation of the true, but in the true of the imitation; that, it seems to me, is the meaning of Horace's verse and of Boileau's. That imitation ought to be practiced only on useful subjects, that is a good precept of morality, but not a rule of poetics. For there are very beautiful pieces whose subject can be of no utility. Such is the *Oedipus* of Sophocles.

---

3. "You are interrogating me on a subject about which I have often thought, and which preoccupies me very much." Cicero, *Academicorum posteriorum*, book 1, chap. 2.4.

4. "This demands the aid of the other and both unite in friendly aid." Horace, *De arte poetica*, lines 410–11.

6. Mathematicians have very well explained the part of music that is within their competence, namely the relations of sounds, upon which also depend the physical pleasure of harmony and song. Philosophers on their side have shown that music taken as one of the fine arts has, as they do, the principle of imitation as the principle of its greatest charms.[5]

7. Musicians are not made to reason about their art. It is up to them to find the things; to the philosopher to explain them.

8. Although the Abbé du Bos has spoken about music as a man who does not understand anything about it, there are, all the same, rules for judging a piece of music as well as a poem or a picture. What would one say about a man who claimed to judge Homer's *Iliad* or Racine's *Phèdre*, or Poussin's *Déluge* like a stew or a ham? The same thing would be done by someone who would like to compare the magic tricks of a ravishing music that brings to the heart the disturbance of all the passions and the sensual pleasure of all the sentiments, with the coarse and purely physical sensation of the palate in the use of food. What a difference for the motions of the soul between trained men and those who are not trained! A Pergolese, a Voltaire, a Titian will have at their disposal, at their will, so to speak, the hearts of an enlightened people; but the peasant insensitive to the masterpieces of these great men finds nothing so beautiful as the *Bibliothèque bleu*,[6] beer labels, and his village dance.[7]

9. I believe then that one can very well dispute over music and even assign relative to language the qualities that it ought to have to be good and to please. For although one cannot explain matters of taste that are only pure sensations, the philosopher can without temerity undertake the explanation of those that modify the soul and belong to the metaphysical beautiful. I will surely refrain from entering into the supposed dispute between simple and composite music until I have learned the meanings of these words, which I do not understand at all. I would think, in the meantime, that sounds and motions must be composed and modified by the musician as lines and colors are by the painter, in accordance with

---

5. The abbé Jean-Baptiste Du Bos published *Reflections on Poetry and Painting* in 1719, and it was reprinted in 1751.

6. A collection of chivalric romances.

7. A sort of dance that involves swaying from side to side.

the tints and nuances of the objects that he wants to render and
the things he wants to express. But to resolve well these questions
that do not fail to have their difficulty,

Vacet oportet, Eutyche, a negociis,
Ut liber animus sentiat vim carminis.[8]

JJRousseau

---

8. "You must, Eutyche, dismiss business, / so that, free from care, your mind can appreciate the reach of my verses." Phaedrus, *To Eutyche*, prologue of book 3, lines 2–3.

Chapter 16

Jean Perdriau

November 28, 1754
Paris
None of Perdriau's letters to Rousseau survive. Rousseau wrote a dedicatory letter to Geneva for the Second Discourse. *The letter describes the country in which Rousseau would have chosen to be born in terms that clearly point to Geneva. Some took the letter as a veiled criticism of Geneva as it really existed. Geneva was plagued by class struggle between the oligarchs who controlled the government and the middle class. Rousseau's letter attempts to mediate in this quarrel in a way that could be interpreted as an attack on the government.*

By responding frankly to your last Letter, by putting my heart and my fate into your hands, I believe, sir, that I am giving you a mark of esteem and confidence less equivocal than the praises and compliments lavished by flattery more often than by friendship.

Yes, sir, struck by the conformities that I find between the constitution of government that follows from my principles and the one that really exists in our republic, I proposed to dedicate my *Discourse on the Origin and Foundations of Inequality* to it, and I seized upon this occasion as a happy means of honoring my fatherland and its leaders by means of just praises, of carrying if possible into the bottom of hearts the olive branch that so far I see only on medals, and at the same time of exciting men to make themselves happy by the example of a people which is happy or which could be so without changing anything in its institution. In doing so I seek, in accordance with my custom, less to please than to make myself useful. In particular, I do not count on the support of anyone who is in some party; for, adopting for myself only that of justice and reason, I hardly ought to hope that any man who follows other rules could approve of mine, and if this consideration has not held me back it is because in everything the blame of the entire universe touches me much less than the admission of my conscience. But, you say, to dedicate a book to the republic, that has never been done. So much the better, sir; in praiseworthy things it is better to give the example than to receive it, and I believe I have reasons that are only too just not to be the imitator of anyone. Thus, your objection is, at bottom, only an additional prejudice in my favor, since for a long time there have not been any bad actions left to attempt, and whatever one might be able to say about it, it would be less a question of knowing whether the thing has been done or not than whether it is good or bad in itself, of which I leave you to be the judge. As to what you add that, after what has happened, such novelties might be dangerous, that is a great truth in other respects; but as to this one, I find, on the contrary, the step I took all the more appropriate after what has happened, for since my praises are for the magistrates and my exhortations for the citizens, it is suitable that the whole be addressed to the republic in order to have the occasion to speak to its various members and in order to deprive my dedication of all appearance of partiality. I know that there are things that should not be called to mind, and I hope that you believe I have enough judgment to use it in this regard only with a reserve, in which I have consulted other people's taste more than my own. For I do not think that it is a skillful policy to push this maxim to the point of scruple. The memory of Erostratus teaches us that removing the freedom of speaking about them is a bad way to cause things to be forgotten.[1] But if you make it so that one speaks about them only with sorrow, you will soon make it so that one will no longer speak about them. There is I know not what kind of pusillanimous circumspection, greatly savored in this century, which, seeing inconveniences everywhere, limits itself out of wisdom to doing neither good nor evil. I much prefer a generous boldness that sometimes shakes off the puerile yoke of decorum to act well.

---

1. In 356 BCE, Erostratus burned down the temple of Artemis in order to become famous. A decree was passed forbidding any mention of him.

That an indiscreet zeal is perhaps misleading me, that taking my errors for useful truths, with the best intentions in the world, I might be doing more harm than good, I have nothing to respond to that, unless it is that such a reason ought to restrain every upright man and leave the universe at the discretion of the wicked and the stupid. For objections taken from the weakness of nature alone have strength against any man whatsoever, and there is no one who ought not to be suspect to himself, if he does not rest the precision of his enlightenment on the uprightness of his heart. That is what I must be able to do without recklessness because, isolated by men, depending on nothing in society, stripped of every sort of pretension, and not even seeking my own happiness except in that of others, I believe at least that I am exempt from those prejudices of station that make the judgment of the wisest men yield to maxims that are advantageous to them. I could, it is true, consult people more skillful than I am, and would do so willingly, if I did not know that their interest will counsel me before their reason. In a word, to speak here straightforwardly, I trust my disinterestedness even more than the enlightenment of anyone whatsoever.

Although in general I set very little store by the etiquette of behavior, and although a long time ago I shook off its yoke, which is heavier than it is useful, I think along with you that it would have been proper to obtain the approval of the republic or of the Council, as is rather the custom in such a case, and I was so much of this opinion that my voyage was made in part with the intention of soliciting that approval. But it took me little time and observation to recognize the impossibility of obtaining it. I felt that to ask for such a permission was to wish for a refusal, and that then my step—which sins at most against a certain decorum with which numerous people have dispensed—would have become by that a condemnable disobedience if I had persisted, or the heedlessness of a fool, if I had abandoned my plan. For having learned that since last May, copies of the work and the dedication had been made without my knowledge, I was no longer the master of preventing their misuse, I saw that neither was I any longer the master of renouncing my project without exposing myself to seeing it executed by others.

Your letter itself teaches me that you do not feel any less than I do all the difficulties that I had foreseen. Now you know that by dint of making oneself difficult about indifferent permissions, one invites men to do without them. That is how the excessive circumspection of the late Chancellor about the printing of the best books finally made it so that manuscripts were no longer presented to him; and books were not printed any less, although that printing made against the laws was actually criminal, while a dedication not communicated is at most only a lack of politeness. And far from such a proceeding being blameworthy by its nature it is, at bottom, more in conformity with honesty than is the established practice. For there is something cowardly in asking people for permission to praise them, and indecent in granting it. Do not believe, either, that such behavior is unprecedented: I can show you books dedicated to the French nation, others to the English people, without it being made into a crime for the authors not to have the consent of the nation for that, or that of the Prince which certainly would have been refused them, because in every monarchy the king wants to be the state all by himself and does not claim that the people are something.

Moreover, if I had had to open myself to someone about this business, it would have been less to M. the Premier than to anyone else in the world. I honor and love this worthy and respectable magistrate too much to have wanted to compromise him in the slightest thing, and to expose him to the sorrow of perhaps displeasing many people by favoring my project, or of being forced, perhaps, to blame it against his own sentiment. You can believe that having reflected for a long time on matters of government, I am not unaware of the strength of these petty maxims of state that a wise magistrate is obliged to follow although he feels all their frivolity himself.

You will agree that I could not obtain the Council's permission without my work being examined. Now do you think that I am unaware what these examinations are, and how much the amour-propre of the best intentioned censors and the prejudices of the most enlightened cause them to put stubbornness and haughtiness in the place of reason and cause them to strike out excellent things, solely because they are not to their manner of thinking and because they have not meditated on them as deeply as the author has? Have I not had a thousand altercations with mine here? Although they are intelligent and honorable people, they have always distressed me with wretched squabbles that have neither common sense nor any other cause than a base pusillanimity, or the vanity of wanting to know everything better than someone else. I have never given in because I only give in to reason. The magistrate has been our judge, and he has always found that the censors were wrong. When I responded to the King of Poland, I ought, according to them, to have sent him my manuscript and published it only with his consent. It was, they claimed, to lack respect for the Queen's father to attack him publicly, above all with the pride they found in my response, and they even added that my safety required some precautions. I did not take any; I did not send my manuscript to the prince; I relied on public decency, as I still do today, and the event proved that I was right. But in Geneva it would not proceed as it does here; my censors' decision would be without appeal; I would see myself reduced to staying silent, or to giving someone else's sentiment under my name, and I want to do neither the one nor the other. My experience has thus caused me firmly to resolve to be my sole censor from now on. I would never have a more severe one, and my principles do not need any others, any more than my morals do. Since all those people are always looking to a thousand alien things about which I do not care at all, I prefer to refer myself to that interior and incorruptible judge who does not let anything bad pass through and does not condemn anything good, and who never deceives when one consults him in good faith. I hope that you will find that he has not done his duty badly in the work in question, with which everyone will be satisfied, and yet which would have obtained approval from no one.

You must also feel that the irregularity that can be found in my proceedings is all to my prejudice and to the government's advantage. If there is anything good in my work, they will be able to take advantage of it; if there is anything bad, they will be able to disavow it; they can approve of me or blame me in accordance with particular interests, or the public's judgment. They could even proscribe my book, if the author and the state were unfortunate enough that the Council were discontented with it. All things they could no longer do after having given approval to the dedication. In a word, if I have spoken well in honor of my fatherland, the glory will be for it; if I have spoken badly, the blame will fall back on me alone. Can a good citizen have any scruples about having to run such risks?

I am suppressing all personal considerations that can concern me, because they ought never to enter into the motives of a good man who is working for the public utility. If the detachment of a heart which depends neither on glory, nor on fortune, nor even on life can render him worthy of proclaiming the truth, I dare to believe myself called to that sublime vocation. It is in order to do men some good in accordance with my power that I abstain from receiving any from them and that I cherish my poverty and my independence. I do not want to suppose that such sentiments could ever do me harm with my fellow citizens, and it is without foreseeing it or fearing it that I am preparing my soul for that final test, the only one to which I can be sensitive. Believe that I want to be honest, true, and a zealous citizen to the grave, and that, if it were necessary to deprive me on this occasion of the sweet abode of the fatherland, I would thus crown the sacrifices I have made for the love of men and the truth, by the one that costs my heart the most of all and that consequently does me the most honor.

You will easily understand that this letter is for you alone. I could have written you one to be shown, in an extremely different style; but aside from the fact that these petty clever measures are repugnant to my character, they would be no less repugnant to what I know about yours. I will be grateful all my life for having taken advantage of this opportunity to open myself to you without reserve, and for confiding in the discretion of a good man who is friendly to me. Good day, sir, I embrace you with all my heart, with tenderness and respect.

JJRousseau

CHAPTER 17

Jean Perdriau

February 20, 1755
Paris
The letter from Perdriau that Rousseau refers to in the first sentence has not been found.

Your last letter, sir, gave me all the more tangible pleasure in that I was extremely anxious about the impression that my preceding one would have made on you. Your friendship has become dearer to me after having found it proof against my frankness. All your observations are very wise, but I assure myself that intentions as pure as mine will not leave anyone the courage to have any others while reading me.

You knew the ill success of my negotiations for the bible of Sixtus Quintus, but you cannot have known all the sorrow that it has caused me, and although it was not my fault, I reproach myself for my bad luck in this circumstance just as I would reproach myself for my wrong in every other. As for the manuscript about which you speak to me, I gave it to M. Vernet more than six weeks ago. I hope that it is not found to be unworthy of the place one is willing to grant it.[1]

---

1. This is a manuscript on the siege of Lyon given by Rousseau to the library of Geneva.

You regret, as I do, the illustrious Montesquieu. It is up to those who have a fatherland and who love it to weep for that great man. He did not need such a long life to be immortal; but he ought to have lived eternally so as to teach peoples their rights and duties. I was in the country when he died,[2] and I learned that out of all the literary people with which Paris swarms, only M. Diderot had accompanied his procession; fortunately, he was also the one who let the absence of the others be least perceived.

During this carnival I had a more pleasant spectacle, but one which is not enough to console for that one. It is the old fellow Fontenelle who opened the ball at Mme. Helvetius's with a four-year-old young maiden. I had advised the mother not to miss this rare occasion.[3] I am persuaded that this will be a memorable anecdote for the little person that she will naturally only forget at thirty, but which she will recollect with pleasure in her old age.

If the cold has been keen in Geneva, it was hardly less so in Paris; but it has been easing for several days, and I hope that we are now completely done with it. I will translate the 4th volume of Giannone all the more willingly in that I will have the pleasure while working on it of thinking that you were occupied with me.[4] I embrace you with respect and with all my heart.

JJRousseau

A thousand respects I beg you, to Monsieur Lullin.

---

2. Montesquieu had died on February 10.

3. Fontenelle danced with both the two-year-old daughters of Mme. Helvétius and the seven-year-old daughter of Mme. d'Épinay.

4. Pietro Giannone wrote a history of Naples published in 1739.

CHAPTER 18

Jacob Vernes

July 6, 1755
Paris
The Second Discourse *was published in April, and, in June, Rousseau sent a copy to the Council of Geneva.*

This, sir, is a long interruption, but since I am not unaware of my wrongs and you are not unaware of our treaty,[1] I have nothing new to tell you as my excuse, and I prefer to take up our correspondence again in the same way, rather than to begin again my apology or my useless excuses each time.

I assume that at present you have seen the writing for which you have shown eagerness. Copies of it are in M. Chappuis's hands. In Geneva I received so many courtesies from everyone that I could not give any preferences to these without making offending exclusions at the same time; but there would be a courtesy to steal from M. Chappuis, of which friendship alone is capable, and which I have some right to expect from those who have given me as much as you have. I cannot express to you the joy with which I learned that the Council had approved the dedication

---

1. See letter 39.

of that work in the name of the Republic. I perfectly feel everything there is of indulgence and grace in that avowal, and henceforth I hope equally to show in my speeches and my conduct that my heart is not unworthy of this favor. I have always hoped that in this epistle the sentiments that dictated it could not fail to be recognized and that it would be approved by all those who share them. I am also counting, then, on your approbation, on that of your respectable father, and on that of all my good fellow citizens. I care very little about what the rest of Europe could think. Moreover, terrible rumors were designedly spread about the violence of this work, and it did not depend on my enemies to give me problems with the government. Fortunately, I was not condemned without being read, and after the examination, entrance was permitted without difficulty.

Give me some news about your journal. I have not forgotten my promise, but for some time now my copying presses me so strongly that it does not give me the leisure to work. Furthermore, I do not want to give you anything that I could have done better, but I will keep my word to you, count on it, and the worst case will be to bring to you myself next spring what I will have been unable to send you earlier. If I know your heart well, I believe that at this price you will not be sorry for the delay.

Good day, sir, prepare yourself to love me more than ever. For that is what I have very much resolved to force you to do upon my return.

JJRousseau

CHAPTER 19

Voltaire

September 7, 1755
Paris
Rousseau had a copy of the Second Discourse *sent to Voltaire, who responded with a letter that began, "I have received, sir, your new book against the human race." He joked that reading the* Discourse *made him want to revert to walking on all fours. Voltaire quickly had this response to Rousseau published, asking for Rousseau's permission only after the fact.*

It is I who must thank you, sir, in all respects. In offering you the sketch of my sad reveries, I did not believe I was giving you a present worthy of you, but rather acquitting myself of a duty and paying you an homage we all owe you as our leader. Moreover, sensible of the honor you confer on my fatherland, I share the gratitude of my fellow citizens, and I hope that it will only increase when they have profited from the teachings you can give them. Enlighten a people worthy of your lessons, and you, who know so well how to portray virtues and freedom, teach us to cherish them within our walls as we do in your writings. All that comes near you must learn from you the path to glory and immortality.

You see that I do not aspire to restore us to our stupidity, although as for myself, I greatly regret the little bit of it that I have lost. With respect to you, sir, this return would be a miracle both so great that only God could perform it and so pernicious that only the devil could wish it. So do not try to go back to walking on all fours. No one in the world would succeed at it less than you. You straighten us all up too well on our own two feet to stop standing up on yours.

I acknowledge all the disfavor that pursues men who are celebrated in literature. I even acknowledge all the ills attached to humanity, which seem independent of our vain knowledge. Men have brought upon themselves so many sources of misery that when chance wards off one of them, they are scarcely happier for it. Besides, there are hidden connections in the progress of things which the common person does not perceive, but which will not escape the philosopher's eye when he will want to reflect on it. It is neither Cicero, nor Virgil, nor Seneca, nor Tacitus who produced the crimes of the Romans and the misfortunes of Rome. But without the slow and secret poison which was imperceptibly corrupting the most vigorous government that history has ever recorded, neither Cicero nor Lucretius nor Sallust, nor all the others, would have existed or written. The pleasant century of Lelius and Terence led from afar to the brilliant century of Augustus and Horace, and eventually to the horrible centuries of Seneca and Nero, Tacitus and Domitian. The taste for the sciences and the arts in a people is born from an internal vice which it soon enlarges in turn. And if it is true that all human progress is pernicious for the species, that of the mind and of knowledge, which enlarges our pride and multiplies our aberrations, soon hastens our misfortunes. But a time comes when the evil is such that the very causes that gave birth to it are necessary to prevent it from increasing. It is the sword that must be left in the wound for fear that the wounded person will die when it is removed. For myself, if I had pursued my first vocation and had neither read nor written, I would doubtless have been happier. However, if letters were abolished now, I would be deprived of the only pleasure remaining to me. It is in their bosom that I console myself for all my ills. It is among their illustrious children that I taste the sweetness of friendship, that I learn to enjoy life and despise death. I owe to them the little that I am. I owe to them even the honor of being known by you. But let us consult interest in our business affairs and truth in our writings. Although philosophers, historians, and learned men are needed to enlighten the world and lead its blind inhabitants, if wise Memnon told me the truth,[1] I know nothing so mad as a people of wise men.

---

1. This is a reference to Voltaire's *Memnon or Human Wisdom*, published in 1749.

Agree, sir: if it is good that great geniuses teach men, it is necessary that the common people receive their teachings. If everyone gets involved in giving them, who will want to receive them? The lame, says Montaigne, are ill-suited to bodily exercise, and those with lame souls to mental exercise.[2] But in this learned century, we see only the lame wishing to teach others to walk. The people receive the writings of the wise in order to judge them, and not to learn. Never have there been so many Dandins.[3] The theater crawls with them, the cafes echo with their pronouncements, the quays overflow with their writings, and I hear the *Orphan* criticized,[4] because it is applauded, by some scribbler so incapable of seeing its faults that he can scarcely feel its beauties.

Let us seek the first source of all of society's disorders, and we will find that all men's ills come far more from error than ignorance, and that what we do not know at all harms us far less than what we believe we know. Now what surer means are there to rush from error to error than the frenzy to know everything? If no one had claimed to know that the earth does not turn, Galileo would not have been punished for having said that it turned. If the philosophers alone had laid claim to the title [of philosopher], the *Encyclopedia* would not have been persecuted. If a hundred Myrmidons did not aspire to glory, you would enjoy yours in peace, or at least you would have only adversaries worthy of you.

Do not therefore be surprised to feel some thorns inseparable from the flowers that crown great talents. The insults of your enemies are the retinue of your glory as satirical acclamations were that of triumphant generals. It is the public's eagerness for all your writings that produces the thefts of which you complain. But falsifications of them are not easy, for neither iron nor lead is easily alloyed with gold. Allow me, sir, to say this because of my interest in your repose and our education. Scorn vain clamors whose intention is less to harm you than to distract you from doing good. The more you are criticized, the more you should make yourself admired. A good book is a devastating reply to printed insults. And who would dare attribute to you writings you did not write, as long as you continue to write only inimitable ones?

I appreciate your invitation, and if this winter leaves me well enough to go and live in my fatherland in the spring, I will profit from your kindnesses. But I would much prefer to drink water from your fountain

---

2. Montaigne, "Of Pedantry," *Essays* 1.25.

3. A reference to Molière's *Georges Dandin*.

4. *The Orphan of China* was a tragedy by Voltaire that was playing at that time.

than milk from your cows, and as for the grasses in your orchard, I fear that I shall find none other than the Lotus, which suits beasts poorly, and the Moly, which prevents men from becoming beasts.

I am, with all my heart and with respect, sir, your very humble and very obedient servant.

JJRousseau

CHAPTER 20

Renée-Caroline de Froullay, marquise de Créqui

September 8, 1755
Épinay[1]
The letter to which Rousseau is responding has not been found. Presumably Mme. de Créqui was concerned that Rousseau was going to be arrested because of the Second Discourse.

I see, madam, that the benevolence with which you honor me is causing you some anxiety over the fate with which some, at the very least indiscreet, people like to threaten me. Please do me the favor of not being alarmed by my calmness when they announce to you that my detention is imminent. If I am doing nothing to prevent it, it is because, having done nothing to deserve it, I would believe that I was insulting the hospitality of the French nation and the equity of the prince who governs it by taking precautions against an injustice.

If I have written, as they claim, on a question of political right proposed by the Academy of Dijon, I was authorized to do so by the program, and since it was not made a crime for that Academy to propose this question, I do not see why anyone would make resolving it into

---

1. Épinay was the country residence of Mme. d'Épinay.

one. It is true that I had to keep myself within the limits of a general and purely philosophic discussion, without personalities and without application: but could you believe, madam, you by whom I have the honor of being known, that I could forget myself for a moment on this point? Even if the most common prudence had not forbidden me every license in that regard, I love frankness and truth too much not to abhor libel and satire; and if I put so little precaution into my behavior, that is because my heart always vouches that I do not need any. Rest well assured then, I beg you, that nothing has ever issued, and nothing ever will issue, from my pen that could expose me to the slightest danger under a just government.

If I were in error about the utility of my maxims, are there not in France prescribed forms for the publication of the works that one has appear there, and if I could deviate from these forms with impunity, would not my respect for the laws be enough by itself to keep me from doing so? You know, madam, to what point I have always been scrupulous in this regard: you are not unaware that my boldest writings, without excepting that fearsome letter on music,[2] have never come to light except with approval and permission. That is how I will continue to act my whole life, and never during my stay in France will any of my works appear there with my acknowledgment except with that of the magistrate.

But if I know what my duties are, I am no less aware of what my rights are. I am not unaware that by obeying faithfully the laws of the country in which I live, I do not owe an account to anyone of my religion or of my sentiments except to the magistrates of the state of which I have the honor of being a member. To wish that every time one sets foot in a state one were obliged to adopt all its maxims, and that in traveling from one country to another it were necessary to change inclinations and principles as one changes language and lodging, would be to establish a very novel law. Wherever one is, one ought to respect the prince and submit to the law, but one does not owe them anything more, and the heart ought always to be for the fatherland. Were it true that, having in view the happiness of my own, I had set forth outside of the kingdom principles more suitable for republican than for monarchic government, where would be my crime? Who ever heard it said that

---

2. Rousseau is referring to the *Letter on French Music*, published in 1753, which stirred up a great controversy—to the point that Rousseau says that this dispute distracted from political events that could have caused a revolution. See *Confessions*, CW 5:322–23.

the law of nations, which one boasts so much of respecting in France, allows punishing a foreigner for having dared to prefer in a foreign country the government of his own country to every other one?

It is true that it is said that this occasion will be nothing but a pretext thanks to which I will be punished for my disdain for French music. How, madam, can a man be punished for his disdain for music? Have you ever heard anything like it? Is one injustice excused by an even more blatant injustice, and at the time of this horrible fermentation worthy of the pen of Tacitus, would it not have been less odious to oppress me based on this serious subject than to return to it after the fact based on an even less reasonable subject?

As for what you tell me, madam, that it is not a question of the good or ill one does, but only of the friends or enemies one has, despite the bad opinion that I have of my century, I cannot believe that things are yet completely at that point: But if that were so, what enemies can I have? Satisfied with my situation, I chase after neither pensions nor employments, nor literary honors. Far from wishing harm to anyone, I do not even seek to avenge myself for the harm done to me. I do not refuse my services to others and never ask them for any. I am not a flatterer, it is true, but I am also not a deceiver, and my frankness is not satirical. All odious personal reflections are banished from my mouth and my writings, and if I attack vices, I do so while respecting men.

Do not fear for me then, madam, because I am not afraid of anything, and I have nothing to fear. If my work were judged based on the rumors spread by calumny I would, I admit, be in very great danger. But in a wise government the fate of men is not disposed of so lightly, and I know very well that I have nothing to fear if I am judged only after I have been read. My sentiments, my conduct, and the King's justice are the safeguard in which I trust; I remain in the middle of Paris in the security that suits innocence and under the protection of laws that I never violated. The shouts of the charlatans will not be listened to any more than they have been. If I am wrong I will be refuted, perhaps; perhaps even if I am right. But an irreproachable man will not be treated as a scoundrel for having honored his fatherland, and for having said that the French do not sing well. In sum, even if a misfortune that decency does not allow me to foresee could happen to me, it would be hard for me to repent having judged the government under which I have to live more favorably than the people who seek to frighten me.

I am with respect, madam etc.

CHAPTER 21

Voltaire

September 20, 1755
Paris

Upon arriving, sir, from the country where I passed five or six days, I find your note which gets me out of a great perplexity, for, having communicated to M. de Gauffecourt, our common friend, your letter and my response, I just now learn that he has himself communicated them to others, and that they have fallen into the hands of someone who is working on refuting me and who proposes, it is said, to insert them at the end of his critique.[1] M. Bouchaud, credentialed in law, who just informed me of this, has not been willing to tell me more; so that I am in no condition to prevent the consequences of an indiscretion that, given the contents of your letter, I committed only for a good end. Fortunately, sir, I see by your project that the harm is less great than I had feared. By approving a publication that does me honor and that can be useful to you, there remains an excuse to make to you about

---

1. It is possible that this was Borde.

what might have been my fault in the promptness with which these letters have circulated with neither your consent nor mine.

I am with the sincerest sentiments of your admirers, sir, etc.

P.S. I assume that you have received my response of the 10th of this month.[2]

---

2. Rousseau is probably referring to the letter of September 7.

CHAPTER 22

Louis de Boissy

[November 29, 1755]

Paris

The work attacking the Second Discourse *referred to here is the* Letter from Philopolis. *It was written by Charles Bonnet who was, in fact, a Genevan. He said that he had published anonymously in order to allow Rousseau more freedom in his response. Rousseau did write a response but decided not to publish it (CW 3:123–26).*

I received, on the 26th of this month, an anonymous letter dated the 28th of last October, which, badly addressed, after having been to Geneva, came back to me in Paris, postage free. To this letter was joined a writing for my defense under the name of Philopolis which I cannot give to the *Mercury* as the author desires, for reasons he ought to feel, if he really has the esteem for me that he indicates. He can therefore have it withdrawn from my hands by means of a note in the same writing, without which his piece will remain suppressed.

The Author ought not to believe so readily that the one he is refuting was a citizen of Geneva, even though he gives himself out as such. For it is easy to date from that country; but some boast of being from there who say the opposite without thinking about it. I have neither the vanity nor the consolation of believing that all my fellow citizens think as I do. But I know the candor of their proceedings; if one of them attacks me, it will be loudly and without hiding himself; they esteem me enough in combating me, or at least esteem themselves enough, to return the frankness that I make use of toward everyone. Moreover, those for whom this work is written, those to whom it is dedicated, those who have honored it with their approval, will not ask me what it is useful for; they will not object to me, along with many others, that, if all that were true, I ought not to have said it, as if the happiness of society were founded on men's errors. They will see in it, I dare to believe it, strong reasons for loving their government, means for preserving it, and if they find in it maxims that are suited to the good and virtuous citizen, they will not disdain a writing that breathes throughout humanity, freedom, love of the fatherland, and obedience to the laws.

As for the inhabitants of other countries, if they do not find anything useful or amusing in this work, it would be better, it seems to me, to ask them why they are reading it rather than to explain to them why it is written. A fine wit from Bordeaux seriously exhorts me to leave political discussions in order to write operas, considering that he, a fine wit, gets much more amusement at the performance of the *Devin du Village* than while reading the *Discourse on Inequality*. Doubtless he is right, if it is true that in writing to citizens of Geneva, I am obliged to amuse the bourgeois of Bordeaux.

Whatever might be the case, in showing my gratitude to my defender, I beg him to leave the field free for my adversaries; I myself very much regret the time that I lost in the past in responding to them. When the search for the truth degenerates into disputes and personal quarrels, it does not delay in taking up the weapons of the lie; let us be afraid of debasing it this way. Whatever value science might have, peace of the soul is worth even more. I do not want any other defense for my writings than reason and truth, or for my person than my conduct and my morals. If these supports fail me, nothing will hold me up; if they hold me up, what do I have to fear?

[JJRousseau]

CHAPTER 23

Louis-Élisabeth de La Vergne, comte de Tressan

December 27, 1755

In November 1755, Charles Palissot's play The Circles, or the Peculiar People *was performed for Stanislas, the former king of Poland (with whom Rousseau had had a respectful exchange over the* First Discourse*), at Lunéville. The play made fun of Rousseau and others connected with the* Encyclopedia. *Stanislas stopped performances of the play and decided to have Palissot expelled from the Academy of Nancy. This letter is to the founder of the academy and head of Stanislas's household. Rousseau wrote the letter after this one to d'Alembert because of his involvement in the affair. Following Rousseau's letter, the king had the academy make a record of Rousseau's request for clemency for Palissot.*

I honored you, sir, as we all do; it is sweet for me to join gratitude to esteem, and I would willingly thank M. Palissot for having procured for me—without thinking about it—testimonies of your kindness which permit me to give you some [testimony] of my respect. If this author was lacking in the respect he owed and which the whole earth owes to the prince he wanted to amuse, who ought to find him more inexcusable than I? But if his whole crime is to have exposed my absurdities, that is the theater's right; I do not see anything reprehensible in that for the decent man and, for the author, I see the merit of having known how to choose a very rich subject. Thus, please, sir, do not listen to the zeal inspired in M. d'Alembert by friendship and generosity on this point, and for this trifle do not distress a man of merit who has not caused me any pain, and who would painfully bear the King of Poland's disfavor and yours.

My heart is moved by the praises with which you honor those of my fellow citizens who are under your orders. Indeed, the Genevan is naturally good, he has a decent soul, he does not lack sense, and he needs only good examples to turn entirely toward the good. Permit me, sir, to exhort those young officers to take advantage of yours, to make themselves worthy of your kindness, and under your eyes to perfect the qualities which they perhaps owe to you and which you attribute to their education. I will myself willingly take the advice I am giving them when you come to Paris. They will study the man of war, I the philosopher: our common study will be the good man, and you will always be our teacher.

I am with respect, sir, your very humble and very obedient servant.

JJRousseau

CHAPTER 24

Jean Le Rond d'Alembert

December 27, 1755

I appreciate, my dear sir, the interest that you are taking in me, but I cannot approve the zeal that makes you pursue this poor M. Palissot, and I would very much regret the time that all this has made you lose, without the testimony of friendship in my favor that results from it. Let this business go, please, once again; I am as obliged to you as if it were finished, and I assure you that the expulsion of Palissot from love of me would cause me more pain than pleasure. As to Fréron, I have nothing to say on my own initiative because the cause is shared; but what is most certain is that your disdain would have mortified him more than your proceedings, and that, whatever their success might be, they will always do him more honor than harm.

I have written to M. de Tressan to thank him and ask him to leave it at that; I will show you my response along with his letter at our first meeting. I cannot doubt that I owe you all the testimonies of esteem with which it is full. Everything accounted for, everything considered, it happens that I gain in every respect in this business. Why would we return harm to this poor man for the real good he has done me? I thank you and embrace you with all my heart.

JJRousseau

CHAPTER 25

Comte de Tressan

January 7, 1756
Paris

Sir, whatever danger there might be of making myself tiresome, I cannot keep myself from joining to the thanks I owe you some remarks about the documentation of the affair of M. Palissot, and to begin with I will take the liberty of telling you that even my admiration for the virtues of the King of Poland does not allow me to accept the testimonial of kindness with which His Majesty honors me on this occasion, except on condition that everything be forgotten. I dare to say that it does not become him to grant an incomplete clemency, and that only a pardon without reservation is worthy of his great soul. Besides, is it granting clemency to make the punishment eternal, and should not the records of an academy extenuate, rather than call attention to, its members' little faults? Finally, whatever little esteem I have for my contemporaries, God forbid that we debase them to this point of inscribing as an act of virtue what is only the simplest proceeding, which any man of letters would not have failed to undertake in my position.

Complete, then, sir, the good work which you have so well begun, so as to make it worthy of you. Let there be no more question of a trifle which has already caused more commotion and given more grief to

M. Palissot than the affair deserved. What will we have done for him, if the pardon costs him as dearly as the penalty?

Permit me not to respond to the extreme praises with which you honor me; these are severe lessons from which I will draw a profit. For I am not unaware—and this letter is evidence of it—that one praises soberly the people whom one esteems perfectly. But sir, we must put off these clarifications until our meetings. I eagerly await the pleasure that you promise me, and one way or another, you will see that you will no longer praise me once we have gotten to know each other.

I am with respect etc.

CHAPTER 26

Jean Perdriau

January 18, 1756
Paris

I do not know, sir, why I am always so very behindhand with you, for in writing to you I occupy myself most pleasantly. But that is not the only thing in which I notice how much temperament often predominates over inclination, and habit even over pleasure.

I begin with what touched me the most in your letter, after the testimonies of friendship that you give me in it, and which are becoming dearer to me each day. It is the sort of lack of confidence you appear to me to have in yourself at the entrance to the new career that is presenting itself to you. I cannot talk to you about your studies and your knowledge because there is nothing of which I am less of a judge than such matters; but I will dare to talk to you about the instrument that makes all that stand out, and of which I find that you make use marvelously. Your mind has subtlety; that is what I have noticed in many of our compatriots, but you join to it the rarer natural disposition, which gives it graces. In all your letters I find an elegant simplicity that goes directly to the heart; nothing of the dryness of letters of pure and fine wit, and all agreeable qualities often lacking in those in which sentiment alone is confided to a friend. I have found the same thing in your conversation; and without thinking about it, I, who fear nothing so much as witty people, attached myself to you because of the turn of yours. With such dispositions you must not be troubled by the caprices of your memory; you will have little need of its resources to cut a figure in the literary world. Reading the ancients will not attach you to the hodgepodge of erudition; you will take in it that interest of the soul that method and precision have chased from our modern writings. If you do not clarify some obscure text, you will make the true beauties felt of those that are understood, and you will make your listeners say that it is better still to imitate the ancients than to explain them. That, sir, is what I predict from your talents applied to the study of belles-lettres. The anxieties that you show and the manner in which you express them teach me that the only faculty that you lack is the courage to put to good use those you possess. It would be very sweet to me, and perhaps it would not be useless to you on this occasion, if the trust you owe to my sincerity gave you a little in your powers.

I think that one must not look for too much precision in the words *modus* and *numerus* used by Horace, any more than in all the technical terms that one finds in the poets.[1] The only place in Horace in which he appears to have chosen specific terms, which only ignorant people understand and explain, is the *sonante mistum* etc. of the ninth Epode. In all the rest he vaguely takes one instrument for music, number for poetry etc., and it is for lack of having made this very simple reflection that so many commentators have tormented themselves so ridiculously about all that.

As for the precise meaning of the two words in question, it is in Boethius and Martianus Capella that one must look for it,[2] for among the ancients they are the only Latins whose writings on music have reached us. You will find there that *Numerus* is taken for the execution of the rhythm, that is, in the case of music, for the regular division of tempos and durations. As to the word *Modus*, it applies to the specific rules of melody, and above all to those that constitute the mode or the tone. Thus, the mode, doing for the intervals or degrees of sounds what the number did for the duration of times, the pace of the song proceeded by *Acutum* and *Grave* in accordance with the first meaning, and by *Arsin* and *Thesin* in accordance with the second.

---

1. Perdriau had asked Rousseau for clarification on this question.
2. Rousseau's note: "If one wants one can add St. Augustine."

Concerning song, for a long time I have forgotten to speak to you about an observation that I made on that of the psalms in our temples; a song whose antique simplicity I praise very much, but whose execution is jarring to delicate ears through a defect that is easy to correct. This defect is that since the cantor is far removed from certain parts of the temple, and the sound travels rather slowly through these great intervals, his voice barely makes itself heard at the extremities when he has already changed tone and begun other notes. This becomes all the more jarring at certain points since the sound arrives even later from one extremity to the other than from the middle where the cantor is, and the mass of air that fills the temple is simultaneously divided into various very discordant sounds, which incessantly cross over each other and strongly jar a practiced ear, a defect that even the organ only causes to increase, because instead of being in the middle of the edifice as the cantor is, it only gives the tone from one extremity.

Now the remedy for this inconvenience seems very easy to me; for as the visual rays are instantly communicated from the object to the eye, or at least with a speed incomparably greater than that with which sound is transmitted from the sonorous body to the ear, it suffices to substitute the one for the other in order to have, in the entire extent of the temple, singing that is simultaneous and perfectly harmonious. For that it is necessary only to place the cantor, or someone charged with that part of his function, in such a way that he is in sight of everyone, and that he use a baton of a size whose motion is easily perceived from afar, as, for example, a roll of paper. For then, with the precaution of prolonging the first note enough so that its intonation is heard everywhere before continuing, all the rest of the singing will advance well together, and the observed discordance will infallibly disappear. Instead of a man one could even employ a chronometer, whose motion would be even more steady.

Two other advantages would result from this: one that, almost without altering the singing of the psalms, one will be able to give it a little rhythm or quantity and at least observe in it the most perceptible longs and shorts; the other that what is languorous and monotonous can be relieved by a precise, masculine, and majestic harmony, by adding to it the base and the parts, in accordance with the first intention of the author who was not a harmonist to be disdained. That, sir, seems to me an important use of the Arsis and Thesis, and of number. But I cannot say more, and I lack paper rather than desire to converse with you. Good day, sir, I embrace you with respect and with all my heart.

PART III

Life in the Country
April 1756–June 9, 1762

The years that Rousseau spent in the country outside Paris were extraordinarily productive. He wrote the *Letter to d'Alembert*, *Julie*, *Emile*, and the *Social Contract*, as well as numerous other works, and planned still others that were begun but not finished. This period was also prolific in letters. In fact, there are almost three times as many letters that survive from these six years as from the preceding forty-four. We are presenting forty-nine of these letters.

The years in the country were marked by very turbulent personal relations, as Rousseau fell in love with Mme. d'Houdetot; broke off relations with Mme. d'Epinay, Diderot, and Grimm; then subsequently established a close friendship with the maréchal and maréchale de Luxembourg. The complications of these relations are well documented in the correspondence. While the publication of *Julie* at the end of 1760 brought about Rousseau's greatest literary triumph, concerns over the preparations for the publication of *Emile* were the warning rumblings of the storm that broke a month after its publication in May of 1762. Some indications of these concerns can be found in Rousseau's correspondence with publishers, censors, and friends. The storm broke on June 9th when the Parlement of Paris condemned the work, and Rousseau was encouraged by his friends to leave France before he could be arrested.

Among the letters presented here are a number that are of the greatest importance for understanding Rousseau's thought. Although Rousseau wrote these letters to specific individuals, he did so with the idea of possible eventual publication. These include his letter to Voltaire on providence, the six so-called moral letters to Sophie d'Houdetot, and four letters to Malesherbes. The first of these is an important statement of Rousseau's view of the philosophic and moral limitations of Voltaire's thought. While Rousseau's earlier letters to Voltaire were deferential, this one is respectful but assertive. Rousseau no longer presents himself as a disciple but as a "friend of the truth" speaking to a philosopher. The letters to Sophie are remarkable in that they present an impressive introduction not only to the major themes of Rousseau's work but also to his reflections on the limitations of philosophy and on the preconditions for a more adequate philosophical account. Finally, the letters to Malesherbes attempt to correct a number of misunderstandings about both Rousseau's character and his thought. They reach their peak with his description of the possibility of happiness.

During this period Rousseau also began to receive letters from admirers who wanted to meet him or sought his advice. Grimpel d'Offreville, for example, wrote to Rousseau to ask whether it was possible to demonstrate that morality is rational, and the Benedictine monk Dom Deschamps initiated what became a prolonged correspondence on questions of metaphysics.

CHAPTER 27

Franz Christoph Scheyb

July 15, 1756
Scheyb had written to a few writers, including Voltaire and Metastasio, to ask them for compositions praising the emperor and empress of Austria for their support of the sciences and the arts.

You ask me, sir, for praises for your august sovereigns and for letters, which they cause to flourish in their states. Find it good that I begin by praising in you a zealous subject of the Empress and a good citizen of the republic of letters. Without having the honor of knowing you, I must judge by the fervor that animates you that you yourself perfectly discharge the duties that you impose on others and that you practice at the same time the functions of a Statesman at the pleasure of Their Majesties, and those of the author in accordance with the pleasure of the public.

With respect to the efforts with which it pleases you to burden me, I know well, sir, that I would not be the first republican who would have heaped praise on the throne, or the first ignoramus who would sing the praises of the arts. But I am so poorly fit to fulfill your intentions in a worthy manner, that my deficiency is my excuse, and I do not know how the great names that you cite have allowed you to consider mine. I see, moreover, from the tone that flattery has in all times made use with vulgar princes, that to praise them soberly is to honor those one esteems, for it is known that the princes praised most excessively are rarely those who most deserve to be. Now it does not suit anyone to put himself in the lineup with the plan of doing less than the others, above all when one must fear doing less well. Allow me then to believe that there is no more true respect for the emperor and the empress-queen in the writings of the celebrated men of whom you speak than in my silence, and that it would be reckless to break it following their example, unless one had their talents.

You also urge me to tell you whether Their Imperial Majesties have done well to dedicate magnificent establishments and immense sums to public lessons in their capital, and after the affirmative response of so many illustrious authors, you also require mine. I do not have, sir, the enlightenment necessary to decide so promptly, and I do not know the morals and talents of your compatriots well enough to make a definite application to your question. But here is the summary of my sentiment on this issue, based on which you will be able to draw the conclusion better than I can.

With relation to morals. When men are corrupt, it is better for them to be learned than ignorant; when they are good, it is to be feared that the sciences might corrupt them.

With relation to talents. When one has some, knowledge perfects and fortifies them; when one lacks them, study also removes reason, and makes a pedant and a fool out of a man of good sense and little wit.

I could add some reflections to this. Whether the sciences are cultivated or not, in whatever century a great man is born, he is always a great man; for the source of his merit is not in his books, but in his head, and often the obstacles he finds and that he overcomes only elevate him and make him even greater. One can buy science and even learned people, but genius that makes knowledge useful cannot be bought; it knows neither money nor the order of princes. Causing it to be born does not rest with them; only honoring it does. It lives and comes to a halt with the freedom that is natural to it, and your illustrious Metastasio himself was already the glory of Italy before being welcomed by Charles VI.[1] Let us therefore try not to confuse the true progress of talents with the protection princes can grant them. The sciences have been ruling, so to speak, in China for two thousand years without being able to leave their

---

1. Pietro Bonaventura Metastasio (1698–1782) was a poet and opera librettist who came to Vienna in 1730. Rousseau praises him highly in his musical writings.

infancy, while they are in their vigor in England where the government does nothing for them. Europe is truly inundated with literary people, and people of merit are still rare there; enduring writings are even more so, and posterity will believe that very few books were written in this century in which so many are written.

As to your fatherland in particular, a very simple observation presents itself, sir. The Empress and her august ancestors did not need to secure historians and poets to celebrate the great things they wanted to do; but they have done great things and they have been dedicated to immortality like those of that ancient people who knew how to act and did not write. Perhaps their labors lacked the worthiest thing to crown them because it is the most difficult. That is to sustain with the aid of letters so much glory acquired without them.

However this might be, sir, enough other people will give to the protectors of the sciences and the arts praises that Their Imperial Majesties will share with most kings; as for me, what I admire in them and what is more truly proper to them, is their love of virtue and of honorable things. I do not deny that your country was barbarous for a long time, but I say that it was easier to establish the arts among the Huns than to make the greatest court of Europe into a school of good morals.

Furthermore, I must tell you that your letter, having been addressed to Geneva before coming to Paris, remained en route nearly six weeks, which deprived me of the pleasure of answering as soon as I would have liked.

I am, as much as a decent man can be to another, sir, your very humble and very obedient servant.[2]

JJRousseau

---

2. Rousseau wrote and crossed out numerous variations of his closing formula before arriving at one that satisfied him.

CHAPTER 28

Voltaire

August 18, 1756

Rousseau's friend Duclos had sent him copies of Voltaire's Poem on the Disaster of Lisbon, or Examination of This Axiom: "All is Good," *as well as the* Poem on Natural Law. *In the first Voltaire had argued that the Lisbon earthquake of November 1, 1755, had proven that there was no divine providence.*

Your last two poems, sir, have reached me in my solitude, and even though all my friends know the love I have for your writings, I do not know from whom these could come to me, unless it is from you. I found in them pleasure along with instruction, and recognized the hand of the master; so I believe that I ought to thank you both for the copy and for the work. I will not say to you that everything in it pleases me equally, but the things in it which pain me only inspire me with more confidence in those that transport me. It is not without effort that I sometimes protect my reason against the charms of your poetry, but it is to make my admiration more worthy of your works that I try not to admire everything in them.

I will do more: I will speak to you directly, not about the beauties that I believed I felt in these two poems—the task would frighten my laziness—nor even about the defects which more skillful people than I may perhaps notice in them, but the displeasures that cloud at this moment the fondness I used to have for your lessons. And I will speak about them to you while still moved by a first reading during which my heart avidly listened to yours, loving you as my brother, honoring you as my teacher, and, finally, flattering myself that you will recognize in my intentions the frankness of an upright soul, and in my speech the tone of a friend of truth speaking to a philosopher. For that matter, the more your second poem enchants me, the more I freely take sides against the first, for if you did not fear to be in contradiction with yourself, why would I fear to share your opinion? I must believe that you do not care very much for sentiments which you refute so well.

All my complaints are therefore against your *Poem on the Lisbon Disaster*, for I was expecting in it effects more worthy of the humanity which seems to have inspired it. You reproach Pope and Leibniz for insulting our ills when they maintain that all is good, and you so enlarge upon the picture of our miseries, that you aggravate our sentiment of them. Instead of the consolations that I hoped for, you only distress me. It is as if you fear that I do not sufficiently see how miserable I am; and you think, it seems, greatly to reassure me by proving to me that all is bad.

Do not be mistaken, sir; exactly the contrary of what you propose happens. That optimism which you find so cruel nevertheless consoles me for the same pains that you depict as insupportable. Pope's poem softens my ills and moves me to patience; yours sharpens my pains, excites me to complain, and taking everything away from me except a shaken hope, reduces me to despair. In this strange opposition which reigns between what you establish and what I experience, calm the perplexity that agitates me, and tell me, which deceives itself, sentiment, or reason.

"Man, be patient," Pope and Leibnitz tell me. "Your ills are a necessary effect of your nature and of the constitution of the universe. The eternal and beneficent Being which governs it would have wanted to protect you from them; of all the possible economies he chose the one that united the least amount of ill with the greatest amount of good or (to say the same thing even more crudely, if one must), if he did not do better, it is because he could not do better."

Now, what does your poem tell me? "Suffer forever, unfortunate wretch. If there is a God who created you, doubtless he is all-powerful. He could have prevented all your ills. Never hope, then, that they will end, for one could not see why you exist, if not to suffer and die." I do not know in what a doctrine like this can be more consoling than optimism, or even fatality itself. As for me, I confess that it seems even more cruel than Manicheanism. If the difficulty regarding the origin of evil forced you to alter some of God's perfections, why justify his power at the expense of his goodness? If one must choose between two errors, I far prefer the first.

You do not want, sir, your work to be viewed as a poem against Providence, and I will take good care not to give it that name, even though you characterized as a book against the human race a writing in which I pleaded the cause of the human race against itself.[1] I know what distinction must be made between an author's intentions and the consequences that can be drawn from his doctrine. A just self-defense only obliges me to have you observe that in depicting human miseries, my goal was excusable, and even laudable, or so I believe. For I showed men how they produced their own ills, and consequently how they could avoid them.

I do not see that one can seek the source of moral evil anywhere but in man, free, perfected, and hence corrupted; as to physical ills, if sensitive and unfeeling matter is a contradiction, as it seems to me, they are inevitable in any system of which man is a part, and then the question is not why is man not perfectly happy, but why does he exist. In addition, I believe that I have shown that except for death, which is an ill almost only because of the preparations which are made to precede it, most of our physical ills are, again, our work. Without departing from your subject of Lisbon, admit, for example, that nature did not assemble twenty thousand houses of six or seven stories there, and that if the inhabitants of this large city had been more equally dispersed and more sparsely lodged, the damage would have been much less, and perhaps null. Everything would have fled with the first shock, and one would have seen them the next day twenty leagues from there, as gay as if nothing had happened. But one must stay, remain obdurately around the ruins, expose oneself to new tremors, because what one leaves behind is more valuable than what one can carry off. How many unfortunate wretches perished in this disaster for having wanted to take, one his clothes, the other his papers, another his money? Do we not know that each man's person has become the least part of himself, and that it is not worth the trouble of saving it when one has lost everything else?

You would have wanted—and who would not have wanted it!—that the earthquake had happened in the depths of a desert rather than in

---

1. The *Second Discourse*.

Lisbon. Can one doubt that some also happen in the deserts? But we do not speak of these, because they do no harm to the gentlemen of the cities, the only men of whom we take account. They do little even to animals and to savages who live, dispersed, in these secluded regions, and who fear neither roofs crashing down nor houses burning.[2] But what does such a privilege signify? Would we have to say that the order of the world must change according to our whims, that nature must be subjected to our laws, and that to forbid an earthquake in a certain place, we only have to build a city there?

There are events that often strike us more or less according to the aspects under which we consider them, and which lose much of the horror they inspire at first sight when one wants to examine them closely. I learned in *Zadig*, and nature confirms from day to day, that an accelerated death is not always a real ill and that it can sometimes pass as a relative good. Among so many men crushed under the ruins of this unfortunate city, some, doubtless, avoided even greater misfortunes, and despite what is moving about such a description and what it furnishes to poetry, it is not certain that one of these unfortunates suffered more than if, in the ordinary course of events, he had waited in long agonies the death which has come to take him unawares. Is there a sadder end than that of a dying man who is tormented by useless treatments, whom a notary and heirs do not let take a breath, whom the doctors assassinate in his bed as they please, and whom barbarous priests artfully cause to savor death? As for me, I see everywhere that the ills to which nature subjects us are far less cruel than those it pleases us to add to them.

But however ingenious we may be in fomenting our miseries by dint of our noble institutions, we have not, until now, been able to perfect ourselves to the point of generally making life a burden, and of preferring nothingness to existence. If that were not so, discouragement and despair would soon have seized upon the greatest number, and the human species could not long have subsisted. Now, if it is better for us to be than not to be, that would be enough to justify our existence, even though we did not have any compensation to expect for the ills that we have to suffer, and these ills were as great as you depict them. But it is difficult to find on this subject good faith among men and sound calculations among philosophers, because the latter, in the comparison

---

2. *Sauvage*, translated here as "savages," can mean "wild" or "uncultivated."

of goods and ills, always forget the sweet sentiment of existing, independent of any other sensation, and the vanity of despising death incites the former to calumny life—a little like those women who, with a stained dress and scissors, claim to prefer holes to stains.

You think along with Erasmus that few would want to be reborn to the same conditions under which they lived. But such a one holds his merchandise at a high price who would reduce it greatly if he had any hope of concluding the deal. Besides, sir, whom should I believe you have consulted on this point? Some rich people, perhaps, replete with false pleasures, but unaware of the genuine ones, always bored with life, and always trembling at the thought of losing it; perhaps men of letters, of all the kinds of men the most sedentary, the unhealthiest, the most reflective, and consequently the most unhappy. Would you like to find better constituted men or, at least, ones who are commonly more sincere and who, making up the greatest number, must, at least on this score, be heard by preference? Consult an honest bourgeois who will have passed an obscure and tranquil life, without projects and without ambition; a good artisan, who lives comfortably from his occupation; even a peasant, not from France, where it is maintained that they must be made to die of misery so that they can make you live, but from the country, for example, where you are,[3] and generally from any free country. I dare to state as a fact that there is perhaps not in the High Valais a single mountain dweller discontented with his almost automatic life, and who would not willingly accept, even instead of paradise, the deal of being ceaselessly reborn in order thus to vegetate perpetually. These differences make me believe that it is often our abuse of life that makes it a burden for us; and I have a much less good opinion of those who are vexed at having lived than of the one who can say with Cato: *Nec me vixisse poenitet, quoniam ita vixi, ut frustra me natum non existimem.*[4] This does not mean that the wise man cannot sometimes willingly move out without complaint and without despair, when nature or fortune very distinctly gives him the order to depart. But, in the ordinary course of things, whatever ills are sown throughout human life it is not, all things considered, a bad present, and if it is not always an ill to die, it is very rarely one to live.

---

3. Voltaire was then living on the outskirts of Geneva.

4. "Nor do I regret that I have lived, since I have lived such that I do not think I was born in vain." Cicero, *Cato Maior de senectute* 84.

Our different ways of thinking on all these subjects teach me why some of your proofs are not conclusive for me. For I am not unaware of the degree to which human reason more easily takes on the mold of our opinions rather than that of truth, and that of two men with contrary opinions, what the first believes to be demonstrated is often nothing but a sophism for the other.

When, for example, you attack the chain of beings so well described by Pope, you say that it is not true that, if one removed one atom from the world, the world could not subsist. You cite on that point M. de Crouzas;[5] then you add that nature is not subject to any precise measure or to any precise form; that no planet moves along an absolutely regular curve; that no known being has a precisely mathematical figure; that no precise quantity is required for any operation; that nature never acts rigorously. Thus, one has no reason to affirm that one atom less on earth would cause the destruction of the earth. I admit that regarding all this, sir, I am more struck by the force of the assertion than of the reasoning, and that, on this occasion, I would yield more confidently to your authority than to your proofs.

As to M. de Crouzas, I have not read his writing against Pope, and I am perhaps not in a condition to understand it. But what is very sure is that I will not concede to him what I would have disputed with you, and that I have as little faith in his authority as in his proofs. Far from thinking that nature is not subject to the precision of quantities and figures, I would believe, on the contrary, that it alone rigorously follows this precision, because it alone knows how to compare exactly the ends and the means and to measure strength against resistance. As to these pretended irregularities, can one doubt that they all have their physical cause, and does it suffice not to perceive it to deny that it exists? These apparent irregularities arise, no doubt, from some laws that we do not know, and which nature follows just as faithfully as those that are known to us; from some agent that we do not perceive, and the obstacle or concurrence of which has fixed measures in all its operations. Otherwise, one would have to say distinctly that there are actions without principle and effects without cause,[6] which is repugnant to all philosophy.

Let us suppose two weights in equilibrium, which are nevertheless unequal; let the quantity by which they differ be added to the smaller one. Either the two weights will remain in equilibrium, and we will have

---

5. Rousseau here cites Voltaire's extended first note to his poem on the disaster of Lisbon.

6. "Principle" here means the fundamental basis or wellspring of a thing.

a cause without an effect; or the equilibrium will be broken, and we will have an effect without a cause. If, however, the weights were made of iron, and if a speck of magnet were hidden under one of them, the precision of nature would then take away the appearance of precision; and by dint of exactitude, it would seem to lack it. There is not a figure, not an operation, not a law in the physical world, to which we could not apply some example similar to the one I just proposed regarding gravity.

You say that no known being has a precisely mathematical figure. I ask you, sir, if there is any possible figure that does not, and whether the most bizarre curve is not as regular in nature's eyes as a perfect circle is in ours. I imagine, furthermore, that if some body could have this apparent regularity, that would only be the universe itself, supposing it to be full and limited. For mathematical figures only being abstractions, they are only related to themselves, whereas all those of natural bodies are relative to other bodies, and to movements which modify them. So this would again prove nothing against the precision of nature, even if we agreed as to what you mean by this word "precision."

You distinguish between events which have effects and those which have none. I doubt that this distinction is solid. Every event seems to me necessarily to have some effect, either moral or physical, or composed of the two, but that one does not always perceive, because the filiation of events is even more difficult to follow than that of men. As in general one must not seek for effects greater than the events that produce them, the smallness of causes often makes examination absurd, even though the effects are certain; and often also several almost imperceptible effects unite to produce a considerable event. Add that this effect does not cease to take place even if it acts outside of the body that produces it. Hence the dust raised by a coach may do nothing to the functioning of the vehicle but have influence on that of the world. But since there is nothing foreign to the universe, everything that is done in it necessarily acts on the universe itself.

Thus, sir, your examples appear to me to be ingenious and unconvincing. I see a thousand plausible reasons why it was perhaps not indifferent to Europe that on a certain day the heiress of Bourgogne had her hair well or badly done; or to the destiny of Rome that Caesar turned his eyes to the right and left, and spit to one side or the other, while going to the Senate, on the day that he was punished. In a word, calling to mind the grain of sand cited by Pascal,[7] I am in some respects of the

---

7. Blaise Pascal, *Pensées*, in *Œuvres complètes*, ed. Jacques Chevalier (Paris: Gallimard, 1914), 1147–48.

same opinion as your Brahmin.[8] However one considers things, if all the events do not have perceptible effects, it appears to me incontestable that all have real ones, the thread of which the human mind easily loses grasp, but which are never confused by nature.

You say that it is demonstrated that celestial bodies revolve in nonresistant space. That was assuredly a fine thing to demonstrate, but, according to the custom of the ignorant, I have very little faith in demonstrations that are beyond my reach. I would imagine that, to construct this one, one would have reasoned more or less in this way: such and such a force, acting according to such law, must give to the stars such and such a motion in a nonresistant medium. Now, the stars have exactly the calculated motion; therefore, there is no resistance. But who can know if there are not, perhaps, a million other possible laws, without counting the genuine one, according to which the same motions would be even better explained in a fluid than in a void according to this one? Has not the abhorrence of vacuum for a long time explained most of the effects that have since been attributed to the action of air? Other experiments having since destroyed the abhorrence of vacuum, has not everything been found to be full? Has not the void been reestablished on the basis of new calculations? Who will vouch that a more exact system will not destroy it once again? Let us leave aside the difficulties without number that a physicist would perhaps raise regarding the nature of light, and lit spaces. But do you believe in good faith that Bayle, whose wisdom and restraint in the matter of opinion I admire as you do, would have found yours to be so fully demonstrated? In general, it seems that the skeptics forget themselves a little as soon as they adopt a dogmatic tone, and that they should use the term "demonstrated" more soberly than anyone. How to be believed, when one boasts of knowing nothing while affirming so many things?

As to the rest, you have made a correction to Pope's system which is very exact, when you observe that there is no proportional gradation between the creatures and the creator, and that if the chain of created beings ends in God, it does so because he holds it, not because he terminates it.

On the good of the whole being preferable to that of the part, you have man say: "I must be as dear to my master, I, a thinking and feeling being, as the planets, which probably do not feel." Doubtless this

---

8. Some scholars believe that this is a reference to a hermit (not a Brahmin) in Voltaire's *Zadig*, but it could refer to his *Dialogue between a Brahmin and a Jesuit on the Necessity and Linkage of Things*, originally published in 1752 and republished often with variants.

material universe must not be dearer to its author than a single think-ing and feeling being. But the system of this universe which produces, preserves, and perpetuates all the thinking and feeling beings must be dearer to him than a single one of these beings. He can therefore, despite his goodness, or rather because of his very goodness, sacrifice something of the happiness of individuals for the preservation of the whole. I believe, I hope, that I am worth more in God's eyes than the earth of a planet; but if the planets are inhabited, as is probable, why would I be worth more in his eyes than all the inhabitants of Saturn? One can ridicule these ideas as much as one wants, but it is certain that all the analogies are on behalf of this population; only human pride is against it. Now, this population being supposed, the preservation of the universe seems to have, for God himself, a morality which is multi-plied by the number of inhabited worlds.

That a man's corpse feeds worms, wolves, or plants is not, I admit, a compensation for the death of this man. But if, in the system of this universe, it is necessary for the preservation of the human species that there be a circulation of substances among men, animals, and plants, then the particular ill for an individual contributes to the general good. I die, I am eaten by worms; but my brothers, my children will live as I lived; and I do by the order of nature for the sake of all men what Codrus, Curtius, the Decemvirs, the Philaeni,[9] and a thousand others did voluntarily for a small part of men.

To return, sir, to the system which you attack, I believe that we cannot properly examine it without distinguishing carefully between particular evil, whose existence no philosopher has ever denied, and general evil, that the optimist denies. It is not a question of knowing whether each one of us suffers or not, but whether it was good that the universe is, and if our ills were inevitable according to its constitution. Thus, the addition of one article, it seems, would make the proposition more precise: and instead of "All is good," it might be better to say, "The whole is good" or "Everything is good for the whole." Then it is very evident that no man could give direct proofs either for or against; for these proofs depend on a perfect knowledge of the constitution of the

---

9. Codrus, legendary king of Athens, renowned for his sacrifice for his city; Marcus Cur-tius, said to have leaped into a chasm to save Rome (Livy, *Ab urbe condita* 7.6); the Decemvirs, the members of the Decemvirate that codified a new set of laws to settle the conflict between the patricians and plebeians in Rome (451 BCE); the Philaeni brothers, who agreed to be buried alive to extend the Carthaginian border against a hostile neighbor (Sallust, *Bellum lugurthinum* 79).

world, and of the aim of its author, and this knowledge is incontest-ably above human intelligence. The real principles of optimism can be derived neither from the properties of matter nor from the mechanism of the universe, but only by induction from the perfections of God who presides over everything. Such that one does not prove the existence of God based on Pope's system, but Pope's system based on the exis-tence of God; and it is, without contradiction, from the question of Providence that the question of the origin of evil is derived. If neither of these two questions has been well treated, that is because Providence has always been so badly reasoned about, and that what was said about it which was absurd has greatly muddled all the consequences that one could draw from this great and consoling dogma.

The first who have blighted God's cause are the priests and the devout, who do not permit that anything be done according to the established order, but always make divine justice intervene in purely natural events, and to be sure of their fact, punish and chastise the bad, test and compensate the good indifferently with goods or with ills, according to the event. I do not know, as for me, if that is good theol-ogy; but I find that it is a bad way of reasoning to found on the pro and con the proofs of Providence, and to attribute to it, without choice, everything that would equally be done without it.

The philosophers, in turn, appear hardly more reasonable to me, when I see them find fault with Heaven that they are not unfeeling, and cry out that all is lost when their teeth ache, or they are poor, or they are robbed, and make God responsible, as Seneca says, for safeguarding their suitcase.[10] If some tragic accident had made Cartouche or Caesar perish in their infancy, it would have been said: what crimes did they commit? These two bandits lived, and we say: why have let them live? On the contrary, a devout person will say in the first case: God wanted to punish the father by taking away his child; and in the second: God preserved the child for the chastisement of the people. Thus, whatever side nature chose, Providence is always right among the devout, and always wrong among the philosophers. Perhaps in the order of human things it is neither wrong nor right because everything depends on the common law, and there is no exception for anyone. One can believe that particular events are nothing in the eyes of the master of the universe, that his Providence is only universal, that he is content with preserving

---

10. Seneca, *De providentia*, 6.i.

kinds and species and with presiding over the whole, without concern about how each individual passes this short life. Does a wise king who wants everyone to live happily within his states need to inform himself whether the inns there are any good? The passerby complains for a night when they are bad and laughs all the rest of his days for such a misplaced impatience. *Commorandi enim natura diversorium nobis, non habitandi dedit.*[11]

In order to think correctly regarding this matter, it seems that things should be considered relatively in the physical order, and absolutely in the moral order: such that the greatest idea I can conceive of Providence is that each material being is disposed as well as possible in relation to the whole, and each intelligent and sensitive being as well as possible relative to himself. Which signifies, in other words, that for whoever feels his existence, it must be better to exist than not to exist. But this rule must be applied to the total duration of each sensitive being, and not to some particular instant in its duration, such as human life, which shows how much the question of Providence depends on the immortality of the soul, in which I have the happiness of believing, without being unaware that reason can doubt it; and on the eternity of suffering, in which neither you nor I, nor any man who thinks well of God, will ever believe.

If I reduce these diverse questions to their common principle, it seems to me that they are all related to the existence of God. If God exists, he is perfect; if he is perfect, he is wise, powerful, and just; if he is wise and powerful, all is good; if he is just and powerful, my soul is immortal; if my soul is immortal, thirty years of life are nothing for me, and are perhaps necessary to the maintenance of the universe. If one grants me the first proposition, one will never shake the subsequent ones. If one denies it, what is the point of quarreling over the consequences?

We are neither of us in this latter case. Very far at least in reading your collected works from being able to presume anything like that on your part, most of them offer me the greatest, the sweetest, the most consoling ideas of the Divinity; and I much prefer a Christian in your manner than one from the Sorbonne.[12]

As for me, I will frankly admit that neither the pro nor the con on this important question seems to me to be demonstrated by the light

---

11. "Nature has willed that we be on earth as guests in passage, not as inhabitants." Cicero, *Cato Maior de senectute* 84.

12. Theological college of the University of Paris.

of reason and that, if the theist founds his sentiment only on prob-
abilities, the atheist, even less precise, seems to me to found his only
on contrary possibilities. Moreover, the objections on both sides are
always insoluble, because they turn on things about which men have
no genuine idea. I grant all this, and yet I believe in God as strongly as
I believe in any other truth; because to believe and not to believe are the
things in the world which depend the least on me; because the state of
doubt is a state too violent for my soul; because when my reason drifts,
my faith cannot for long stay in suspense and determines itself without
it; because, finally, a thousand subjects of preference draw me to the
most consoling side and join the weight of hope to the equilibrium of
reason.[13]

Here then is a truth from which we both begin, in the support of
which you feel how easy optimism is to defend and Providence to justify. And it is not you to whom one has to repeat the rehashed but solid
reasonings which have so often been made on this subject. As to the
philosophers who do not agree with the principle, one must not argue
with them on these matters, for what is only a proof of sentiment for
us cannot become a demonstration for them, and because to say to
a man, you must believe this because I believe it, is not a reasonable

---

13. The following significant paragraph was first included as a previously unpublished
part of this letter in an 1861 edition of Rousseau's works overseen by George Streckeisen-
Moulton: "I remember that what struck me the most strongly in my whole life, regarding the
fortuitous arrangement of the universe, is the twenty-first philosophic thought, in which it
is shown by the laws of the analysis of chance that when the quantity of throws is infinite,
the difficulty of the outcome is more than sufficiently compensated for by the multitude of
throws; and that consequently the mind ought to be more astonished by the hypothetical
duration of chaos than by the actual birth of the universe.—It is, assuming that movement is
necessary, what has never been said more strongly to my liking on this dispute; and, as for me,
I declare that I do not know the slightest response that accords with common sense, neither
true, nor false, if not to deny as false what one cannot know, that motion might be essential
to matter. From another perspective, I do not know that the generation of organized bodies
and the perpetuity of seeds have ever been explained by materialism. There is, however, this
difference between the two opposed positions, that although both seem equally convincing
to me, the latter alone persuades me. As for the former, let someone come to tell me that the
Henriade was composed from a fortuitous throw of letters, I deny it without hesitating. It
is more possible for chance to bring it about than for my mind to believe it, and I feel that
there is a point for me at which moral impossibilities are equivalent to physical certainty. You
may well speak to me about the eternity of time, I have not traversed it; about the infinity of
throws, I have not counted them; and my incredulity—as little philosophic as you want—will
triumph over demonstration itself. I do not prevent what I call here 'proof of sentiment' from
being called 'prejudice'; and I do not present this obstinacy of belief as a model. With a good
faith perhaps without precedent, however, I present it as an invincible disposition of my soul,
that nothing will ever be able to overcome, about which I have nothing to complain up to now
and which cannot be attacked without cruelty."

speech. They, on their side, must not argue with us either on these same subjects, because they are only corollaries of a central proposition that a decent adversary hardly dares to oppose to them. In their turn, they would be wrong to require that we prove the corollary independently of the proposition which serves as its basis. I believe that they ought not to also for another reason, which is that there is inhumanity in troubling peaceful souls and in desolating men to no purpose, when what one wants to teach them is neither certain nor useful. I think, in a word, that, following your example, one could not attack the superstition that disrupts society too strongly, nor respect the religion which supports it too much.

But, like you, I am indignant that each one's faith is not in the most perfect freedom, and that man dares to control the inside of consciences where he could not penetrate, as if it depended on us whether to believe or not to believe in matters where demonstration does not take place, and as if one could ever subject reason to authority. Do the kings of the world then have some right of inspection in the other, and are they in the right to torment their subjects here below so as to force them to go to paradise? No, every human government is limited by its nature to civil duties, and whatever the sophist Hobbes may have said about it, when a man serves the State well, he does not owe an account of the way he serves God to anybody.

I do not know whether this just Being will not one day punish every tyranny exercised in his name; I am at least very sure that he will not share it, and that he will not refuse eternal happiness to any unbeliever who is virtuous and of good faith. Can I, without offending his goodness and even his justice, doubt that an upright heart makes amends for an involuntary error, and that irreproachable morals are in his eyes well worth a thousand bizarre cults prescribed by men and rejected by reason? I will say more: if I could purchase works at the expense of my faith, and compensate by dint of virtue for my supposed incredulity, I would not hesitate for an instant, and I would rather be able to say to God: "I did, without thinking of you, the good that pleases you, and my heart followed your will without knowing it" than to say to him, as I will have to one day: "Alas! I loved you and never stopped offending you; I knew you and did nothing to please you."

There is, I admit, a kind of profession of faith that the laws can impose, but apart from the principles of morality and of natural right, it must be purely negative, for religions that attack the foundations of society can exist, and one must begin by exterminating these religions so as to assure the peace of the State. Of these dogmas to be proscribed, intolerance is easily the most odious. But it must be taken hold of at its source, for the most bloodthirsty fanatics change their language according to fortune and preach only patience and gentleness when they are not the most powerful. I thus call intolerant on principle every man who imagines that one cannot be a good man without believing everything he believes, and pitilessly damns all those who do not think as he does. Indeed, the faithful are rarely in the mood to leave the reprobates in peace in this world, and a saint who lives in the mist of the damned willingly anticipates the work of the devil. If there were intolerant unbelievers, who would want to force the people to believe nothing, I would banish them no less severely than those who want to force it to believe everything that pleases them.

I would like, therefore, that in each State there were a moral code, or a kind of civil profession of faith, which would positively contain the social maxims that each would be held to accept, and negatively the fanatical maxims that one would be held to reject, not as impious, but as seditious. Hence any religion which could accord with the code would be accepted; every religion which could not accord with it would be proscribed; and each would be free to have none other than the code itself. This work, done with care, would be, it seems to me, the most useful book that would ever have been composed, and perhaps the only one necessary for men. There, sir, is a subject worthy of you. I would passionately wish that you would want to undertake such a work, and even adorn it with your poetry, so that, everyone being able to learn it easily, it would carry from infancy into all hearts those sentiments of gentleness and humanity which shine in your writings, and which the devout always lacked. I exhort you to meditate on this project, which must at least please your soul. In your *Poem on Natural Religion*, you gave us man's catechism: now give us, in the one I propose to you, the citizen's catechism. It is, furthermore, a matter to be meditated at length, and perhaps to reserve for the last of your works, so as to bring to a close, by a benefit to the human species, the most brilliant career that man of letters ever traversed.

I cannot prevent myself, as I finish, from noting a very singular opposition between you and me regarding the subject of this letter. Replete with glory, disabused of vain grandeurs, you live free in the bosom of abundance; quite sure of immortality, you tranquilly philosophize on the nature of the soul, and if either the body or the heart suffers, you have Tronchin as doctor and friend. Yet you find nothing but evil on earth. And I, an obscure and poor man, tormented by an ill without remedy, I meditate with pleasure in my retreat, and find that all is good. Whence these apparent contradictions? You have explained it yourself: you enjoy; but I hope, and hope embellishes everything.

I have as much trouble in leaving this tiresome letter as you will have in finishing it. Pardon me, great man, for a perhaps indiscreet zeal, but which would not express itself to you if I esteemed you less. God forbid that I would want to offend the one among my contemporaries whose talents I honor the most, and whose writings speak best to my heart, but it is a question of the cause of Providence, from whom I expect everything. After having for so long drawn consolations and courage from your lessons, it is hard for me that you now take away all of that, to leave me with nothing but an uncertain and vague hope, rather as a palliative for the present than as a compensation to come. No, I have suffered too much in this life not to await another one. All the subtleties of metaphysics may well sharpen my pains, but they will not at all shake within me faith in the immortality of the soul. I feel it, I believe it; I want it, I hope for it, I will defend it until my last breath, and it will be, in all the disputes that I have sustained, the sole one in which my interest will not be forgotten.

I am with respect, sir, yours etc.

CHAPTER 29

Louise Florence Pétronille Tardieu d'Esclavelles, madame d'Épinay

December 1, 1756

Mme. d'Épinay had given Rousseau a packet of salt and an English flannel petticoat that she had worn so he could have it made into a waistcoat. See Confessions, *book 9, CW 5:367. Rousseau acknowledged the gifts, saying that he had not understood a reference to an icebox, Giants of the North, and goblins in her accompanying note. She wrote a letter explaining her motives for sending the gifts and mentioned that she had, at last, met Rousseau's friend Diderot. Her letters have been lost.*

Let the petticoat pass, but the salt! Never has a woman given warmth and prudence at the same time. In the end you will make me put my bonnet on crosswise, and I will not set it straight again.[1] Have you not done enough for yourself? Now do something for me and let yourself be loved in my own way.

Oh, how good you are with your explanations! Ah! this dear rheumatism? Now that you have explained your note to me, explain the commentary; for that icebox about which I understand nothing returns

---

1. The expression Rousseau uses is "mettre mon bonnet de travers," which means "put me in a bad mood."

in it, and as for me, I do not know of any icebox of yours other than a collection of French music.

Finally: you have seen the man. That is always so much gained; for I am of your opinion, and I believe that this is all that you will have of him. Yet I easily suspect what a perfumed bear should tell you about the effect of this first discussion,[2] but as for me, I think that the Diderot of the morning will always want to go see you and that the Diderot of the evening will have never seen you. You know that rheumatism also comes over him sometimes, and when he is not soaring close to the sun on his two great wings one finds him on a heap of grass crippled in his four paws. Believe me, if you have another petticoat left, you will do well to send it to him. I did not know that papa Gauffecourt was sick, and I was even made to hope that I would see him today; what you informed me about will make me extremely sad if he does not come.

More new plans? The devil with plans, and *plan plan relantanplan.* Without a doubt a plan is a very fine thing, but made of details and theatrical scenes, that is all that is needed for the success of a piece at a reading, and sometimes even in performance. May God preserve you from making a good enough one for that.

I have reread your letter to look for spelling mistakes in it and did not know how to find one, although I do not doubt that they are there. I do not hold it against you for making them, but for having taken note of them. As for me, I wanted to make some on purpose to make you ashamed and did not think about it anymore when I was writing to you.

Good day, my friend of the present time and even more again in the time to come. You tell me nothing about your health which makes me predict that it is good.

Apropos of health, I do not know if there is accurate spelling in this rag, but I find that there is not very much sense; which makes me believe that I would not have done any harm by making out of your petticoat a good, very thick skullcap, rather than a waistcoat; because I feel that rheumatism holds me by the head rather than by the heart.

---

2. There have been numerous guesses about the object of the reference to "a perfumed bear," including Grimm, d'Holbach, and Gauffecourt. Mme. d'Épinay was fond of nicknames and called Rousseau *ours* (bear), which is both an anagram of the first four letters of his name and a reference to his unsociability. Thus, it seems possible that Rousseau is distinguishing himself (a bear) from a domesticated "perfumed" bear.

I ask you please to be willing to ask the tyrant the meaning of a package that he had sent to me containing two crowns of six francs.[3] That appears to me to be a slightly large advance on the chess matches he must lose to me.

Diderot is leaving here, I showed him your letter and mine. I told you; he has conceived a great esteem for you and will not see you . . . You have done enough; even for him. Believe me, let him go. Mother Levasseur has returned and feels a little better.

____

3. "The tyrant" is a nickname that was given to Grimm by Gauffecourt. See *Confessions, CW* 5:392.

CHAPTER 30

Denis Diderot

March 24, 1757

Rousseau's quarrel with Diderot began when Diderot sent him a copy of his play The Natural Son. *This play has a character, Dorval, who resembles Rousseau in some ways. When Dorval wants to retire to the country, a friend says, "Only the wicked man lives alone." Rousseau thought that people would apply this phrase to him.*

I would like to summarize the history of our quarrels in a few words. You sent me your book. I wrote you the most tender and honorable note about it that I have written in my life,[1] and in which I complained with all the gentleness of friendship about a maxim that is very fishy and of which people could make a very injurious application to me. In response I received a very dry letter, in which you claim to pardon me by not considering me a dishonorable man, and that solely because I have an eighty-year-old woman in my home, as if the country were fatal at that age and eighty-year-old women were only in Paris. My answer had all the liveliness of a decent man insulted by his friend; you rejoined with an abominable letter. I defended myself again and very strongly;

---

1. Neither this note nor the response to which Rousseau refers immediately below has been found.

but distrusting the rage in which you had put me, and in that state even dreading to be in the wrong with a friend, I sent my letter to Mme. d'Épinay, whom I made the judge of our difference of opinion. She returned that same letter to me imploring me to suppress it, and I suppressed it. Now you write me another one in which you call me wicked, unjust, cruel, ferocious. That is the summary of what has happened on this occasion.

I would like to ask you two or three very simple questions. Who is the aggressor in this business? If you want to submit to the judgment of a third party, show my first note; I will show yours.

Assuming that I received your reproaches badly and was wrong at bottom, which of the two of us was more obliged to take on the tone of reason so as to bring the other back to it? I have never resisted a gentle word; you might be unaware of that, but you may know that I do not give way willingly to insults. If your plan in all this business had been to irritate me, what more would you have done?

You complain a great deal about the harms I have done you. What are they then, in the end, these harms? Would it be not to put up patiently enough with those you like to do me, not to let myself be tyrannized as it pleases you, to grumble when you affect to fail to keep your word to me and never to come when you have promised? If I have ever done you other harms, articulate them. Me, do harm to my friend! As cruel, as wicked, as ferocious as I am, I would die of sorrow if I believed I had ever done to my cruelest enemy as much as you have done over the past six weeks.

You speak to me about your services; I had not forgotten them. But do not fool yourself. Many people have rendered me some who were not my friends. A decent man who feels nothing renders a service and believes he is a friend; he is fooling himself; he is only a decent man. All your eagerness, all your zeal in procuring for me things I do not care about touch me very little. I want only friendship, and that is the only thing I am refused. Ingrate, I have not rendered you any service, but I have loved you, and you will not pay me in your life for what I felt for you for three months. Show this item to your wife, who is more equitable than you are, and ask her if, when my presence was sweet to your afflicted heart, I counted my steps and considered the weather to go to Vincennes to console my friend.[2] Insensitive and harsh man, two

---

2. Diderot was imprisoned in the Chateau of Vincennes for slightly over three months in 1748 as a result of the publication of the *Letter on the Blind*. Rousseau visited him almost every day.

tears shed in my bosom would have been worth more to me than the throne of the world; but you refuse them to me and content yourself with wresting them from me. Eh, well! keep all the rest: I no longer want anything from you.

It is true that I engaged Mme. d'Épinay to keep you from coming last Saturday. We were both irritated: I do not know how to measure my words, and you, you are mistrustful, touchy, weighing rigorously words let out inconsiderately, and subject to giving to a thousand simple things a subtle meaning of which one had not dreamed. It was dangerous to see each other in this condition. Moreover, you wanted to come on foot; you were risking making yourself ill and would, perhaps, not have been too sorry about it. I did not feel that I had the courage to risk all the dangers of that interview. This fright assuredly did not deserve your reproaches; for whatever you might do, the tie of our old friendship will always be sacred to my heart, and even were you to insult me again, I will always see you with pleasure when anger does not blind me.

As to Mme. d'Épinay, I have sent her your letters and mine; I would be stifled with sorrow without this communication and, no longer having any reason, I needed advice. You always appear to be so proud of your behavior in this business that you ought to be very satisfied to have a witness who can admire it. It is true that she is serving you well, and if I did not know her motive, I would believe her to be as unjust as you.

As for me, the more I think about it, the less I can understand you. How? Because, apropos of I do not very well know what, you said that the wicked man is alone. Is it absolutely necessary to make me wicked and sacrifice your friend to that saying? For other authors, the alternative would be dangerous, but you! Moreover, that alternative is not necessary; your saying, however obscure and fishy, is very true in one sense, and in this sense it does me nothing but honor; for whatever you might say about it, I am much less alone here than you in the middle of Paris. Diderot! Diderot! I see it with a bitter sorrow; ceaselessly among the wicked, you are learning to resemble them; your good heart is being corrupted among them, and you are forcing mine to detach itself insensibly from you.

CHAPTER 31

Madame d'Épinay

March 26, 1757

Diderot has written me a third letter upon sending me back my papers. Although you notified me by yours that you are sending me this packet, it reached me later and in another way, so that when I received it my response to Diderot was already finished. You must be as bored by this long commotion as I am exasperated by it. So let us not speak of it any longer, I beg you.

But what has made you assume that I would complain about you too? If I had to complain it would be because you are too cautious with me and treat me too gently. I often need to be rebuked more than that; a tone of scolding pleases me greatly when I deserve it; I believe that I would be the man to regard it sometimes as a sort of cajolery of friendship. But one quarrels with one's friend without disdaining him; one will indeed tell him that he is a beast; one will not tell him that he is a scoundrel. You will never make me understand that you believe you are doing me a favor by thinking well of me; you will never insinuate that in considering it closely, there would be much esteem to reduce. You will not tell me: there would be more to say about that.[1] That would

---

1. Diderot had said this in his letter to Rousseau.

not only be to offend me; that would be to offend yourself, for it is not suitable for decent people to have friends of whom they think ill. If it happened to me to misinterpret on this point something you said, you would certainly hasten to explain your idea, and you would keep from maintaining this same statement harshly in the wrong way in which I would have understood it. How, madam, do you call that a form, an exterior?

I would like, since we are discussing this subject, to make you my declaration on what I require of friendship and on what I want to put into it in my turn. Correct freely what you will find to blame in my rules, but expect not to see me depart from them easily; for they are taken from my character, which I cannot change.

First, I want my friends to be my friends, and not my masters; for them to advise me without claiming to govern me; for them to have every sort of right upon my heart, none upon my freedom. I find very singular people who under this name claim always to meddle with my business without telling me anything about theirs.

For them always to speak to me freely and frankly; they can tell me everything. Aside from disdain I allow them everything. The disdain of an indifferent person is indifferent to me; but if I would put up with it from a friend, I would be worthy of it. If he has the misfortune to disdain me, let him not tell me so; let him leave me—that is his duty to himself. Aside from that, when he remonstrates with me, whatever tone he adopts to do so, he is making use of his right; when, after having listened to him, I do my will, I am making use of mine; and I find it bad that anyone harp on eternally about something that is done.

Their great eagerness to render me a thousand services about which I do not care is burdensome to me; I find in it a certain air of superiority that displeases me. Besides, everyone can do as much. I prefer that they love me and let themselves be loved; that is what friends alone can do. I am indignant above all when the first comer compensates them for me, while I cannot put up with anyone but them in the world. Only their caresses can make me tolerate their benefits, but when I do so much as to receive some from them, I want them to consult my taste, and not theirs. For we think so differently about so many things that often what they esteem as good appears to me bad.

If a quarrel arises, I could very well say that it is up to the one who is in the wrong to get over it first. But that says nothing, because each always believes that he is right; wrong or right, it is up to the one who began the quarrel to end it. If I receive his censure badly, if I become embittered without any subject for it, if I get angry inappropriately, he ought not to get angry following my example, or he does not love me. On the contrary, I want him to caress me well, to kiss me. Do you understand, madam: in a word, let him begin by calming me down, which surely will not take long. For there has never been a blaze at the bottom of my heart that a tear would not extinguish. Then, when I have been moved, calmed, ashamed, confused, let him rebuke me well, let him give me a piece of his mind, and surely he will be satisfied with me. If it is a question of a minutia that is not worth clarification, let it go; let the aggressor be quiet first, and not make it a foolish point of honor always to have the advantage. That is what I want my friend to do toward me and that I am always ready to do toward him in the same case.

I could cite on this point a sort of little example which you do not suspect, even though it concerns you. It is about a note that I received from you some time ago in response to another, from which I saw that you were not pleased, and in which you did not, it seemed to me, understand my thought very well. I made a rather good reply, or at least it appeared so to me. It certainly had the tone of genuine friendship, but at the same time a certain liveliness from which I cannot stop myself, and I feared, upon rereading it, that you would not be any more pleased with it than with the first. Instantly I threw my letter into the fire. I cannot tell you with what satisfaction of heart I saw my eloquence burning. I did not speak to you about it anymore, and I believe I have acquired the honor of being defeated. Sometimes it takes nothing more than a spark to light a blaze. My dear and good friend, Pythagoras said that one ought never to stir up a fire with a sword.[2] This saying appears to me to be the most important and most sacred of the laws of friendship.

I require from a friend even much more than everything I just said to you; more even than he ought to require from me, and which I would not require from him, if he were in my place and I were in his. As a solitary, I am more sensitive than someone else; if I have committed some wrong with a friend who lives in the social world, he ponders it for a moment and a thousand distractions make him forget it for the rest of the day; but nothing distracts me from his. Deprived of sleep, I occupy myself with it for the entire night; alone on a walk, I occupy myself with it from sunrise to sunset; my heart does not have a moment of relaxation, and the harshness of a friend gives me years of suffering in

---

2. Diogenes Laertius, *Lives of Eminent Philosophers* 8, chap. 1, secs. 17–18.

a day. As a sick man, I have a right to the consideration that humanity owes to the weakness and humor of a man who is suffering. Who is the friend, who is the decent man, who ought not to fear to afflict a wretch tormented by an incurable and painful malady? I am poor, and it seems to me that this condition also should be respected. All these considerations that I require, you have had them without me speaking to you about it; and surely never will a genuine friend need me to ask him for them. But my dear friend, let us speak sincerely, do you know me to have any friends? My word, I was right to learn to do without them. I know many people who would not be sorry that I had an obligation toward them, and many to whom I in fact have one. But hearts worthy of answering mine, ah, it is quite enough to know one.

Do not be surprised if I hate Paris more and more. Aside from your letters nothing comes from it but distressing things. They will never see me there again. If you want to make me your remonstrances on this point, and even in as lively a way as you please, you have the right to do so. They will be well received and useless; after that you will not make any more of them.

Do everything that you judge appropriate regarding M. d'Holbach's book,[3] except burden yourself with editing it. This is a way to have a book bought by force, and to call upon one's friends. I do not want any of that.

I thank you for *Anson's Voyage*; I will send it back to you next week.[4]

Excuse the crossing out. I am writing to you from the corner of my fireplace where we are all gathered, along with the gardener; the housekeepers are using up the stories of all the people hanged in the country;[5] and today's gazette is so abundant that I no longer know at all what I am saying. Good day, my good friend.

---

3. D'Holbach had proposed that Rousseau take charge of the publication of a book of chemistry for which the latter would receive the profits.

4. Rousseau is referring to a translation of *The Voyage around the World in the Years 1740, 1, 2, 3 and 4 by George Anson Esq*. He had asked Mme. d'Epinay to see if she could arrange for him to borrow d'Holbach's copy. This account of Anson's expedition against the Spanish, which resulted in the taking of an enormous prize from a galleon off the Philippines, was used by Rousseau in *Julie*. In the interval between the first and second halves of *Julie*, Saint-Preux participates in Anson's voyage and renounces the wealth he acquired from it. In part 4, letter 3, he describes his experiences and attacks both the slave trade and the conquest of Native Americans.

5. "The housekeepers" was the nickname for Thérèse and her mother.

Chapter 32

Élisabeth-Sophie-Françoise Lalive de Bellegarde, comtesse d'Houdetot

December 17, 1757
Montmorency

At last I am free. I can take on again the character of frankness and independence that nature gave me. If I had always kept it, everyone would be satisfied with me, and I would be even more so. My entire fault is to have given way to the solicitations of a feigned and deceitful friendship. I resisted for a long time; I should always have resisted. But I did not know the trap into which this siren's voice was attracting me. I might not, it is true, have found a false and perfidious friend, but I would still have found irons, and could never have been anything but a wicked slave. It was just that, after having allowed myself to be dragged in spite of myself to someone else's house, I had the shame of being dismissed from it, and the trouble of leaving it in the heart of winter. Let us speak of Mme. d'Épinay no longer. Since I no longer depend on her, I want to forget her wrongs, and am ready to put up with the blame of her friends and mine for having comported myself with the uprightness and frankness that suits me and has given me what I owed myself. If I had some reproach to make myself, it would be that I dissimulated my just indignation for too long; but I esteem myself all the more for a restraint that I would not have imposed on myself if honor and faith had been less inviolable to me.

You wish that I went without noise to live with my friend.[1] Why that? What then, for having lodged for eighteen months in someone else's house, must I wander for the rest of my days from refuge to refuge without daring any longer to reside in my own home? One ought not to have made a rupture public? Eh, have I done so? Has anyone heard me speak about Mme. d'Épinay except with praise—not those ironic and bitter praises of me in which she engages in Geneva, but those that arise from truths that do her honor and from the justice which I love to render to her? I have spoken about the inconveniences of the stay at the Hermitage during the winter, and I have spoken about them in a natural enough way not to make any other motive for my departure suspected. That was my duty. The rest does not concern me. You know that I had resolved, not out of duty, but to please you, to make a trip in the spring so as better to cover my departure, but since Mme. d'Épinay did not consent to let me stay in her house until that time, was I supposed to stay there despite her? Withdraw to my friend's home! It was necessary then to dissolve my little household entirely or transport it to his home. Do you know my situation, his, the mood of his wife, well enough to be sure that this was practicable, or was this duty of such importance that every other consideration was supposed to yield to it? On this point, I have one further word to say . . . All those whom I have loved know whether I forget them during their adversities; I believe I am allowed to be a little less zealous during my own. One does not have to fear importuning one's friends when they are suffering; but when one is suffering oneself, and they know it, one must be a little more discreet.

"I believe that you are an honorable man because you are among my friends."[2] Madam, whatever value I place on your friendship, I place even more on virtue; it was dear to me before you were, and this love is not the fruit of the sentiments with which you honor me but is what has given birth to them. May they be able to remain as long as their cause. You assure me of this yourself; you promise to love me so long as you believe me to be estimable; that is a condition that is always understood in the friendship of decent people, but which one rarely expresses without a particular motive. Would this motive lie in the difference that you are assuming between our principles? That would be

---

1. Rousseau rented a house belonging to Jacques-Joseph Mathas.
2. This is a quotation from Mme. d'Houdetot's letter of December 14 to Rousseau.

very strange, because it seems to me that probity does not allow two sorts; only the consequences can adapt to the diversity of characters. However that might be, here are mine on the point at issue. Love of oneself, as well as friendship, which is only the sharing of it, has no other law than the sentiment that inspires it. One does everything for one's friend as for oneself, not out of duty but out of delight; all the services that one renders him are goods that one does to oneself; all the gratitude inspired by those one receives from him is a sweet testimony that his heart responds to ours. That, madam, is what suits all friendship. As for me, I admit it; make in all this distinctions that are less common. Devoured by the need to love and to be loved, and hardly sensitive to all others, I do not want my friends to torment themselves any more than I do about my poverty, but to love me such as I am. I do not want them to turn their attachment into officious cares but into sentiments. I want them to make the worth of their friendship felt only by the signs that are so proper to it that they cannot have any other motive. That is why, of all the testimonies of friendship, services are the least precious to me, for every decent man renders them for people to whom he is indifferent, and merit alone has the right to expect them from humanity. That is why, again, out of all services, those that are taken from the purse and that are rendered with money are the ones to which I give the least importance, above all when they are public. For of all the sorts of sacrifices, money is the one that costs the least to give and the most to receive. Thus, between two friends, the one who gives is without contradiction very much obliged to the one who receives; without friendship, a thousand suspect intentions can poison the purity of the benefit: vanity, ostentation, interest in acquiring for oneself a slave at little expense and to stir up a great gratitude with small benefits, all of that can play its role in that feigned generosity. Is it not then only a question of pursuing, money in hand, a man who does not care about it and gives more importance to an hour of his time and his freedom than to all the treasures in the world? Is it not only a question of giving, to the despicable gifts that one constrains him to accept, a value of which he is unaware, and of which one informs him only when it is no longer time to retract one's word, like those unfortunate people who find themselves enrolled after having received their engagement as a pure gift? Oh friendship, are those your true testimonies! No, you have gentler ones, more tangible ones, less equivocal ones that vanity does not imitate! Oh my friend, whoever you may be, if there is in the world a heart made to be one and to feel everything that it can inspire in me, leave there all that apparatus of benefits, and love me. Do not build me a house on your land so as no longer to come see me, while saying within yourself, I have got that one, and no longer need to cultivate him. Build me one in the depths of your heart. There I will establish my residence, there I want to inhabit all my life, no more tempted to leave it than you are to dismiss me. Seek me out ceaselessly and let yourself be sought; may I read in your eyes upon approaching you the joy that my presence causes you; let us take a thousand delightful walks in which the sun always sets too soon upon a day passed in innocence and simplicity. Console me in my troubles, shed yours in your turn in my bosom, so that even our woes might be a source of pleasures for us; and let our common life be a web of reciprocal benefits and true signs of friendship. What does the difference of fortune and rank have to do with all that, if it is not to render more estimable two friends who make each other forget their wealth and their poverty? Their friendship counts sentiments, not services, and the one of the two who loves the other the most is his true benefactor. But you will say, when one is so little sensitive to gifts, why allow anyone to give us any. Doubtless one must not, when one wants to stay free? But whose is the sensitive heart that is never weak, and can always resist the importunities of an unsatisfied friend? When one has loudly declared one's sentiments to the whole world, as I have always done, and particularly to Mme. d'Épinay; when one has thoroughly testified that one has no need of gifts or money, but of friendship; when one has openly and frankly rejected that mercenary morality that multiples the duties of a self-interested gratitude in order to attract new benefactors to oneself; if all those who are dear to us, and who do not want to dishonor us, represent to us a present accepted as a duty toward a decent man whom a refusal would afflict, I believe that decency itself brings us to consent. And to what will amour-propre ever give way if it is not to tender friendship? That was my case, some time ago, in relation to M. d'Holbach. I was forced to receive from him the profit from a book of which his fortune did not allow him to take advantage, and from which his bookseller alone would have profited. This gift was not from a friend to a friend but from a well-to-do decent man to an indigent decent man. He had done similar things to people he hardly knew. It was a loan made to humanity; it is to humanity that one must repay it. To what do you think then that such a benefit engages me? It is not basely to pay my court to M. d'Holbach. It is to imitate his behavior and to return to others at the expense of my bare necessities what he did for me at the expense of his superfluity. You, whom I sometimes dared to call my friend, excuse this admission that justice and truth tear from a demeaned honorable man. I do not pay my court to the rich, but I do not turn away the poor. My door has never been closed to the unfortunate; all types have come to implore my influence, my efforts, my purse, or my advice; none left me dissatisfied. That is how I endeavor to maintain, in accordance with my power, that circulation of benefits that makes up the tie of society. So long as calumny does not take my friends' hearts from me, I will let myself be publicly called an ingrate without complaint, but I will try to be a man and beneficent in secret. I know that there are benefits that require direct recognition, and never did a heart give itself over to it in a livelier way than mine. But why would benefits that I in no way feel demand the same return as those that are so sweet to me? Will I pay with the same sentiments the onerous savings of two years of rent and the salutary advice that sends me back into the arms of my friend? I am mistaken, they also wanted to return a friend to me.[3] A friend! Perfidious man! He was waiting only for the return of my trust to put the crown on his ingratitude and his foul deeds. Let us speak about it no longer. They have ruined me; they will ruin others who are unsuspecting, and this will be the most strongly felt stroke of their rage against me.

Although it is not a question here of knowing whether he who serves me in his fashion and not in mine has my interest or his own in view, or up to what point I must hold myself as engaged in such a case, I believed I ought to expose to you my principles on this point so that you could know upon what the difference is founded between my principles and those of that multitude of ingrates who preach the miser's gratefulness out of a vile self-interest, not even being acquainted with that of the sensitive man. As for me, I am touched only by benefits that bear the true character of friendship; for someone who renders me services that are dear to me, I am the most grateful of men; but if one chained me with millions, my heart would be as free as previously. Why do I owe a return for what does not give me the slightest pleasure? I do not know whether these maxims are those of ingratitude, but surely, they are not those of greed, and I honor myself for having a heart that is not for sale.

The friendship that is no longer still has rights, I know it. But how does a genuine friendship end? Alas, when one has had the misfortune to be mistaken in one's choice, it is a second misfortune to recover from

---

3. The reference is to Grimm.

such a sweet error. When one finds calumniators and traitors among those whom one believed to be one's friends, what sentiment can one return to them, and were one to find only those who are wicked toward others, does the wicked person know how to love something, and can he be lovable to good people? How would I hold on to connections that I find already broken? How would I love again what I cannot esteem? What would I do to satisfy rules of conduct? Will I affect sentiments that I no longer have? Shall I be false to be a decent man, and shall I sacrifice frankness to the proprieties? No, madam, no, I know that in the social world rules have been established in place of sentiments, but mine are as they ought to be and do not need to be disguised. I do not know how to give signs of attachment and esteem any longer to people whom I no longer love and whom I disdain, and if I owe them gratitude, I am ready to do everything for them, aside from continuing to be in their debt and give them testimonies of friendship contradicted by my heart. There do not cease to be substantial differences in the behavior I impose on myself toward them, and that which I should have with the rest of the world. For trust, outpourings, familiarity, and everything the intimacy of relations could have shown me about defects and vices in my friend, as well as the secrets that he could have confided in me, should eternally be hidden from the public even after our broken connections, and I should not even make them into weapons for my defense, if he happens to calumniate me. It is a duty to unmask and pursue the wicked in everything and everywhere; but I no longer have this right regarding the wicked man whom I had the misfortune to love without knowing him. The reason for this is that one would destroy all the charm of friendship if one could fear that it might ever become harmful, and how could the sweetest sentiment in the world serve as an instrument of hatred? "Do not soak your knife in milk," said Pythagoras; it seems to me that this mysterious precept ought to be applied to broken friendships.[4] What decent and sensitive soul could adopt that horrible maxim of living among friends as if they were to be enemies one day? Quite the contrary, when they have become enemies, they should ceaselessly remember their former friendship, and that is enough to dispense friends from that horrible prudence which carries distrust and reserve into the bosom of intimacy.

---

4. In the letter to Mme. d'Épinay above from March 26 of the same year, Rousseau refers to the Pythagorean maxim of not stirring up a fire with a sword. There is no record of this version of the maxim in Pythagoras.

I do not know, madam, if there is anything you will understand in all this verbiage; as for me, I have just reread it, and I understand nothing in it. But my head is going, my soul and my reason are at the end of their tether, and I feel myself in no condition to begin over again. Excuse my disorder: I have not learned how to conduct my defense, and I should not have had to foresee that one day I would need to.

I return to your letter, in which you base the esteem that you appear still to leave me on the fact that I am among your friends. No, madam, it is not among your friends that I ought to be, but your friend. Since you yourself offered me this title, I believe I have deserved it well enough that I should never lose it. I must grant the first place to the one who is dear to you.[5] You forewarned me of this, I consented to it. But aside from him alone, the second after any other is unworthy of my heart, and I refuse it. It is impossible for me to forget the esteem that you owe me and the attachment you promised me. I have too sensitive a soul and am too unhappy not to be proud. It is not a favor I ask of you, but justice, and if you refuse it to me, from whom in the world should I hope for it?

Let us speak plainly. My friendship is becoming onerous to you, and I am aware of it. I also penetrate the cause of this, and my fatal presentiments will be too well verified. I knew it, and I told you what fate I was preparing for myself in obeying your orders; I was sure that in giving you back a friend so little worthy of this name, that so sensitive and so grateful a friend would act with you as he does with everyone, and would continue to deprive me of all those [friends] I had given him; that is to say, all of his were formerly all mine; at last he is satisfied, and I no longer have any left.[6] If I had spent a hundred francs for him, he would be an ingrate. But I have given him goods of an inestimable value; I shared with him everything that constituted the happiness of my life; for my recompense he has deprived me of everything, he has reduced me to despair, and he is a very decent man. O worldly people, worthy estimators of virtues, vices, gratitude, and friendship, if those are your decent people, you deserve similar friends.

Let us come back to you, madam. After having spoken to you about him in one of my letters,[7] I predicted from your silence what I ought to expect, and the tone of your last letter perfectly confirmed it for me. No

---

5. Her lover, Saint Lambert.
6. The reference is to Grimm.
7. From December 5, less than two weeks before this letter.

longer use with me, then, proprieties and proceedings that I do not use with anyone; do not spin out an unfeeling rupture, but do it plainly, in a manner worthy of your frankness and of the esteem that you owe me. You ought to know my heart better than anyone. I have just set forth my principles to you; I believe, moreover, that you are not unaware that my attachment for you is henceforth independent of any return on your part, and that it is equally impossible for me to hate you and to forget you, however you act toward me. Render me at least enough justice to believe that I will be able to bear my ills and your indifference with the same heart that could taste its happiness and your friendship. Sophie, I do not say anymore to you about it. I can lose that friendship that was so sweet to me, but I would not know how to cease to be worthy of it.

Consider also how many circumstances invite you to rid yourself of the remnants of an importunate liaison. Alone and relegated to my retreat, it is through you alone that I am attached to the world, and by abandoning me as the others have, you will only imitate many decent people whom I love and whom I honor, even though I am abandoned by them. My widespread enemies, adroit, skillful, and less delicate than I, will know how to make their cause good at my expense. I, alone, far away, without correspondence, without any other defender than the hidden truth, I will remain exposed to universal blame, without knowing or worrying about it. You are not one of those who let their friends be insulted in their presence without saying anything. Why would you uselessly make enemies for yourself by taking my defense alone, and will you expose yourself fruitlessly to sharing the blame, instead of freeing me from it? Would that not provide a new foothold for calumny, and a proof that my accusers were right, by endeavoring to justify me?

Add to all that the fact that my misfortunes have made me more difficult and prouder. I do not want any friend who hides himself, or who is generous by halves. I want one to be honored by my friendship even though the whole world disdains it, and I find it more decent to break off with me entirely, than to support me feebly. Above all, I ask for all the esteem that is due me. The time of my adversity is not the one for putting conditions on the friendship one shows me, and whatever time it might be, my friend ought not to assume that I can ever cease to deserve his esteem. In a word, I believe that the duties of friendship increase with the peril of fulfilling them. As for me, that is the way I love; and whoever does not have the courage to love me in the same way ought rather to renounce me; there would be less trouble in it, and I would complain less about him.

Perhaps in the state in which I find myself it is good for me that all my friends abandon me this way. It is by them alone that I was attached to life, and feeling myself so close to leaving it, is it not time to renounce everything that could render it dear to me?

I conceive that it could cost something to your good heart to declare to the friend whom you sought out that he has lost this title. I have found the way to provide for that. Keep silent as your only response; I will understand that language and I will not importune you anymore. If, against my expectation and my advice, your friendship perseveres against my misfortune, the first letter that comes to me from you will proclaim my happiness to me even before I open it, and after so many torments and anguish, upon seeing your writing, I will have at least one more moment of pure joy in my life.

Farewell Sophie; farewell, my dear and worthy friend. Give my tender farewells to your friend. I will never forget that the two of you have taught me to esteem myself and to value all my worth. May you taste forever, each by means of the other, the charms that I have found in your friendship! May you be able to find in all your attachments hearts more true, more upright, more sensitive, and greater friends of virtue, or at least happier than I am.

C H A P T E R 33

Comtesse d'Houdetot—Moral Letters 1

Late 1757–Early 1758

These letters, known as the Moral Letters, were written to the Comtesse d'Houdetot. Although Rousseau informed her that he was writing these letters, and she expected to receive them, it is not clear whether he ever sent copies to her.

Come, my dear and worthy friend, listen to the voice of the one who loves you. It is not, as you know, that of a vile seducer. If ever my heart went astray in wishes for which you have made me blush, my mouth at least did not attempt to justify my going astray. Reason travestied into sophisms did not lend its offices to error. Humiliated vice fell silent at the sacred name of virtue. Faith, honor, and holy truth were not outraged in my speeches. By refraining from giving my faults decent names, I prevented decency from leaving my heart; I kept it open to the lessons of wisdom that you deigned to make me understand. It is now my turn, O Sophie, it is up to me to give back to you the cost of your cares, since you preserved my soul for the virtues that are dear to you. I want to fill yours with those which are still perhaps unknown to it. How fortunate I consider myself never to have prostituted my pen or my mouth to lies. Because of this, I feel less unworthy of being today the instrument of the truth near you.

As I remember the circumstance in which you asked me for rules of morality for your use, I cannot doubt that you then practiced one of the most sublime of them, and that in the danger to which a blind passion exposed me, you thought even more of my instruction than of yours. Only a villain could endanger the duties of another while trampling on his own, or bend morality to his passions, and you, who honor me with your friendship, know well that with a soft heart, I do not have the soul of a wicked man. By endeavoring today to fulfill the noble task that you have imposed upon me, I offer you an homage which is due to you. Virtue is dearer to me since I learned it from you.

In subjecting to duty and to reason the sentiments that you had inspired in me, you have exercised the greatest, the worthiest empire that heaven gave to beauty and wisdom. No, Sophie, a love like mine could not give way except to itself. You alone, like the Gods, could destroy your work, and it belonged only to your virtues to erase the effect of your charms.

Far from my heart detaching itself from yours while purifying itself, to blind love succeeded a thousand enlightened sentiments which make it a charming duty to me to love you all my life, and you are only dearer to me since I ceased to adore you. My desires, far from cooling in changing object, become only more ardent as they become more decent. If they dared to violate your charms in the secret of my heart, they have thoroughly atoned for this outrage. They incline toward nothing but the perfection of your soul and to justifying, if it is possible, all that mine has felt for you. Yes, be perfect as you can be, and I will be happier than if I had possessed you. May my zeal help to elevate you so high above me that amour-propre compensates me in you for my humiliations and consoles me in some way for not having been able to attain you. Ah! If the attentions of my friendship can encourage your progress, consider sometimes all that I have a right to expect from a heart that mine has not been able to deserve.

After so many days lost pursuing a vain glory, telling the public truths which it is not in a condition to understand, I finally see myself being proposed a useful object. I will fulfill the cares to which you oblige me. I will occupy myself with you, your duties, the virtues that suit you, and the means to perfect your fortunate natural disposition. I will always have you before my eyes. No, were I to pass my life seeking a pleasant task, I could not find one more in accordance with my heart than the one you impose on me.

Never was a project formed under sweeter auspices, never did an enterprise promise a happier success. Everything that can ignite one's courage and nourish hope is united to the most tender friendship to excite my zeal. The path to perfection is open to you without obstacle. Nature and fate have done so much for you, that what you still lack no longer depends on anything but your will, and your heart vouches for it in everything related to virtue. You bear an illustrious name that your fortune sustains and that your merit honors; a nascent family only awaits your cares to make you one day the happiest of mothers; your Husband, welcomed at court, esteemed in war, intelligent in affairs, enjoys a constant happiness which began with his marriage. The taste for pleasures is not foreign to you. Restraint and moderation are even more natural to you. You have the charms which lead to success in society, the enlightenment which makes one disdain it, and the talents which compensate for it. You will be everywhere where you will want to be, and always in your place.

That was still not enough. A thousand others enjoy all these advantages and are only common women. More precious goods are your amiable endowment. A just and penetrating mind, an upright and sensitive heart, a soul enamored by the love of the beautiful, an exquisite sentiment to recognize it, these are the guarantors of the hopes that I have conceived for you. It is not I who wants you to be the best, the worthiest, the most respectable of women. It is nature that wanted it; do not deceive her plans, do not bury her talents. I ask you only to examine your heart, and to do what it prescribes to you. Listen to my voice, O Sophie, only as much as you feel that mine confirms its voice.

Amid all these gifts that Heaven has accorded you, dare I count that of a faithful friend? There is one, you know, who, not contented with cherishing you as you are, is gripped by a lively and pure enthusiasm for all that can be hoped for from you. He contemplates you with an avid eye in all the conditions that you might be. He sees you at every instant of his life, in the past, in the present, in the future. He would like to gather at once all your being at the bottom of his soul. He knows no other pleasure than to occupy himself with you ceaselessly; his dearest desire is to see you perfect enough to inspire the whole universe with the same sentiments he has for you. Near the end of my short career, it seems by the ardor with which I feel myself inflamed that I am receiving a new life to employ it in guiding yours. My mind is illuminated by the fire of my heart; I experience in myself the invincible impulsion of genius. I believe that I am sent by Heaven to perfect its most worthy work. Yes, Sophie, if you deign to listen to me, the occupations of my last days will honor my sterile youth; what I will have done for you will compensate for the uselessness of my entire life. And I will become better myself because of it, by striving to give you the example of virtues the love of which I want to inspire in you.

Even if we have stopped seeing one another, we will not stop loving one another, I feel it, for our mutual attachment is founded on relations that do not perish. It is in vain that fate and the wicked separate us. Our hearts will always be close, and if they were so well attuned when two contrary passions inspired in them incompatible desires, what will they not do today, joined in the worthiest object that could fill them?

Recall the beautiful days of this summer, so charming, so short, and so suited to leaving long memories. Recall the solitary walks that we loved to repeat along the shaded slopes where the most fertile valley in the world spread before our eyes all the riches of nature, as if to disgust us with the false goods of opinion. Think about those delicious conversations during which, in the effusion of our souls, confiding our pains mutually soothed them, and in which you poured the peace of innocence upon the sweetest sentiments that the heart of man has ever tasted. Without being united in the same bond, without burning with the same flame, I do not know what celestial fire still animated us with its ardor and made us sigh together after unknown goods which we were made to enjoy together. Do not doubt it, Sophie, these so desired goods were the same whose image I come today to offer you, the same inclination for everything that is good and decent attached us one to the other, and the same sensibility joined together made us find more charms in the common object of our adorations. How we would be changed and how we would have to be pitied if we could ever forget moments so dear, if we could stop recalling each to the other with pleasure, sitting together at the foot of an oak, your hand in mine, your eyes moved to pity fixed upon mine and shedding tears purer than the dew of heaven. No doubt a vile and corrupt man could from far away interpret our conversation according to the baseness of his heart. But the witness beyond reproach, the eternal eye that one does not deceive, perhaps saw with indulgence two sensitive souls encourage each other mutually to virtue and nourish by a delicious outpouring all the pure sentiments with which it filled them.

Those are the guarantees of the success of my cares, those are my rights for daring to take them on. In explaining to you my sentiments on the use of life, I intend less to give you lessons than to make my profession of faith to you. To whom can I better confide my principles than to the one who knows my sentiments so well? Doubtless along with important truths of which you will know how to make use, you will find here involuntary errors which your uprightness of heart and mind will know how to cure in me and preserve in you. Examine, discern, choose, deign to explain to me the reasons for your choice, and may you derive as much profit from these letters as the author expects from your reflections. If sometimes I take with you the tone of a man who believes he is giving instruction, you know, Sophie, with this air of a schoolmaster I am only obeying you, and I would give you similar lessons for a long time before paying you the cost of those I received from you.

Had this writing no other use than that of bringing us closer sometimes and of renewing at a distance those sweet conversations which filled my last days and constituted my last pleasures, this idea would suffice to pay me for the labors of the rest of my life. I console myself amid my ills when I think that when I will be no more, I will be something for you still, that my writings will take my place near you, that you will acquire in rereading them the taste you had for conversing with me, and that if they do not bring new enlightenment to your mind, they will at least nourish at the bottom of your soul the memory of the most tender friendship there ever was.

These letters are not made to see the light of day, and I do not need to tell you that they will never see it without your consent. But if circumstances permitted you to accord it one day, how much the purity of the zeal which attaches me to you would make its public declaration voluntary! Without appearing in this work, neither your name nor mine would perhaps escape the suspicions of those who have known us. As for myself, I would be prouder than humiliated by this penetration and I would only obtain more esteem by showing that which I have for you. With respect to you, amiable Sophie, although you do not need my approbation to be honored, I would like the whole world to have its eyes on you. I would like to see everyone instructed as to what I expect from the qualities of your soul, to inspire in you more courage and strength to fulfill this expectation in the eyes of the public. They will say that neither my attachment nor my esteem have ever been lavished on anyone, especially on women. They will therefore be even more curious to consider the one who so perfectly joined one and the other. I make you responsible for my glory, O Sophie. Justify, if possible, the honor I have received from good people. Make it so that it will be said one day upon seeing you and recalling my memory: Ah, that man loved virtue and was knowledgeable about merit.

CHAPTER 34

Comtesse d'Houdetot—Moral Letters 2

The object of human life is the felicity of man, but who among us knows how to reach it? Without principle, without any assured goal, we wander from desires to desires, and those that we manage to satisfy leave us as far from happiness as before we obtained anything. We have no invariable rule, neither in reason which lacks support, a hold, and consistency, nor in the passions which succeed and destroy one another incessantly. Victims as we are of the blind inconstancy of our hearts, the enjoyment of desired goods only prepares for us privations and pains. Everything we possess only serves to show us what we lack, and for lack of knowing how one must live, we all die without having lived. If there is some possible means to deliver oneself from this terrible doubt, it is to extend it for a time beyond its natural limits, to mistrust all of one's inclinations, to study oneself, to carry to the bottom of one's soul the torch of truth, to examine for once everything one thinks, everything one believes, everything one feels, and everything that one must think, feel, and believe in order to be as happy as the human condition allows. That, my charming friend, is the examination I propose to you today.

But what are we going to do, O Sophie, but what has already been done a thousand times? All the books speak to us of the sovereign good, all the philosophers show it to us, each teaches the others the art of being happy. None has found it for himself. In this immense labyrinth of human reasonings you will learn to speak about happiness without knowing it. You will learn to hold forth, and not to live. You will lose yourself in metaphysical subtleties; the perplexities of philosophy will besiege you from every side; you will see everywhere objections and doubts; and by dint of instructing yourself, you will end by knowing nothing. This method exercises one at speaking about everything, at shining in a circle. It produces learned people, fine wits, talkers, arguers, happy people in the judgment of those who are listening, unfortunates as soon as they are alone. No, my dear child, the study that I am proposing to you does not give knowledge for show that one can display for the eyes of others, but it fills the soul with everything which makes the happiness of man. It makes not others, but us, content with it. It does not bring words to one's mouth but sentiments to the heart. In submitting to it one grants more trust to the voice of nature than to that of reason, and without speaking about wisdom and happiness with so much emphasis, one becomes wise inside and happy for oneself. Such is the philosophy which I seek to teach you; it is in the silence of your study that I want to converse with you. So long as you feel that I am right, I care little to prove it to you. I will not teach you how to resolve objections, but I will endeavor that you have none to make to me. I trust your good faith more than my arguments, and without burdening myself with the rules of the school, I will call on your heart alone to give witness to everything I have to say to you.

Look at this universe, my amiable friend. Cast your eyes upon this theater of errors and miseries which, in contemplating it, makes us deplore man's sad fate. We live in the climate and in the age of philosophy and reason. The enlightenment of all the sciences seems to unite at once to light the way for our eyes and to guide us in this obscure labyrinth of human life. The noblest geniuses of all ages collect their lessons to instruct us; immense libraries are open to the public; multitudes of colleges and universities offer us from childhood onward the experience and the meditation of 4,000 years. Immortality, glory, even wealth and often honors are the prize for the worthiest in the art of instructing and enlightening men. Everything concurs in perfecting our understanding and in lavishing upon each of us everything that can form and cultivate reason. Have we thereby become better or wiser for it; do we know better which is the way and what will be the term of our short course; are we in better agreement regarding the first duties and the true goods of the human species? What have we acquired from all this vain knowledge except quarrels, hatreds, incertitude, and doubts? Each sect is the only one to have discovered the truth. Each Book exclusively contains the precepts of wisdom; each author is the only one who teaches us what is good. One proves to us that there is no body, another that there are no souls, another that the soul has no relation to the body, another that man is a beast, another that God is a mirror. There is no maxim so absurd that some reputable author has not advanced it, no axiom so evident that it has not been combated by one among them. All is good so long as one says otherwise than others, and one always finds reasons to support what is new in preference to what is true.

Let them admire as they please the perfection of the arts, the number and greatness of their discoveries, the extent and sublimity of human genius. Shall we congratulate them for knowing all of nature except themselves, and for having found all the arts save that of being happy? We are happy, they cry out sadly. So many resources for well-being; such a crowd of commodities unknown to our fathers; how many pleasures we savor of which they were ignorant. It is true, you have softness, but they had felicity; you are reasoners, they were reasonable; you are polite, they were humane; all your pleasures are outside of you, theirs were in themselves. And what is the cost of these cruel sensual delights which the few buy at the expense of the multitude. The luxury of the towns brings misery, hunger, and despair to the countryside. If a few men are happier, humankind is only more to be pitied. By multiplying the commodities of life for a few rich people, one has only forced most men to consider themselves miserable. What is this barbarous happiness that one feels only at the expense of others? Sensitive souls, tell me, what is happiness that is bought at the cost of money?

Knowledge makes men gentle, they say again. The age is less cruel, we spill less blood. Ah, unfortunate people! Do you cause fewer tears to be shed, and would not the wretches whom one causes to die of languor for an entire life prefer to lose it once on the scaffold? Because you are gentler, are you less unjust, less vindictive; is virtue less oppressed, power less tyrannical; are the people less overburdened; do we see fewer crimes, are evildoers rarer, are prisons less full? What then have you gained by letting yourselves become softer? For the vices that are the marks of courage and vigor, you have substituted those of little souls. Your gentleness is base and pusillanimous; you torment silently and under cover those you would have attacked openly by force. If you are less bloodthirsty, it is not virtue but weakness. It is in you only one vice the more.

The art of reasoning is not reason; often it is its abuse. Reason is the faculty of suitably ordering all the faculties of our soul to the nature of things and to their relations with us. Reasoning is the art of comparing known truths, in order to constitute, from them, other truths we did not know, and that this art makes us discover. But it does not teach us to know those primitive truths which serve as elements of the others, and when in their place we put our opinions, our passions, and our prejudices, it blinds us. It does not elevate the soul; it enervates it and corrupts the judgment which it ought to perfect.

Within the chain of reasonings which serve to form a system, the same proposition will return a hundred times with almost imperceptible differences which will escape the philosopher's mind. These differences, so often multiplied, will finally modify the proposition to the point of changing it completely without his perceiving it. He will say of one thing what he will believe he is proving about another, and his consequences will be so many errors. This inconvenience is inseparable from the spirit of system, which alone leads to grand principles and consists in always generalizing. Inventors generalize as much as they can: this method extends discoveries and gives an air of genius and of force to those who make them. And, because nature always acts by general laws, in establishing general principles in their turn they believe that they have penetrated its secret. By dint of extending and abstracting a little fact, one thereby changes it into a universal rule. One believes one is ascending to principles, one wants to gather within one sole object more ideas than human understanding can compare, and one affirms of an infinity of beings what is often found hardly true of one. The observers, less brilliant and cooler, then arrive, adding exception upon exception, until the general proposition has become so particular that one can no longer infer anything from it, and distinctions and experience reduce it to the sole fact from which it was drawn. It is thus that systems are established and destroy one another, without discouraging new reasoners from erecting on their ruins others which will last no longer.

Everyone thus losing their way by diverse roads, each believes that he arrives at the true goal because no one perceives the tracks of all the detours he has made. What then will the one who sincerely seeks the truth do among these crowds of the learned, all of whom claim to have found it and give each other the lie mutually? Will he weigh all the systems? Will he leaf through all the books, will he listen to all the Philosophers, will he compare all the sects, will he dare to pronounce between

Epicurus and Zeno, between Aristippus and Diogenes, between Locke and Shaftesbury? Will he dare to prefer his enlightenment to that of Pascal and his reason to that of Descartes? Hear a mullah discourse in Persia, in China a Buddhist monk, in Tartary a lama, a Brahmin in India, in England a Quaker, in Holland a rabbi. You will be astonished by the force of persuasion that each one of them knows how to give to his absurd doctrine. How many people as sensible as you has each of these not convinced? If you barely deign to listen to them, if you laugh at their vain arguments, if you refuse to believe them, it is not reason in you that resists their prejudices, it is your own [prejudice].

Life will have flowed away ten times before one has discussed down to their foundation a single one of these opinions. A Parisian bourgeois makes fun of Calvin's objections which frighten a doctor of the Sorbonne. The more deeply one goes the more one finds subjects for doubt, and whether one opposes reasons to reasons, authorities to authorities, votes to votes, the more one advances, the more one finds subjects for doubt. The more one learns, the less one knows, and one is totally astonished that instead of learning what one did not know, one loses even the knowledge one believed one had.

CHAPTER 35

Comtesse d'Houdetot—Moral Letters 3

We know nothing, my dear Sophie, we see nothing; we are a crowd of blind men, cast by chance into this vast universe. Each one of us, not perceiving any object, makes of all of them a fantastic image which he subsequently takes as the rule of what is true; and this idea, not resembling that of any other person, no two among this appalling multitude of philosophers whose babbling confuses us can be found who agree regarding the system of this universe that they all claim to know, or regarding the nature of things that all make sure to explain.

Unfortunately, what is precisely least known to us is what matters most to us to know, namely man. We see neither the soul of another, for it hides itself, nor our own, because we have no intellectual mirror. We are blind men at every point, but blind men from birth who do not imagine what sight is and, believing that there is no faculty we lack, want to measure the ends of the earth, while the brief light of our understanding, like our hands, reaches a mere two feet from us.

If we plumb this idea more deeply, we might perhaps find it to be no less exact literally than figuratively. Our senses are the instruments of all our knowledge; from them all of our ideas come; or at least all are occasioned by them. The human understanding, constrained and enclosed within its envelope, cannot so to speak penetrate the body which compresses it, and acts only through sensations. They are, shall we say, five windows through which the soul would like to see the light; but the windows are small, the glass is blurred, the wall thick, and the house very badly lit. Our senses are given to us not to instruct but to preserve us, to warn us of what is useful or not, and not of what is true or false. They are not at all destined to be used to research into nature: when we use them for that purpose, they are insufficient; they deceive us, and we can never be sure of finding the truth through them.

The errors of one sense are corrected by another. If we had only one, it would forever deceive us. We therefore have only faulty rules for correcting each other. If two false rules came to agree, they would deceive us by their very agreement, and [if] we lacked the third, what means remain to discover the error?

Sight and touch are the two senses which serve us most for the investigation of the truth, because they offer objects to us more wholly and in a state of perseverance more suited to observation than that in which these same objects provide a hold for the other three senses. The first two also seem to share between them the whole of the philosophic spirit. Sight, which with one glance measures the whole hemisphere, represents the vast capacity of systematic genius. Touch, slow and progressive, which assures itself of one object before passing on to another, resembles the spirit of observation. Each one also has the defects of the faculties they represent. The more the eye fixes itself on faraway objects, the more it is subject to optical illusions, and the hand, always attached to some part, could not embrace the whole.

It is certain that sight is of all our senses the one from which we receive at the same time the most instruction and the most errors. It is through sight that we judge almost all of nature, and it is sight which ·suggests to us almost all our false judgments. You have heard speak of the famous operation on the man born blind to whom not a saint but a surgeon had restored sight; it took him a great deal of time to learn how to make use of it. According to him, everything he saw was in his eye; when he looked at unequal bodies at a distance, he had no idea either of sizes or of distances; and when he began to discern objects, he still could not distinguish a portrait from an original; they forgot to certify whether he saw objects reversed.

With all experience acquired, there is no man who is not subject to bring to bear false judgments by sight on objects at a distance, and falsely to measure those he has in front of his eyes; and what is even more astounding, these errors are not even always within the rules of perspective.

If, however, sight so often deceives us and touch alone corrects it, touch itself deceives us on a thousand occasions. Who will assure us that it does not always deceive us and that we would not need a sixth sense to correct it? The experiment of a little ball rolled between two crossed fingers shows that we are no less slaves of habit in our judgments than in our inclinations. Touch, which prides itself on judging figures so well, judges none of them precisely; it will never teach us if a line is straight, if a surface is even, if a cube is regular. It judges degrees of heat no better: the same cave seems cool to us in summer and warm in winter without any change in temperature. Expose your right hand to the air, the left to a big fire; then dip both in warm water: this water will seem hot to your right hand and cold to your left. Everyone reasons about gravity, but no one feels its most general effect, which is the pressure of the air; we can barely feel the fluid which surrounds us, and we believe that we only feel the weight of our bodies, whereas we carry that of all the atmosphere. If you want to experience some small indication of this, while in your bath, lift your arm slowly out of the water in a horizontal position; and in measure as the air presses upon your arm, you will feel your muscles tiring from this terrible pressure, about which you had perhaps never had any idea. A thousand other similar observations would teach us in how many ways the most certain of our senses misleads us, either by concealing or altering effects which exist, or by supposing some which do not exist. No matter how hard we try to unite sight and touch to judge extension, which is within the competence of both, we do not even know what largeness and smallness are. The apparent size of objects is relative to the stature of the one who measures them. The gravel which a mite finds on its path presents itself to him as the mass of the Alps. One foot to us is a toise in the eyes of a pygmy and an inch to those of a giant.[1] If that were not so, our senses would be disproportionate to our needs, and we could not subsist. In every sense each of us bases the measure of all things upon himself. Where then is absolute size; do all deceive themselves, or none? One does not have to tell you more to have you glimpse to what point one could push these reflections. All geometry is founded only upon sight and touch, and these two senses perhaps need to be rectified by others that we lack.

---

1. A toise is approximately six and a half feet.

What is the most demonstrated for us is therefore still suspect, and we cannot know whether Euclid's *Elements* is not a web of errors.

It is not so much reasoning that we lack as the hold for reasoning. Man's mind is in a condition to do much, but the senses furnish it with few materials, and our soul, active within its bonds, would rather exert itself upon chimeras which are within its reach than stay idle and without movement. Let us therefore not be astonished to see arrogant and vain philosophy lose itself in its reveries, and the finest geniuses exhaust themselves on puerilities. With what distrust must we deliver ourselves to our feeble enlightenment, when we see the most methodical of the philosophers, the one who has best established his principles and reasoned the most consequently, lose his way with his first steps and sink from errors to errors into absurd systems. Descartes, wanting to cut all at once the root of all prejudices, began by calling everything into question, submitting everything to reason's examination. Beginning from this unique and incontestable principle, "I think, therefore I exist," and proceeding with the greatest precautions, he believed that he was going toward truth and found only lies. Based on this first principle, he began by examining himself. Then, finding within himself very distinct properties which seemed to belong to two different substances, he first applied himself to knowing these two substances thoroughly and, setting aside everything which was not clearly and necessarily contained in their idea, he defined one as the extended substance and the other the substance that thinks. Definitions that were all the wiser in that they in a way left the obscure question of the two substances undecided, and in that it did not absolutely follow that extension and thought could not unite in and penetrate the same substance. Well, these definitions, which seemed incontestable, were destroyed within less than a generation. Newton showed that the essence of matter did not at all consist in extension, and Locke showed that the essence of the soul did not at all consist in thought. Farewell to all the philosophy of the wise and methodical Descartes. Will his successors be happier, will their systems last any longer? No, Sophie, they are beginning to totter, they will fall likewise; they are the work of men.

Why can we not know what is mind and matter? Because we know nothing save through our senses, and they are insufficient to teach us. As soon as we want to deploy our faculties, we feel them all constrained by our organs. Even reason, submitted to the senses, is like them in contradiction with itself: geometry is full of demonstrated theorems that are impossible to conceive. In philosophy, substance, soul, body, eternity, motion, liberty, necessity, contingency, etc. are so many words that one is constrained to use at every moment and that no one has ever conceived. Simple physics is no less obscure to us than metaphysics and morality. The great Newton, the interpreter of the universe, did not even suspect the wonders of electricity, which appears to be the most active principle of nature. Its most common operations and the easiest to observe, namely the multiplying of plants through their germs, remains to be known, and one discovers every day regarding them new facts which overturn all our reasonings. The Pliny of our century, wanting to develop the mystery of generation, saw himself forced to have recourse to a principle which was unintelligible and irreconcilable with the known laws of mechanics and motion. Try as we may to explain everything, we find everywhere inexplicable difficulties that show us that we have no certain notion of anything.

You may have seen in the abbé de Condillac's statue what degree of knowledge would belong to each sense if they were given to us separately, and the bizarre reasonings that beings endowed with fewer organs than we have would make about the nature of things. In your opinion, what in turn would other beings, endowed with other senses unknown to us, say about us? How to prove that these senses cannot exist, and that they would not shed light on the obscurity that ours cannot destroy? There is nothing fixed about the number of senses necessary to give the sentiment of life to a corporeal and organized being. Let us consider the animals: several have fewer senses than we do; why would others not have more? Why would they not have some which will be eternally unknown to us because they offer no hold for ours, by which we could explain what seems to us inexplicable in several actions of beasts? Fish do not hear, birds and fish have no sense of smell, snails and worms have no eyes, and touch seems to be the oyster's only sense; but how many animals take precautions, have foresight and inconceivable ruses which it might be better to attribute to some organ foreign to man, than to that unintelligible word *instinct*? What a puerile pride to regulate the faculties of all beings according to our own, while everything gives the lie before our very eyes to this ridiculous prejudice. How can we assure ourselves that we are not, among all the reasoning beings that diverse worlds can contain, the least favored by nature, the least provided with organs suited to the knowledge of truth, and that it is not to this insufficiency that we owe the incomprehensibility which stops us at every moment regarding a thousand demonstrated truths?

With so few means of observing matter and sensitive souls, how do we hope to be able to judge about the soul and spiritual beings? Let us suppose that such really exist; if we are ignorant of what a body is, how will we know what a mind is?[2] We see ourselves surrounded by bodies without souls, but which of us has ever perceived a soul without a body and can have the least idea of a purely spiritual substance? What can we say of the soul about which we know nothing save what acts through the senses? How do we know if it does not have infinite other faculties which, for their development, are waiting only for a suitable organization or the return of freedom? Does our understanding come to us from outside to the inside through the senses according to the materialists, or does it escape from within outward as Plato claimed? If daylight enters the house through the windows, the senses are the seat of the understanding. On the contrary, if the house is lit within, you could close everything and the light, even if muted, would no less exist; but the more you open windows, the more light will come out, and the easier it will be for you to distinguish surrounding objects. It is therefore a very puerile question to ask how a soul can see, hear, and touch, without hands, without eyes, and without ears; I would rather a lame man ask how one can walk without crutches. It would be much more philosophical to ask how with hands, eyes, and ears, a soul can see, understand, and touch; for how the body and the soul act upon one another was always the despair of metaphysics, and there is even more difficulty in giving sensations to pure matter.

Who knows if there are not minds of different degrees of perfection, to each of which nature has given bodies organized according to the faculties of which they are capable, from the oysters up to us on this earth and, from us, perhaps, all the way to the most sublime species in the various worlds? Who knows whether what distinguishes man from beast is not that the soul of the latter has no more faculties than its body has sensations, while the human soul, compressed in a body which hinders most of its faculties, wants at each instant to break out of its prison, and joins an almost divine daring to the weakness of humanity? Is it not thus that those great geniuses, the wonder and honor of their species, in a way cross the barrier of the senses, launch themselves into the celestial and intellectual regions, and raise themselves as much above the common man as nature raised the latter above the animals?

---

2. *Esprit* means either "spirit" or "mind."

Why would we not imagine the vast bosom of the universe full of an infinity of minds of a thousand different orders, eternal admirers of the play of nature and inevitable spectators of men's actions? O, my Sophie, how sweet it is for me to think that sometimes they were present at our most charming discussions, and that a murmur of applause would arise among these pure intelligences upon seeing two tender and decent friends making sacrifices to virtue within the hidden depth of their hearts.

That these are only conjectures without probability, I admit, but it is enough for me that one cannot prove the contrary to deduce from them the doubts that I wish to establish. Where are we? What do we see, what do we know, what exists? We only run after shadows that escape us. A few light specters, a few chimerical phantoms flutter before our eyes, and we believe we are seeing the eternal chain of beings. We do not know one substance in the universe, we are not even sure of seeing its surface, and we want to plumb the abyss of nature. Let us leave such puerile work to those children we call philosophers. After having gone over the narrow circle of their vain knowledge, one must end where Descartes had begun: "I think, therefore I exist." That is all we know.

Chapter 36

Comtesse d'Houdetot—Moral Letters 4

The more man looks at himself, the more he sees himself small. But the lens that diminishes is made only for good eyes. Is it not a strange pride, my dear Sophie, that one gains in feeling all one's misery. Yet that is the only kind one can draw from healthy philosophy. As for me, I would a hundred times rather forgive the fake wise man for being vain about his pretended knowledge than the real one for being so about his ignorance. That a madman rises up as a demi-God, his madness is at least consistent; but to believe oneself to be an insect and to crawl proudly under the grass, that to my mind is the crowning absurdity. What then is the first lesson of wisdom, O Sophie? Humility! Humility, about which the Christian speaks, and which man knows so little, is the first sentiment which should arise within us from the study of ourselves. Let us be humble about our species, so as to be able to take pride in ourselves as individuals. Let us not say in our imbecile vanity that man is the king of the world, that the sun, the stars, the firmament, the air, the earth, the sea are made for him, that the plants germinate for his subsistence, that the animals live so that he may devour them. With this way of reasoning, this devouring thirst for happiness, for excellence and perfection, why will each not believe that the rest of the human species was created to serve him? And will he not see himself personally as the unique object of all the works of nature? If so many beings are useful for our preservation, are we sure that we are less useful to theirs? What does that prove if not our weakness, and how do we know their purpose better than ours? If we were deprived of sight, in what way could we learn that there are birds, fish, and insects almost imperceptible to touch; several of these insects appear in their turn to have no idea about us. Why then could not other, more excellent species exist that we will never perceive for lack of senses suitable to discovering them, and for whom we are perhaps as contemptible as the maggots are in our eyes? But enough of lowering man, made arrogant by gifts he does not have; enough remain to him to nourish a worthier and more legitimate pride.[1] If reason crushes and debases him, the inner sentiment elevates and honors him. The involuntary homage that the wicked man gives the just one in secret is the true title of nobility that nature has engraved in the heart of man.

Have you never felt that secret disquiet which torments us at the sight of our misery, and which becomes indignant at our weaknesses as an outrage to the faculties that elevate us? Have you never experienced these involuntary transports which sometimes seize a sensitive soul when it contemplates the morally beautiful and the intellectual order of things, that devouring ardor which suddenly sets the heart ablaze with love of the celestial virtues, those sublime wanderings which raise us above our being, and carry us to the empyrean by the side of God himself? Ah, if this sacred fire could last, if this noble delirium animated our entire life, what heroic actions would frighten our courage, what vices would dare come near us, what victories could we not win over ourselves, and what great thing could we not obtain by our efforts? My honorable friend, the principle of this strength is within us; it shows itself for a moment to excite us ceaselessly to seek it. This holy enthusiasm is the energy of our faculties extricating themselves from their terrestrial bonds, and which it would perhaps only be up to us ceaselessly to maintain in this state of freedom. However this may be, we at least feel within ourselves a voice which forbids us to despise ourselves. Reason crawls, but the soul is elevated; if we are small by our enlightenment, we are great by our sentiments, and whatever rank may

---

1. Two French terms, *orgueil* and *fierté*, can be translated as "pride." Rousseau distinguishes the first of these from vanity. Although he usually gives it a positive connotation, he sometimes uses it negatively, in the sense of arrogance. *Fierté* is always positive and is the word used in the phrase we have translated as "worthier and more legitimate pride."

be ours in the system of the universe, a being who is a friend of justice and sensitive to the virtues is not abject by his nature.

I have nothing more to demonstrate to you, O Sophie, and if it were only a question of philosophizing, I would come to rest at this point and, seeing myself stopped at every turn by the limits of my mind, I would finish instructing you before having started to do so. But as I have already said, my goal is not to reason with you, and it is from the bottom of your heart that I want to draw the only arguments that must convince you. Let me tell you then what is happening in mine; and if you experience the same thing, the same principles ought to suit us, the same road must lead us in the search for true happiness.

During the span of a rather brief life, I have experienced great vicissitudes. Without leaving my poverty, I have tasted something of every condition; well-being and ill-being made themselves felt to me in every way. Nature gave me the most sensitive soul. Fate subjected it to every imaginable affection, and I believe that I can say along with one of Terence's characters that nothing human is foreign to me.

In all these diverse situations, I always felt myself affected in two different, and sometimes contrary, ways, one coming from the state of my fortune, and the other from that of my soul, such that sometimes a sentiment of happiness and peace consoled me in my misfortunes, and sometimes an importunate malaise would trouble me during my prosperity.

These inner dispositions, independent of fate and of events, made upon me an even more vivid impression as my inclination toward a contemplative and solitary life led to their further development. I felt within me, so to speak, a counterweight to my destiny; I would go to console myself for my pains in the same solitude in which I shed tears when I was happy. As I sought the principle of this hidden strength which counterbalanced the empire of my passions in this way, I found that it came from a secret judgment that, without thinking of it, I made on the actions of my life and the objects of my desire. My ills tormented me less when I thought that they were not my doing. And my pleasures lost all their worth when I considered coolly in what I made them consist. I believed that I felt within me a seed of goodness which compensated me for misfortune, and a seed of greatness which elevated me above good fortune. I saw that it is in vain that one seeks one's happiness afar when one neglects to cultivate it in oneself. For all that it comes from outside, it can make itself felt only as long as within, it finds a soul fit to taste it.

This principle about which I am speaking with you serves me not only to direct my present actions according to the rule that it prescribes me, but also to make an exact assessment of my past conduct: often blaming it even though it was good in appearance; approving of it sometimes even though it was condemned by men; and recalling the events of my youth only as a local memory of the various affections that they occasioned in me.

In measure as I advance toward the end of my course, I feel weakening in me the motions which for so long submitted me to the empire of the passions. After having exhausted everything that a sensitive being can experience of good and bad, I am little by little losing sight and the expectation of a future which no longer has anything in it to gratify me. Desires extinguish themselves along with hope; my existence is no longer except in my memory; I only live from my past life, and its duration has ceased to be dear to me since my heart no longer has anything new to feel.

In this state it is natural that I like to turn my eyes toward the past, from which I now take all my being. It is then that my errors correct themselves and that the good and the bad make themselves felt in me without admixture and without prejudices.

All the false judgments that the passions have made me make vanish along with them. I see the objects which have most affected me, not as they seemed to me during my delirium, but as they really are. The memory of my good or bad actions causes me a durable well-being or ill-being more real than he who was its object. Thus, the pleasures of a moment have often prepared long repentances for me; thus, the sacrifices made to decency and justice compensate every day for what they once cost me, and for brief privations, give me eternal enjoyment.

With whom can I better speak about the charms of these memories than with the one who makes me taste them again so fully? Only you, Sophie, could make dear to me the memory of my last derangements by that of the virtues that brought me back from them. You made me blush too much for my faults for me to be able to blush about them now, and I do not know what makes me most proud: the victories won over myself; or the help which made me win them. If I had only listened to a criminal passion, if I had been vile for an instant and had found you weak, how dearly I would be paying today for transports that would have appeared so sweet to me; deprived of all the sentiments that had united us, we would have ceased to be so. Shame and repentance would have made us odious to one another; I would hate you for having loved you too much; and what intoxication from voluptuousness could ever have compensated my heart for such a pure and tender attachment? Instead of this fatal separation, I remember nothing about you that does not make me happier with myself, and which does not add to the friendship that you have inspired in me, honor, respect, and gratitude of having kept myself worthy of loving you. How could I think without pleasure of those moments which were painful to me only by sparing me eternal pains? How today could I not enjoy the charm of having listened to everything from your lips that can elevate the soul and give value to the union of hearts. Ah, Sophie, what might I have become after having been insensitive near you to everything by which I had acquired your esteem, and having shown you in the friend you had chosen a wretch whom you ought to despise?

It is everything most touching in the image of virtue that you were placing before my eyes; it is the fear of defiling so late a life without reproach, of losing in one moment the prize for so many sacrifices; it was the sacred trust of friendship that I had to respect; it is from all that is most inviolable in faith, honor, and probity that the invincible barrier which you ceaselessly opposed to all my desires was formed. No, Sophie, there is not one of my days during which your speeches do not come to move me again and wrest delicious tears from me. All my sentiments for you are beautified by the one which overcame them. They are the glory and sweetness of my life. I owe all this to you; or it is through you at least that I feel what they are worth. My dear and honored friend, I sought repentance, and you made me find happiness.

Such is the state of a soul which, daring to propose itself to you as an example, offers you in doing so only the fruit of your efforts. If this inner voice that judges me in secret and makes itself ceaselessly heard in my heart also makes itself heard in yours, learn to listen to it and to follow it, learn to draw from yourself your primary goods. These alone do not depend at all on fortune and can supplement others. That is my whole philosophy and, I believe, the whole art of being happy which is practicable for man.

CHAPTER 37

Comtesse d'Houdetot—Moral Letters 5

The whole morality of human life is in man's intention. If it is true that the good is good, it must be so at the bottom of our hearts as it is in our works, and the first prize of justice is to feel that one practices it. If moral goodness is in conformity with our nature, man could be healthy or well constituted only as long as he is good. If it is not, and man is naturally wicked, he cannot cease to be so without becoming corrupt. Goodness would be in him only a vice against nature. Made to harm his fellows like a wolf to slaughter its prey, a humane man would be an animal as depraved as a pitying wolf, and virtue alone would leave us with remorse.

Would you believe that there is in the world an easier question to resolve? What is required for that except to return to oneself and to examine, all personal interest aside, what our natural inclinations carry us toward? What sight delights us more, that of the torments, or of the happiness, of others? What is the sweetest for us to do and leaves us with a more pleasant impression after having done it, an act of beneficence or an act of malice? Who interests you in your theaters? Is it in heinous crimes that you take pleasure? Is it for those who commit them that you shed tears? Between the unhappy hero and the triumphant tyrant, to which of the two do your secret wishes ceaselessly bring you closer; and which of you, if forced to choose, would not prefer to be the good man who suffers than the bad man who prospers, so much does horror at doing bad naturally prevail in us over that of suffering it?

When one sees in a street or on a path some act of violence and injustice, in an instant a movement of anger and indignation arises at the bottom of our hearts, and leads us to take on the defense of the oppressed person; but a more powerful duty restrains us, and the laws take away our right to protect the innocent.

On the contrary, if some act of clemency or generosity strikes our eyes, what admiration, what love it inspires in us. Who does not say to himself: I would like to have done as much? The most corrupt souls cannot completely lose this primary inclination: the thief who despoils passersby nevertheless covers the poor man's nakedness; there is no ferocious assassin who does not support a fainting man; even traitors, while plotting among themselves, clasp one another's hands, give their word, and respect their faith. Perverse man, try as you may, I see in you only a wicked man who is inconsistent and clumsy, for nature did not make you one.

They talk about the cry of remorse that secretly punishes hidden crimes, and so often places them in evidence. Alas! Who among us has never known this importunate voice. They speak from experience, and would like to erase this involuntary sentiment which gives us so many torments. But let us obey nature. We will know with what gentleness she approves of what she has commanded, and what charm one finds in tasting the inner peace of a soul content with itself. The wicked man fears himself and flees from himself; he amuses himself by casting himself outside of himself; he looks around with anxious eyes and seeks an object which makes him laugh; without insulting mockery he would always be sad. On the contrary, the serenity of the just man is internal; his laughter arises not from malignity but from joy; he carries its source within himself. Alone, he is as cheerful as amid a circle; and this unalterable contentment that one sees reign in him, he does not draw it from those who approach him, he communicates it to them.

Cast your eyes over all the nations of the world, glance through all the histories. Among so many inhuman and bizarre forms of worship, among that prodigious diversity of morals and characters, everywhere you will find the same ideas of justice and decency, everywhere the same principles of morality, the same notions of good and bad. Ancient paganism gave birth to abominable gods who would have been punished here below as heinous criminals, and who offered as a picture of supreme happiness only felonies to be committed and passions to satisfy. But vice, dressed up in sacred authority, descended in vain from the eternal abode; nature repulsed it from human hearts. Jupiter's debaucheries were celebrated, but Xenocrates's temperance was admired; chaste Lucretia adored shameless Venus, the intrepid Roman sacrificed to fear, the great Cato was considered more just than providence. The immortal voice of virtue, stronger than that of the gods themselves, made itself respected on earth, and seemed to relegate crime along with the guilty to heaven.

There is therefore at the bottom of all souls an innate principle of justice and of moral truth anterior to all national prejudices, to all the maxims of education. This principle is the involuntary rule according to which, despite our own maxims, we judge our actions and those of others as good or bad, and it is to this principle that I give the name conscience.

But with this word I hear from every side rise the voice of the philosophers: errors of infancy, prejudices of education, they all cry out as if in concert. There is nothing in human understanding that is not introduced into it by experience, and we judge nothing save through acquired ideas. They go further: they dare to reject this evident and universal accord of all the nations, and against this resounding uniformity of men's judgments, they go seek in the shadows for some obscure example known only to themselves, as if all the natural inclinations were annihilated by the perversity of a few individuals, and as soon as there are a few monsters the human species is no longer anything. But how does it benefit the skeptic Montaigne to give himself pains to unearth in some corner of the world a custom opposed to the notions of justice? Of what benefit is it to him to give to the most contemptible and suspect traveler an authority he refuses to the most respectable writers? Will some uncertain and bizarre usages, founded upon particular causes which are unknown to us, destroy the general inference drawn from the agreement of all peoples, who are in opposition regarding everything else? O Montaigne, you who pride yourself on frankness and truth, be sincere and true, if ever a philosopher can be, and tell me if there is any region where it is a crime to keep one's word, to be clement, beneficent, and generous, where the good man is despicable, and the heinous criminal honored.

I do not plan to enter here into metaphysical discussions which lead nowhere. I have already told you that I did not at all want to dispute with the philosophers, but to speak to your heart. Were all the philosophers in the world to prove that I am wrong, if you feel that I am right,

I want nothing more. For this purpose all that is needed is to have you distinguish our acquired perceptions from our natural sentiments; for we necessarily feel before we know, and since we do not learn to seek our personal good and to flee what is bad for us, but hold this will from nature, in the same way the love of good and the hatred of bad are as natural to us as our own existence. Thus, although ideas come to us from outside, the sentiments that appreciate them are within us, and it is by them alone that we know the suitability or lack of suitability which exists between us and the things that we ought to seek or flee.

To exist for us is to feel; and our sensitivity is incontestably anterior to our reason itself. Whatever may be the cause of our existence, it has provided for our preservation by giving us sentiments in conformity with our nature; and one could not deny that at least those are innate. For the individual, these sentiments are the love of oneself, the fear of pain and of death, and the desire for well-being. But if, as one cannot doubt, man is an animal who is sociable by nature or at least made to become one, he cannot be so except by innate sentiments relative to his species. And it is from the moral system formed by this double relation to himself and to his fellows that the natural impulsion of conscience is born.

Do not therefore think, O Sophie, that it was impossible to explain by the consequences of our nature the active principle of the conscience, independent of reason itself. And were that impossible, it would still not be necessary. For the philosophers who combat this principle do not prove that it does not exist, but are satisfied with affirming it. When we affirm that it exists, we are therefore just as advanced as they are, and we have in addition all the strength of the inner witness and the voice of the conscience, which testifies for itself.

My dear friend, how these sad reasoners are to be pitied. By erasing in themselves all the sentiments of nature they destroy the source of all their pleasures, and do not know how to free themselves of the weight of conscience except by making themselves insensitive. Is it not a very clumsy system which removes remorse for voluptuousness by stifling both? If the faith of lovers is only a chimera, if the modesty of the female sex consists in vain prejudices, what will become of all the charms of love? If we no longer see anything in the universe except matter and motion, where will be the moral goods for which our soul is always avid? And what will be the worth of human life if we enjoy it only to vegetate?

I return to this sentiment of shame that is so charming and so sweet to conquer, perhaps still sweeter to respect, which combats and inflames the desires of a lover and gives back to the heart so many pleasures for those it refuses to the senses. Why would we reject the inner reproach which veils with an impenetrable modesty the secret wishes of a modest girl and covers her cheeks with an enchanting rosiness upon hearing the tender speeches of a loved lover? What then, attack and defense are not laws of nature? Is it not nature which permits resistance to the sex which can cede as much as it likes? Is it not [nature] which prescribes pursuit to the one which she takes care to make discreet and moderate? Is it not [nature] which during their pleasures, in a state of weakness and forgetfulness of themselves which delivers them to any aggressor, puts them under the guard of shame and mystery? You will therefore feel how false it is [to say] that shame does not have its sufficient reason and is only a chimera in nature. And how would it be the work of prejudices, if the very prejudices of education destroy it, if you see it in all its force among ignorant and rustic peoples, and if its sweet voice is stifled only in more cultivated nations by reason's sophisms?

If the first glimmerings of judgment dazzle us, and begin by confounding all objects in our sight, let us wait until our weak eyes reopen, strengthen themselves, and soon we will see again these same objects in the light of reason as nature first showed them to us. Or rather, let us be more simple and less vain. Let us limit ourselves in everything to the first sentiments that we find in ourselves, since it is always to them that study brings us back when it has not misled us.

Conscience, conscience, divine instinct, immortal and eternal voice, certain guide of an ignorant and limited but intelligent and free being, infallible judge of good and bad, sublime emanation of the eternal substance, which makes men like the Gods: it is you alone which is the excellence of my nature.

Without you I feel nothing in me which raises me above the beasts, other than the sad privilege of losing my way from error to error with the aid of an understanding without rule and of a reason without principle. Attach yourself to doing the things that you like to see others do.

CHAPTER 38

Comtesse d'Houdetot—Moral Letters 6

Finally, we have a certain guide in this labyrinth of human errors; but it is not enough that it exists, one must know how to recognize it and follow it. If it speaks to all hearts, O Sophie, why then are there so few who hear it? Alas, it speaks to us in the language of nature that everything has made us forget.

The conscience is timid and fearful; it seeks solitude; the world and noise terrify it, the prejudices of which it is said to be the product are its most mortal enemies; it flees or becomes silent before them; their loud voices stifle its voice and prevent it from making itself heard. By dint of being turned away, it is repelled in the end; it no longer speaks to us; and after such a long contempt for it, it costs one as much to recall it as it cost to banish it.

When I see each of us ceaselessly occupied with public opinion extend so to speak our existence all around ourselves, while reserving almost none of it in our own heart, I believe I see a tiny insect form from its own substance a great web by which alone it seems to be sensitive, while one might believe it dead in its hole. Man's vanity is the spider's web which he spreads over everything around him. One is as solid as the other; the smallest thread one touches makes the insect move. It would die languishing if one left the web alone, and if with one finger one tears it, it ends by exhausting itself rather than not remaking it instantly. Let us begin by becoming ourselves again, by concentrating ourselves within ourselves, by circumscribing our soul within the same limits that nature has given to our being. In a word, let us begin by gathering ourselves where we are, so that in seeking to know ourselves everything that composes us comes to present itself at once to us. As for me, I think that the one who knows best what the human I consists in is the closest to wisdom and that, just as the first line of a drawing is formed from the lines that complete it, the first idea of man is to separate himself from all that he is not.

But how is this separation accomplished? This art is not so difficult as one might think or, at least, the difficulty does not lie where one believes it does. It depends more upon the will than upon enlightenment; one does not at all need an apparatus of studies and research to attain it. Daylight illuminates us, and the mirror is before us; but to see it one has to cast one's eyes on it and have the means to fix one's glance there, and to set aside the objects which divert us from it. Collect yourself, seek solitude, that is to begin with the whole secret, and through it alone one soon discovers yours. Do you think that philosophy, in fact, teaches us to return to ourselves? Ah, how much pride, under its name, leads us away from it! It is entirely the opposite, my charming friend, one must begin by returning to oneself to learn to philosophize.

Do not be frightened, I entreat you; my plan is not to relegate you to a cloister and to impose upon a fashionable woman the life of an Anchorite. The solitude at issue is less that of closing your door and of staying in your apartment than that of drawing your soul away from the crowd, as the abbé Terrasson used to say,[1] and to close off access to the foreign passions which assail it at every instant. But one of these means can aid the other, especially at the beginning. It is not the work of a day to learn how to be alone amid society, and after such a long-held habit of existing in everything that surrounds you, the concentration of your heart must begin with that of your senses. At first, you will have enough to do to contain your imagination without being obliged as well to shut your eyes and your ears. Push away the objects which must distract you until their presence no longer distracts you. Then, live ceaselessly in their midst; you will surely know when you will have to find yourself again with yourself. I am therefore not at all saying to you: leave society.

---

1. The remark is quoted by d'Alembert in his preface to Jean Terrasson's *Philosophy Applicable to All the Objects of the Mind and Reason*, but it originally comes from Montaigne, *Essays* 3.3.

I do not even say to you: renounce dissipation and the vain pleasures of society. But I say to you: learn to be alone without boredom. If you do not, you will never hear nature's voice, you will never know yourself. Do not fear that the exercise of these brief retreats will make you taciturn and savage, and detach you from habits which you would not want to renounce. On the contrary, they will only be sweeter for it.

When one lives alone one loves men better; a tender interest brings us closer to them. The imagination shows us society through its charms, and even the boredom of solitude turns to the profit of humanity. You will gain twice over from the taste for this contemplative life. You will find in it more attachment for what is dear to you so long as you have it, and less pain in losing it when you are deprived of it.

Every month, for example, take an intermission of two or three days from your pleasures and business, so as to consecrate it to the greatest of all. Make it a law for yourself to live alone during these two or three days, even if you must at first be very bored. It is better to pass them in the country than in Paris. It will be, if you like, a visit you will go make: you will go see Sophie. Solitude in the city is always sad. Since everything around us shows the work of men and some social object, when one does not have this society, one feels out of place, and a room in which one is alone seems very much like a prison. It is entirely the reverse in the country: objects are cheerful and pleasant; they excite one to concentration and reverie; one feels at liberty outside of the sad walls of the city and the constraints of prejudice. The woods, the streams, the greenery take men's gaze away from our hearts; the birds flitting here and there according to their caprice offer us in solitude the example of freedom; one hears their warbling, one smells the scent of prairies and woods. The eyes, struck only by the sweet images of nature, bring it closer to our heart.

It is therefore here that one must begin to converse with nature and to consult its laws within its own empire. At least boredom will not so soon come to pursue you, and it will be easier to bear during the exercise of walks and the variety of pastoral objects, than on a deck chair or in an armchair. I would like for you to avoid choosing times when your heart, vividly affected by some sentiment of pleasure or pain, would retain the emotion of it in your retreat, where your imagination, too moved, would bring you closer despite yourself to the beings which you believed you had fled, and your mind, too preoccupied, would refuse the light impressions of your first returns to yourself. On the contrary, so that you will have less regret about going to be bored alone in the country, take the moments when you will be reduced to being bored in the city. The life most occupied with cares and amusements leaves only too many such voids, and this way of filling the first that will present themselves will soon make you impervious to all the others. I do not ask that at first you give yourself over to profound meditations; I ask only that you can maintain your soul in a state of languor and calm that allows it to withdraw into itself and brings back from it nothing foreign to you.

In this state, you will say to me, what will I do? Nothing. Let the natural uneasiness which in solitude is not slow to occupy each with himself for all he can do, take its course.

Nor am I saying that this state ought to produce a complete subsidence, and I am far from believing that we have no way of awakening in us the inner sentiment. Just as one warms a numbed part with gentle rubbing, the soul, deadened by a long inaction, reanimates itself with the gentle warmth of a moderate movement. It must be touched by pleasant memories related only to it, it must be made to recall affections that delighted it, not by the intermediary of the senses, but by a sentiment particular to it and by intellectual pleasures. If there existed in the world a being so miserable that he had never done anything in the whole course of his life the memory of which could give him an inner contentment and give him joy to have lived, this being, having nothing but sentiments and ideas which would take him away from himself, would be unable ever to know himself, and for lack of knowing in what consists the goodness which suits his nature, would remain forcibly bad and would be eternally unhappy. But I maintain that on earth there is no man so depraved as never to have abandoned his heart to the temptation to do good. This temptation is so natural and so sweet that it is impossible always to resist it, and it is enough to give in to it once never to forget the pleasure one tastes through it. O dear Sophie, how many of your life's actions will follow you into solitude to teach you to love it. I do not need to seek any that are foreign to me. Think of the heart that you preserved for virtue, think of me; you will love to live with yourself.

These are the ways to work in society at pleasing yourself in reclusion, by preparing pleasant memories for yourself, by procuring your friendship for yourself and making yourself good enough company for yourself so you can do without any other. But what exactly must one do to achieve this? On that point it is not at all yet time to enter here into details which suppose knowledge that we are proposing to acquire.

I know that one must not begin a moral treatise by its end, nor give as first precept the practice that one wants to teach. But again, in whatever condition a soul may be, there remains a sentiment of pleasure in doing good which is never erased, and which serves as the first hold for all the virtues. It is by this cultivated sentiment that one arrives at loving oneself, and at liking to be with oneself. The exercise of beneficence naturally flatters amour-propre by an idea of superiority. One recalls all of its acts as so many pieces of evidence that, over and above one's own needs, one has still more strength to relieve those of others. That air of power makes one take more pleasure in existing and live more willingly with oneself. That is, at first, all I ask of you. Attire yourself to present yourself to your mirror; you will more willingly look at yourself. Always think of arranging for a sentiment of well-being while you are alone, and in the objects of your pleasures, always give preference to those that one still enjoys when one no longer possesses them.

A woman of quality is always too much surrounded by her position. I would wish that you could renounce yours for a few moments; that would be another means of talking more immediately with yourself. When you go into reclusion, leave behind all the retinue of your house; bring neither cook nor butler. Take a servant and a maid. That is already too many. In a word, do not convey the city to the country; go there truly to taste the retired and rustic life. But the proprieties. Ah! Always these fatal proprieties! If you always want to listen to them, you need no other guide; choose between them and wisdom. Go to bed early, get up in the morning; more or less follow the course of the sun and of nature. No toilette, no reading, eat simple meals at the people's hours. In a word, be in everything a woman of the fields. If this manner of living becomes pleasant to you, you will have one more pleasure; if it bores you, you will take up again with more taste for it the one to which you have accustomed yourself.

Do even better. Use a part of these short intervals in which you will be willing to live in solitude to make the other part pleasant. You will have long mornings free of your ordinary occupations: reserve them for errands in the village. Inform yourself about the sick, the poor, the oppressed. Seek to give each the help he needs, and do not think that it is enough to assist them with your purse if you do not also give them your time and do not help them with your cares. Impose upon yourself this function, that is so noble, to act so that there are fewer ills on this earth; and if your intentions are pure and real, you will soon find wherewith to fulfill them. I know well that a thousand obstacles will in the beginning distract you from such an effort. Unkept houses, loutish people, objects of misery will in the beginning disgust you. But when you enter these unfortunate wretches' houses, say to yourself: I am their sister, and humanity will triumph over your repugnance. You will find them liars, self-serving, and full of vices which will discourage your zeal, but interrogate yourself in secret about your own to learn to forgive those of others; and consider that, in covering them with a more decent appearance, education only makes them more dangerous. Boredom, above all, that tyrant of people in your position, which makes them pay so dearly for exemption from work—and of which one makes oneself even more the prey by making efforts to avoid it—boredom alone will at first turn you away from these salutary occupations, and in making them insupportable to you will furnish you with pretexts to dispense with them. Consider that taking pleasure in doing good is the prize for having done well, and that one does not obtain it before having deserved it. Nothing is more lovable than virtue, but it shows itself this way only to those who possess it. When one wants to embrace it, like the Proteus of the fable it at first takes on a thousand frightening forms, and finally shows itself in its own [form] only to those who did not lose hold. Resist, therefore, the sophistries of boredom. Do not push away objects made to move you; detest that cruel pity which turns its eyes away from the ills of others to dispense itself from relieving them. Do not rest from these honorable cares [by handing them] to mercenaries. Be sure that servants always take a contribution for the good deeds of masters; that they know how to appropriate in one way or another a part of what one gives through their hands; and that they demand a very onerous gratitude for everything that the master did freely. Make it your duty to carry everywhere with genuine assistance that interest and those consolations which give it worth, and which often take its place. May your visits never be fruitless! May everyone jump with joy at your approach, may public benedictions ceaselessly accompany you. Soon such a sweet procession will enchant your soul, and in the new pleasures that you will learn to taste, if sometimes you lose the good that you would have thought to do, you will at least not lose the one you will have drawn from it.

CHAPTER 39

Jacob Vernes

February 18, 1758
Montmorency
D'Alembert's article "Geneva" in the Encyclopedia *had stated that the Genevan clergy were no longer really Calvinists. The clergy debated making a response to this charge.*

Yes, my dear fellow citizen, I still love you and, it seems to me, more tenderly than ever. But I am overwhelmed by my illnesses, I have a great deal of trouble living in my retreat from labor that is hardly lucrative. I have only the time I need to earn my bread, and the little that I have left is used in suffering and resting. My malady has made such a progression this winter, I have felt so many pains of every sort, and I find myself so weakened, that I begin to fear that I will lack strength and means at the same time for executing my project. I console myself for that impotence by considering the condition I am in. What use would it be to me to go die among you? Alas, it was necessary to live there! What does it matter where one leaves one's corpse? I would not need to have my heart carried back to my fatherland; it has never left it.

I have not had an opportunity to execute your commission with M. d'Alembert. As we never saw each other very much, we do not write to each other, and confined in my solitude I have not preserved any sort of relation with Paris. It is as if I am at the other end of the earth, and I do not know what happens there any more than in Peking. Moreover, if the article that you mention is indiscreet and reprehensible, it is certainly not offensive. Nevertheless, if it can harm your corps, perhaps it will be good to respond to it; although, to speak to you truly, I have a bit of aversion for the details into which that can lead, and in general I hardly like to have the conscience subjected to formulas in matters of faith. I have religion, my friend, and that has worked out well; I do not believe that any man in the world needs it as much as I do. I passed my life among unbelievers without letting myself be shaken;[1] loving them, esteeming them very much, and not being able to bear their doctrine. I always told them that I did not know how to combat them, but that I did not want to believe them. On these matters, philosophy, having neither bottom nor shore, lacking primitive ideas and elementary principles, is only a sea of uncertainty and doubt, from which the metaphysician never extricates himself. Thus, I left reason behind, and I consulted nature, that is, the interior sentiment that directs my belief independently of my reason. I let them arrange their chances, their lots, their necessary motion, and while they were building the world by casting dice, I saw in it that unity of intention which in spite of them showed me a single principle; exactly as if they had told me that the *Iliad* had been formed by a fortuitous throw of letters, I would have said to them very resolutely: that is possible, but it is not true; and I have no other reason for not believing any of it except that I do not believe any of it. "What prejudice!" they say. So be it. But what can that overbearing reason do against a prejudice more persuasive than it is? Another endless argumentation against the distinction of the two substances; another persuasion on my part that there is nothing in common between a tree and my thought; and what amused me in this was to see them corner themselves by means of their own sophisms to the point of preferring to give feeling to stones than to grant a soul to man.[2]

My friend, I believe in God, and God would not be just if my soul were not immortal. That, it seems to me, is everything that is essential and useful in religion. Leave the rest to the disputers. As to the eternity of punishments, it cannot be accorded with man's weakness, or with God's

---

1. In the *Reveries,* Rousseau says that the philosophers among whom he lived "had shaken all the certainty I thought I had concerning the things that were most important for me to know." *CW* 8:21.

2. This position is defended by Diderot in his *D'Alembert's Dream.*

justice. Therefore I reject it. It is true that there are souls so black that I cannot conceive that they can ever savor that eternal beatitude whose sweetest sentiment, it seems to me, must be contentment with oneself. That makes me suspect that it could very well be that the souls of the wicked are annihilated at their death, and that to be and to feel are the first rewards for a good life. However this may be, what does it matter to me what the wicked will be. It is enough for me that in approaching the end of my life, I do not see that of my hopes, and that I expect a happier one after having suffered so much in this one. If I deceive myself in this hope, this is itself a good that will have caused me to bear all my ills more easily. I peacefully await enlightenment on these great truths that are hidden from me, thoroughly convinced nonetheless that, in any event, if virtue does not always make man happy, at least he could not be happy without it; that the afflictions of the just are not without some compensation; and that even the tears of innocence are sweeter to the heart than the prosperity of the wicked.

It is natural, my dear Vernes, for a solitary man who is suffering and deprived of all society to pour out his soul into the bosom of friendship, and I do not fear that my confidences displease you. I should have begun by speaking about you and your project on the history of Geneva, but there are times of pain and ills in which one is forced to be occupied with oneself, and you know very well that I do not have a heart that wants to disguise itself. All that I can tell you about your enterprise, with all the circumspection that you want to put into it, is that it is that of an intrepid wise man or of a young man. I advise you to think about it well. Give my love to our friend Roustan. Farewell, my dear fellow citizen. I am writing you with as great an effusion of heart as if I were separating myself from you forever, because I find myself in a condition which can still take me very far, but that still lets me doubt whether each letter that I write will not be the last.

CHAPTER 40

Denis Diderot

March 2, 1758
This is the last letter that Rousseau ever wrote to Diderot, who did not reply to it. One week later Rousseau finished writing the Letter to d'Alembert, *to which he added a note announcing his definitive rupture with his old friend. See CW 10:256.*

I must, my dear Diderot, write to you one more time in my life. You have dispensed with my doing so only too well; but the greatest crime of that man whom you sully in such a strange manner is to be unable to detach himself from you.

My plan for now is not to enter into explanations about the horrors that you impute to me. I see that this explanation would be useless at present. For, although born good and with a frank soul, you nevertheless have an unfortunate inclination to misinterpret your friends' speeches and actions. Prejudiced against me as you are, you would turn into evil everything that I could say to justify myself, and my most ingenuous explanations would do nothing but provide your subtle mind with new interpretations at my expense. No, Diderot; I feel that this is not the place to start. First, I want to propose to your good sense prejudices that are simpler, truer, better founded than yours, and in which at least I do not think you can find new crimes.

I am a wicked man, is that not so?[1] You have the most certain testimonies of this; it has been well attested to you. When you began to learn it, it had been sixteen years that I was, for you, a good man, and forty years that I was so for everyone. Can you say as much about those who have communicated this fine discovery to you? If one can falsely wear the mask of a decent man for so long, what proof do you have that this mask does not cover their faces as well as mine? Is charging in secret an absent man in no condition to defend himself a very suitable way to give weight to their authority? But that is not the issue.

I am a wicked man. But why am I one? Take good care, my dear Diderot, this deserves your attention. One is not maleficent for nothing. If there were some monster made this way, he would not wait forty years to satisfy his depraved inclinations. Consider then my life, my passions, my tastes, my inclinations. Seek out, if I am wicked, what interest could have brought me to be so? I who for my misfortune always bore a too sensitive heart, what did I gain by breaking with those who were dear to me? To what place did I aspire, to what pensions, to what honors has anyone seen me lay claim, what competitors do I have to set aside, what return can come to me from doing ill? I who seek only solitude and peace, I whose sovereign good consists in laziness and idleness, I whose indolence and ills barely leave me the time to provide for my subsistence, to what aim, to what good would I go plunge myself into the agitations of crime and embark upon the eternal maneuverings of scoundrels? Whatever you might say about it, one does not flee men when one seeks to harm them; the wicked man can meditate on his blows in solitude, but it is in society that he strikes. A cheat has skill and sangfroid, a perfidious man is master of himself, and does not get carried away: do you recognize anything of all that in me? I get carried away in anger and am often thoughtless in sangfroid. Do these defects make up the wicked man? No, doubtless; but the wicked man takes advantage of them to ruin the one who has them.

I would wish that you could also reflect a little on yourself. You trust your natural goodness; but do you know to what point example and error can corrupt it? Have you never feared being surrounded by skillful

---

1. This is a reference to the line "Only the wicked man lives alone," from Diderot's play *The Natural Son*. Rousseau had complained that audiences would apply it to him, and Diderot did not deny that that had been his intention.

admirers who avoid praising crudely to your face only to take possession of you more skillfully under the lure of a feigned sincerity? What a fate for the best of men to be led astray by his very candor, and, in the hands of the wicked, to be innocently the instrument of their perfidy! I know that amour-propre revolts against this idea, but it deserves the examination of reason.

There are some considerations that I beg you to weigh well. Think about them for a long time before answering. If they do not touch you, we no longer have anything to say to each other; but if they do make some impression on you, then we will begin clarifications; you will find again a friend worthy of you, and who perhaps will not have been useless to you. I have a weighty motive for urging you to that examination, and here is that motive.

You may have been seduced and deceived. Nevertheless, your friend groans in his solitude, forgotten by all that was dear to him. He might fall into despair there, finally die there, cursing the ingrate whose adversity made him shed so many tears and who unworthily overwhelms him in his own. It might be that the proofs of his innocence will finally reach you, that you will be forced to honor his memory, and that the image of your dying friend will not leave you with tranquil nights. Diderot, think about it, I will not speak about it any longer.

CHAPTER 41

Jacob Vernes

May 25, 1758
Montmorency

I do not write to you punctually, my dear Vernes, but I think about you every day. The illnesses, the periods of languishing, the troubles ceaselessly increase my laziness; I no longer have anything that is active but my heart. Aside from God, my fatherland, and the human race, there is no longer any particular attachment in it except for you; and I have known men on the basis of such sad experiences that if you deceive me like the others, I would be afflicted by it, doubtless, but I would no longer be surprised by it. Fortunately, I do not presume anything like it on your part, and I am persuaded that if you make the trip that you promise me, the habit of seeing each other and of becoming better acquainted will forever strengthen that genuine friendship that I have so much inclination to contract with you. If it is true, then, that your business and your fortune allow you this trip and your heart desires it, announce it to me in advance so that I can prepare myself for the pleasure of pressing a decent man and a friend against my breast at least once in my life.

In relation to my belief, I have examined your objections,[1] and I will tell you naturally that they do not persuade me. I find that for a man convinced of the immortality of the soul you give too much value to the goods and evils of this life. I have been better acquainted than you with the latter, and better, perhaps, than any man who exists. I do not adore the equity of Providence any less and would believe that I am as ridiculous for murmuring about my misfortunes during this short life as for crying misfortune because I spent a night in a bad inn. Everything that you say about the impotence of the conscience can be turned back more vigorously against revelation; for what do you want to be thought about the author of a remedy that does not cure anything? Would one not say that all those who are acquainted with the Gospel are extremely holy personages, and that a bloodthirsty and faithless Sicilian is worth much more than a stupid and coarse Hottentot? Do you want me to believe that God has given his law to men only to have a double reason for punishing them? Beware, my friend, you want to justify him for a chimerical fault, and you aggravate the accusation. Remember above all that in this dispute, you are the one who is attacking my sentiment, and I am not doing anything but defending it; for as a matter of fact I am extremely far from disapproving of yours, so long as you will not want to constrain anyone to embrace it.

What! This lovable and dear sister-in-law is still in her bed.[2] Why am I not near her? We would console each other mutually for our ills, and I would learn from her to suffer my own with constancy. But I no longer hope to make such a desired journey; from day to day I feel less in a condition to sustain it. It is not that summer has not given me back vigor and courage; but the localized illness has not made any less progress for it. It even begins to make itself very perceptible externally; a swelling that grows when I walk almost deprives me of the pleasure of walking, the only one that was left me, and I reacquire strength only to suffer; God's will be done! I hope that will not keep me from showing you the surroundings of my solitude; the only thing they lack is to be around Geneva to appear delightful to me. I embrace dear Roustan, my so-called disciple. I read his examination of the four fine ages with

---

1. These are presumably objections to the previous letter, but Vernes's letter has not been found.

2. Dorothée, the wife of Vernes's brother Pierre.

pleasure,[3] and I maintain my sentiment with more confidence seeing that it is also his. The only thing that I would like to ask him would be not to practice virtue at my expense, and not to show himself modest by flattering my vanity. Farewell, my dear Vernes, from day to day I find more pleasure in loving you.

If you want to spare me the cost of letters, you can write to me enclosed in the letters of M. de Chenonceaux, farmer general of the king, at the tax farming office, Paris.[4]

---

3. Roustan wrote *Critical Examination of the Four Golden Ages of Voltaire*. He declared himself to be Rousseau's disciple in a letter dated March 5, 1757. Later, however, he expressed serious reservations about the *Social Contract* and the second half of the *Profession of Faith*.

4. Generally the recipient of a letter had to pay the cost, which led Rousseau ultimately not to accept much mail. By sending the letter to a government office in care of Rousseau's friend Chenonceaux, Vernes would save Rousseau the expense.

CHAPTER 42

Jean Le Rond d'Alembert

June 25, 1758
Montmorency

I had, sir, to respond to your article *Geneva*. I have done so, and I have addressed this writing to you. I am grateful for the testimonies of your remembrance, and to the honor that I have received from you on more than one occasion; but you give us a pernicious piece of advice, and if my father had done as much, I neither could nor should remain silent. I have tried to accord what I owe you with what I owe to my fatherland; when it was necessary to choose, I would have committed a crime by hesitating. If my boldness offends you, you will only be too well avenged for it by the weakness of the work. In it you will look in vain for the remnants of a talent that is no longer, and that perhaps was nourished only by my disdain for my adversaries. If I had consulted only my reputation, I would certainly have suppressed this writing. But it is not a question here of what can please us or honor me; in doing my duty I will always be satisfied enough with myself and justified enough toward you.

CHAPTER 43

Toussaint-Pierre Lenieps

November 8, 1758
Montmorency

Here, my friend, is my response to M. the abbé de la Porte.[1] Please seal it before handing it to him. I would give a hundred to one odds that his falling out with M. Fréron is a feigned falling out, and that they have arranged this little game between them to double their revenue and pull the public's strings more pleasantly. This idea makes me die of laughter and seems to me to be one of the best tricks that has ever been played.

I am quite disposed to agree with you about my errors. Above all, it is possible that I am mistaken about the circles;[2] find some other way for men not to live with women, and I abandon that one. It is true that they maintain a sort of external decency, but it is dearly bought.

It can also be the case that public balls might not be suited to Geneva for the very good reasons that you allege at the end of the item that concerns them; but when you condemn dancing in general, you are very assuredly mistaken. Dancing is an inspiration of nature, and nature is never wrong. It is only a matter of regulating it. That is accordingly

___

1. Neither this response nor the abbé's letter has been found.
2. The circles were men's clubs devoted to hunting and conversation.

what I proposed to do. Why, you say, make girls and boys learn what will be forbidden to them when they are married? Because girls and boys must necessarily live differently than husbands and wives; because, being married, they will no longer need to get married. Because the inclinations of each age require different amusements. Because reasons of health require that one let young people be given over to the exercises that nature asks of them. There is a time to be young, the author of nature wishes it so; it is an injustice and a harshness to deprive youth of the amusements of its age, and to deprive them of these because that age will not last forever is to reason badly. Let us be what we ought to be at all times of life and let us not make old people at twenty. You speak of learning to dance as if a great science were in question: but not at all. I do not want a Marcel in Geneva. Let them walk, let them leap in cadence, let a master give several months of lessons to learn how to walk and to present oneself gracefully: that science is appropriate at all times. That is enough for pleasure and utility; I do not ask for anything more. Why, you continue, divert each of them from their occupations and their duties? But one of their duties is to get married. Respond to what I have said about that in my book; so then you do not want to grant any sort of amusement to youth? Dear Lenieps, that appears very harsh to me, and I warn you that if you deprive it of everything, it will give itself some despite you, and that those that it chooses will be worth less than those I leave it.

Neither do I agree with you when you say that if we are corrupt, it is not women's fault, it is ours. But my whole book is employed in showing how it is their fault, and I do not believe that there is anything to respond to that. In every country, men are what women make them, that is inevitable, that is the law of nature. To philosophize well about morals, one must never separate the two sexes, for morals always depend on their relation. We renounce our sex only because women renounce theirs; restore women, and we will be men.

I did not want to dispute with you, but the subjects draw me along. I wish with all my heart that we could finish one of these days glass in hand. I was at Clichy on November 1,[3] and had I been here, I would not have received your letter in time to be able to go dine with you, which I do not despair of doing, either this winter, or at least in better weather. It seems to me that your celebration and mine are the only times that

---

3. Rousseau had been paying one of his rare visits to Paris, visiting Mme. Dupin.

we see each other.[4] I admit to you that the small word "Escalade" that you said to me utterly delighted my heart, and if the only thing necessary to celebrate it with you is to consent that you bring your dish, I consent to it with pleasure, come both of you: you and your dish, one will be caressed and the other eaten, and I hope *cé qu'é l'aino* will keep us all in joy.[5] You are not unaware how much I appreciate the memory, the esteem, and the friendship of Madame your daughter; I am very certain that my book does not displease her. In general, the only women who take offense at it are those who cannot recognize themselves in the first lines of page 161.[6] Farewell my good and dear friend, you see that I lack paper more than babbling.

---

4. Lenieps and Rousseau celebrated the Escalade, Geneva's repulse of the attack on it by Charles-Emmanuel of Savoy, December 12, 1602.

5. "Cé qu'é l'aino" means "the one who is above," which is the opening of a song celebrating the Escalade.

6. In this passage Rousseau refers to mothers surrounded by their children. See *CW* 10:315.

Chapter 44

Théodore Tronchin

November 26, 1758
Montmorency
On November 13, Tronchin had written Rousseau a letter congratulating him on the Letter to d'Alembert, *although he also argued that Genevan morals were more corrupt than Rousseau thought.*

Your letter, sir, would have given me great pleasure at any time, and gives me even more today; for I see in it that, having judged the absent man without hearing him, you have not judged him quite as severely as I had been told. The more indifferent I am about the public's judgments, the less I am about those of men of your order. Although I aspire to deserve the esteem of good people, however, I do not know how to beg for anyone's, and I admit that being just or unjust toward me is the least important thing in the world.

I did not doubt that you would be of my opinion, or rather that I would be of yours regarding M. d'Alembert's proposal, and I am charmed that you wanted to confirm this opinion yourself. It will be unfortunate if your credit and your wisdom do not keep the comedy from being established in the city and from being kept at our gates.

Regarding the circles, I agree about their abuse; I did not doubt it; that is the fate of human things. But I believe that from the destruction of the circles will follow even greater abuses. You draw a very judicious distinction regarding the difference between the Greek republics and ours as to public education. Be that as it may, however, this education could not take place among us, and could not do so even because of the sole force of things, whether one wants it to or not. The proof is that there is a great difference between the artisans of other countries and ours. A watchmaker from Geneva is a man to present anywhere; a watchmaker from Paris is good only for talking about watches. The education of a workman tends to form his fingers, nothing more. Nevertheless, the citizen remains; for well or ill the head and the heart are formed; one always finds the time for that, and that is what instruction must provide for. Here, sir, I have the advantage over you as an individual that you have over me in general observation. This station of artisans is my own, that in which I was born, in which I should have lived, and that I left only for my misfortune. I received there that public education; not through formal instruction, but by means of traditions and maxims which, being transmitted from age to age, early on gave to youth the enlightenment that suits it and the sentiments it ought to have. At twelve, I was a Roman; at twenty, I had run around the world and was no longer anything but a scamp. Times have changed, I am not unaware of it; but it is an injustice to shift the public corruption onto the artisans. It is known only too well that it did not begin with them. Everywhere the rich man is always the first corrupted, the poor follows, and the middle station is touched last. Now with us, the middle station is watchmaking.

Too bad if children remain abandoned to themselves; but why are they? It is not the circles' fault; on the contrary, that is where they should be brought up, girls by mothers, boys by fathers. There is precisely the average education that suits us, between the public education of the Greek republics and the domestic education of monarchies, where all the subjects must remain isolated and have nothing in common except obedience.

Nor must one confuse the exercises that I am counseling with those of ancient gymnastics; the latter formed a genuine occupation, almost a profession; the former ought to be nothing but relaxation, festivals, and I have proposed them only in this sense. Since there must be amusements, these are the ones that ought to be offered to us. An observation that was made in my times is that the most skillful workmen of Geneva were precisely those who shone the most in these sorts of exercises, at that time in honor among us. This proves that these diverse occupations do not harm each other, but on the contrary mutually aid each other.

Farewell, sir, I embrace you and respect you with all my heart. May you honor your fatherland and do good for the human species for a long time.

JJRousseau

CHAPTER 45

Louis Phélypeaux, comte de Saint-Florentin, Duc de la Vrillière

February 11, 1759
Memorandum

At the beginning of the year 1753, I presented at the Opera a little work titled *The Village Soothsayer*, which had been performed before the king at Fontainebleau the preceding autumn. I declared to Masters Rebel and Francoeur, then inspectors of the Royal Academy of Music, in the presence of M. Duclos of the French Academy, historiographer of France, that I was not asking for any money for this little opera, that I was satisfied as its price with my free entry in perpetuity, but I stipulated that expressly, to which it was responded to me by the said master Rebel in the presence of the same M. Duclos that this was by right, in conformity with custom, and that in addition I was owed the honoraria that they would take care to have me paid.

The Village Soothsayer was played, and although I had also required that the first four performances would be done by good actors, which was granted, it was done by understudies from the third performance on; and the piece was performed 31 times in a row before Easter, without counting the three capitations for which it was also given.[1]

As for the honoraria which were due to me, and for which I had not asked, twelve hundred francs were brought to my home, the receipt for which I signed as soon as it was presented to me.

The Village Soothsayer was repeated after Easter and continued for the whole year, and even during the following carnival almost without interruption, but in a state which, not leaving me the courage to put up with the spectacle, always forced me to be absent from it; and that is a year of non-enjoyment of my right of which I would be only too well founded to demand an account.

Finally at the time that, delivered from this distress, I believed I could take advantage of the privilege of my free admission without disgust, Master de Neuville declared to me at the gate of the Opera that he had been ordered by the City Office to refuse it to me, agreeing at the same time that such a proceeding was unprecedented. And, in fact, if such is the distinction that the City Office reserves for those who compose the words and music of an opera at the same time, and for the authors of works that are played a hundred times in a row, it is not surprising that it is rare.[2]

Based on this simple and faithful exposition I believe I have the right to ask for the restitution of my manuscript, and that it be forbidden to the Royal Academy of Music ever to perform *The Village Soothsayer*, over which it has lost its right, by violating the contract by which I had granted it. For by depriving me of the agreed price, it returns ownership to me; that is incontestable in all justice.

1. It would not be an answer to oppose to me a so-called regulation which, they say, limits to one year the free admission for the authors of a one-act opera: a regulation that they allege without showing it; which is known to no one and has never been put into practice against an author before me; a regulation which, finally, after a careful verification, is found not to have existed when my agreement was made and which, had it since been established, can have no retroactive effect.

---

1. At the end of each annual season, performances, or capitations, were given for the benefit of the actors in the company.
2. These events, which followed Rousseau's criticism of French music in the *Letter on French Music*, are described in book 8 of the *Confessions* (*CW* 5:323–24).

2. Were this regulation to exist, were it in effect, it can have no force concerning me, a foreigner who was not acquainted with it, and to whom it was not opposed when, master of my work, I granted it only while stipulating a contrary condition. Did they not depart from this regulation by negotiating with me? That was when it was necessary to speak to me about it. Who ever heard it said that one annuls an express agreement through the secret intention of not keeping it?

3. Why would the Royal Academy of Music take advantage against me of a regulation that it itself violated to my prejudice? If the author of the words and that of the music of a one-act opera each have admission for a year, he who is both at the same time ought to have them for two, unless the union of the talents that contribute to their perfection is a title against the one who brings them together.

4. If the intention of the City Office was to make use of it in all strictness with me, it had to begin then by paying me strictly what was due me. The product of a grand opera for each of the two authors is two thousand livres when it continues for thirty consecutive performances, and fifty francs each for twenty others. Now, the third of four thousand francs is more than twelve hundred francs. If I did not ask for the surplus, it was not out of ignorance of my right; but it is that having stipulated another price for my work, I did not want to haggle over that one.

If one adds to these arguments that, against what was promised me, my work was played by understudies from the third performance on, one will find that the management of the Opera, not having observed with me either the conditions that I stipulated or its own regulations, has stripped itself, as if willingly, of every sort of right over my piece. It is true that I received twelve hundred francs that I am ready to return upon receiving my score; hoping that in its turn the Royal Academy of Music will indeed want to account for the one hundred performances that it made of a work that it knew did not belong to it, because it did not want to pay the agreed upon price.

If this Academy has complaints to make against me, let it make them before the tribunals, and not establish itself as the judge in its own case, nor believe it has the right because of them to seize hold of my possession. As soon as one is dissatisfied with a man it does not follow that one is allowed to rob him.

CHAPTER 46

Charles-François-Frédéric de Montmorency-Luxembourg, maréchal-duc de Luxembourg

April 30, 1759
Montmorency

Sir,

I have forgotten neither the favors you have heaped upon me, nor the engagement that respect and gratitude have not allowed me to refuse.[1] I have lost neither the will to keep my word, nor the sentiment with which it suits me to accept the honor that you have done me. But Monsieur le maréchal, this engagement could only be conditional, and in the extreme distance that exists from you to me, it would be an inexcusable rashness to dare to live in your house, without knowing whether I would be viewed by both you and Madame la maréchale with the same benevolence that brought you to offer it to me.

Your kindnesses have put me in a perplexity that increases the desire not to be unworthy of them. I conceive how one rejects with a cold and repellent respect the advances of the great whom one does not esteem; but how, without forgetting myself, will I behave with you, sir, whom my heart honors? With you whom I would seek out if you were my

---

1. The duke had offered Rousseau the use of a house on his estate while repairs were being made to Rousseau's lodging.

equal? Having never wanted to live with anyone but my friends, I have only one language, that of friendship, of familiarity. I am not unaware how much one must modify this language from my station to yours. I know that my respect for your person does not dispense me from that which I owe to your rank, but I know even better that poverty that demeans itself soon becomes despicable. I know that it also has its dignity that even love of virtue obliges it to preserve. Thus, I am always uncertain whether I am lacking in respect to you or to myself, whether I am familiar or groveling; and this very danger that preoccupies me keeps me from doing anything or saying anything appropriate. Already, without wanting to, I might have committed some fault, and this fear is very reasonable in a man who does not know how one ought to conduct oneself with the great, who did not trouble to learn it, and who will have only once in his life regretted not knowing it.

Forgive then, Monsieur le maréchal, the timidity that makes me hesitate to benefit from a favor which I must hardly have expected, and which I would not like to abuse. I have not, as for me, changed my resolution, but I fear that I have given you grounds to change your sentiment on my account. If M. Chassot informs me on your behalf and that of Madame la maréchale that I am still welcome,[2] you will see from my eagerness to take advantage of your favors that it is not the fear of being ungrateful that has made me hesitate.

Whether I live in your house and am sometimes admitted near you, or I remain at the distance that suits me, the kindnesses with which you have honored me and the way I have tried to respond to them have henceforth placed a common interest between us. Reciprocal esteem brings all stations nearer to one another; however elevated you may be, however obscure I may be, the glory of each of the two ought no longer to be indifferent to the other. I will tell myself all the days of my life: remember that Monsieur le maréchal-duc de Luxembourg honored you with his visit and came to sit on your straw chair in the middle of your broken pots. This is neither for your name nor for your fortune, but for some reputation of probity that you have acquired for yourself; never make him blush for the honor he has done you. Deign, Monsieur le maréchal, to say to yourself also sometimes: in the patrimony of my fathers there is a solitary man who takes an interest in me, who is touched by the reputation of my beneficence, who joins the

---

2. M. Chassot was one of the servants in the duke's household.

benedictions of his heart to those of the wretches whom I relieve, and who honors me, not because I am great, but because I am good.

Receive, Monsieur le maréchal, the humble testimonies of my gratitude and my profound respect.

CHAPTER 47

Madeleine Angélique de Neufville, duchesse de Luxembourg

May 6, 1759
Petit-Chateau of Montmorency

Madame,

My entire letter is contained in its date. How this date honors me! How wholeheartedly I write it! I do not praise you, madam, I do not thank you; but I live in your house. Each has his language, and I have said everything in mine.

Deign, Madame la maréchale, to accept my profound respect.

JJRousseau

CHAPTER 48

Duc de Luxembourg

May 27, 1759
Petit-Château

Sir,

Your house is charming; its abode is delightful. It would be even more so if the magnificence that I find in it and the attentions that follow me there let me notice a little less that I am not in my own home. That aside, the only thing lacking to the pleasure with which I live in it is that of seeing you as its witness.

You know, Monsieur le maréchal, that solitary people all have a romantic spirit. I am full of that spirit; I feel it and am not afflicted by it. Why would I seek to be cured of such a sweet folly, since it contributes to making me happy? People of society and of the court, do not go thinking that you are wiser than I am: we differ only in our chimeras.

Here then is mine on this occasion. I think that if we are both the way that I love to believe, we can form a rare and perhaps unique spectacle in relations of esteem and friendship. You suggested this word to me, between two men of stations so diverse that they did not seem made to have the slightest relation between them. But for that, sir, you must remain as you are, and leave me as I am. Do not wish to be my patron; as for me, I promise you not to be your panegyrist. I promise you in addition that we will both have done a very fine thing and that our society, if I dare to use this word, will be for both of us a subject of praise preferable to all those that adulation lavishes. On the contrary, if you want to protect me, give me gifts, obtain favors for me, draw me out of my station, and I acquiesce in your benefits, you will have sought out nothing but a maker of phrases, and you will be nothing but a grandee in my eyes. I hope that the kindnesses with which you honor me will not lead to this reciprocal opinion.

But sir, I must admit all my perplexity to you. I do not imagine the possibility of seeing only you and Madame la Maréchale amid the crowd inseparable from your rank and with which you are ceaselessly surrounded. That is, nevertheless, a condition from which it would be hard for me to depart. I want neither to please the curious, nor to see, for even a moment, other men than those who suit me, and if I had believed I made an exception for you, I would never have done it. My mood, which cannot abide any bother; my discomforts which could not bear it; my maxims, based on which I do not want to constrain myself, and which surely would offend anyone else but you; above all peace and the repose of my life, everything imposes on me the sweet law of ending as I began. Monsieur le maréchal, I wish to see you, to cultivate your esteem, to learn from you how to deserve it; but I cannot sacrifice my reclusion to you. Make it so I can see you alone; and find it good that I see you only that way.

I would never forgive myself for having thus set my terms of surrender to you before accepting the honor of your offers, and it is another honor that I believe I owe to your generosity to tell you my whims only after having put myself in your power. For in feeling what duties I was going to contract, I engaged myself to them without fear. I am not unaware that my abode here, which is nothing for you, is extremely consequential to me. I know that had I slept there only one night, the public, posterity perhaps, would demand an account from me of that single night. Doubtless they will demand it from me for the rest of my life; I have no trouble providing a response. Sir, it is not up to me to make it. In naming you I must be justified, or I never could be.

I do not believe I need an excuse for the tone that I am taking with you. It seems to me that you must understand me, Monsieur le maréchal. I could, it is true, speak to you in more respectful terms, but not in more honorable ones.

CHAPTER 49

Duchesse de Luxembourg

August 13, 1759

Madame,

How cruel your kindnesses are! Why do you come to disturb the peace of a solitary who renounced the sweet things in life in order not to feel its troubles any longer? I have spent my days uselessly seeking solid attachments. I have not been able to form any in the walks of life I could reach; is it in yours that I am to find them? Never have I been able to resist caresses; why are you jointly attacking me at a weak point that I ought to overcome, since in the distance that separates us outpourings of sensitive hearts must not bring mine closer to you? What gratitude can it return to you, this heart that does not know two ways of giving itself, and feels itself capable only of friendship? Of friendship, Madame la maréchale! Ah! There is my misfortune! It is fine for you, for Monsieur le maréchal to use that term; but how insane I am to take you at your word! You are diverting yourselves. I, I am becoming attached, and the end of the game prepares new regrets for me. How I hate all your titles, and how I pity you for bearing them. You seem to me so worthy of tasting the charms of private life! Why do you not live at Clarens?[1] I would seek out the happiness of my life there. But the chateau of Montmorency, but the hotel de Luxembourg! Is that where one should see Jean-Jacques? Is that where a friend of equality should bring the affections of a sensitive soul who, paying in this way for the esteem that is shown it, believes it returns as much as it receives? Yours is loving and sensitive also; I have seen it, I know it, I regret that I was not able to believe it earlier. But in the rank in which you find yourself, with your manner of living, nothing can make a durable impression; so many new objects are successively erased that not one remains. You will forget me, Madame, after having made me unable to imitate you. You will have done much to render yourself inexcusable.

JJRousseau

---

1. The home of Rousseau's character Julie. Rousseau read his novel to the duchess prior to its publication.

CHAPTER 50

Jean-Ami Martin

September 14, 1759
Montmorency
A reprinting of d'Alembert's response to the Letter to d'Alembert *was accompanied by a response to d'Alembert from the Genevan clergy and by anonymous notes attacking their declaration. Martin had written a refutation of the notes and forwarded the manuscript to Rousseau. Ultimately Martin followed Rousseau's advice to consult his fellow clergymen, who advised him not to publish it.*

Driven to distraction without respite by a thousand troublesome people, I could, sir, read your writing only very hastily; all the more reason why I cannot make the small observations about it that might come to me, and which would require much writing to say rather little. Overall, I was extremely satisfied with it. I do not know whether everyone will find its doctrine very orthodox, but I know very well that one will see everywhere in it the sentiments of a decent man and a true Christian. Nevertheless, because of the consequences, I believe that it is proper to give this work to the public only after having well consulted MM. your colleagues. Above all, although I understand nothing of theology, it seems to me that to attribute divinity to Jesus Christ only by communication is to declare him purely a man. If, without entering into the explanation of dogmas, you had been satisfied with showing the injustice, the incompetence, and the dishonesty of those who demand that things be this way, I believe that you would have done the same good without running the same risks. Would it not have been child's play for you, especially against the notes of the true or false theologian who, remaining anonymous in a cowardly way, protects himself while making others run risks and impudently cites a whole company before the tribunal of a nobody? Nevertheless, I would not like you to let the imputation of being the author of these notes fall on M. d'Alembert himself, unless you are very certain of the fact. If he were in fact their author, which I cannot believe, he would be a man to stifle; and see what an advantage one would have against him by turning back against him his manner of reasoning, and above all his note *b*.[1] However that might be, it seems clear to me that these notes are by a Catholic who, not satisfied with damning us in the other world, would not be sorry to torment us in this one. For since he proscribes the Socinians and the Calvinists equally, what does it matter to him to know by what title we are going to hell? A Catholic theologian who meddles in the quarrels of the Protestants, and who has the impertinence to ask them for an account of their doctrine, appears to me to be playing a very despicable and very ridiculous role. He is encroaching on the devil's profession; I would wish that you had made that better sensed. In a word, show the baseness and the wickedness of the accusers: the accusation will fall by itself, and honorable people will always be ashamed to make common cause with wicked people.

Good day, sir, I thank you for your confidence. I have read your work with all the more pleasure in that it has redoubled my esteem and friendship for you.

JJRousseau

---

1. This note said that the entire church of Geneva inclined toward Socinianism.

CHAPTER 51

Paul-Claude Moultou

January 29, 1760
Montmorency

If I have wronged you, sir, I am not doing so by not feeling it and not reproaching myself for it. My silence is indeed more against myself than against you; for how to respond to a letter that honors me so strongly, and in which I recognize myself so little? I will leave out of your letter what does not suit me; I will not return to you the praises you give me; I assume that you would not like to hear them, and I will seek to deserve in what follows that you think the same of me.

It is somewhat M. Favre's fault that I am responding to you so late. He had promised me to come back to see me and I had promised myself, after having chatted with him for a short time, to give him a letter for you. I waited for him, and he did not come back. I received him with simplicity but with joy; I do not imagine that such a reception could rebuff a Genevan and a friend of M. Moultou. If that could be, my intention would be very poorly fulfilled, and I would be genuinely afflicted by it.

M. Favre had an extract of your sermon on luxury. He read it to me, and I asked him to lend it to me to copy it. Do you understand me, sir?

Moreover, you are the first that I know who has shown that the feigned charity of the rich person is, in him, only an additional luxury; he feeds the poor like dogs and horses. The harm is that dogs and horses serve his pleasures, and in the end the poor bore him. In the end it is an affectation to let them perish, as it was one at first to assist them.

I am afraid that in showing the incompatibility of luxury and equality you may have done the opposite of what you wanted to do. You cannot be unaware that the partisans of luxury are all enemies of equality; by showing them how the former destroys the latter, you will only make them love it more. To the contrary, it was necessary to make it seen that opinion turned in favor of wealth and luxury annihilates the inequality of ranks, and that all the credit gained by the rich is lost for the magistrates. It seems to me that on that point there would be a much more useful, more profound, even more politic, sermon to be made, and in which in paying your court you would state very important truths with which everyone would be struck.

You speak to me about that Voltaire! Why does the name of that wandering buffoon soil your letters? The wretch has ruined my fatherland; I would hate him more if I despised him less. In his great talents I see only an additional disgrace that dishonors him because of the unworthy use he makes of them. His talents, like his wealth, serve him only to nourish the depravation of his heart. O Genevan, he is paying you well for the asylum that you have given him! He no longer knew where to go to do harm; you will be his final victims. I do not believe that, after you, many other wise men will be tempted to have such a guest.

Let us stop kidding ourselves, sir. I was wrong in my *Letter to M. d'Alembert*. I did not believe our progress so great or our morals so advanced. Our ills are henceforth without remedy; we no longer need anything but palliatives, and comedy is one. Good man, do not lose your ardent eloquence in preaching equality to us; you would no longer be understood. We are still merely slaves; teach us, if possible, not to be wicked. *Non ad vetera instituta, quae jam pridem, corruptis moribus, ludibrio sunt, revocans,*[1] but by retarding the progress of the evil through reasons of interest which alone can touch corrupt men. Farewell, sir, I embrace you.

---

1. Sallust, *Epistolae, ad Cesarum* 5: "Not by recalling the ancient institutions that our corrupt morals have rendered ridiculous for a long time."

Chapter 52

Voltaire

June 17, 1760
Montmorency
Upon learning that his letter to Voltaire from 1756 had been published, Rousseau wrote to Malesherbes, the head of the book trade in France, asking him to forbid the republication of the letter in France. Malesherbes answered that he could not prevent republication and advised Rousseau to republish it himself in Paris. This is the last direct letter between Rousseau and Voltaire.

I did not think, sir, that I would ever find myself in correspondence with you again. But learning that the letter that I sent you in 1756 has been printed in Berlin, I ought to give you an account of my conduct in that regard, and I will fulfill this duty with truth and simplicity.

Having really been addressed to you, this letter was not intended for publication. I passed it on, conditionally, to three people to whom the rights of friendship did not allow me to refuse anything of this sort, and who were even less allowed by the same rights to take advantage of what was entrusted to them by violating their promise. These three people are Mme. de Chenonceaux, daughter-in-law of Mme. Dupin; Mme. la comtesse d'Houdetot; and a German named M. Grimm. Mme. de Chenonceaux wished that this letter be printed and asked my consent for that; I told her that it depended on yours. It was asked of you, you refused it, and there was no longer any question of it.

M. the abbé Trublet, however, with whom I have no sort of connection, just wrote to me out of an attentiveness full of decency that, having received the sheets of a journal by M. de Formey, he had read this same letter with a notice in which the editor says on October 23, 1759, that "he found it several weeks ago at the booksellers in Berlin, and that since it is one of those passing sheets that soon disappear without coming back, he believed he ought to give it a place in his journal."

That, sir, is all I know about it. It is very certain that up until now no one had even heard this letter spoken of in Paris. It is very certain that the copy, either manuscript or printed, that fell into M. de Formey's hands could have come to him mediately or immediately only from you, which is not plausible, or from one of the three people that I have named. Anyway, it is very certain that the two ladies are incapable of such an infidelity. I am unable to know anything more about it from my retreat. You have correspondences by means of which it would be easy for you, if the thing were worth the trouble, to go back to the source and verify the fact.

In the same letter, M. the abbé Trublet indicates that he is holding the sheet in reserve and will not lend it without my consent, which I certainly will not give; but it could happen that this copy is not the only one in Paris. I wish, sir, that this letter were not printed there, and I will do my best that it not be. But if I could not avoid that, and informed in time, could I do what I prefer, then I would not hesitate to have it printed myself. That seems to me just and natural.

As for your response to the same letter, it has not been passed on to anyone, and you can count on it never being printed without your avowal,[1] for which I will not be so indiscreet as to ask, knowing well that what a man writes to another he does not write to the public. But if you would like to write one for publication and address it to me, I promise to join it faithfully to my letter, and not to respond to it with a single word.

I do not love you, sir. You have done me wrongs that I could feel the most, to me your disciple and your enthusiast. You have ruined Geneva

---

1. To his copy of this letter, Rousseau added the following note: "During his lifetime, it is understood, and certainly the strictest proceedings, above all toward an enemy who crushes them underfoot, could not require anything further."

as the price of the asylum that you received there; you have alienated my fellow citizens from me as the price of the applause for you that I lavished among them. It is you who make residence in my country unbearable for me. It is you who will make me die in a foreign land, deprived of all the consolations of the dying and honored only with being thrown into a dump while, living or dead, all the honors that a man can expect will accompany you in my country.[2] I hate you, finally; you have wanted it so. But I have hated you as a man even more worthy of loving you if you had wanted it. Of all the sentiments with which my heart was filled for you, the only one left is the admiration one cannot refuse your fine genius, and love for your writings. If I cannot honor in you anything but your talents, that is not my fault. I will never fail in the respect that I owe them, or in the conduct that this respect requires. Farewell, sir.

---

2. "Thrown into a dump" refers to the fact that, in much of France, Protestants could not be buried in hallowed ground.

CHAPTER 53

Chrétien-Guillaume de Lamoignon de Malesherbes

November 5, 1760
Montmorency
A week earlier, Malesherbes had replied to a letter from Rousseau asking him to suppress counterfeit editions of Julie *in France. He explained that, as director of the book trade and therefore as someone interested in promoting French publishers, he could not object to a French publisher printing a counterfeit edition of a book published in another country. He suggested that Rousseau arrange for republication with a French publisher of his choice.*

I see, sir, from the response with which you have honored me, that without knowing it I committed an indiscretion for which I owe you, along with my humble excuses, my justification insofar as it is possible. Thus, taking the discussion you are willing to begin with me as permission to begin it in my turn, I will make use of that freedom to set forth to you the reasons for my sentiment, which I judged was also yours, about the business in question.

To begin with I will note that, regarding the law of nations, there are many uncontested maxims, which nevertheless are and will always be vain and without effect in practice, because they bear on an assumed equality among States as among men; a principle which for the former is true neither of their size nor of their form, nor consequently of the relative right of the subjects which derives from both of these. Natural right is the same for all men, who have all received from nature a common measure, and limits they cannot surpass. The law of nations, however, stemming from measures of human institution, which do not have an absolute limit, varies and must vary from nation to nation. Large States overawe small ones and make themselves respected by them; yet they need them and, perhaps, need them more than the small do the large. Thus, they must grant them something as an equivalent for what they require of them. Taken individually, the advantages are not equal, but they make up for one another; and from that is born the true law of nations, established, not in books, but between men. The ones have for themselves honors, rank, power; the others, ignoble profit and small utility. When the large States will want to have their advantages to themselves alone, and to share in those of the small, they will want something impossible, and whatever they might do, they will never succeed in establishing in small things that parity they do not put up with in large ones.

The differences born from the nature of the government no less necessarily modify the respective rights of the subjects. The freedom of the press established in Holland requires different regulations in the policing of the book trade than those given to it in France, where this freedom neither does nor can take place. And if one wanted, by means of treaties between powers, to establish uniform policing and the same regulations on this matter between the two States, these treaties would soon be without effect, or one of the two governments would change its form, considering that in every country there are never any laws observed but those that pertain to the nature of the government.

The book trade's sales are prodigious in France, almost as large as in the entire rest of Europe. In Holland it is almost nothing. On the contrary, proportionally more books are printed in Holland than in France. Thus, one could say in some respect that the consumption is in France and the fabrication in Holland, even if France sent more books to Holland than it receives from the same country; because where the Frenchman is the consumer the Dutch is only the merchant: France receives for itself alone; Holland receives for someone else. Such is the relative state of that part of commerce between the two powers; and that state, forced by the two constitutions, will always come back whatever one does. I understand very well that the government of France would like the manufacturing to be where the consumption is: but that cannot be, and it prevents this itself by the rigor of censorship. It could not, even if it wanted to, soften that rigor: for a government that can do everything cannot remove from itself the chains it is forced to give itself to continue to be able to do everything. If the advantages of arbitrary power are great, a moderate power also has its own which are not fewer; that is to do without inconvenience everything that is useful to the nation.

Following one of the maxims of the government of France, there are many things one ought not to allow, and which are suitable to tolerate. From which it follows that one can and one ought to put up with the entry of some books the printing of which one ought not to allow. And in fact, without that, France, reduced almost to its own literature alone, would secede from the body of the republic of letters, would soon fall into barbarism, and would even lose other branches of commerce to which that one serves as counterweight. But when a book, printed in Holland because it could not or ought not to be printed in France, is nevertheless reprinted there, the government then sins against its own maxims and puts itself in contradiction with itself. I add that the parity that it authorizes for itself is illusory, and the consequence it draws from it, although just, is not equitable. For since one prints in France for France, and in Holland also for France, and since counterfeit editions based on those of the country are not allowed to enter the kingdom, the reprinting done in Holland of a book printed in France does little harm to the French bookseller, and the reprinting done in France of a book printed in Holland ruins the Dutch bookseller. If this consideration does not affect the government of France, it affects the government of Holland, and it will very well know how to put it forward, if ever the first proposes to it to put the thing on par.

I know too well to whom I am speaking, sir, to enter into a detailed account of consequences and applications with you. The magistrate and the statesman versed in these matters does not need the clarifications that would be necessary for a private man. But here is a more direct observation, and one that brings me nearer to the particular case. When a Dutch bookseller deals with a French bookseller, as they say, in exchange, that is to say, when he receives the payment for his books in books, then the profit is double and shared by them; and aside from the expenses of transportation, the effect is absolutely the same as if the books they reciprocally send each other were printed in the places where they are sold. That is the way that Rey previously dealt with Pissot and Durand regarding what he has published for me until now. Moreover, the Dutch bookseller, who fears counterfeiting, covers himself and deals with the French bookseller so that the latter is burdened with his perils and risks for the sale of the copies he receives, the number of which is agreed upon between them. That is also the way that Rey negotiated for *Julie*. He puts his French correspondent in his place and position and, without knowing it, following the advice you were willing to give me for him, he is sending him half his edition at once. By this means, the counterfeiting, if it does take place, will not harm the Amsterdam bookseller, but the Parisian bookseller who is substituted for him. It will be one French bookseller who will ruin another; or it will be two French booksellers who will mutually ruin each other.

From all this are deduced only the reasons that led me to believe that you would not permit the reprinting in France of a book first printed in Holland against the first publisher's will. It remains for me to set forth to you those which keep me both from consenting to this reprinting, and from accepting any benefit from it if it is done despite me. You say, sir, that I should not regard myself as bound by the engagement that I made with the Dutch bookseller, because I could grant him only what I had, and that I did not have the right to keep the booksellers of Paris from copying or counterfeiting his edition. But equitably I can draw from that only one consequence, for which I am responsible, for I dealt with the bookseller on the footing of the value that I gave to what I granted him. Now it happens that instead of selling him a right that I really had, I have sold him only a right that I believed I had. If then, this right is found to be less than I had thought, clearly far from drawing profit from my error, I owe him compensation for the harm that he can suffer from it.

If I received again from a Parisian bookseller the benefit I have already received from the one from Amsterdam, I would have sold my manuscript twice; and how would I have this right of consent of the one with whom I dealt, since he even disputed with me the right to make a general and unique edition of my writings, reviewed and augmented with new pieces? It is true that, never having thought of depriving myself of this right when I granted him my manuscripts, I believe that in this matter I can pass over his opposition, of which he has made me the judge, by the same principle that keeps me, sir, from acquiescing on this occasion to your advice. Since I feel myself held to everything that I either stated or understood to put into my bargains, I believe myself to be bound to nothing beyond that.

Whether then, you judge it appropriate to allow or to prevent the counterfeiting or reprinting of the book at issue I can, in my position as editor, neither choose a French bookseller for that reprinting, nor much less receive from him any sort of benefit, in peace of conscience. But an advantage that is more precious to me and from which I profit with satisfaction with myself, is to receive on this occasion new testimonies of your kindness for me, and to be able to repeat to you, sir, those of my gratitude and profound respect.

JJRousseau

I ask your forgiveness, sir, for having troubled your relaxation by my preceding letter. I will wait to get this one sent for your return from the country. Nor have I given M. Guérin my little manuscript yet.[1] I find a cowardice that is repugnant to me in wanting to excuse a frivolous book in advance in public. It is better to let the book appear and be judged; and then I will state my reasons. T.S.V.P.[2]

Rey appears to me very troubled not to have received, sir, the permission he requested of you. I have notified him that he ought not to be anxious about this delay; that by its type, the book could not experience any difficulty, and that on every suspicious matter, it was the most circumspect of all the writings I have published up to now. I hope that nothing was found in the sheets that made you think differently about them.[3]

---

1. This manuscript is the preface in dialogue form to *Julie* that was originally published separately.

2. Rousseau had reached the bottom of his page and indicated that he continued on the other side.

3. In fact, the French censors had many reservations about Rousseau's novel.

CHAPTER 54

Jacob Vernet

November 29, 1760
Montmorency
Vernet had written to Rousseau about an anonymous attack that Voltaire had published against both Protestant and Catholic clergy: Christian Dialogues, or Preservative against the Encyclopedia.

If I had received fifteen days earlier, sir, the letter with which you honored me on the 4th of this month, I would rather happily have been able to make mention of the matter about which you had the goodness to inform me.[1] And I could have done this even more opportunely, in that in the book in which I would have spoken of it, which was not made to be seen by you, I could have honored you more at my ease than in the writings which must pass under your eyes.[2] It is a kind of insipid and dull novel of which I am the editor, and of which whoever has the courage to do so, can believe me the author if he wishes. Here and there in

---

1. In his letter, Vernet had informed Rousseau that Voltaire's anonymous brochure had come out in August.

2. The book to which Rousseau refers here is presumably his epistolary novel, *Julie, or the New Heloise*, which he contrasts with the more serious writings that someone like Vernet would read.

this collection of letters I sowed a few notes on different subjects, and the one on the *Preservative* would have suited it marvelously. But it is too late, and I would not have been able to make this addition arrive in Holland before the book finished printing there. The solitary life that I lead here during the winter gives me no resource to supplement that of conversation, and what society comes to my neighborhood in summer takes so little part in literary matters that I do not hope to be within range of transmitting through them the just indignation which seized me upon reading your letter. I will not neglect the occasion to do so if I find it. While I wait, I rejoice with all my heart that the evidence of your justification has confounded the calumny and made the opprobrium with which they would like to cover all the defenders of faith, mores, and virtue fall back on its authors.

So, in this way satire, the black lie, and libels have become the weapons of philosophers and of their partisans! That is how M. Voltaire repays the hospitality with which, by a baneful indulgence, Geneva treats him! This braggart of impiety, this noble genius and this base soul, this man so great by his talents, and so vile by the use he makes of them, will leave us with long and cruel memories of his stay among us. The ruin of morals, and the loss of liberty which is its inevitable result, will be among our descendants the monuments of his glory and of his gratitude. If there remains in their hearts some love for the fatherland, they will detest his memory, and he will be more often cursed than admired by them.

It is not, sir, that I have such a bad opinion of the present state of our city as you appear to believe. I know that many true citizens remain there who have sense and virtue, who respect the laws, the magistrates, who love morals and liberty. But these dwindle every day, and the others increase, *mox daturos progeniem vitiosiorem.*[3] The decline is given. Nothing from now on can arrest the progress of the ill. The present generation began it; the one to come will complete it. The youth who are arising will soon dry up the remains of the patriotic blood that circulates among us. Each citizen who dies is replaced by some pleasant fellow. Ridicule, that poison of good sense; satire, the enemy of public peace; softness, arrogant pomp, and luxury, form for us in the future only a people of little jokers, buffoons, strolling players, philosophers of the bedchamber, and fine wits of the store counter who, from the

---

3. Horace, *Odes* 3.6: "Our progeny will be worth even less."

consideration our literary types used to have, will raise them to the glory of the academies of Marseilles or Angers; who will find it much more beautiful to be courtiers rather than free, comedians rather than citizens; who would never have wanted to get out of their beds at the Escalade, less because of cowardice than for fear of catching a cold. I confess to you, sir, that all this is hardly appealing for a man who has the zeal and perhaps the folly of patriotism, and to whom there is no other resource left than to look away from the ills that he cannot cure. I love peace, rest: hatred of trouble and cares constitutes all my moderation, and a lazy temperament has until now taken the place of virtue in me. Less intoxicated than suffocated by I do not know what little puff of smoke, I have cruelly felt its bitterness without being able to acquire a taste for it, and I aspire to the return of that happy obscurity which allows one to enjoy oneself. Seeing literary people tear each other apart like wolves, and feeling the remnants of the warmth which had put the pen into my hand at nearly forty to be entirely extinguished, I have put it down before fifty, never to take it up again. It remains for me to publish a kind of treatise on education, full of my customary reveries, and the last fruit of my country walks, after which, far from the public and given over entirely to my friends and to myself, I will peaceably await the end of a career already too long for my troubles, and regarding which it is indifferent to everyone and to me where the remnants of it end.

I am enchanted by the trip to the Montagnons.[4] This shows that my testimony has some authority with persons for whom I have so much respect, and I am delighted for them, for myself, and above all for the Montagnons not to have been found to be a liar. I am not astonished that luxury has made some progress among these good people. This is the general downward path; it is the chasm in which everything perishes in the end. But the incline becomes steeper according to events; that is what, advancing us by two hundred years, has accelerated our ruin by as much.

---

4. Rousseau describes the Montagnons, a people who lived outside Neuchâtel, in the *Letter to d'Alembert*. Vernet had said that his brother had recently visited the area.

CHAPTER 55

Claire Cramer

February 12, 1761
Montmorency
This is a response to a letter that the wife of the Genevan publisher wrote to con-
gratulate Rousseau on the success of Julie.

You have much wit, Madam, and you had it before reading *Julie*; nevertheless, I did not find anything but that in your letter; from which I conclude that this reading was not suited to you, since it did not inspire you with anything. I do not esteem you any less for it, Madam. Tender souls are often weak, and it is always a crime for a woman to be weak. It is not with my consent that this book reached all the way to Geneva. I did not send a single copy of it there, and although I do not think much of our present morals, I do not believe them bad enough yet for them to gain by rising back up to love. Receive, Madam, my humble thanks, and the assurance of my respect.

JJRousseau

CHAPTER 56

Chrétien-Guillaume de Lamoignon de Malesherbes

February 19, 1761
Montmorency
On February 16, Malesherbes sent Rousseau a list of cuts demanded by the censors to permit publication of a French edition of Julie. *Most of the cuts concerned religious matters. Rousseau responded with this and the following letter, both written on the same day. In this letter Rousseau refers to Malesherbes in the third person, probably because he is dealing with him in his official capacity as head of the office of the book trade.*

I was not able to judge very well the effect of the cuts, the note about and reasons for which Monsieur de Malesherbes was kind enough to send me, because I do not have the Paris edition under my eyes.[1] I believe, however, that this mutilation must be very shocking to read and produce many ill-assorted passages.

Some of the cuts would appear to me rather appropriate and suitable, even according to my manner of thinking; but the majority and most important are those to which I cannot acquiesce, because they go directly against the object of the book, and because the images that are

---

1. Malesherbes is addressed in the third person because, as the next letter clarifies, this one would presumably be seen by the censors of *Julie*.

too free, but necessary to the effect of the rest, are no longer compensated for by anything useful. A good book that I thought I was bringing out becomes nothing more than a free and scandalous novel that I would suppress myself, if I had the power to do so. I do not care whether I am read in France, if one must make use of six volumes of insipidities to that end, solely to serve as secretary of love for youth, and to give readers bedtime erudition.[2]

A common devout person, humbly submissive to her director, a woman who begins with libertinism and ends with devotion, is not an object rare enough, instructive enough to fill up a fat book; but a woman at the same time lovable, devout, enlightened, and reasonable is a newer object and, according to me, more useful. Yet it is this novelty and this utility that the required cuts make disappear. It is true that it is precisely on the supposition of this enlightened piety that Monsieur de Malesherbes does not want her to have sentiments different from the doctrine of the Church. But this word "Church" needs explanation. The Roman Church does not require an enlightened piety, it requires a blind piety; and as to the Protestant Church, it is precisely because it requires an enlightened piety that it leaves to each the use of her reason. Does one see the book that alarms Catholic theologians so much also alarming ours? This is a new sort of intolerance, which the priests had not yet taken into their heads, to want a Protestant to be a Protestant in their way rather than hers.

Monsieur de Malesherbes thinks that the doctrine put into the mouth of the dying Julie is that of the author or editor of the book. Nevertheless, he wants this profession of faith to be truncated. Now, it is clear that any deletions in an edition made by my efforts would be a tacit disavowal on my part. What! Does Monsieur de Malesherbes want me to renounce my faith? Either the courage that I believe I feel in myself deceives me; or were I to see the apparatus of torture in front of me, I would not remove a word of this speech.

I will not enter into the detail of the motives that have determined M. de Malesherbes to order these cuts. These motives, drawn as they are from principles that I do not adopt, have no authority for me. I did not imagine that a Genevan novel had to be approved by the Sorbonne, and since I did not want it to be published in France, nothing obliges me to subscribe to the conditions under which it can be printed. I will

---

2. Rousseau borrowed this expression from a letter that Mme. de Créqui had written him.

only note that these cuts are done with such care that nothing is left to my Calvinists in point of doctrine that the most superstitious Catholic cannot avow. One might as well require that every Protestant who comes to Paris recant at the border. The novels of the abbé Prévost, above all *Cleveland*, are far from being treated with so much severity. Now it appears to me rather strange that in his novels a Catholic priest can make Protestants speak in accordance with their ideas more freely than a Protestant can in his.

Monsieur de Malesherbes raises scruples with me about the sentiments of Julie and St-Preux that he did not raise against my own in my *Discourse on Inequality* or even in my *Letter to M. d'Alembert*, the first ten or twelve pages of which contain without detour, directly, and under my name sentiments at least as bold and as harshly expressed. Instead of which, in the novel those contested among the interlocutors can be imputed with certainty neither to me nor to anyone.

I have thought about the proposed changes, and I have seen that I cannot substitute anything for the things cut out without also changing the object of this book and without spoiling it, which I do not want to do. That if I wanted only to soften these same things I would never succeed, having neither that talent nor the taste that makes it useful. In truth there are many bad notes that I would like not to be in it, but those are not what Monsieur de Malesherbes requires to be cut. I could consent that absolutely all of them be removed, provided that the entire text remains as it is in the first edition. Even this sacrifice would cost me a lot.

I very humbly thank Monsieur de Malesherbes for his goodwill, but I neither know nor want to learn how one must prepare a book to put it in condition to be printed in Paris.

CHAPTER 57

Chrétien-Guillaume de Lamoignon de Malesherbes

February 19, 1761
Montmorency

There,[1] sir, is my response to the observations that you were kind enough to send me about *The New Heloise*. You have raised her to the honor she hardly expected of occupying theologians; that is perhaps a fate attached to this name, and to those who bear it, always to have to pass through the hands of those Gentlemen. I see that they labored on the conversion of this one with great zeal, and I do not doubt that their pious efforts would have made her into a very orthodox person, but I find that they have treated her a little roughly. They have withered her charms, and I admit that she pleased me more, lovable if heretic, than bigot and sullen as she is now. I ask that she be given back to me as I gave her, or I abandon her to her directors.

Receive, sir, the assurances of my profound respect.

JJRousseau

---

1. This refers to the letter above from the same day.

CHAPTER 58

Chrétien-Guillaume de Lamoignon de Malesherbes

March 10, 1761

Malesherbes had replied to Rousseau's refusal to make changes to Julie *for the French edition by urging him to reconsider, arguing that he was not requiring Rousseau to renounce his Protestant faith but only not to say everything that he thought. As he had in letter 56 above, Rousseau refers to Malesherbes in the third person.*

I. Since M. le président de Malesherbes requires me to enter into discussion about the articles cut from *Julie*, I obey, without, however, seeing the utility of this discussion. I shall remark only, before entering into the subject, that M. de Malesherbes, grounding all these cuts on the ideas of the Catholics, or even on those of the reformed, and I, reasoning uniquely on my own, it is not a miracle if we have few meeting points.

II. I do not disagree that M. de La Bédoyère has done a heroic deed in recognizing his daughter-in-law. I do not believe any less, however, that he did a barbarous deed in disinheriting his son. There is no prejudice, however universal it might be, that prescribes against nature; and to disinherit his son is not an act of weakness, but of cruelty.[1]

The station of the person who loved M. de La Bédoyère's son, the law of prejudices, even honor, could determine the father to oppose his son's marriage with all his strength. Once the marriage has taken place and is consummated, however, the son, by abandoning his wife, by stripping his children of their legitimate condition, became a dishonorable man; and the father who repudiated his son for not having disgracefully violated his pledge, was a disgraceful father. Everyone would have said so if this father had been a man of the people. That was only truer since the father was a magistrate, obliged by station to be just, and especially to protect the oppressed.

I have consented before to what regards M. de La Bédoyère. Thus M. de Malesherbes can return to it only to reproach me for it; and so, not esteeming myself guilty, I must justify myself.

III. The answer that Saint-Preux makes to M. de Wolmar is everything that one can say is most moderate, most sensible, about the Christian religion and its mysteries. The Catholics who persist in wanting to play at double or nothing are very wrong; they will certainly not do well out of this deal. Now, why would we be held to be in the wrong as they are? The reformed begin to feel the necessity of sacrificing some branches to preserve the trunk, and it is in this spirit that theological subjects are treated in *Julie*. Moreover, if Saint-Preux is not a Calvinist, he will be, if you wish, Socinian. That is still to be a heretic. What more is being asked of him? Would the Sorbonne like to make us intolerant despite ourselves, or to prescribe to us in what manner it is pleased that we go to hell? What right, what inspection does the Catholic Church claim to have over anyone who does not recognize its authority? Do as it will: intolerance, even theological, is against our principles, and has never been able to introduce itself among us except by abuse. Now, I maintain that it belongs to all the faithful to cry out against this abuse. Every formula of profession of faith is contrary to the spirit of reform; and I do not acknowledge any heterodox doctrine other than the one that does not establish good morality, or which leads to bad.

---

1. Cf. *CW* 7:169–70.

It remains to know whether that of Julie or of Saint-Preux is such a one. Julie and Saint-Preux being the heroes of the novel, says M. de Malesherbes, their manner of thinking can make an impression, and will always be taken for that of the author. Author or not, if that manner of thinking is taken as mine, and can make an impression, so much the better; that is one more reason for me not to change anything. Every other objection from Catholics is incompetent and does not touch me from anyone at all.

As to the phrase "by chance,"[2] I do not know how it is out of place in M. de Wolmar's mouth, but I know very well that it would be a great chance if there were a single Christian on the earth. Nevertheless, if it depends only on sacrificing that phrase, I consent to it. Let one substitute an equivalent one, if one can, provided that this phrase is short, concise, and within Wolmar's principles. Let it not spoil the harmony of the sentence, and let it be possible for Saint-Preux's answer to be related to it.

IV. I agree that there are some harsh epithets that one can soften. One will remove the note, if one wants; perhaps it is not even impossible to modify the text without weakening it, provided nevertheless that M. de Wolmar's disbelief continues to bear on the same foundation, and that Saint-Preux still says that in the Greek and Catholic religions, it is impossible to be reasonable and believe in God.

V. I have no doubt that there are people whom the note displeases. If it did not displease anyone, it would not be worth the trouble to leave it. As for me, I believe that every persecutor is a rogue, or a fool. If the note is not new, that matters little; it is useful, that is the essential. Nevertheless, if one wants to remove the last three lines, I consent to it.[3]

VI. M. de Malesherbes proposes an expedient that wounds me. Up until now I have sought the truth in good faith, preferring nevertheless useful truths. But however that may have been, I never knew the art of weakening objections, and I am not

---

2. Wolmar, a nonbeliever, asks Saint-Preux sarcastically whether he is "by chance" a Christian. See *Julie*, 5.3 (*CW* 6:477).

3. The note in question here reads, "How much more natural is this eminently humane sentiment than the terrible zeal of persecutors, forever busy tormenting unbelievers, as if to damn them even in this life, and acting as forerunners of the demons! I will never stop repeating that such persecutors are no believers, they are scoundrels" (*CW* 6: 487).

tempted to learn it. Moreover, this would be a very sure way of setting off that of M. de Wolmar to good advantage, rather than weakening it, after having begun by exposing it in all its strength: it is necessary then to leave it.

As to Saint-Preux's response, which M. de Malesherbes finds very weak, it seems very strong to me, even unanswerable; and I believe I find in it the solution for all the difficulties of the Manichaeans. In that, I might be wrong: but what to do about it? I can only make use of my own head to reason. Since, then, that response is good for me, I do not consent that it be removed; but I do consent wholeheartedly that one add a better one to it, if one knows one.

VII. I consent that the phrases excised from the text be modified a little if one wants, but not that they be removed. They are useful, because they pertain to good morals: and this is a very correct example of which Julie is right to take advantage. As for the note, it does not matter to me more than the others; it is a conclusion one likes to draw from the text, even if I said nothing about it.

The pages should remain exactly as they are. If Saint-Preux wants to be a heretic on the question of Grace, that is his business. Moreover, he very well must defend man's freedom, since he elsewhere makes the abuse of that freedom the cause of moral evil. He absolutely must be a Molinist,[4] in order not to be a Manichaean, and then, no worse ought to happen to him among the Catholics for rejecting the decisions of Calvin, than for rejecting those of the pope. As for what M. de Malesherbes calls a revolt against the authority of Scripture, I call it, I do, a submission to the authority of God and reason, which ought to go before that of the Bible, and which serves as its foundation. And as for Saint Paul, if he does not allow one to argue against him, he ought not to argue himself, or at least he ought to argue better.

If one wants to excise the note,[5] so be it; but if one leaves it, it is also necessary to leave that to err is a petty evil, because I believe that. I can be wrong, without a doubt; but when I speak

---

4. Luis Molina (1535–1600) was a Jesuit who argued that human freedom was compatible with divine omniscience.

5. *CW* 6:562.

in my name, it is my sentiment that I ought to say, above all when that serves to resolve objections. One can remove the note if one wants. I say as much for the other one.[6] That note, thank God, is not yet useful.

---

6. This concerns a footnote that Rousseau had added to *Julie*. See *CW* 7:158–59.

CHAPTER 59

Dom Léger-Marie Deschamps

May 8, 1761
Montmorency
Dom Léger-Marie Deschamps (1716–74) was a Benedictine monk. He wrote to Rousseau about his manuscript, The True System or the Key to the Metaphysical and Moral System.

I was ill, sir, when I received your preface, and I was deferring to burn it and answer you until a time when I would be in a condition to read it without distraction.[1] But this time not arriving at the end of eight to ten days, I am taking the course, whatever may happen, of conforming to your intention. After having read it with all the attention of which I was capable, it remains only to burn it, which will be done before this letter is sealed.

If you formed the design in it to embarrass and trouble the reader by the strangest enigma, you have perfectly succeeded in relation to me. And perhaps you could well have dispensed with impairing in this way the tranquility of a solitary who has no consolation amid his ills of every kind other than the simplicity of his faith, and for whom the hope

---

1. Burning was a necessary and common precaution when correspondence on unorthodox topics could be punished if discovered.

of another life can alone console him for this one. You believe that you are addressing a philosopher, and you are mistaken. I am a man of very little instruction who has never troubled himself to be one, but who sometimes has good sense and who always loves the truth.

You wish, nevertheless, that I speak to you about your preface. What will I say to you? The system you announce in it is so inconceivable, and promises so many things, that I do not know what to think of it. If I had to render the confused idea that I conceive of it through something that is known, I would relate it to that of Spinoza. But if some morality issued from his, it was purely speculative, whereas it appears that yours has practical laws, which supposes some sanction for these laws.

It appears that you establish your principle on the greatest of abstractions. Now the method of generalizing and abstracting is very suspect to me, as too little proportional to our faculties. Our senses show us only individuals. Attention finishes separating them, judgment can compare them one by one; but that is all. To want to unite everything exceeds the power of our understanding; it is to want to push the boat in which one is without touching anything outside of it. We make judgments by induction about the whole up to a certain point by means of the parts. It seems on the contrary that from the knowledge of the whole you want to deduce that of the parts. I conceive nothing of this. The analytical route is good in geometry, but in philosophy it seems to me to be worth nothing. The absurdity to which it leads by false principles does not sufficiently make itself felt.

Your style is very good, it is that of the thing, and I do not doubt that your book is well written. You have a thinking head, enlightenment, philosophy. Your manner of announcing your system makes it interesting, even disquieting. But even with all that, I am persuaded that it is a reverie. You wanted my sentiment; there it is. I salute you, sir, with all my heart.

JJRousseau

CHAPTER 60

Duchesse de Luxembourg

June 12, 1761

How many things would I have to tell you before leaving you! But time presses; I must abridge my confession and pour my last secret into your beneficent heart. You will know, then, that for sixteen years I have lived in the greatest intimacy with this poor girl who resides with me, except since my retreat to Montmorency, when my condition has forced me to live with her as with my sister. My tenderness for her, however, has not diminished, and without you, the idea of leaving her without resource would poison my last moments.

From these relations have come five children, who have all been put in the Foundling Hospital, and with so little precaution for recognizing them one day, that I did not even keep the date of their birth. For several years now, remorse over this negligence troubles my repose, and I am dying without being able to make up for it, to the mother's great regret and mine. I had put into the swaddling clothes of the oldest only a mark whose duplicate I have kept; he must have been born, it seems to me, in the winter of 1746 to 47, or thereabouts. That is all that I remember. If there were a means of finding that child again, this would cause the happiness of his tender mother; but I despair of it, and

I do not carry that consolation away with me. The ideas with which my fault has filled my mind have contributed in great part to making me meditate on the *Treatise on Education*, and you will find, in the first book, a passage that can indicate this disposition to you.[1] I have not married the mother, and I was not obliged to, since before tying myself to her, I declared to her that I would never marry her. Even a public marriage would have been impossible for us, because of the difference of religion;[2] nonetheless, I have always loved and honored her as my wife, because of her good heart, her sincere affection, her unparalleled disinterestedness, and her stainless fidelity, about which she has not even occasioned the slightest suspicion in me.

There, Madame la maréchale, is the too just reason for my solicitude about the fate of this poor girl after she will have lost me, so much so that if I had less confidence in your friendship for me, and in that of Monsieur le maréchal, I would leave filled with suffering about the abandonment in which I am leaving her. I entrust her to you, however, and I die in peace in that respect. It remains for me to tell you what I think would suit her situation and her character the best, and what would give the least purchase for her faults.

My first idea was to ask you to give her asylum in your house, or with the child who is its hope, until he left the hands of the women; but infallibly that would not succeed. There would be too many intermediaries between you and her, and in your house there are people with malice toward her, which she has assuredly not attracted through her fault, and who would infallibly find the art of disgracing her sooner or later with you or with Monsieur le maréchal. She is not supple and prudent enough to maintain herself with so many different minds, and to lend herself to the little ploys with which one wins the masters' trust, however enlightened they are. Once again, that would not succeed. Thus, I ask you not to consider it.

Nor would I want her to reside in Paris in any manner at all, being certain that, fearful and easy to subjugate, she would become there the prey and the victim of her numerous family, people of an unlimited avidity and wickedness, from whom I myself had much difficulty in tearing her away, and who are in large part the cause of my retirement to the country. If she ever resides in Paris, she is lost. For even if she

---

1. See *CW* 13:175.

2. Catholics and Protestants were not allowed to intermarry, although Rousseau was officially a Catholic until 1754.

were hidden from them, since she has a good natural disposition, she will never be able to abstain from seeing them, and in little time they will suck her blood to the last drop, and then will make her die of bad treatment.

I have no less strong reasons to wish that she not go reside with her mother, abandoned to my cruelest enemies, nourished by them to bad intention, and who are looking only for the opportunity of punishing that poor girl for not having wanted to lend herself to their plots against me. She is the only one who has had nothing from her mother, and the only one who nourished and cared for her in her poverty; and if I have given asylum to that woman for twelve years, you surely understand that it is for the daughter that I have done it. I have a thousand reasons too long to spell out to desire that she not go back with her; so I ask you even to interpose your authority, if necessary, to keep her from it.

I see only two courses of action that are suitable for her: one, to continue to occupy my lodging,[3] and to live in peace at Montmorency, which she can do at little expense with your assistance and protection, as much from the product of my writings as from that of her labor. For she sews very well, and nothing is lacking for her but occupation, which you will kindly give her or procure for her, wishing only that she not be at the discretion of the chambermaids, for their tyranny and their monopoly are known to me.

The other course of action is that she be placed in some community in the provinces where one lives cheaply, and where she could very well earn her living by her labor. I would like this course of action less than the other because she would thus be too far away from you, and for other reasons also. You will choose for the best, Madame la maréchale; but whatever choice you make, I beg you to act so that she always has her freedom, and that she be the mistress of changing residence as soon as she does not find herself well. Finally, I beg you not to disdain to take care of her small affairs, so that, whatever happens, she has bread until the end of her days.

I have asked Monsieur le maréchal to consult you about the choice of the person whom he would charge with watching over the poor girl's interests after I am deceased. You are not unaware of the unjust

---

3. Rousseau added the following note: "I do not propose that you give her one yourself at Montmorency, because of Chassot and his family, who would make her pay cruelly for it. Since my rent is only fifty livres, it will not be more onerous to her than a room in Paris."

partiality that is shown by the one who naturally would be chosen for that. Whatever esteem I have conceived for his probity, I would not want her to remain at the mercy of a man whom I must believe to be honest, but whom I see abandoned, through an inconceivable blindness, to the interests and the passions of a rogue.

You see, Madame la maréchale, with what simplicity, with what confidence I pour out my heart before you. All the rest of the universe is already no longer anything in my eyes; this heart that loved you sincerely already no longer lives except for you, for Monsieur le maréchal, and for the poor girl. Farewell, tender and cherished friends, love my memory a little, As for me, I hope to love you also in the other life. But whatever the case may be regarding that obscure and formidable mystery, in whatever hour death might surprise me, I am sure that it will find me thinking of you.

JJRousseau

CHAPTER 61

Jacob Vernes

June 24, 1761

Vernes had written to Rousseau to express his admiration for Julie, *as well as his reservations about Wolmar, whose atheism troubled him. Vernes found it impossible to believe that an atheist could be moral and wished that he had been converted at the end of the book.*

I was almost in extremity, dear fellow citizen, when I received your letter. And now that I am answering it, I am in a state of continuous suffering that, according to all appearances, will not leave me except with life. My greatest consolation in the state I am in is to receive testimonies of interest from my compatriots and above all from you, dear Vernes, whom I have always loved and whom I will always love. My heart laughs and it seems to me that I come back to life again at the project of going to share with you that charming retreat that tempts me even more by its inhabitant than by itself. Oh! if God bolstered my health enough for me to be able to undertake the trip, be sure that I would not die without having embraced you one more time!

I have never claimed to justify the innumerable defects of *The New Heloise*. I find that it has been received too favorably, and in the public's judgments I have to complain much less about its rigor than to praise myself for its indulgence. But your grievances against Wolmar show me that I have fulfilled the object of the book poorly, or that you have not grasped it very well. This object was to bring the opposed parties closer by means of a reciprocal esteem, to teach the philosophers that one can believe in God without being a hypocrite, and the believers that one can be a nonbeliever without being a scoundrel. One would have done much for civil peace if one could remove from partisan spirit the disdain and hatred that comes much more from self-importance and pride than love for the truth. The devout Julie is a lesson for philosophers, and the atheist Wolmar is one for the intolerant. There is the true goal of the book: it is up to you to see whether I diverged from it. You reproach me for not having made Wolmar change systems at the end of the novel; but my dear Vernes, you have then not read that end. For his conversion is indicated there with a clarity that could not undergo greater development without wanting to make a dull sermon.

Farewell, dear Vernes, I am grasping an interval of doing better to write to you. I ask you to inform those of your friends who take an interest in me about this improvement, and among others, Messieurs Moultou and Roustan, whom I embrace with all my heart as well as you.

JJRousseau

Chapter 62

Dom Deschamps

June 25, 1761
Montmorency

You will pardon me, sir, for the delay in my answer when you know that I have been very ill, and that I continue to be plagued by pains without respite which hardly leave me the liberty to write.

The truth I love is not so much metaphysical as moral. I love the truth because I hate lies. I cannot be inconsequent on that point unless I were in bad faith. I would also very much love metaphysical truth if I believed that it was within our reach. But I have never seen that it was in books and, despairing of finding it there, I scorn their instruction, persuaded that the truth which is useful to us is closer to us, and that one does not need such a great scientific apparatus in order to acquire it. Your work, sir, can provide this demonstration, promised and missed by all philosophers, but I cannot change my maxim on the basis of reasons that I do not know. Yet your confidence impresses me. You promise so much, and so boldly. And I find moreover so much precision and reason in your manner of writing that I would be surprised if there were none in your philosophy, and I should hardly be surprised, with my shortsightedness, that you see where I did not believe one could see. Now this doubt makes me uneasy, because the truth that I know or that I take as such is very pleasant, a very sweet state results from it for me, and I do not conceive how I could change it without losing by the change. If my sentiments were demonstrated, I would hardly be uneasy about yours. But to speak sincerely, I am much more persuaded than I am convinced. I believe, but I do not know. I do not even know if the knowledge that I lack will be good or bad for me, and if perhaps after having acquired it one will not have to say *alto quaesivi coelo lucem ingemuique reperta.*[1]

Such, sir, is the solution to, or at least the clarification of, the inconsistencies for which you reproach me. Still, it seems hard to me that I must justify myself for having told you my sentiment when you asked me to. I only took the liberty of judging you to accommodate you. I may have been mistaken, doubtless. But error in this is not a wrong.

You nevertheless also ask me for advice on a very serious subject, and I am perhaps again going to answer you all amiss. But luckily this piece of advice is among those that an author hardly asks except when he has already adopted his course of action.

I will note first that the supposition that your work contains the discovery of the truth is not peculiar to you; it is common to all philosophers. Based on this motive they publish their books, and truth remains to be discovered.

I will add that it does not suffice to consider the good that a book contains in itself, but one must also weigh the bad to which it can give rise. One must consider that it will find fewer well-disposed readers than bad hearts and badly made heads. Before publishing it, one must compare the good and the bad that it can do, and uses with abuses. It is based on which of these two effects will prevail over the other, that it is good or bad to publish.

If I knew you, sir, if I knew your fate, your condition, your age, I might also have something to say regarding you. One can run risks while one is young, but it is not sensible to expose the tranquility of one's life after having attained maturity. I have often heard the late M. de Fontenelle say that never has a book given as much pleasure as griefs to its author. It was the happy Fontenelle who said this. Until forty I was wise. At forty I took up the pen and I lay it down before fifty, cursing all the days of my life that day when my foolish pride made me

---

1. "She sought above the light of the sky and she shuddered at having found it" (Virgil, *Aeneid* 4.691–92).

take it up and I saw my happiness, my tranquility, and my health go up in smoke, without any hope of ever recovering them. This is the man of whom you are asking advice on the publication of a book. I salute you, sir, with all my heart.

JJRousseau

CHAPTER 63

Dom Deschamps

August 12, 1761
Montmorency
*Dom Deschamps replied to Rousseau to ask his advice about what he should do
with his work on the assumption that it was completely true and that it contained
the most incontestable morality.*

I am very glad, sir, that my letters give you some benevolence for me. It
is a return you owe me for the effect that yours have on me. In no condition to act and write, I no longer answer almost anyone and especially
not literary people, whom in general I do not esteem. Nevertheless, it is
always my pleasure and my duty to answer you promptly. There is the
fact, it is up to you to draw the consequence from it.

From your first letter and especially from your preface I have passionately desired to see your work, and this desire does not leave me,
even though application is almost impossible for me given the condition I am in. If I have not more positively shown this eagerness, I did
not believe that discretion allowed it for a work which you noted to me
yourself ought not to leave your hands. Although I have advised you
and still advise you to think about it fully before giving it to the public,
for myself, I wish that it will appear soon, so as to be able to read it and

meditate on it at my ease. Hence if you had the goal in your letters of inspiring this desire in me, you have succeeded long since.

I would gain, you say, in adopting your principles, if I lived among men who would adopt them as I do? I believe it; but with this condition all morality would be demonstrated. If one gave back good for good, it is as clear as day that virtue would constitute the happiness of humankind. But the real and worldly advantage of being good among the wicked, that is the philosophical stone which must be found.

Believe, sir, that if my writings have given me grief, it is neither from the public, regarding whom I have only to praise myself, nor from the critics, regarding whose works I have made it an inviolable law never to read a single line, and who consequently do not trouble my rest. My pains are much closer to my heart. It is most cruel for a man who has sought happiness only in his attachments, to see that a fume of reputation has shattered all of them, that the friends he adored have become his rivals, his most mortal enemies, and that instead of the chains of friendship which made up his happiness, he saw himself entwined by the snares of perfidy on every side. Those, sir, are the ills for which a heart like mine never consoles itself, and which will make me curse all the days of my life the one when I took up the pen for the first time. When I was obscure and loved I was happy. Now with a name, I live and will die the most miserable of beings. Good day, sir, I salute you and embrace you with all my heart.

JJRousseau

CHAPTER 64

Dom Deschamps

September 12, 1761
Montmorency
Dom Deschamps wrote to Rousseau to tell him that he planned to publish his work and sent him two prefatory epistles, one dedicated to Rousseau (in verse) and the other to humankind in general. He also sought Rousseau's permission to publish their correspondence.

What you tell me, sir, in your last letter, makes me tremble about the publication of your work. If I had ten reasons to divert you from it, I now have ten thousand. I understand how tempted you must be, but you who have such a judicious head could not disagree with yourself that such a step is very injudicious. I am almost certain that you would bring about the unhappiness of your life. I cannot beseech you too much to reflect well on it.

If it were only a matter of procuring for you abilities that you do not have, that is a little service that I could render you and perhaps the public, but that you ought never to expect from me unless you have proven to me that you are not risking anything at all.

Your epistles have given me pleasure, but one is too many. You cannot dedicate your book to the public and to your best friend at the same time; that would be to make fun of one of the two, or rather of both of them. The phrase the gods in the one in verse is quite alarming; I do not hate that frankness that goes to the point of audacity. Sometimes I engage in it with impunity because I do not depend on anything, and I boldly say the worst about everyone; but you cannot say the same thing.

That idea of the protection of men seems to me a little novelistic. A man whom the human race protected would be extremely badly protected, because the human race is nothing; the powers are the only thing that are anything. Then, doubtless, you are not unaware that the powers neither are nor can be of the public's opinion on anything in the world.

I had already noticed in several places in your preface, and again I noticed in your epistle to men, that your sentences are sometimes a little tangled up. Watch out for that, above all in a book of metaphysics. I am not acquainted with any style clearer than yours; but it will become even more so if you can cut your sentences a little and remove some pronouns.

Based on your letters I love you, based on your portrait I love you even more. I do not even much distrust the author's partiality, precisely because he says directly about himself the good that he thinks about it. I remember that you praised me for being modest. Splendid. But I admit to you that I will always very much like people who have the courage not to be so. I am persuaded that you resemble your portrait, and I am extremely glad. Furthermore, I am persuaded that one is always very well depicted when one depicts oneself, even if the portrait did not resemble at all.

You are very good to scold me about my imprecisions in acts of reasoning. Are you good about noticing that I see certain objects very well, but that I cannot compare; that I am fertile enough in propositions without ever seeing consequences; that order and method which are your gods are my furies; that nothing ever offers itself to me except in isolation, and that instead of linking my ideas in my writings, I make use of a charlatanry of transitions that imposes most of all on all you other great philosophers. It is because of this that I set myself to despising you, seeing very well that I cannot reach your level.

Writing this to you is enough of a response to the article that involves printing our letters; you ought to see that a man who writes such follies does not write them to be printed, not even to be reread, still less copied. I want to be free, incorrect, without consistency in my letters, as in my conversation. I would no longer want relations in which it would ceaselessly be necessary to be an author. Nevertheless, if you have enough time and efforts to waste to want to keep and copy my letters, I will not bother you about that, provided that it is never a question of printing them. As for yours, I have always been faithful about burning them and have not copied them, and you ought to believe that I will not use them any more negligently in the future, as long as you continue to require it, since I feel the consequence of it better. Good day, sir, I embrace you.

CHAPTER 65

Grimprel d'Offreville

October 4, 1761
Montmorency
Very little is known about Offreville. He was born around 1737 and published Rousseau's letter in 1780. Rousseau's opening lines summarize the letter Offreville had sent him.

The question you propose, sir, in your letter of September 15th, is important and serious. On its solution depends knowing if there is a demonstrated morality or if there is none.

Your adversary maintains that no man acts, whatever he does, except relative to himself, and that even to the acts of the most sublime virtue, even to the purest works of charity, each relates everything to himself.

You, sir, you think that one must do good for the sake of the good itself, without any return of personal interest, and that good acts that one relates to oneself are no longer acts of virtue, but of amour-propre. You add that our alms are without merit if we give them only through vanity or with the aim of dismissing from us the idea of human miseries, and in that you are right.

But regarding the foundation of the question, I must admit that I share your adversary's view. For when we act, we must have a motive for acting, and this motive cannot be foreign to us, since it is us which it sets to work. It would be absurd to imagine that being myself, I would act as if I were another. Is it not true that if one said to you that a body is pushed without anything touching it, you would say that this is not conceivable? It is the same thing in morality when one believes one is acting without any interest.

But this word "interest" must be explained. For you could give it such a meaning, you and your adversary, that you would agree without understanding one another, and he himself could give it one so crude that then it would be you who would be right.

There is a sensual and palpable interest which is related uniquely to our material well-being, to fortune, to consideration, to the physical goods which can result for us from the good opinion of others. Everything one does for such an interest produces only a good of the same order, as a merchant achieves his good by selling at the best price he can. If I oblige another man with a view to acquiring rights over his gratitude, I am in doing that only a merchant engaged in commerce, and even one who makes use of surprise with the buyer. If I give alms to make myself esteemed as charitable, and to enjoy the advantages attached to this esteem, I am still only a merchant who buys some reputation. It is just about the same if I give these alms only to free myself from the importunity of a beggar or the sight of his misery. All the acts of this kind which have in view an external advantage cannot bear the name of good deeds, and one does not say of a tradesperson who conducts his business well that he behaves virtuously in them.

There is another interest which is not attached to the advantages of society, which is relative only to us, to the good of our soul, to our absolute well-being, and which for that reason I call spiritual or moral interest, in contrast to the first. Interest which, despite not having sensible objects, material ones, is no less true, no less great, no less solid, and to say everything in a word, the sole one which, as it is intimately attached to our nature, tends toward our genuine happiness. That, sir, is the interest that virtue proposes itself and that it must propose itself, without taking anything away from the merit, the purity, and the moral goodness of the actions it inspires.

First, following the system of religion, namely of the punishments and rewards of the other life, you see that interest in pleasing the Author of our being and the supreme judge of our actions is of an importance that prevails over the greatest ills and that makes true believers rush to martyrdom; and, at the same time, of a purity which can ennoble the most sublime duties. The law of doing good is drawn from reason itself, and the Christian only needs logic to have virtue.

But aside from this interest, which one can look upon as in some way foreign to the matter, as being connected to it only by the express will of God, you will perhaps ask me if there is another interest linked more immediately, more necessarily to virtue by its nature, and which must make us love it for itself. This is connected to other questions, the discussion of which goes beyond the limits of a letter, and which therefore I will not attempt to examine here. Such as: whether we have a natural love for order, for the morally beautiful; whether this love can be lively enough by itself to take precedence over all our passions; whether the conscience is innate in man's heart, or whether it is only the fruit of prejudices and education. For in the latter case, it is clear that no one, having in himself any interest in doing good, can do any good, save for the profit that he expects from another; that consequently there are none but fools who believe in virtue and dupes who practice it. Such is the new philosophy.

Without launching here into this metaphysics which would lead us too far, I will content myself with proposing to you a fact that you could put into question with your adversary, and which, thoroughly discussed, will perhaps teach you more about his real sentiments than you could learn by remaining within the generality of your thesis.

In England, when a man is criminally accused, twelve jurors, shut up in a room to opine, based on the examination of the procedure, whether he is guilty or not, no longer leave this room and receive nothing to eat there until they are all in agreement, such that their judgment is always unanimous, and decisive for the fate of the accused.

During one of these deliberations, the proofs seeming convincing, eleven of the jurors condemned him without hesitation. But the twelfth insisted so obstinately on absolving him, without wanting to allege any other reason than that he believed him to be innocent, that seeing this juror determined to die of hunger rather than to be of their opinion, all the others, so as not to suffer the same fate, came back to his opinion, and the accused was dismissed as absolved.

The affair over, some of the jurors secretly pressed their colleague to tell them the reason for his obstinacy. Finally, he confessed to them that it was he himself who did the deed of which the other was accused, and that he was less horrified of death than of making the innocent, who was charged with his own crime, perish.

Propose the case to your man and do not fail to examine with him the state of this juror in all its circumstances. He was not a just man, since he had committed a crime, and in this affair the enthusiasm for virtue could not elevate his heart and make him disdain life. He had the most real interest in condemning the accused, to bury along with him the imputation of the misdeed. He had to fear that his invincible obstinacy would lead to suspicion of the genuine cause and would be the beginning of evidence against him. Prudence and care for his safety demanded, it seems, that he do what he did not do, and one can see no palpable interest which must have led him to do what he did. There was, however, only one very powerful interest which could have determined him like this, in the secret of his heart, to every kind of risk. What then was this interest for which he was sacrificing his very life?

To engage in denial of this fact would be to fail badly. For one can always establish it by supposition, and seek, all extraneous interest set aside, what in a similar case any man of good sense, who would be neither virtuous nor villainous, would do for the sake of his own interest.

Setting down these two cases successively, one that the juror had pronounced the accused's sentence and had made him die in order to secure himself, the other that he had absolved him, as he did, at his own risk, then following in these two cases the rest of the juror's life and the probability of the fate that he would have prepared for himself, press your man to pronounce conclusively on this conduct, and to set out distinctly on one side or the other the interest and the motives of the side that he would have chosen. Then, if your argument is not over, you will at least know if you understand one another, or if you do not understand one another.

If he distinguishes between the interest in a crime to be committed or not to be committed, and that of a good deed to do or not do, you will easily make him see that according to this hypothesis the reason for abstaining from an advantageous crime that one can commit with impunity, is of the same kind as that of doing, between heaven and one-self, a costly good deed. For, besides the fact that whatever good we may do, in doing so we are only just, one can have no interest in oneself not to do wrong and not have a similar interest in doing good. Both derive from the same source and cannot be separated.

Above all, sir, consider that one must not exaggerate things beyond the truth, nor confound, as did the stoics, happiness with virtue. It is certain that doing good for the sake of the good is to do it for oneself, for one's own interest, since it gives the soul an inner satisfaction, a contentment with itself without which there is no real happiness. It is also certain that the wicked are all miserable, whatever may be their apparent fate. For happiness poisons itself in a corrupt soul like the pleasures of sense in an unhealthy body. But it is false that the good are always happy in this world. Just as it is not enough for the body to be healthy to have enough to eat, neither does it suffice for the soul to be healthy to obtain the goods it needs. Even though only good people can live contentedly, this is not to say that every good person lives contentedly. Virtue does not give happiness, but it alone teaches how to enjoy it when one has it. Virtue does not guarantee us from the ills of this life and does not procure its goods; that is what vice does not do either, with all its ruses. But virtue makes one patiently bear the ones and more delightfully enjoy the others. We therefore in any event have a genuine interest in cultivating it, and we always do well to work for this interest, even though there are cases where this interest would be insufficient by itself, without the expectation of a life to come. That is my sentiment on the question that you proposed to me.

Thanking you for the good you think of me, I advise you all the same, sir, to lose no more time defending or praising me. All the good or ill one says of a man that one does not know does not signify much. If those who accuse me are wrong, it is up to my conduct to justify me; any other apology is useless or superfluous. I should have answered you earlier. But the sad condition in which I live must excuse this delay. In the few intervals that my ills leave me, my occupations are not of my choice, and I confess to you that were they, my choice would not be to write letters. I do not answer congratulatory ones, nor would I answer yours either, if the question that you proposed in it had not made it my duty to tell you my opinion.

I salute you, sir, with all my heart.

CHAPTER 66

Duc de Luxembourg

October 20, 1761
Rousseau had written to the duke saying that he did not want to bother him but that a short or even blank note would reassure him about the duke's well-being. The duke responded with a blank page.

I do not tire, Monsieur le maréchal, of rereading your last letter. What abundance, what eloquence! I never take it up without finding in it a thousand ideas, a thousand sentiments that I had not noticed at first; it seems that it renews itself each time I return to it. That letter is a library; but a library that one can skim over, exhaust, leaf through incessantly, without fatigue, without boredom, without repetitions; a library as one would wish all others to be. Unfortunately, that is what one could not obtain, and it is in vain that the most illustrious authors would want to struggle with you over precision, energy. No, Monsieur le maréchal, never have Montesquieu, Pascal, Tacitus, said so many things in fewer words. But it must also be admitted that you do not have a bad interpreter, and that it is about this letter that one must say, "To the good listener, few words."

Confess the truth: although it is easy for you to draw from yourself many more things than all that, for having done it so soon, did you not have yourself helped a little with this epistle? I believed I found in it here and there some of Madame la maréchale's phrases; I believed it because I desired it; also because the correspondence with which she honors me is rather often in that tone. Frankly, if I were wrong, I would not consider her to have settled up; she owes me a response, and I do not mean to spare her trouble any more than you. Perhaps what holds her back is the fear of entrusting herself to the reader's discretion, but it seems to me that this discretion could be a little indiscreet and make me seek more things in her letter than she would have put into it. But it would be too strict for her to complain to me about a usurpation that costs her nothing and which she can avoid. However that may be, be our arbiter, and if you do not find it good for her to compromise herself too much, engage her, I beg you, also to give me something to interpret.

CHAPTER 67

Jean Ribotte

October 24, 1761
Montmorency
Ribotte had written to Rousseau to implore his intervention on behalf of several Protestants who had been arrested for clandestinely practicing their religion and had been threatened by a mob in September 1761. In 1762 the Protestant minister was hanged, three Protestant gentlemen were beheaded, and three other Protestants were sentenced to hard labor. Ribotte also wrote to Voltaire, who gave a supportive, but somewhat lukewarm, response.

Your letter, sir, of September 30 having passed by way of Geneva—that is to say, having crossed France twice—reached me only the day before yesterday. In it I saw with a sorrow mixed with indignation the horrible treatment that our unfortunate brothers are suffering in the country where you are, and which surprises me all the more in that the interest of the government would be, it seems to me, to leave them in peace, at least for the present. I understand very well that the madmen who are oppressing them consult their bloodthirsty mood much more than the interest of the government; but I nevertheless find it somewhat difficult to believe that they would bring themselves to this point of cruelty if the behavior of our brothers did not give some pretext for it. I feel how hard it is to see oneself ceaselessly at the mercy of a cruel populace, without support, without resource, and without even having the consolation of hearing the word of God in peace. But even so, sir, this same word of God is definite about the duty of obeying the laws of princes. Forbidding assemblies is incontestably included in their rights; and after all, since these assemblies are not of the essence of Christianity, one can abstain from them without renouncing one's faith. The enterprise of seizing a man out of the hands of justice or its ministers, even if he is unjustly being held, is still a rebellion which one cannot justify and which the powers always have the right to punish. I understand that there are vexations so harsh that they tire out even the patience of the just. Nevertheless, someone who wants to be a Christian ought to learn to suffer, and every man ought to behave in a way consistent with his doctrine. These objections might be bad. Even so, if someone made them to me, I do not see very well what I would have to answer.

Unfortunately, I am not in the position to run the risk of doing so. I am hardly known by M. de Richelieu, and I am so only by some wrong he formerly did me,[1] which would not dispose him favorably for what I would have to tell him. For as you must know, sometimes the offended person forgives, but the offender never forgives. I do not have a better reputation with the ministers, and when I had to ask one of them—not for favors, I do not ask for them—but for the clearest and the most owed justice, I did not even receive an answer.[2] I would, due to an indiscreet zeal, only spoil the cause in which I would want to take an interest. Friends of the truth are not welcome in courts and ought not to expect to be. Each has his vocation on the earth; mine is to say to the public harsh but useful truths. I try to fulfill it without troubling myself about the harm that the wicked want to do me for it, and that they do to me when they can. I have preached humanity, gentleness, tolerance as much as it depended on me to do so; it is not my fault if I was not listened to. Moreover, I have made it a law for myself always to keep myself to general truths. I write neither lampoons nor satires, I do not attack a man but men, nor an action but a vice. I could not, sir, go beyond that.

You have chosen a better expedient by writing to M. de Voltaire. He is extremely friendly with M. de Richelieu and would certainly make himself listened to if he spoke to him for our brothers; but I doubt that

---

1. Richelieu was governor of Languedoc. For his failure to keep a promise to Rousseau, see *Confessions*, CW 5:280–86.

2. See letter 45.

he will put great zeal into his recommendation. My dear sir, he lacks will, I lack power, and nevertheless what is just suffers. I see from your letter that you have learned to suffer as well as I have from the school of poverty. Alas, it makes us empathize with the misfortunes of others, but makes us unfit to ease them. Good day, sir, I salute you with all my heart.

JJRousseau

CHAPTER 68

Marie-Anne Alissan de La Tour and Marie-Madeline Bernardoni

October 26, 1761

At the end of September, Mme. Bernardoni wrote an anonymous letter to Rousseau, saying that she had read Julie *and that she had a friend who resembled Julie perfectly. Rousseau responded somewhat warily, but a long correspondence ensued, particularly with Mme. de La Tour. Over the next ten years they exchanged around a hundred letters, most of them from Alissan de La Tour, who also published pamphlets defending Rousseau in his quarrel with Hume.*

To the inseparables,[1] men or women,

I must admit it to you, Gentlemen or Ladies, I am entirely as mad as you wanted me to be. Relations with you become more interesting to me than is suitable for my age, for my station, for my principles. Despite that, my poorly cured suspicions do not permit me to continue any longer without distrust. That is why I do not write to Julie in particular, because in fact if she is what you say she is, which I desire, or rather which I ought to fear, the offense is less not to write to her, than to write to her differently than would be necessary. If she is a woman, she is more than an angel; she must have adorations. If she is a man,

---

1. In *Julie*, Claire and Julie are referred to this way.

this man has much wit; but wit is like power, one always abuses it when one has too much of it. Once more, this is becoming too lively to continue anonymously. Make yourself known, or I will keep silent. This is my last word.

CHAPTER 69

Paul-Claude Moultou

December 23, 1761
Montmorency
This letter, written during the height of Rousseau's physical suffering, was not sent and was found in his papers after his death. In Julie, *Lord Eduard and Saint-Preux debate justifications for suicide. The former argues that it is justified in cases of extreme incurable suffering.*

That is it, dear Moultou, we will not see each other anymore except in the abode of the just: my fate is decided by the consequences of the accident about which I spoke to you previously, and when it is time for it I will be able without scruple to take from Lord Eduard the counsels of virtue itself.

What humiliates and afflicts me is an end so little worthy, I dare say of my life, and at least of my feelings. For six weeks I have been committing only iniquities and imagining only calumnies against two honest booksellers, one of whom has no wrong other than some involuntary delays, and the other a zeal full of generosity and disinterestedness that I have paid, for all gratitude, with an accusation of treachery. I do not know what blindness, what somber mood inspired in solitude by a frightful illness, made me invent, to blacken my life and other people's honor, this tissue of horrors, the suspicion of which, changed in my biased mind almost into certitude, was no better disguised to others than it was to you. I feel nevertheless that the source of this madness was never in my heart. The delirium of pain made me lose my reason before my life; in committing the actions of a wicked man, I was only an insane one.

Even so, in the state of derangement my head is in, no longer trusting anything that I see and believe, I made the decision to finish the copy of the piece about which I spoke to you previously, and even to send it to you, very persuaded that it will never be necessary to make use of it, but even more certain that I risk nothing by entrusting it to your probity.[1] It is with the greatest repugnance that I extort from you the immense expenses that this package will cost you by post. But time is pressing, and everything well weighed, I thought that of all the risks the one I could regard as the smallest was that of a little money. Certainly, I would have done better if I had been able to without danger. But, furthermore, by assuming, as I hope, that it will never be necessary to spread this business, I ask you for secrecy about it, and I put my last faults under the safeguard of the wing of your charity. The package will be put tomorrow December 24 in the post without a letter, and even there is some appearance that this one is the last that I will write you.

Farewell, dear Moultou, you will easily conceive that the profession of faith of the Savoyard vicar is mine. I desire too much for there to be a God not to believe it, and I die with the firm confidence that I will find in his bosom the happiness and peace that I was unable to enjoy here below.

I have always loved my fatherland and my fellow citizens tenderly; I dare to expect on their part some testimony of goodwill for my memory. I am leaving behind a housekeeper almost without recompense after seventeen years of services and very difficult cares for a man who was almost always suffering. It would be frightful for me to think that, having dedicated to me her finest years, she would spend her old age in poverty and abandonment. I hope that that will not happen; I leave her as protectors and support all those who have loved me during my life. Even so, if this assistance happened to fail her, I believe I can hope that my compatriots would not let her beg for her bread. Engage, I beg you, those among them whom you know to have the Genevan soul never to

---

1. *The Profession of Faith of the Savoyard Vicar.*

lose sight of her, and to join together if necessary to help her to have her days flow in peace sheltered from poverty.

Here is a letter for my very honored disciple.[2] I believe that I would have been his master in friendship; in all the rest I would have been glorified to take a lesson from him. I very much hope that he will accept the proposal of writing the preface of the collection of my works, and in this case, you will kindly make with M. the maréchal de Luxembourg the arrangements for making him accept a present upon publication. Moreover, if things did not turn out as I hope for an edition in France, I have no complaint about Rey's probity and I believe that he has no complaint to make either about my writings. One could address oneself to him.

Farewell one more time. Love your duties, dear Moultou; do not go looking for dazzling virtues. Bring up your children with great care, edify your new compatriots without ostentation and without harshness, and sometimes think that death loses much of its horrors if one approaches it with a heart satisfied with one's life.

JJRousseau

Keep for me both of you the secret of these letters, at least until after the event about whose time I am unaware, although surely not very distant; I am beginning with friends and business, to see afterward in repose with Jean-Jacques whether he has by chance forgotten anything.

If you come, you will find the piece that I intended for you among what I still have left of little manuscripts. If you do not come and they neglect to send it to you, you can ask for it, for your name is written on it. It is, as I believe I have already notified you, a *Funeral Oration for the late M. the Duke of Orleans*.[3]

---

2. Roustan.
3. For this piece, see *CW* 12:252–63.

Chrétien-Guillaume de Lamoignon de Malesherbes

January 4, 1762
Montmorency
When troubles arose over the publication of Emile, *Malesherbes became concerned about Rousseau's mental state and indicated that he believed that Rousseau's country life had made him depressed and suspicious. The four following letters constitute Rousseau's reply.*

I would have delayed less, sir, in thanking you for the last letter with which you honored me if I had proportioned my diligence in answering to the pleasure which it gave me. But besides it costing me a great deal to write, I thought that a few days should be given to the importunities of these times so as not to weigh you down with mine. Although I do not console myself about what has just happened, I am very happy that you know of it since it has not deprived me of your esteem. It will be more my own when you do not believe me to be better than I am.

The motives to which you attribute the resolutions that I have been seen to take since I bear a kind of name in the world perhaps honor me more than I deserve, but they are certainly closer to the truth than those attributed to me by literary men who, ascribing everything to reputation, judge my sentiments by their own. I have a heart too sensitive to other attachments to be so very much attached to public opinion.

I like my pleasure and independence too much to be a slave to vanity to the point they suppose. He for whom fortune and the hope of succeeding never weighed against a rendezvous or a pleasant supper, must not naturally sacrifice his happiness to the desire to make others talk about him. And it is not at all believable that a man who feels that he has some talent, and who delays until 40 to make himself known, is crazy enough to go bore himself the rest of his days in a desert, uniquely to acquire the reputation of a misanthrope.

But sir, although I sovereignly hate injustice and wickedness, this passion is not dominant enough to alone determine me to flee men's society, if in leaving them I had a great sacrifice to make. No, my motive is less noble and closer to me. I was born with a natural love for solitude which has only increased in measure as I have known men better. I get more out of being with the chimerical beings that I gather around me than with those I see in the world, and the society which my imagination furnishes me in my retreat completes the disgust I feel for all those I have left. You suppose me unhappy and consumed by melancholy. Oh! sir, how mistaken you are! It was in Paris that I was. It was in Paris that a black bile was eating away at my heart, and the bitterness of this bile makes itself felt only too well in all the writings I published so long as I remained there. But sir, compare those writings to the ones I did in my solitude. Either I am mistaken, or you will feel in the latter a certain serenity of soul that cannot be played at, and based on which one can pass a sure judgment on the inner state of the author. The extreme agitation which I have just experienced may have made you pass a contrary judgment. But it is easy to see that the principle of this agitation is not in my actual situation, but in a disordered imagination ready to take fright at everything and to carry everything to the extreme. Continual successes have made me sensitive to glory, and there is no man who has some loftiness of soul and some virtue who could think, without the most mortal despair, that after his death a pernicious work, apt to dishonor his memory and to do a great deal of harm, would be substituted under his name for a useful work. It may be that such an upheaval accelerated the progress of my ills, but supposing that I had been gripped by such a fit of folly in Paris, it is not sure that my own will would not have spared nature the rest of the work.

For a long time, I was mistaken as to the cause of this insurmountable disgust I have always experienced in commerce with men. I attributed it to chagrin at not having a prompt enough wit to show in conversation the little I have, and as an indirect consequence of not occupying the place in society that I believed I deserved. But when, after having scribbled on some paper, I was very sure that even when I was making foolish remarks I would not be taken for a fool, when I saw myself sought out by everyone, and honored with much more respect than my ridiculous vanity would have dared to aspire to, and that despite that I felt the same disgust rather increased than diminished, I concluded that it arose from another cause, and that these kinds of enjoyments were not the ones that I needed.

What then finally is this cause? It is nothing other than this indomitable spirit of liberty that nothing has been able to conquer, and before which honors, fortune, and even reputation are nothing to me. It is certain that this spirit of liberty comes to me less from pride than from laziness. But this laziness is incredible. Everything frightens it; the slightest duties of civil life are unbearable to it. A word to say, a letter to write, a visit to make, as soon as one must, are tortures to me. That is why, even though the ordinary commerce of men is odious to me, intimate friendship is so dear to me, because there are no longer any duties to it. One follows one's heart and all is done. That is also why I have always dreaded benefits so much. For every benefit demands gratitude, and I feel that my heart is ungrateful from the sole fact that gratitude is a duty. In a word, the kind of happiness I need is not so much to do what I want as not to do what I do not want. The active life has nothing which tempts me. I would rather consent a hundred times never to do anything than to do something despite myself. And I have thought a hundred times that I would have lived not too unhappily in the Bastille, if I were held to nothing at all except to stay there.

I nevertheless made some efforts to succeed in my youth. But these efforts have never had as a goal anything but retirement and rest in my old age, and because they were made only in jolts, like those of a lazy person, they have never had the least success. When ills came, they furnished me with a fine pretext to abandon myself to my dominant passion. Finding it to be folly to torment myself for an age at which I would never arrive, I dropped everything, and I hurried to enjoy. That, sir, I swear to you, is the genuine cause of this retreat, for which our literary men went seeking motives of ostentation, which supposes a constancy or rather obstinacy to stick to what costs me that is directly contrary to my natural character.

You will say to me, sir, that this supposed indolence harmonizes badly with the writings that I have composed for ten years, and with this desire for glory which must have stimulated me to publish them.

That is an objection to be resolved which obliges me to prolong my letter and which consequently forces me to finish it. I will come back to it, sir, if my familiar tone does not displease you, for in pouring out my heart I could not adopt any other. I will paint myself without makeup and without modesty. I will show myself to you such as I see myself, and such as I am, for passing my life with myself I must know myself, and I see by the way in which those who think they know me interpret my actions and my behavior that they understand nothing about it. No one in the world knows me except myself alone. You will pass judgment on it when I have said everything.

Do not send me back my letters, sir, I beg you. Burn them, for they are not worth the bother of keeping, but not by regard for me. Do not consider either, I beg you, taking back those that are in Duchesne's hands. If the traces of all my follies had to be erased from the world, there would be too many letters to take back, and I would not move the tip of my finger for that. Whether to be charged or discharged, I do not fear to be seen such as I am. I know my great defects, and I keenly feel all my vices. With all this I will die full of hope in the supreme God, and very persuaded that of all men that I have known in my life, none was better than I.

Chrétien-Guillaume de Lamoignon de Malesherbes

January 12, 1762
Montmorency

I am continuing, sir, to give you an account of myself, since I started to. For what can be most unfavorable to me is to be known halfway. And since my faults have not taken away your esteem, I do not assume that my frankness must take it away.

It seems that a lazy soul which is frightened by every care, and an ardent, irritable temperament which is easily affected and sensitive to excess to everything that affects it, could not be allied in the same character. And yet these two contraries compose the foundation of mine. Although I cannot resolve this contradiction on the basis of principles, it nevertheless exists; I feel it. Nothing is more certain; and I can at least provide a kind of historical account based on the facts which can serve to conceive it. I was more active in infancy, but never like another child. This ennui with everything threw me early on into reading. At six I came across Plutarch, at eight I knew him by heart. I had read all the novels; they had made me shed buckets of tears before the age when the heart takes an interest in novels. From this was formed in mine this heroic and romantic taste which has only grown until now, and which ended by disgusting me with everything save that which resembled my follies. In my youth, when I believed that I would find in the world the same people that I had known in my books, I would surrender myself without reservation to whoever knew how to impress me by a certain jargon of which I have always been the dupe. I was active because I was mad. As I was disabused, I changed tastes, attachments, projects, and in all these changes I would always lose my trouble and my time because I was always seeking what was not there. In becoming more experienced I almost lost hope of finding it, and consequently the zeal to seek it. Soured by the injustices I had suffered, by those that I had witnessed, often afflicted by the disorder into which example and the force of things had carried me away, I came to despise my century and my contemporaries. And feeling that I would not find among them a situation which could content my heart, little by little I detached it from the society of men, and I made myself another one in my imagination, which charmed me all the more since I could cultivate it without effort, without risk, and always find it trustworthy and such as I needed it.

After having passed 40 years of my life thus discontented with myself and others, I was uselessly seeking to break the bonds which held me fastened to this society which I esteemed so little, and which chained me to the occupations the least to my taste by needs that I judged to be those of nature, and which were only those of opinion. Suddenly a happy chance came to enlighten me about what I had to do for myself and to think of my fellows, regarding whom my heart was incessantly in contradiction with my mind, and for whom I still felt myself brought to love with so many reasons to hate them. I would like, sir, to be able to depict for you this moment which has made such a singular epoch in my life, and which will always be present to me should I live eternally.

I was going to see Diderot, who was then a prisoner at Vincennes. I had in my pocket a *Mercure de France* which I began to leaf through along the way. I fall upon the question from the Academy of Dijon which occasioned my first writing. If anything has ever resembled a sudden inspiration, it is the motion which took place within me upon this reading. Suddenly I feel my mind dazzled by a thousand insights. Crowds of vivid ideas presented themselves at the same time with a force and disorder which threw me into an inexpressible turmoil. I feel my head gripped by a giddiness similar to drunkenness. A violent palpitation suffocates me, makes my chest heave. No longer being able to breathe while walking, I let myself fall under one of the trees on the avenue, and I pass there half an hour in such agitation that when I get up again, I notice the entire front of my vest wet with my tears without having felt that I was shedding any. Oh! Sir, if I could have written a quarter of what I saw and felt under that tree, with what lucidity I would have caused the contradictions of the social system to be seen, with what force I would have exposed all the abuses of our institutions, with what simplicity I would have demonstrated that man is naturally good and that it is through these institutions alone that men become wicked. All that I have been able to remember of these crowds of great truths which in a quarter of an hour illuminated me under that tree, has been very feebly scattered in my three principal writings, namely that first *Discourse*, the one on *Inequality*, and the treatise on education, which three works are inseparable and together form the same whole. All the rest has been lost, and there was nothing written at that very place but the prosopopeia of Fabricius. That is how, when I was thinking of it least, I became an author almost despite myself. It is easy to conceive how the appeal of a first success and the critiques of the scribblers threw me into the career in earnest. Did I have some real talent for writing? I know not. A lively persuasion has always taken the place of eloquence in me, and I have always written feebly and badly when I was not strongly persuaded. Thus, it is perhaps a hidden return of amour-propre which made me choose and merit my motto,[1] and has so passionately attached me to the truth, or to everything I took for it. If I had written only to write, I am convinced that I would never have been read.

After having discovered or having believed that I discovered in men's false opinions the source of their misery and of their wickedness, I felt that none but these same opinions had made me miserable myself, and that my ills and my vices came to me much more from my situation than from myself. At that same time an illness of which I had felt the first attacks since infancy having revealed itself as absolutely incurable despite all the promises of the false healers of whom I was not for long the dupe, I judged that if I wanted to be consistent, and for once to shake the heavy yoke of opinion off my shoulders, I did not have a moment to lose. I abruptly resolved on my course with quite enough courage, and I have sustained it quite well until now with a firmness the worth of which I alone can feel, because I alone know what obstacles I had and still have to combat every day to hold myself ceaselessly against the current. I nevertheless feel very well that for ten years now I have drifted a little. But if I judged that I had only four more to live, one would see me give a second heave, and go back up at least to my first

---

1. Rousseau's motto was "Vitam impendere vero" (Juvenal, *Satires* 4.91). Rousseau translated it as "to consecrate one's life to truth."

level so as hardly ever to descend again. For all the great trials have been undergone, and it is from now on demonstrated for me by experience that the state in which I have placed myself is the only one in which man can live good and happy, because it is the most independent of all and the only one in which one never finds oneself under the necessity to harm someone else for one's own advantage.

I admit that the name that my writings have made for me very much facilitated the execution of the course I adopted. One must be believed to be a good author to become a bad copyist with impunity and yet not lack for work for all that. Without this first title, one might have taken me too much at my word on the other, and perhaps that would have mortified me. For I easily brave ridicule, but I would not bear contempt so well. But if some reputation gives me a little advantage in this respect, it is well compensated for by all the inconveniences attached to this same reputation, when one does not want to be a slave, and one wants to live isolated and independent. It is these inconveniences which have in part chased me from Paris, and which, still following me into my refuge, would most certainly chase me even further away if my health happened to strengthen itself. Another one of my scourges in this great city was these crowds of so-called friends who had taken hold of me, and who judging my heart by their own wanted absolutely to make me happy in their fashion, and not in mine. In desperation at my retreat, they pursued me there to draw me away from it. I could not remain there without breaking everything off. I am truly free only since then.

Free! No, I am not yet. My last writings are not yet printed, and given the deplorable state of my poor machine, I no longer hope to survive the impression of the collection of all of them. But if, against my expectation, I can last until then and for once take leave of the public, believe, sir, that then I will be free or that never has any man been so. *O utinam!*[2] O thrice happy day! No, it will not be granted me to see it.

I have not said everything, sir, and you will perhaps have at least one more letter to endure. Luckily, nothing obliges you to read them, and perhaps you might be very burdened in doing so. But pardon, I beg you. To write out this long hodgepodge again it would have to be redone, and in truth I do not have the courage for it. I surely take a great deal of pleasure in writing to you, but I take no less in resting, and my condition does not permit me to write for a long time continuously.

---

2. If only!

Chrétien-Guillaume de Lamoignon de Malesherbes

January 26, 1762
Montmorency

After having set out, sir, the real motives of my behavior, I would like to speak to you about my moral state in my retreat. But I feel that it is very late. My soul, estranged from itself, is all in my body. The decay of my poor machine holds it more bound to it from day to day, until it finally suddenly separates itself from it. It is of my happiness that I would like to speak to you, and one speaks badly about happiness when one is suffering.

My ills are the work of nature, but my happiness is mine. Whatever one may say about it, I have been wise because I have been as happy as my nature allowed me to be. I did not go seeking my felicity afar, I sought it near me and found it there. Spartianus says that Similis, a courtier of Trajan's, having without any personal dissatisfaction left the court and all his posts to go live peaceably in the country, had these words put on his tomb: "I remained seventy-six years on earth, and I have lived seven." That is what I can say in some respects, although my sacrifice would have been less. I began to live only on the 9th of April 1756.

I would not know how to tell you, sir, how touched I was to see that you consider me to be the most miserable of men. The public will no doubt judge it as you do, and that too distresses me. Oh! That the fate that I have enjoyed could be known to all the universe! Each would want to make a similar one for himself; peace would reign on earth; men would no longer think of harming one another; and there would be no more wicked men when none would have interest in being so. But what, in the end, was I enjoying when I was alone? Myself, the entire universe, everything that is, everything that can be, everything that is beautiful in the sensible world, and imaginable of the intellectual world. I gathered around me everything that could caress my heart; my desires were the measure of my pleasures. No, never have the most voluptuous known similar delights, and I have enjoyed my chimeras a hundred times more than they do their realities.

When my pains make me sadly measure the length of the nights, and the agitation of fever prevents me from tasting a single instant of sleep, I often distract myself from my present condition by thinking about various events of my life, and the repentances, sweet memories, regrets, and tender feelings share the charge of making me forget my sufferings for a few moments. What times would you believe, sir, that I remember the most often and the most willingly in my dreams? They are not the pleasures of my youth: they were too rare, too mingled with bitterness, and are already too far from me. They are those of my retreat, they are my solitary walks, they are those rapid but delightful days that I passed entirely with myself alone, with my good and simple housekeeper, with my beloved dog, my old cat, with the birds of the countryside and the does of the forest, with the whole of nature and its inconceivable author. By getting up before the sun to go see, [and] contemplate its rise in my garden, when I saw a beautiful day begin, my first wish was that neither letters nor visits would come to disturb its charm. After giving the morning over to various tasks, all of which I carried out with pleasure because I could put them back to another time, I hastened to lunch so as to escape importunate people and arrange for a longer afternoon. Before one o'clock, even on the most scorching days, I would leave at the sun's zenith with my faithful Achates,[1] quickening my step for fear that someone would come and take hold of me before I could

---

1. Rousseau refers to his dog using the name of the faithful companion of Aeneas. The dog was named Turk.

get away. But once I was able to round a certain corner, with what a beating of my heart, with what ebullient joy I would begin to breathe as I felt saved, saying to myself: Here I am master of myself for the rest of the day! I would then go at a more tranquil pace to look for some wild place in the forest, some deserted place where nothing showing the hand of men announced servitude and domination, some refuge where I could believe I had penetrated first and where no importunate third party could interpose between nature and me. It was there that it seemed to deploy to my eyes an always novel magnificence. The gold of the brooms and the purple of the heathers struck my eyes with a lavishness which touched my heart. The majesty of the trees which covered me with their shade, the delicacy of the shrubs surrounding me, and the stunning variety of grasses and flowers I was pressing beneath my feet kept my mind in a continual alteration between observation and admiration. The concurrence of so many interesting objects contesting for my attention, attracting me ceaselessly from one to the other, encouraged my dreamy and lazy humor, and would often make me repeat within myself, No, Solomon in all his glory was not clothed like one of these.[2]

My imagination did not for long leave deserted the earth so adorned. I soon peopled it with beings according to my heart, and chasing opinion, prejudices, all the artificial passions far away, I transported into the refuges of nature men worthy to inhabit them. I formed from them a charming society for which I did not feel unworthy. I made myself a golden age to my fancy, and filling these beautiful days with all the scenes of my life which had left me with sweet memories, and all those which my heart could still desire, I was moved to tears by the true pleasures of humanity, pleasures so delicious, so pure, and which are henceforth so far from men. O, if in these moments some idea of Paris, of my century, and of my little author's vainglory came to trouble my reveries, with what disdain I chased it away on the instant to deliver myself without distraction to the exquisite sentiments with which my soul was full! Nevertheless, amid all that, I admit, the nothingness of my chimeras would sometimes suddenly grieve it. If all my dreams had turned themselves into realities, they would not have been enough for me. I would have imagined, dreamed, desired again. I found in myself an inexplicable void that nothing could have filled; a certain soaring of

---

2. Matt. 6:29.

the heart toward another sort of enjoyment about which I had no idea, and for which I yet felt the need. Eh! Well, sir, that itself was enjoyment, because I was filled by it with a sentiment so keen and of such an alluring sadness that I would not have wanted not to have.

Soon, from the surface of the earth I raised my ideas to all the beings of nature, to the universal system of things, to the incomprehensible Being which encompasses everything. Then, the mind lost in all this immensity, I did not think, I did not reason, I did not philosophize. With a sort of voluptuousness I felt myself overcome by the weight of this universe. I would surrender myself with rapture to the confusion of these grand ideas. I liked to lose myself in imagination in space; my heart restricted within the limits of beings found itself too constricted there. I was suffocating in the universe. I would have liked to soar into the infinite. I believe that if I had unveiled all the mysteries of nature, I would have felt myself to be in a less delightful situation than this dizzying ecstasy to which my mind surrendered without restraint and which, in the agitation of my transports, would make me sometimes cry out. O great Being! O great Being, without being able to say or think anything more.

In this way flowed in a continual delirium the most charming days that human creature ever spent, and when the setting of the sun made me think of retiring, astonished by the rapidity of time, I believed that I had not turned my day to best account. I thought that I could enjoy it still more, and to make up for the lost time I would say: I will come back tomorrow.

I came back slowly, head a little tired, but heart content. I would rest pleasantly upon my return, surrendering myself to the impression of objects but without thinking, without imagining, without doing anything other than feeling the calm and happiness of my situation. I would find my place set on my terrace. I dined with a hearty appetite in my little household. No image of servitude or dependence disturbed the goodwill which united us all. My dog himself was my friend, not my slave; we always had the same will, but never did he obey me. My gaiety all evening testified that I had lived alone all day. I was very different when I had seen company: I was rarely satisfied with others and never with myself; at night I was grumbling and taciturn. This remark is from my housekeeper, and since she told it to me, I have always found it accurate when I observed myself. Finally, after having taken a few more turns in my garden or sung some tune on my spinet, I found in my bed repose of body and soul a hundred times sweeter than sleep itself.

Those are the days which have made the true happiness of my life, happiness without bitterness, without troubles, without regrets, and to which I would have voluntarily limited all that of my existence. Yes, sir, may similar days fill eternity for me, I ask for no others, and do not imagine that I am much less happy in these ravishing contemplations than the celestial intelligences. But a body that suffers takes away the mind's liberty. From now on I am no longer alone; I have a guest who importunes me. I must set myself free from it to belong to myself, and the trial I have made of these sweet enjoyments no longer serves except to make me wait with less fear the moment of tasting them without distraction.

But here I am already at the end of my second sheet. Yet I would need one more. One more letter therefore, and then no more. Pardon, sir. Although I love talking about myself too much, I do not like to talk about this with everyone. That is what makes me take advantage of the occasion when I have it and it pleases me. That is my wrong and my excuse. I pray you accept it.

Chrétien-Guillaume de Lamoignon de Malesherbes

January 28, 1762
Montmorency

I showed you, sir, within the secret recesses of my heart, the true motives of my retreat and of all my conduct; motives that are less noble, doubtless, than you had supposed them, but such, however, as to make me content with myself and to inspire in me the pride of soul of a man who feels himself to be well ordered and who, having had the courage to do what needed to be done to be so, believes that he can attribute the merit of it to himself. I was answerable, not for making myself another disposition or character, but for taking advantage of mine to make myself good for myself and in no way bad to others. That is a great deal, sir, and few men can say as much. So I will not hide from you that, despite the sentiment of my vices, I have high esteem for myself.

Your literary people may well clamor that a solitary man is useless to everyone and does not fulfill his duties to society. I at least consider that the peasants of Montmorency are more useful members of society than that whole heap of idlers paid with the fat of the people to go chatter six times a week in some academy; and I am happier to be able on occasion to give some pleasure to my poor neighbors, than to help those crowds of little schemers of which Paris is full—all of whom aspire to the honor of being rascals with posts—to succeed; and for the public good, as well as for theirs, they should be sent back to plow the earth in the provinces. It is something to set an example to men of the life they should all lead. It is something, when one no longer has strength or health to work with one's arms, to dare from one's retreat to make the voice of truth heard. It is something to warn men of the folly of the opinions which make them miserable. It is something to have been able to contribute to preventing or at least delaying the pernicious establishment which, to court Voltaire at our expense, d'Alembert wanted to have brought about among us.[1] If I had lived in Geneva, I could not have published the dedicatory letter to the *Discourse on Inequality*, nor even speak against the establishment of the theater in the tone in which I did. I would be much more useless to my compatriots were I living among them than I can be, on occasion, from my retreat. What does it matter where I live if I act or must act? Besides, are Montmorency's inhabitants less men than the Parisians are, and when I can dissuade someone from sending his child to be corrupted in the city, do I do less good than if I could from the city send him back to the paternal hearth? Would not my indigence alone prevent me from being useless in the way these smooth talkers understand it, and since I only eat as much bread as I earn, am I not forced to work for my subsistence, and to pay society for all the need I may have of it? It is true that I have refused occupations I did not think suitable for me. Not feeling within myself the talent that could have made me deserve the good you wanted to do me, to accept it would have been to steal it from some other writer as indigent as I and abler to do that work. In offering it to me you supposed that I was in a condition to do an excerpt, that I could busy myself with matters indifferent to me, and that not being the case, I would have cheated you. I would have made myself unworthy of your kindness if I had behaved otherwise than I did; one is never excusable for doing badly what one does voluntarily. I would now be unhappy with myself and you too, and I would not taste the pleasure I take in writing to you. Lastly, as much as my strength permitted, in working for myself, I did everything I could, according to what was within my reach, for society. If I did little for it, I required even less of it, and I believe that I am so even with it in my condition that if, from now on, I could entirely rest and live for myself alone, I would do it without scruple.

---

1. Rousseau refers to d'Alembert's article "Geneva" in the *Encyclopedia*, to which Rousseau responded with the *Letter to d'Alembert on the Theatre*.

I would at least drive away from me with all my strength the importunity of public rumor. If I lived another hundred years, I would not write one line for the press, and would believe that I truly begin to live again only when I am entirely forgotten.

Yet I admit that it would not have taken much to find myself reengaged in the world and to have left my solitude, not out of distaste for it, but because of a no less lively taste that I almost preferred to it. You would, sir, have to know the state of neglect and abandonment by all my friends in which I found myself, and the profound pain by which it affected my soul when Monsieur and Madame de Luxembourg wanted to become acquainted with me, to judge the impression made on my afflicted heart by their advances and their caresses. I was dying; without them I would infallibly have died from sadness. They gave me back my life. It is very just that I use it to love them.

I have a very loving heart, but which can suffice to itself. I love men too much to need a choice among them; I love them all, and I hate injustice because I love them; I flee them because I love them; I suffer less from their ills when I do not see them. This interest in the species is enough to nourish my heart. I do not need particular friends; but when I have some, I greatly need not to lose them, for when they detach themselves, they rend me. In this, [they are] even more culpable in that I only ask them for friendship; as long as they love me and I know it, I do not even need to see them. But in place of sentiment, they always wanted to put efforts and services that the public saw and about which I could not care less. When I loved them, they wanted to appear to love me. As for me who disdains appearances in everything, I was not satisfied with this, and finding nothing but that, I took it as read. They did not exactly stop loving me; I only discovered that they did not love me.

For the first time in my life, then, I suddenly found myself with a heart that was alone, and at that, alone also in my retreat, and almost as ill as I am today. It is in these circumstances that this new attachment began, which has so thoroughly compensated me for all the others and for which nothing will compensate me; for it will last, I hope, as long as my life; and whatever happens, it will be the last. I cannot hide from you, sir, that I have a violent aversion for all the stations that dominate the others. I am even wrong to say that I cannot hide it from you, for I have no trouble admitting it to you, you born of an illustrious bloodline, son of the chancellor of France and first president of a sovereign court, yes, sir, you who have given me a thousand benefits without knowing me and to whom, despite my natural ingratitude, it costs me nothing to be obligated. I hate the great, I hate their station, their harshness, their prejudices, their pettiness, and all their vices; and I would hate them even far more if I despised them less. It was with this sentiment that I was as if swept away to Montmorency Chateau; I saw its masters, they loved me, and I, sir, I loved them and will love them as long as I live, with all the strength of my soul. For them I would give, I do not say my life, the gift would be a feeble one in my condition; I do not say my reputation among my contemporaries, about which I hardly care; but the only glory which ever touched my heart, the honor I await from posterity and which it will give me, because it is my due, and posterity is always just. My heart which does not know how to attach itself by half gave itself to them without reserve, and I do not repent it. I would even repent uselessly, for it would no longer be the moment to recant. In the heat of enthusiasm they inspired in me I have been a hundred times on the point of asking them for an asylum in their house, to pass the rest of my days near them; and they would joyfully have granted it, even if in the way they went about it I must not consider myself as having been forestalled by their offers. This project is certainly one of those I have meditated on the longest and with the greatest agreeableness. Yet I had reluctantly to feel, in the end, that it was not good. I was only thinking of the attachment between persons, without considering the intermediaries who would have kept us distant from one another, and there were so many kinds of these, especially involving the inconvenience attached to my ills, that such a project is excusable only because of the sentiment that had inspired it. Besides, the manner of life that would have had to be adopted shocks my tastes, my habits, too directly; I could not have stood firm against it for even three months. Finally, we may well have brought our dwellings closer; the distance between the stations remaining the same, that delightful intimacy which is the great charm of a closely knit society would always have been missing in ours. I would not have been either the friend or the servant of Monsieur le maréchal de Luxembourg; I would have been his guest. Not feeling at home, I would often have yearned for my old sanctuary, and it is a hundred times better to be far away from the people one loves and want to be near them, than to expose oneself to making the opposite wish. A few degrees closer would perhaps have revolutionized my life. In my dreams I have a hundred times imagined M. de Luxembourg not a duke, not marshal of France, but a good country gentleman living in some old chateau, and J.-J. Rousseau not an author, not a maker of books, but with a mediocre mind and a little acquired knowledge, presenting himself to the lord castellan and to the Lady, pleasing them, finding near them the happiness of his life, and contributing to theirs. If, to make the dream more pleasant, you would permit me to shove the chateau of Malesherbes to half a league away from there, it seems to me, sir, that in dreaming this way I will not for long want to wake up.

But it is done. Nothing remains but to end the long dream, for the others are from now on out of season, and it is a great deal if I can still promise myself a few of the delightful hours I spent at the castle of Montmorency. However this may be, here I am, such as I am affected. Judge me based on all this hodgepodge if I am worth the trouble; for I could not order it better and I do not have the courage to start again. If this overly veracious portrait takes your benevolence from me, I will have ceased to usurp what did not belong to me. But if I keep it, it will become dearer to me, as being more mine.

CHAPTER 74

Jean Néaulme

June 5, 1762
Montmorency

I received, sir, just now and in the same package along with six printed sheets and five cartons,[1] your four letters of May 20, 22, 24, and 26. I am displeased to see the continuation of your complaints regarding your two colleagues in them. Having entered into neither the contracts nor the reciprocal negotiations, however, what right would I have to interfere in a business that is not mine, and what else can I desire other than that justice be observed and that you are all satisfied? I will add only that I would have wished, and wholeheartedly, that everything had passed through your hands alone and that you were the only one dealt with; but not having been consulted in this business, I cannot answer for what was done without me knowing.

I have told you, sir, and I repeat, that *Emile* is the last writing that has left and that ever will leave my pen for publication. I do not understand what enables you to infer the contrary. It is enough for me to have told you the truth. You will believe what you want about it.

---

1. Cartons were separate sheets making corrections usually for proof sheets with many errors. They would be pasted into the book in the proper places.

I am very sorry about the trouble you say you are in about the *Profession of Faith*. I declare to you again, however, once and for all, that there is neither disapproval, nor danger, nor violence, nor power on earth that would ever make me cut one syllable. Since you did not consult me about the contents of my manuscript in negotiating for its publication, you have nothing for which to blame me in the obstacles that are stopping you, and all the less since the bold truths sown in all my books should have made you presume that this one would not be exempt from them. I have neither surprised you nor misled you. I am incapable of it. I would even like to please you, but what you require of me on this point cannot happen, and I am astonished that you could believe that a man who takes so many measures for his work not to be altered after his death would let it be mutilated during his life.

As to the reasons you set forth, you could, sir, skip this display and assume that I had thought about what it suited me to do. You say that even people who think as I do disapprove of me. I answer you that that cannot be, for I who surely think as I do, I approve of myself, and have done nothing in my life of which my heart was as content. By rendering glory to God and speaking for the true good of men I have done my duty. Let them take advantage of it or not, let them disapprove or approve of me, that is their business; I would not give a straw to change their disapproval into praise. Moreover, they can do their worst; what will they do to me that nature and my illnesses might not do soon without them? They will not give me nor deprive me of my recompense; it does not depend on any human power. You see very well, sir, that my decision is made, whatever happens. Thus, I advise you not to speak to me about it anymore, for that would be perfectly useless. But as for the declaration that you are asking for your discharge, nothing is more just than to grant it to you. You have only to draw up the formula yourself, send it to me with your last sheets, and I will send it back to you written and signed in my hand.

I have not yet been able to read the sheets that you just sent me. As soon as I have the whole, I will send you the notes of the mistakes I noticed, and what I had not noticed previously. I assume you to be informed about the publication and suppression of my book;[2] therefore I will not speak to you about it. They say that the Parlement proposes to prosecute the author, but I do not think that so wise and so enlightened a body would commit such a stupidity. I embrace you with all my heart.

---

2. The *Social Contract*.

CHAPTER 75

Paul-Claude Moultou

June 7, 1762
Montmorency

I would keep myself from making you uneasy, dear Moultou, if I believed that you were tranquil on my account. The fermentation is too strong for the rumor not to have reached you, and I judge by the letters that I receive from the provinces that the people who love me are even more alarmed for me there than in Paris. My book appeared in unfortunate circumstances. It is said that to justify its zeal against the Jesuits, the Parlement of Paris also wants to persecute those who do not think as they do, and the only man in France who believes in God must be the victim of the defenders of Christianity. For several days all my friends are vying with each other in doing their utmost to frighten me. I am being offered refuge everywhere, but since they do not give me any reasons that are good for me to accept them, I remain, for your friend Jean-Jacques has not learned to hide himself. I also think that they exaggerate the evil before my eyes to try to rattle me. For I could not conceive by what title I, a citizen of Geneva, can owe an explanation to the Parlement of Paris for a book that I had printed in Holland with a privilege from the Estates General. The only means of defense that I intend to use if they interrogate me is to challenge the impartiality of my judges, but this means will not satisfy them. For I see that, entirely full of its supreme power, the Parlement has little idea of the law of nations and will hardly respect it in a little private individual like me. In all bodies there are interests to which justice is always subordinate, and to the Parlement of Paris there is no more inconvenience in burning an innocent person than there is to the Parlement of Rouen in breaking one on the wheel.[1] It is true that in general the magistrates of the former of these bodies love justice and are always equitable and moderate when too strong an influence is not opposed to it; but if this influence acts in this affair, as is probable, they will not resist. Such are men, dear Moultou, such is that so vaunted society; justice speaks and the passions act. Moreover, even though I had only to declare openly the truth of the facts, or on the contrary to make use of some lie to get out of trouble, even despite them, very resolved to say nothing except what is true and not to compromise anyone, always hampered in my answers, I will give them the easiest time in the world to ruin me at their pleasure.

But, dear Moultou, if the motto I have taken is not empty chatter, this is the occasion to show myself worthy of it, and to what better use can I put the little life I have left. In whatever manner men treat me, what will they do to me that nature and my illnesses would soon have done to me without them. They will be able to take away from me a life that my condition makes a burden to me, but they will not take away my freedom. I will preserve it, whatever they might do, in their bonds and in their walls. My career has ended; nothing is left for me but to crown it. I have rendered glory to God, I have spoken for the good of men. O friend, neither you nor I will ever refuse to suffer for such a great cause. It is today that the Parlement reconvenes; I am waiting in peace for what it will be pleased to ordain for me.

It is several days ago already that MM. Voullaire undertook to have a copy of my book sent to you; but at present I am in no position to send any others to Geneva as I had proposed to do. They say that since it has been suppressed, it is being sold at an exorbitant price. Someone told me yesterday they had seen someone pay 42 livres. Farewell, dear Moultou, I embrace you tenderly. As soon as my fate has been decided, I will instruct you if I remain free. If not, you will be informed through public channels.

---

1. This is an allusion to the Calas affair. Jean Calas was executed on March 10.

PART IV

Exile

June 9, 1762–May 1767

When he left Montmorency after the warrant was issued for his arrest, Rousseau intended to go to Geneva, but Geneva, Bern, and other communities imitated the French in condemning his work. Ultimately Rousseau sought refuge in Môtiers, near Neufchâtel, under the protection of Frederick the Great and his representative Lord Marshal Keith, with whom Rousseau formed a friendship. While at Môtiers, Rousseau wrote two major works defending *Emile* and the *Social Contract*, which were published in quick succession. The first of these was the *Letter to Beaumont* (1763) in reply to the pastoral letter written by the archbishop of Paris against *Emile*. The second was the *Letters Written from the Mountain* (1764). The latter work not only defended Rousseau's books but also entered into discussion of Genevan politics. From the time of the condemnation of *Emile*, Rousseau's native city had been divided between his opponents and his supporters. Rousseau's intervention generalized the stakes by arguing that his case revealed a deep-seated constitutional crisis. He kept his writing of the *Letters* a secret from all but a few of his supporters. The publication of this work led to a break with Pastor Montmollin, who gave sermons stirring up the populace against Rousseau.

During this tumultuous period, Rousseau also engaged in correspondence with representatives of Corsica, which had just gained its independence from Genoa. Some Corsican leaders asked Rousseau to serve as a sort of master legislator for their new government. Rousseau entertained the idea of seeking refuge in Corsica and working there. He compiled a dossier of information about Corsica and completed a part of a project toward a new Corsican government.

When the public furor rose to such a pitch that the public authorities told him that they could not guarantee his safety, Rousseau had to leave his refuge, and he eventually made his way to England under the protection of David Hume. Although Hume and Rousseau began with protestations of admiration for each other, their relations soured as Rousseau became suspicious of what he regarded as Hume's efforts to control, as well as to defame, him, and Hume became worried that Rousseau would make his complaints public. Their famous quarrel also involved very different views about intellectual independence and solitary versus social life. Hume decided to preempt Rousseau (who does not actually seem to have intended to make his complaints public) by publishing a pamphlet describing their relations. This led to an international pamphlet war in which partisans of both men took sides. Their worsening relations caused Rousseau to fear repercussions from the British government and ultimately led him to make a sudden decision to return to France.

During these years, Rousseau continued to be a very active correspondent. There are more than one thousand extant letters from this period. We are presenting eighty-one. Although some of Rousseau's letters from his time in England show acute anxiety on his part, others show him enjoying his new hobby of botanizing. He also wrote the first half of his *Confessions* while living at Wootton in Staffordshire. Although the publication of *Emile* and the *Social Contract* led to condemnations by governments and ecclesiastical authorities, these books added to Rousseau's authority as an intellectual and moral exemplar among many readers. Some aspiring writers wrote to him for advice. Other people, such as the Prince de Wurtemberg, the woman known only as "Henriette," Séguier de Saint-Brisson, and Carondelet wrote to Rousseau for advice about their personal and familial lives.

CHAPTER 76

Paul-Claude Moultou

June 15, 1762
Yverdun

You judged better than I did, dear Moultou. The event justified your foresight, and your friendship saw my dangers more clearly than I did. After the resolve in which you saw me in my preceding letter, you will be surprised to know that I am now at Yverdun. But I can tell you that it is not without difficulty nor without very serious considerations that I could make up my mind to a course of action so little to my taste. I waited until the last moment without letting myself be frightened, and it was only a courier who arrived during the night of the 8th and 9th from M. le prince de Conti to Madame de Luxembourg, who brought the details, based on which I immediately made my decision. It was no longer a question of myself alone, who certainly never approved the turn that was taken in this business, but of persons who out of love of me found themselves involved in it. Once I was arrested, even my silence—since I did not want to lie—might have compromised them. Thus, it was necessary to flee, dear Moultou, and to expose myself in a rather difficult retreat to all the convulsions of scoundrels, leaving the Parlement joyful at my evasion, and very resolved to follow the refusal to appear in court as far as it could go. It is not, believe me, that this body hates me and does not very well feel its iniquity. Wanting to shut the mouths of the devout by pursuing the Jesuits, however, they would make me, without regard for my sad condition, suffer the cruelest tortures, they would have burned me alive with as little pleasure as justice, simply because that suited them. However that might be, I swear to you, dear Moultou, before that God who reads in my heart, that I have done nothing against the laws in all this, that not only was I perfectly in order, but that I had the most authentic proofs of this and, before leaving, I voluntarily got rid of these proofs for someone else's tranquility.[1]

I arrived here yesterday morning, and I am going to wander in the mountains until I find a wild enough asylum to spend the rest of my miserable days there in peace. Perhaps someone else would ask me why I do not retire to Geneva; but either I poorly know my friend Moultou, or he will certainly not pose that question. He will feel that it is not in the fatherland that an unfortunate outlaw ought to take refuge; that he ought not to bring his ignominy there, nor make it share his affronts. Why can I not from this instant cause my memory to be forgotten there! Do not give my address to anyone there; do not speak about me any longer there; no longer name me there. May my name be effaced off the earth. Ah Moultou! Providence was mistaken; why did it cause me to be born among men, while making me of a different species than they are?

Wherever I am, you will always be able to write to me care of: M. Daniel Roguin at Yverdun.

---

1. Rousseau refers here to Mme. de Luxembourg, who would have been implicated for her role in the publication of *Emile* in France.

CHAPTER 77

Marie-Thérèse Levasseur

June 17, 1762
Marie-Thérèse replied to this letter by saying that she would cross seas and precipices to be with Rousseau.

My dear child, you will learn with great pleasure that I am safe. May I learn soon that you are well and that you still love me. I occupied myself with you while leaving and during my entire trip; at present I am occupying myself with the effort to reunite us. See what you want to do, and do not follow anything but your inclination in that. For however repugnant it might be to me to be separated from you after having lived together for so long, yet I can do it without inconvenience, although with regret; even your stay in this country happens to have difficulties that will still not stop me if you agree to come. Consult yourself then, my dear child, and consider if you will be able to bear my retreat. If you come I will try to make it sweet for you, and I will even provide as much as possible for you to be able to fulfill the duties of your religion as often as you please. But if you prefer to stay, do so without scruple, and I will always contribute with all my power toward making life convenient and pleasant for you.

I do not know anything about what is happening, but the Parlement's iniquities can no longer surprise me, and there are no horrors for which

I am not already prepared. My child, do not despise me because of my wretchedness. Men can make me unhappy, but they could not make me wicked or unjust, and you know better than anyone that I have done nothing against the laws.

I do not know how the effects that have remained in my house will have been disposed of; I have every confidence in the obligingness that M. Dumoulin has had in being willing to be their guardian. I believe that that can remove many difficulties that others could have made. I do not presume that the Parlement, as completely unjust as it is, would be base enough to confiscate my rags. Nevertheless, if that happened, come with nothing, my child, and I will be consoled for everything when I have you near me. If, as I believe to be the case, they close their eyes and let you dispose of everything, consult Messieurs Mathas, Dumoulin, and de La Roche about the way to get rid of all that, or the greater part of it, above all the books and the large pieces of furniture, the transportation of which would cost more than they are worth, and have the rest packed up carefully so that it is sent to me by a way that is known to M. le maréchal. But above all, try to have a trunkful of linen and clothing sent to me, for which I have a very great need, giving with the trunk an exact memorandum of everything it contains. If you come you will keep with you what is best and takes up the least volume, to carry it with you, as well as the money that the rest will have generated which you will make use of for your trip. For, against my expectation, I have found that it is very expensive to live here, that everything costs a lot and that if we must absolutely set ourselves up again in furnishings and clothing, that will not be a small matter. You know that there is the spinet and some books to return, and M. Mathas, the butcher, and my barber to pay, I will send you a memorandum about all that. You must have found in the lid of the candy box three or four crowns that ought to be enough for the butcher's payment.

I have not yet decided about the asylum that I will choose in this country. I am waiting for your answer to settle things, for if you did not come, I would manage differently. I beg you to share with MM. Mathas and Dumoulin, Mme. de Verdelin, MM. Alamanni and Mandard, M. and Mme. de La Roche, and generally with all the people who will appear to you to take an interest in my fate, how much it cost me to leave so brusquely all my friends and a country where people were well disposed toward me. You know the true motive for my departure. If no one had been compromised in this unfortunate affair, I would surely never have left, having nothing for which to reproach myself.

Do not fail also to see M. the curate on my behalf and show him with what edification I always admired his zeal and all his behavior, and how much I regretted distancing myself from so respectable a pastor whose example made me better. M. Alamanni had promised to have a truss made for me similar to a model that he showed me, except that what was on the right ought to be on the left. I think that this truss can very well be made without exact measurement by not opening the stitches, so that I could have them opened here to my measurement. If he were willing to take the trouble to have two similar ones made for me, I would be markedly obliged to him. You will take care to reimburse him for the price, and to have them sent to me in the first trunk that you have sent to me. Also, do not forget the cases of catheters, and be attentive to wrap all of that up with the greatest care.

Farewell, my dear child, I console myself a little for the trouble in which I am leaving you with the kindness and protection of M. le maréchal and Mme. la maréchale, who will not abandon you in need. M. and Mmes. Dubettier appeared to me well disposed toward you; I would wish you to make the advances to patch things up to which they will surely lend themselves. If only I could make things up the same way with M. and Mme. de La Roche. If I had stayed, I would have attempted that good work, and I have it in mind that I would have succeeded. Farewell once again, I recommend everything to you, but above all to preserve yourself and take care of yourself.

CHAPTER 78

André Maucourant de Morancourt

June 25, 1762
Maucourant de Morancourt was editor of the Gazette of Bern, *which published a copy of the indictment by the Parlement of Paris for Rousseau's arrest. He had also praised Rousseau's talents and morals.*

In speaking, sir, in your gazette of June 23, about a paper called an indictment published in France against the best and most useful of my writings, you have fulfilled your office, and I do not hold it against you. I do not even complain that you have transcribed the imputations with which this paper is full, and to which I abstain from giving what they deserve.

But when you add on your own initiative that I am blameworthy beyond what they can say for having composed the book in question, and above all for having put my name on it, as if it were allowed and honorable to hide oneself when speaking to the public, then, sir, I have the right to complain about what you are judging without knowing. For it is not possible for an enlightened man and a good man to bring such an inequitable judgment on a book in which the author maintains the cause of God, morals, virtue, against the new philosophy with all the force of which he is capable. You have given too much authority to procedures that are irregular and dictated by private motives that everyone is acquainted with. My book, sir, is in the public's hands. It will be read sooner or later by reasonable men, perhaps finally by Christians, who will see with surprise and doubtless with indignation that a disciple of their divine master is treated among them as a scoundrel.

Thus I beg you, sir, and this is a reparation that you owe me, to read the book, about which you have spoken so lightly and so badly, yourself; and when you have read it, to want then to give an account to the public without favor and without mercy of the judgment you will have made of it. I salute you, sir, with all my heart.

JJR

CHAPTER 79

Marie-Charlotte-Hyppolite de Campet de Saujon, comtesse de Boufflers

July 4, 1762
Yverdun

Touched by the interest you take in my fate, I wanted to write to you, madam, and I would like to do so more than ever; but my ever-worsening situation leaves me barely a moment to steal from the most indispensable efforts. Perhaps in two days I will be forced to leave here, and so long as I do stay, I avouch that I will not be left without any occupation. One must wait for me to be able to breathe, so that I can give you an account of myself. Mademoiselle Levasseur had already spoken to me about your kindness to her, and that of M. le prince de Conti. I carry away in my heart all the feelings they have inspired in me; may less stormy days let me enjoy them more at ease.

You amaze me, madam, by reproaching me for my indignation against the Parlement of Paris. I regard it as a troop of thoughtless children who in their games do much harm to men without knowing it; but that does not alter the fact that by accusing it only of iniquity toward me, I made use of the gentlest word possible. Since you have read the book, you know well, madam, that the advocate general's indictment is only a tissue of calumnies, which could save its author from the punishment due him were he only a private individual, only because of their stupidity. What must be the case with a man who dares to use the sacred character of the magistracy to carry on the trade he should be punishing?

It is nevertheless based on this lampoon that they hasten to judge me in all of Europe before the book has arrived there. It is based on this lampoon that, without summoning me or hearing me, they began by issuing a warrant for my arrest in Geneva; and when my book finally arrived there, its reading caused the emotion, the fermentation that still reigns there to such a point that the magistrate disavows his decree, even denies that he issued it, and has denied upon my family's request the communication of the judgment rendered in the council on that occasion.[1] A proceeding which perhaps has never had a precedent since tribunals have existed.

It is true that M. de Voltaire's credit in Geneva contributed very much to this violence and precipitation. It is at M. de Voltaire's instigation that the cause of God has been avenged against me.[2] But in Berne, where the same indictment was printed in the Gazette, it produced such an effect that I know from M. the bailiff himself that he expects, perhaps as soon as tomorrow, the order to make me leave the territory of the Republic, and I can say that he fears it. I know very well that when my book reaches Bern it will excite the same indignation as in Geneva against the author of the indictment. In the meantime, however, I will be expelled. They will not want to go back on what they said, and if they would like to, it would not suit me to return. Thus, successively, air and water will be refused me everywhere. That is the effect of those so regular procedures whose equity you want me to admire.

You can certainly judge, madam, that all these circumstances can only make the offers of Mme. de La Marck even more precious to me.[3] If I have the honor of being known by you, you could easily make her understand to what point I am touched by it. But madam, where is this chateau? Must I still make voyages, I who can no longer drag myself

---

1. Rousseau's cousins Jean-François Rousseau and Theodore Rousseau had made the routine request for a copy of the judgment, which was denied without comment.

2. While it was the case that Voltaire frequently bitterly attacked Rousseau after the publication of the *Letter to d'Alembert*, and that he was on excellent terms with many of those responsible for the judgment against Rousseau, there is no direct evidence that he urged them to undertake this course. Nevertheless, Rousseau was not alone in holding Voltaire responsible.

3. Mme. de Boufflers had relayed from the Countess de La Marck an offer of asylum on an estate in Germany, as well as the suggestion that Rousseau go to England with David Hume.

around? No: in my condition, all that is left is to let myself be expelled from border to border until I can no longer go on; then the last one will do with me what he pleases. Regarding England, you judge very well that henceforth it is for me like the other world. I will never see it again in my life.

Now I should speak to you about your own offers, madam, about my gratitude, about the chevalier de Lorenzy, about Miss Becquet,[4] and about a thousand things that, in your kindnesses to me, it is important for me to tell you. But this is the way the world is, I lack paper and the post will soon leave; one must finish for today.

---

4. Miss Becquet later married Lorenzy.

CHAPTER 80

Frederick II, King of Prussia

July 10 or 11, 1762
This letter was probably never sent.

Sire,

I have spoken much ill of you, perhaps I will say more. Yet driven out of France, of Geneva, of the canton of Bern, I come to seek asylum in your States.[1] My fault is perhaps not to have begun with that. This praise is among those that are worthy of you. Sire, I have deserved no favor from you, and I do not ask any. But I believed I ought to declare to Your Majesty that I was in his power, and that I wanted to be so. He can dispose of me as he pleases.

---

1. Frederick was the ruler of Neuchâtel.

CHAPTER 81

Isaac-Ami Marcet de Mézières

July 24, 1762
Môtiers-Travers

Your letter, sir, about the affair of M. Pictet is judicious; it gets to the point well. Allow me to add to it some ideas, so as to finish determining the state of the question.

1. Is the doctrine of the *Profession of Faith of the Savoyard Vicar* so obviously contrary to the religion established in Geneva, that this could not even constitute a question, and that the Council, when it was a question of the honor and fate of a citizen, ought not even to have consulted the theologians on this point?

2. Assuming that this doctrine is contrary to it, is it very certain that J. J. R. is its author? Is it even certain that he is the author of the book that bears his name? Can one not falsely publish the name of a man at the head of a book that is not by him? Was it not appropriate to begin by having either proofs, or the declaration of the accused, before proceeding against his person? One would say that they were in a rush to pass a decree without hearing him, out of fear of finding him innocent.

3. The case of the Parlement of Paris is completely different and does not authorize the Council of Geneva's procedure. The Parlement, having claimed, on what foundation I do not know, that the book was published in the kingdom with neither approval nor permission had, or believed it had, on these grounds, inspection over the book and the author. Nevertheless, everyone agrees that it committed a shocking irregularity, by passing an arrest warrant against the one it should first have summoned to be heard. If this procedure were legitimate, the freedom of every honorable man would always be at the mercy of the first publisher. It will be said that the public voice is unanimous, and that the one to whom the book is attributed does not disavow it. But once again, before sullying the honor of an irreproachable man, before infringing upon the freedom of a citizen, some positive proof would be necessary. Now, the public voice is not one, and no one is held to answer when he is not questioned. If then the procedure of the Parlement of Paris is irregular on this point, as is incontestable, what will we say about that of the Council of Geneva, which does not have the slightest pretext on which to found it? Sometimes one hastens to issue a writ carelessly against an accused when one can seize him, and one fears that he might escape; but why issue a writ against him when he is absent, unless the offense is cut and dried? This violent proceeding is as without pretext as it is without reason. When the public judges without thinking, it is even less permitted to tribunals to imitate it, since the public recants as it judges. Instead of which, the premier maxim of all the governments of the world is to heap stupidity upon stupidity, rather than ever to admit that they have committed one—still less to rectify it.

4. Now let us assume the book to be entirely acknowledged as being by the author whose name it bears; it is then a question of knowing whether the profession of faith also is by him. Another positive and juridical proof, indispensable on this occasion: for in the end, the author of the book does not present himself in it as that of the profession of faith. He declares that it is a writing that he is transcribing in his book, and in the preamble that writing appears to be addressed to him by one of his fellow citizens. That is all that one can infer from the work itself. To go further is to guess, and once one gets mixed up in guessing on tribunals, what will become of the private individuals who will not be fortunate

enough to please the magistrates? If then the one who is named at the head of the book in which the profession of faith is found ought to be punished for having published it, it is as editor, and not as author. One has no right to regard the doctrine it contains as being his own, above all after the declaration he makes himself that he does not give this profession of faith as a rule for the sentiments that one ought to follow in matters of religion, and he says why he gives it. But in Geneva every day Catholic books are published, even controversial ones, without the Council looking for a quarrel with the editors. By what unjust partiality does one punish the Genevan editor of a work claimed to be heterodox printed in a foreign country, without saying anything to Genevan editors of incontestably heterodox works, printed in Geneva itself.

5. Regarding the *Social Contract*, the author of this writing claims that a religion is always necessary to the good constitution of a State. This sentiment might very well displease the poet Voltaire, the mountebank Tronchin,[1] and their satellites, but it is not from that direction that they will dare to attack the book in public. Subsequently the author examines the civil religion without which no State can be well constituted. He seems, it is true, not to believe that Christianity, at least that of today, is that civil religion, indispensable to all good legislation. And, in fact, up until now many people have regarded the republics of Sparta and Rome as well constituted, even though they did not believe in J.C. Let us assume, however, that the author is mistaken in that; he will have committed a political error, for there is no question here of anything else. I do not see where the heresy will be; still less the crime to punish.

6. As for the principles of government established in this work, they are reduced to these two principal ones: the first, that legitimately sovereignty always belongs to the people; the second, that aristocratic government is the best of all. Perhaps it would matter a great deal to the people of Geneva and even to its magistrates to know precisely in what respect one of them finds this book blameworthy, and its author criminal. If I were procurer general of the

---

1. The term *jongleur*, translated here as "mountebank" and which usually means "juggler," also was used to refer to healers who gained status by combining simple medical treatments with claims that they had spiritual sources of healing ability. Diderot's *Encyclopedia* uses the term in this sense. Other possible translations would be "charlatan" or "quack."

Republic of Geneva, and a bourgeois, whoever he might be, dared to condemn the principles established in this work, I would oblige him to explain himself clearly, or I would pursue him criminally as a traitor to the fatherland and criminal of lèse-majesté.

They persist, nevertheless, in saying that there is a secret writ by the Council against J. J. R., and even that when his family demanded communication of this writ by petition it was refused to them. This shadowy manner of proceeding is frightening. It is unprecedented in all the tribunals of the world, except that of the State inquisitors of Venice. If it were ever established in Geneva, it would be better to be born Turkish than Genevan.

Moreover, I cannot believe that the tribunal you mention is being set up against M. Pictet. In any event, that will be to provide a man who is firm, who has some sense, health, enlightenment, the occasion to play a very fine role and to give great lessons to his fellow citizens.

He who is writing these remarks to you loves you and salutes you with all his heart.

CHAPTER 82

Lord Marshal George Keith

August 18, 1762

My Lord,

It is very just that I owe to you the permission that the king gives me to live in his States, for it is you who make it precious to me; and if it had been refused to me, you would have been able to reproach yourself for having changed my departure into exile. As to the commitment I have made with myself not to write anymore, I hope this is not a condition that His Majesty means to put on the asylum that he is willing to grant me. To him and Your Excellency, I commit myself only, and very wholeheartedly to respect, as I have always done, in my writings and my conduct, the laws, the prince, decent people, and all the duties of hospitality. In general, I have esteem for few kings, and I do not like monarchic government; but I have followed the rule of the Bohemians who in their excursions always spare the house they live in. While I lived in France, Louis XV had no better subject than me; and surely, I will not be seen to be less faithful to a prince of a different caliber. But as to my manner of thinking in general on any matter whatsoever, it is mine, born republican and free. And so long as I do not divulge it in the State where I live, I owe no account of it to the sovereign, for he is not a competent judge of what is done away from his home by a man who was not born his subject. Those are my sentiments, My Lord, and my rules. I have never departed from them, and I will never depart from them. I have said all that I had to say, and I do not like to keep harping. Thus, I have promised myself and I promise myself not to write any longer: but once again I have promised it only to myself.

No, My Lord, I do not need the pleasant folk of Môtiers to drive me from it to want to inhabit the square tower, and if I were to live there it would surely not be to make myself invisible, for it is better to be a man and your fellow than the god of the vulgar and the Dalai Lama.[1] But I have begun to settle myself in my habitation and I could not change it before winter without an indisposition that frightens my laziness and can harm my health. To mark festival days, one must also have other days. If my pilgrimages are not troublesome to you, I will make a very pleasant division of my time, just about the way you mark it out for the king. Here I will crochet along with some women; at Colombier, I will go think along with you.

Everything written to you from Bern that M. de Voltaire has done in Geneva and there against me through the mountebank's credit is not unknown to anyone in the country.[2] Tolerant for atheists alone, he wants whoever dares to believe in God to be burnt. The clergy of Geneva who have sense and enlightenment have not been his dupe. But do you not find it funny to see this new missionary get together all the gang of ministers of Bern and of the pays de Vaud to avenge insulted atheism? Not satisfied with that, he writes me anonymous letters that he would like to be gay and that are only foolish.[3] He is continually kind enough to worry about me. When the poor man will have taken the trouble to lift me up on his shoulders, I will be hardly any taller for it.

---

1. Keith had invited Rousseau to live in his summer residence, the Chateau of Colombier. He had offered to let Rousseau be invisible there, "like the Dalai Lama," who was held to have the power to make himself invisible.

2. "The mountebank" refers to Dr. Tronchin.

3. Rousseau had, in fact, received at least one anonymous letter that he believed originated from Voltaire, who later did write anonymous works attacking Rousseau.

CHAPTER 83

Comtesse de Boufflers

August 20, 1762

The comtesse had written to Rousseau to urge him to seek refuge in England, where Hume had agreed to assist him. As alternatives, she suggested living with her friend Mme. de La Marck in the Rhineland, or in Trie, a property of the Prince de Conti. Ultimately, after a stay in England, Rousseau did live in Trie for a time.

I have received in a timely way, madam, your two letters of 21 and 31 July, with the extract by duplicate of a P.S. from Mr. Hume that you joined to them. The esteem of that rare, and perhaps unique, man erases many insults; he had all mine even before I heard you speak of him, and your sentiments about him have increased it by clarifying it. Mr. Hume is the truest philosopher that I know and the only historian who has ever written with impartiality. He has not loved the truth more than I, I dare to believe it, but I have sometimes put passion into my research, and he has put into his only his intelligence and his fine genius. Amour-propre has often led me astray by my very aversion for what is evil or seemed to me to be so: I have hated despotism as a republican and intolerance as a theist. Mr. Hume has said: here is what intolerance does and what despotism does; he has seen by all its facets the object that passion allowed me to see only on one side. He has measured, calculated the errors of men as a being who is above their weaknesses. A hundred times I have wanted, and still want, to see England either for itself, or to converse there with the one who is now its honor, and to deserve his friendship. But this project becomes less practical from day to day, if only because of the greater distance, and the long detours that would have to be made in not passing through France. For that matter, dwelling in England is very costly, and if I do not draw my resources from it, I will need more there than elsewhere. Whatever Mr. Hume might say, I do not believe that at my age and in my condition, he would seriously advise me to go seek my fortune at the court of London, he who refused it when it sought him out. Habit has so much attached me to dwelling in the country that I die of sadness as soon as I cease seeing meadows, bushes, trees. That is not a good disposition for going to breathe in the black vapors of the streets of that large city, in which it is not even certain that my last work and the note about the "good natured people" does not erase the effect of *Heloise* which could have made me hope for a favorable welcome there.[1] It is better, I agree, to depend on a government rather than a man when one has the freedom to choose. But when one does not want to give anything to fortune one must begin by taking the present away from it, and it has all the holds on me that it can have on a man accustomed to defying it from my youth, and will have them until my death. As for the general edition of my writings to be produced in London, that is a very good idea, above all if this project can be executed with me absent. Nevertheless, the expenses of printing are so great in England, that this cannot fail to make the execution of this project more difficult, and the profit much less great.

Being less far away, the chateau of Schleyden would be more within my reach, and the advantage of living cheaply that I do not have here would be a great reason for preference. I do not know M. and Mme. de la Marck well enough, however, to know if it suits me to have this obligation to them; it is up to you, madam, and to Madame la maréchale to make me decide on that point. Regarding the situation, I do not know any dwelling with greenery that is sad and ugly; but if there is nothing there but sand or totally naked rocks, let us not speak of it. As to the rest, so long as my feet can drag me, I will not be led anywhere by compulsion, and when they will no longer drag me, I prefer to stay on the spot.

---

1. "Good natured people" is in English in the original. Rousseau's note is in *Emile, CW* 13:297.

As for the third asylum about which you speak, madam, I am very grateful for that offer, but very determined not to take advantage of it. We will have time to deliberate again about the others; for I am not now in a condition to travel, and although the winters might be long and severe here, I am forced to pass this one here at all risks, since I cannot suppose that the king of Prussia, whose response has not yet come, will refuse me the asylum that he has often granted to people who hardly deserved it.

There, madam, as for the present, is what I can tell you about the efforts relative to me with which you are willing to occupy yourself. Be persuaded that my fate depends less on the effect of these efforts themselves than on the interest that inspires you with them. Your kindness in thinking of Mlle. Levasseur authorizes her to assure you of her profound respect. There is not a day when she does not move me to tears by speaking to me about you and your kindnesses. Madam, I would bless a misfortune that has taught me so well to know you, if it had not taken me so far from you at the same time.

Chapter 84

Frédéric-Guillaume de Montmollin

August 24, 1762
Môtiers

Before I approach the Holy Table, the respect that I bear for you, and my duty, as your parishioner, oblige me, to make to you a declaration of my sentiments in the matter of faith which has become necessary from the strange prejudice taken against one of my writings, based on a calumnious indictment whose detestable principles are not noticed.

It is regrettable that on this occasion the ministers of the Gospel make themselves the avengers of the Roman Church, whose intolerant and bloodthirsty dogmas alone are attacked and destroyed in my book, thereby following a suspect authority without examination, for lack of having wanted to listen to me, or for lack of even having read me. Since, sir, you are not in that case, I expect a more equitable judgment from you. However this may be, the work carries all its clarifications in itself and, since I could explain it only by itself, I abandon it, such as it is, to the blame or approval of the wise, wanting neither to defend nor to disavow it.

Limiting myself, then, to what concerns my person, I declare respectfully to you, sir, that, since my reunion with the Church in which I was born,[1] I have always made of the reformed Christian religion a profession, all the less suspect since in the country where I lived, I was required only to keep silent and to leave some doubt in that respect, in order to enjoy the civil advantages from which I was excluded by my religion. I am attached to that genuine and holy religion in good faith, and I will be so until my last breath. I want to be always united to the Church outwardly, as I am at the bottom of my heart and, however consoling it might be for me to participate in the communion of the faithful, I want it, I protest to you, as much for their edification and for the honor of the worship as for my own advantage. For it is not good that one think that a man of good faith who reasons cannot be a member of Jesus Christ.

I shall go, sir, to receive a verbal response from you, and to consult with you over the way I ought to conduct myself on this occasion to give neither surprise to the pastor whom I honor, nor scandal to the flock that I would like to edify.

Accept, sir, I beg you the assurances of all my respect.

JJRousseau

---

1. Rousseau had converted to Catholicism but returned officially to Protestantism when he reacquired his Genevan citizenship in 1754.

CHAPTER 85

Marie-Madeleine, marquise de Verdelin

September 4, 1762
Môtiers-Travers

Before giving myself over, madam, to the pleasure of writing to you, it was necessary to find an asylum to be able to breathe, and that was not easy. Pursued by Master Voltaire, by his worthy friend the mountebank Tronchin, and by their numerous clique in Paris and Geneva, I have been successively proscribed from my fatherland, from the canton of Bern, and I was even to be so from this State, if the Lord Marshal's protection and the King of Prussia's orders had not repressed, at least for some time, the rage of the Voltaireans, violent defenders and avengers of the cause of God against my irreligion. But even though they are working strongly at the court of Berlin, and sparing nothing to circumvent the prince, I have grounds for hoping that he will at least let me pass the winter in this village before prohibiting fire and water to me. In the meantime, they are not losing a moment and forget nothing to finish crushing me, as if I were worth all the pains they give themselves. They cause action to be taken in all States, they make everyone write, above all to my friends, and overwhelm me with anonymous letters to turn me against them. They have taken over all the gazettes, all the newspapers, even those of England, and do not allow in them anything relative to me that does not cooperate with their [goal]. Innocence and truth no longer have any voice to make themselves heard. No man in Europe dares to take up my defense, and were I vile enough to want to take it up myself, I would not be allowed to speak. Such is, madam, the terrible effect of that indictment drawn up at leisure by two exiled priests who edit the ecclesiastical gazette at Montmorency and who reside with M. d'Alembert in Paris. The moment appeared favorable; it was seized. All the parties together swooped down on me. I do not know how all this will end, but I would never have believed that a poor invalid without asylum and without bread could be the object of such a terrible conjuration. Be that as it may, let them dispose of the time I have left to live; they will not keep me from dying in peace.

The pleasure I had in seeing Mlle. Levasseur again was increased by everything that she has told me about you and your kindnesses. You give me, madam, you and a very small but very precious number of friends, the only pleasure that remains to me in this life, that of still having hearts to love. I am keenly touched by the asylum that you have given to my venerable duenna.[1] The poor old thing passed peaceful days with me; she will not end them less peacefully with you; she will be happier than her host. I beg you above all that she always has her freedom and that no dog worries her, for she is gentle, fearful, and very easily frightened.

Oblivion among men, peace, precious rest, where are you? Ah, if I could at least find you in these mountains, I would not leave them in my life. I am attempting to lose every memory of the past in them. I have adopted the long outfit, and I make laces: behold me more than half woman. Why was I not always so! Madam, I have tried not to dishonor my sex; I hope not to be rejected by yours. A thousand salutations to Monsieur le marquis. Good day, madam, be assured that my pure and tender attachment for you will end only with me. I do not know if I will be able to write to you often, but I am beginning to feel keenly the approach of winter, very harsh in this country for as poor a machine as mine.

When one wants to write to me, letters ought to be addressed to me at Môtiers-Travers by Pontarlier, and the postage paid to Pontarlier, without which they do not pass.

---

1. Rousseau's cat.

CHAPTER 86

Caspar Hess

October 12, 1762
Môtiers

You made me pass, sir, a pleasant day during your passage through Môtiers, and by means of the testimony of your memory and of your friendship you give me a new pleasure to which I am no less sensitive. I congratulate myself for having in Zurich two friends such as you and M. Usteri, who attract to me the esteem and kindness of so many men of merit with whom your city is full. Be persuaded that if the rigor of winter, which I am beginning to feel, leaves my poor rickety machine in a condition to make that pleasant trip next summer, it is impossible that I could find among you purer and more lively pleasures than the ones I promise myself there.

I read with gratitude and, I can say, with surprise, Mlle. Bondeli's letters, the copies of which you sent me, and which M. Usteri also sent me along with the dissertation on the moral sense. I say "with surprise," because she joins what is found rarely anywhere and which I would not have looked for in Bern: solidity and coloring, precision and agreeableness, the reason of a man and the intelligence of a woman, Voltaire's pen and Leibniz's head. She refutes my censors as a philosopher and scoffs at them as a woman who follows fashion. Her critique is as well reasoned as her bons mots are salient. The way she defends *Heloise* makes me almost love its defects and, based on the only one that she has noticed, I am very lucky that she was willing not to find any others. Regarding the writing on moral sense, I did not understand it well everywhere, and I believe that is my fault. Be that as it may, I will always be honored to have such an advocate and I would be very sorry not to be attacked, as long as I will be defended by her.

I beg you, sir, to make all my respect acceptable to Madame your worthy spouse, as well as that of Mlle. Levasseur, who thanks you both very humbly for the honor of your remembrance. I salute you, sir, with all my heart.

JJRousseau

CHAPTER 87

Comtesse de Boufflers

October 31, 1762

In announcing, madam, in your letter of 22 September (it is I believe the 22 October) an advantageous change in my fate, you at first made me believe that the men who persecute me had grown weary of their wicked deeds; that the Parlement of Paris had lifted its iniquitous edict, that the magistracy of Geneva had acknowledged its wrong, and that the public was finally doing me justice. But far from that, I see from your letter itself that new accusations are being instituted against me. The change of fate that you announce is reduced to offers of subsistence that I do not need at present. And since, even when healthy, I have always counted for nothing a future as uncertain as human life, for me, I swear to you, it is the most indifferent thing to have the wherewithal to dine on three years from now.

I am very far, nevertheless, from being insensitive to the king of Prussia's kindnesses. On the contrary, they augment a very sweet sentiment, namely the attachment that I have conceived for this great prince. They flatter my amour-propre and would flatter it far more if he had not sometimes lavished them with more generosity than selectivity. As for the use I must make of them, there is no rush to decide, and I have time to think about it.

As to Mr. Stanley's offers, since they are all on your behalf, madam, it is for you to be obliged to him for them. I have not heard the letter that he tells you he has written me spoken of.[1]

I come now to the final point in your letter, about which I hardly understand anything, and which surprises me to such a degree, above all after the conversations we have had on this matter, that I looked at the handwriting more than once to see whether it was really from your hand. I do not know of what you could disapprove in the letter I have written to my pastor on a necessary occasion. To listen to you along with your angel,[2] one would say that it was a question of embracing a new religion, whereas it was only a question of remaining as before within the communion of my fathers and of my country from which they were seeking to exclude me; no other angel was necessary for that than the Savoyard vicar. If he performed consecration in simplicity of conscience in such an extravagant form of worship, I do not see why J.J. Rousseau would not take communion in the same way in such a reasonable form of worship, and I see even less why, after having professed my religion up to now among the Catholics without anyone making a crime of it for me, one suddenly takes it into one's head to make it into an extremely strange one for me not to leave it in a Protestant country.

But why this affectation of writing a letter? Ah why, here is the reason. Seeing me oppressed by the Parlement of Paris, with the generosity natural to him and his party, M. de Voltaire seized this moment to have me oppressed in the same way in Geneva, and to oppose an insurmountable barrier to my return to my fatherland. One of the surest means that he employed for that was to make me looked upon as a deserter from my religion; for on that point our laws are categorical, and every citizen or bourgeois who does not profess the religion authorized by the laws, by that very thing, loses his civic right. Thus, they labored with all their strength, he and the mountebank, to provoke the ministers. They did not succeed with those of Geneva who know them, but they aroused those of the land of Vaud so much that, despite the protection and friendship of M. the bailiff of Yverdon and of several magistrates, it was necessary to leave the canton of Bern.

---

1. Hans Stanley, a member of British Parliament, had written to the countess saying that he was offering Rousseau asylum in Hampshire.

2. The countess had written, "Even if an angel had come from heaven to make the scales fall from your eyes, the very good of the religion whose truth you had discovered required that you wait for other circumstances to profess it."

The same thing was tried in this country. The municipal magistracy of Neuchâtel forbade my book, the Classis of ministers brought it before the court,[3] the Council of State was going to forbid it in the entire state, and perhaps proceed against my person. But the orders of the Lord Marshal and the declared protection of the king stopped it short; it was necessary to leave me in peace. Nevertheless, the time for communion was approaching, and that period was going to decide whether I was separated from the Protestant church or whether I was not. In that circumstance, wanting neither to expose myself to a public affront, nor tacitly to certify the desertion for which I was being reproached by not presenting myself, I decided to write to M. de Montmollin the pastor of the parish a letter that he had circulated, but of which the Voltaireans were careful to falsify many copies. I was very far from expecting from that letter the effect that it produced; I regarded it as a necessary protestation and one that would have its use in the proper time and place. What was my surprise and joy to see M. Montmollin at my home the next day, to declare to me that not only did he approve my approaching the Holy Table, but that he requested that I do so, and that he requested it by the unanimous consent of the entire consistory for the edification of his parish, whose approval and esteem I had! Afterward we had several meetings in which I frankly expanded on my sentiments to him just about as they are set out in the *Profession of the Vicar*, leaning with truth on my constant attachment to the Gospel and to Christianity, and not disguising to him either my difficulties or my doubts. He on his side, being well enough acquainted with my sentiments through my books, prudently avoided the points of doctrine that might have stopped me or compromised him. He did not even pronounce the word "retraction," did not insist on any explanation, and we separated satisfied with each other. Since then, I have the consolation of being acknowledged as a member of his Church. One must be oppressed, ill, and believe in God to feel how sweet it is to live among one's brothers.

Having to justify his behavior before his colleagues, M. de Montmollin had my letter circulate. In Geneva it had an effect that sent the Voltaireans into despair and that redoubled their rage. Crowds of Genevans rushed to Môtiers, embracing me with tears of joy, and loudly calling M. de Montmollin their benefactor and their father.[4] It is even

---

3. A classis is the governing body of a Calvinist church.

4. Two Genevan ministers who supported Rousseau had preached from Montmollin's pulpit in early October.

certain that this business would have consequences if I were at all in the mood to lend myself to them. Yet it is true that many of the ministers are discontented. There is so to speak the *Profession of Faith of the Vicar* approved on every point by one of their colleagues. They cannot stomach that: some grumble, others threaten to write, others are in fact writing, all absolutely want retractions and explanations that they will never have. What should I do at present, madam, in your opinion? Will I leave my worthy pastor in the traps into which he put himself for love of me, will I abandon him to the censure of his colleagues, will I authorize this censure by my behavior and by my writings and, giving the lie to the step that I have taken, will I leave to him all the shame and all the repentance for having lent himself to it? No, no, madam; one can call me a hypocrite as much as one likes, but I will be neither a traitor nor a coward. I will not renounce the religion of my fathers, that religion that is so reasonable, so pure, so much in conformity with the simplicity of the Gospel, to which I returned in good faith some years ago and which I have always loudly professed since then. I will not renounce it when it makes up all the consolation of my life and when it matters to the honorable man who has maintained me in it that I remain sincerely attached to it. Nor will I preserve exterior ties as dear as they are to me at the expense of the truth, or of what I take for it, and I could be excommunicated and have decrees issued against me many times before being made to say what I do not think. Moreover, I will console myself for an imputation of hypocrisy without plausibility and without proof. An author who is banished, against whom decrees are issued, or who is burned for having stated his sentiments boldly, for having given his name, for not wanting to give himself the lie. A citizen cherishing his fatherland who prefers to renounce his country rather than his frankness and to expatriate himself than to give himself the lie, is a rather novel species of hypocrite. In this condition I know of only one way to prove that one is not a hypocrite. But this expedient, to which my enemies want to reduce me, will never suit me, whatever happens: that is to be openly an impious man. For pity's sake explain to me, then, madam, what you want to say with your angel and what you find to correct in all that.

You add, madam, that I had to wait for other circumstances to profess my religion (you wanted to say to continue to profess it). Perhaps I have waited only too long out of a pride of which I would not know how to rid myself. I did not take any step so long as the ministers persecuted me. But once I was under the king's protection and they could no longer do anything to me, then I did my duty, or what I believed it to be. I am waiting for you to inform me in what I was mistaken.

I am sending you the extract from a dialogue by M. de Voltaire with a worker from this country who is in his service. I have written this dialogue from memory following M. de Montmollin's account, who reported it to me only from the worker's account, more than two months ago. Therefore, the whole might not be absolutely precise; but the principal strokes are faithful, for they struck M. de Montmollin, he retained them, and you can very well believe that I have not forgotten them. You will see that M. de Voltaire did not wait for the proceeding about which you are complaining to tax me with hypocrisy.

Conversation of M. de Voltaire with one of his workers from the county of Neuchâtel.

M. DE V.: Is it true that you are from the county of Neuchâtel?
WORKER: Yes, sir.
[M. DE V.]: Are you from Neuchâtel itself?
WORKER: No, sir, I am from the village of Buttes in the valley of
   Travers.
M. DE V.: Buttes! Is that far from Môtiers?
W.: A short league.
M. DE V.: You have in your country a certain character from this
   one who has made a lot of trouble.
W.: Who then, sir?
M. DE V.: A certain J.J.R. Do you know him?
W.: Yes, sir; I saw him one day at Buttes in the carriage of M. de
   Montmollin who was making a promenade with him.
M. DE V.: What, this lout goes in a carriage. There he was, then,
   very proud.
W.: Oh! sir, he also takes a promenade on foot. He runs like a
   skinny cat and climbs all our mountains.
M. DE V.: Someday he could very well climb on a ladder. He would
   have been hanged in Paris if he hadn't escaped. And he will be
   here if he comes.
W.: Hanged, sir, he has the air of such a good man, and my God,
   what has he done, then?
M. DE V.: He has written abominable books. He is an impious
   man, an atheist.

W.: You surprise me. He goes to church every Sunday.

V.: Ah! the hypocrite, and what do they say about him in the country? And is there anyone there who wants to see him?

W.: Everyone, sir, everyone loves him. He is sought out everywhere and they say that My Lord also gives him many caresses.

V.: That's because My Lord does not know him, or you either. Wait only two or three months and you will know the man. The people of Montmorency, where he resided, built bonfires when he escaped in order not to be hanged. He is a man without faith, without honor, without religion.

W.: Without religion: sir, but they say that you don't have much of it yourself.

M. DE. V.: Who, me, great God! And who says that?

W.: Everyone, sir.

M. DE V.: Ah! what a horrible calumny. I who studied with the Jesuits, I who spoke of God better than all the theologians!

W.: But sir, they say that you have written many bad books.

M. DE V.: They are lying. Let them show me a single one that bears my name, the way those of this bumpkin bear his, etc.

CHAPTER 88

Frederick II

November 1, 1762

Sire,

You are my protector and my benefactor, and I bear a heart made for gratitude. I want to settle accounts with you if I can.

You want to give me bread: are there none of your subjects who lack it?

Take away from in front of my eyes that sword that dazzles and wounds me. It has done its service only too well, and the scepter is abandoned. The career of kings of your stuff is great; you are still far from the end. Yet time presses, and you do not have a moment to lose to reach it. Sound your heart well, oh Frederick! Could you resolve to die without having been the greatest of men?

May I see Frederick the just and the dreaded, finally cover his States with a happy people whose father he is, and Jean-Jacques Rousseau, the enemy of kings, will go die of joy at the feet of his throne.

May Your Majesty, sire, deign to accept my zeal and my very profound respect.

JJRousseau

CHAPTER 89

Frédéric-Guillaume de Montmollin

November 14, 1762

When I reunited myself to the Church nine years ago, sir, I did not lack censors who blamed the step I took, and I do not lack them today when I stay united to it under your auspices, against the hope of so many people who would like to see me separated from it. There is nothing very surprising in that; everything that honors and consoles me displeases my enemies, and those who would like to make religion despicable are angry that a friend of the truth professes it openly. You and I know men too well to be unaware for how many human passions feigned zeal for the faith serves as a cloak, and one ought not to expect to see atheism and impiety more charitable than is hypocrisy or superstition. I hope, sir, having now the good fortune of being better known to you, that you see nothing in me that, giving the lie to the declaration that I made to you, might make the step I took suspect, nor make you regret yours. If there are people who accuse me of being a hypocrite, that is because I am not an impious man. They have come to an arrangement to accuse me of the one or the other, doubtless because they do not imagine that one can sincerely believe in God. You see that, however I behave, it is impossible for me to escape from one of the two imputations. But you also see that, if both are equally destitute of proofs, that of hypocrisy is nevertheless the most inept, because a little hypocrisy would have saved me from many disfavors, and my good faith costs me dearly enough, it seems to me, that it should be above all suspicion.

When we had, sir, conversations about my work, I told you with what intentions it was published, and I repeat the same thing to you in sincerity of heart. These intentions encompass nothing but what is praiseworthy; you agreed to this yourself, and when you inform me that they attribute to me that of having wanted to cast ridicule upon Christianity you feel at the same time how ridiculous this imputation is itself, since it bears solely on a dialogue in a language blamed on both sides in the work itself, and where one certainly finds nothing applicable to the true Christian. Why do the reformed thus take up the cause of the Roman Church, why are they becoming so heated when one records the vices of its argumentation that have not been theirs up to now? Do they want then to draw near, little by little, to its ways of thinking, as they are already drawing near to its intolerance, against the fundamental principles of their own communion?

I am very persuaded, sir, that if I had always lived in a Protestant country, then either the profession of the Savoyard vicar would not have been written, which certainly would have been an evil in many respects; or to all appearances, in its second part it would have had an extremely different turn from the one it has. I do not think, nevertheless, that it would be so necessary to suppress objections that one cannot resolve, for that stealthy cleverness has an air of bad faith that revolts me and makes me fear that there are at bottom few true believers. All human knowledge has its obscurities, its difficulties, its objections that the too limited human mind cannot resolve. Geometry itself has some, that the geometers do not take it into their heads to suppress, and which do not for all that render their science uncertain. Objections do not prevent a demonstrated truth from being demonstrated, and one must know how to keep oneself to what one knows, and not to want to know everything, even in the matter of religion. We will not serve God any less wholeheartedly by it, we will not be any less true believers, and we will be more humane, more gentle, more tolerant for those who do not think as we do, in everything. Considering the *Profession of Faith of the Savoyard Vicar* in this sense, it can have its utility even in what has been most blamed in it. In any case one had only to resolve the objections as suitably, as decently as they were proposed, without getting angry as if one were wrong, and without believing that an objection is sufficiently resolved when one has burned the paper that contains it.

I will not go on about the quibbles without number and without foundation that have been raised with me, and that are raised with me every day. I know how to bear in others manners of thinking that are not my own, provided that we are all united in J.-C.; that is the essential thing. I want only to renew to you, sir, the declaration of the firm and sincere resolve in which I am, of living and dying within the communion of the Christian Reformed Church. Nothing has consoled me more in my disfavors than to make its sincere profession to you, to find my pastor in you, and my brothers in your parishioners; I ask you and them for the continuation of these same kindnesses. And since I do not fear that my behavior might cause you to change your sentiment on my account, I hope that the wicked acts of my enemies will not do so either.

CHAPTER 90

Paul-Claude Moultou

February 17, 1763

I hastened to burn your letter of the 4th as you desired. I will do more, I will try to forget it. I do not know what has happened to you, but you have changed your language very much. Six months ago you were indignant with M. de Voltaire for assuming me to be capable of one quarter of the base actions that you are now advising me to do. Your counsels might be good, but they are not suitable. I know well that after having flogged children, very often wrongly, one still makes them ask for forgiveness. But in addition to the fact that this practice has always appeared extravagant to me, it does not go with my gray beard. It is not up to the offended one to ask forgiveness for the insults he has received: I am sticking to that. I must forgive, and that is what I am doing wholeheartedly even without being asked. But it appears peculiar to me that you imagined it possible for me to go at my age to solicit, like a schoolboy, certificates from the consistory. Your ministers and I are far from agreeing. Based on my letter to M. de Montmollin they believed they had found favorable occasion to have me crawl beneath them. They will have all the time for disabusing themselves. Since they have deprived themselves of my esteem, they will put up, if they please, with my disdain. I gave them public testimonies of that esteem, I was wrong; and that is the only wrong for which it remains for me to make amends.

My dear, I am tolerant out of principle in my religion, for I am a Christian; I tolerate everything, except intolerance; but every inquisition is odious to me. I look upon all inquisitors as so many satellites of the devil. For that reason I would no more want to live in Geneva than in Goa.[1] Only atheists can live in peace in those countries, because all professions of faith cost nothing to anyone who has none in his heart, and however little I am attached to life, I am not curious to go seeking Servet's fate.[2] Farewell, then, Gentlemen burners, Rousseau is not your man. Since you do not want him because he is tolerant, he does not want you for the opposite reason.

I believe, dear Moultou, that if we had seen each other and talked things over, we would have spared ourselves many misunderstandings in our letters. You cannot put yourself in my place, nor see things from my point of view. Geneva always remains under your eyes and distances itself from mine more every day. I have made my decision.

I am afraid that my condition, which is ceaselessly worsening, prevents me from executing our project. In that case it will be necessary for you to come to see me, and in any event, it would always be a preliminary that would give me great pleasure. Farewell.

I approve very strongly that you are not considering publishing what you have written. All that would no longer be of any use, and you would only be compromising yourself.

---

1. The seat of the Inquisition in the East Indies.
2. Michel Servet (1509–53) was burned alive in Geneva.

CHAPTER 91

David Hume

February 19, 1763
Môtiers-Travers

I received only here, sir, and a short time ago, the letter with which you honor me from London last July 2, supposing that I had arrived in that capital. Without a doubt I would have sought my retreat in your nation and as close to you as possible, had I foreseen the welcome that was waiting for me in my fatherland. It was the only place I could prefer to England, and that predisposition, for which I have been only too punished, was very forgivable in me at the time. I have found only affronts and insults where I was hoping for consolations and even gratitude. How many things have made me regret the asylum and philosophic hospitality that was waiting for me with you! Nevertheless, even my misfortunes have brought me near them in a way. The protection and the kindnesses of your illustrious and worthy compatriot, the Lord Marshal, have made me find, so to speak, Scotland in the middle of Switzerland. He has put you among us by his conversations; he made me acquire knowledge of your virtues which I had previously had only of your talents; he inspired me with the tenderest friendship for you and the most ardent desire to cultivate it, even before I knew you were disposed to honor me with yours. No, sir, I was giving you only half of what is due to you when I had only admiration for you. Your great vision, your astonishing impartiality, your genius would raise you too much above men, if your good heart did not draw you near them. By teaching me to see you as even more lovable than sublime, the Lord Marshal makes relations with you more desirable to me every day, and nourishes in me the eagerness he caused to be born in me to end my days near you. Sir, if only better health, if only a more convenient situation put me within reach of making the voyage as I would like to! If only I could hope to see us gathered one day near My Lord in your common fatherland, which would become mine! In such a charming society I would bless the misfortunes by which I was led there, and I would believe that I had begun to live only on the day that it began! May that happy day, more desired than hoped for, arrive! With what transports of joy would I cry out upon touching the happy land in which David Hume and the Marshal of Scotland were born!

> *Salve fatis mihi debita tellus!*
> *Hic domus, haec patria est.*[1]

---

1. Virgil, *Aeneid*, 7.120, 122: "Hail, land promised by the fates, Here is our home, here is our fatherland."

CHAPTER 92

Jacques-François Deluc

February 26, 1763
Môtiers

I do not, my dear friend, have any declaration to make to M. the first syndic, because they began by judging me without reading me or listening to me, and because a declaration after the fact could not undo what had been done. There, however, is where it would be necessary to begin to restore things to the case of the declaration you are asking for.

I cannot say that I am sorry for having written what it is not true that I am sorry for having written, since on the contrary if what I have written and published were to be written and published, I would write it today and publish it tomorrow.

I could say, at the very most, that I am sorry that they could draw from my writings pretexts for persecuting me; but this phrase "animadversion of the Council" will never suit me. "Iniquity and violation of the laws" is necessary; I do not know how to name things except by their name.

I neither can nor want to say anything nor do anything in any manner whatsoever that has the air of reparation or excuse, because it is infamous and ridiculous for it to be up to the offended party to give satisfaction to the offender.

The clarifications that you propose to me are good and well turned. I could have given them if they had not wanted to constrain me to do so. But I am tired of playing the child, and indignant at seeing Genevans play at being inquisitors so stupidly. The necessary clarifications are all in my writings and in my behavior: I have no other to give.

Your Genevans, you say, ask themselves, "What will Rousseau do?" I find that those who say, "He will do nothing," speak very sensibly, because in fact he has nothing to do. As for those who say, "He will make himself known," I do not know what they expect, but I know very well that if that has not been done, it never will be. I too asked myself, "What will the Genevans do?" I answered, "They will make themselves known"; that is also what they have done.

I am surprised that my friend Deluc can advise me to commit base actions in Bern that I do not want to commit in Geneva. I swear to you that the proceedings of the Bernese hardly affect me; it is those of the Genevans that have saddened me. If they want to be the last to repair their wrongs, I dispense them from doing so.

I am in no condition to go to Geneva. I do not have the slightest desire to do so, and if I ever do go (which, given the fate that awaits me there, is to be desired neither for my repose, nor for my safety, nor for the Genevans' honor), it will certainly not be as a suppliant.

I was a citizen so long as I believed I had a fatherland. I was deceiving myself. I have been disabused. The insult done to me is shared, as you say extremely well, with the laws and religion. The affronts one shares with them are triumphs. Nevertheless, the members of the State remain calm spectators in this business, as if it did not concern them. So be it. As for me, I declare to you that henceforth it concerns me even less. If I stubbornly played the Don Quixote by myself, what up to now has been the zeal of a patriot would become the obstinacy of a madman. No one knows better than the Genevans whether I am good for anything for them. As for me, I know by experience that they are not good for anything for me.

Here are your books, dear friend. I forced myself to read them, but I admit to you that your Ditton overwhelms my poor head;[1] he drowns me in a sea of words from which I cannot extricate myself. All I seem to glimpse is that he is holding in the air a fat club that he waves about

---

1. Humphrey Ditton, *Discourse concerning the Resurrection of Jesus Christ.*

in a terrible and threatening manner; and when he happens to strike, which he rarely does, and for cause, one feels that the club is only made of cotton. Good day, good man, I embrace you and, Genevan or not, I will always be your friend.

JJRousseau

Chrétien-Guillaume de Lamoignon de Malesherbes

March 6, 1763
Môtiers

I have had, sir, the imprudence of reading the *Pastoral Letter* that M. the archbishop of Paris wrote against my book, the weakness of responding to it, and the stupidity of sending this response right away to Rey. Having returned to myself, I wanted to withdraw it. It was too late; the printing had begun, and there is no longer a remedy for a silly act. I hope at least that this will be the last in this genre. I take the liberty of having two copies of this wretched writing addressed to you by post; one that I beg you to accept, and the other for M. Duclos to whom I ask you please to be willing to pass it on, not as reading for either him or you to do, but as a duty of which I acquit myself toward both of you. Moreover, I am persuaded, given my particular position, given the constraint by which I was enslaved in so many respects, given the ecclesiastical chatter to which I was forced to conform, given how indecent it would be to get heated while speaking about oneself, that it would have been easy for others to do better, but impossible to do well. Thus all the harm comes from having taken up the pen when I should not have.

Receive sir, the assurances of all my respect.

JJRousseau

CHAPTER 94

Lord Marshal Keith

March 21, 1763

In your letter of the 19th there is an item that gave me palpitations; it is the one about Scotland. I will say only one word to you on that point; it is that I would give half the days that I have left to pass the other [half] there with you. But as for Colombier, do not count on me. I love you, My Lord, but my residence must please me, and I cannot abide that country. You ought to know from experience that one is no more sheltered from fools and haranguers at the Chateau of Colombier than at that of Neuchâtel.

There is nothing equal to Frederick's position. It seems that he feels all its advantages and that he will know well how to turn them to account. Everything hard and difficult is done, everything that required the cooperation of fortune is done. At present nothing remains for him to do but to fulfill cares that are agreeable, and whose effect depends on him. It is from this moment that he is going to erect, if he wants, a unique monument to himself in posterity, for up to now he has labored only for his century. Henceforth, the only dangerous trap that remains for him to avoid is that of flattery. If he allows himself to be praised, he is lost. Let him know that there are no longer any accolades worthy of him than those that will come out of the huts of his peasants.[1] More-over, he still has one stain to erase, and he can cover it with a monument of glory. He will guess what it is, and he will do well; for no one will tell it to him.

Do you know, My Lord, that Voltaire is seeking to reconcile with me. He had a long discussion with Moultou about me in which he played his role in a superior manner. There is nothing alien to the talent of this great comedian, *dolis instructus et arte Pelasga.*[2] As for me, I cannot promise him an esteem that does not depend on me; but aside from that, I will be, if he wants, always ready to forget everything. For I swear to you, My Lord, that of all the Christian virtues there is none that costs me less than forgiveness of injuries. It is certain that if the protection of Calas did him great honor, the persecution that he caused me to endure in Geneva did him little honor in Paris; they have stirred up a universal cry of indignation there. Despite my misfortunes, I enjoy there an honor of which he will never have any part; that is to have left my memory esteemed in the country where I lived. Good day, My Lord.

---

1. Frederick had just abolished serfdom on royal lands.

2. "Instructed in Pelagian art" (Virgil, *Aeneid* 2.152). This refers to Sinon, who persuades the Trojans to accept the horse.

CHAPTER 95

Paul-Claude Moultou

April 30, 1763

If it is true, dear friend, that my *Letter* has succeeded as you say it has, you have seen better than I have. The future will teach us which of the two of us is mistaken. Meanwhile, I am ready to give you a mark of confidence by accompanying you to Geneva if you want and if I am able. Be very sure that no one but you would have obtained this mark. I can remain there for you for 24 hours, as much, if necessary, for the fellow Deluc. Beyond that, do not speak to me about it anymore; only force could hold me there longer. They have let me make my decision, and it is made.[1]

I see that you have distributed a large number of copies. I have done as much in this country, and they were received with unprecedented arrogance. I can assure you that these are so many very ardent satellites of the archbishop of Paris, and they are in despair that France is not picking a fight with me all the way into their country. Without fear of the king of Prussia, they would not balk at disposing of me. To cap the misery, I am losing My Lord Maréchal, and I remain here without

---

1. Rousseau decided to renounce his citizenship.

support and, what is worse, without a friend, among the people who love virtue the least of any on earth. I beg you to notify me when I will see you; I console myself in advance, in the hope of consoling myself with you. But to come back to our copies, you have bought yours; that is an item to add to the open account that I must settle with you upon your arrival here. Nevertheless, I do not see why, when a work is public, you and I should become the suppliers for those who do not want to take the trouble of buying it. Send it, nevertheless, to the advocate-general Fleury, if that is what you want, but you can be sure that he is not asking for it for any good use. He is a fool who believes himself extremely eloquent and who, so as to put some phrases in an indictment, would with pleasure issue a decree against, hang, and burn the whole universe. I find very thoughtless this remark of M. Quesnel. "M. J.J. seems to me to be going back toward being a little bit Christian?" Where did he find that I was less of one?

This is the third and last time that I have given my profession of faith in my writings, and this last is certainly the one in which I have spoken most openly and with the most boldness. I have said much more in it than in the *Profession of Faith of the Vicar*; but I have always been a Christian, I am one, and will not cease being one. If M. the abbé Quesnel does not know how to read, that is not my fault.

If M. Mallet comes, I will receive him as a man whom you love. What is more, having no secret, I have no need to be reserved. I will speak about the mountebank as a mountebank, of Geneva as a city whose inhabitants I will always love despite their insults, but where I will never reside, and of Moultou as my friend.

Your last letter was certainly opened; but I do not know whether it was in Geneva or here.

CHAPTER 96

Jacob Favre

May 12, 1763

Sir,

Having recovered from the long stupefaction into which I was thrown by the proceeding which I ought least to have expected from the Magnificent Council, I am finally making the decision that honor and reason prescribe to me, however dearly it costs my heart. I therefore declare to you, sir, and I beg you to declare on my behalf to the Magnificent Council, that I abdicate in perpetuity my right of bourgeoisie and citizenship in the City and Republic of Geneva. Having fulfilled as well as I could the duties attached to this title without enjoying any of its advantages, I do not believe I am still indebted to the State in leaving it.

I have tried to honor the Genevan name. I have tenderly loved my compatriots; I have omitted nothing to make myself loved by them. One could not succeed any worse. I want to please them even in their hatred. The final sacrifice that remains for me to make to them is that of a name that has been so dear to me.

But sir, by becoming alien to me, my fatherland cannot become indifferent. I remain attached by a tender memory, and I forget nothing about it except its insults. May it always prosper and see its glory increase. May it abound in citizens better and above all happier than I!

Receive, sir, I beg you, the assurances of my profound respect.

JJRousseau

CHAPTER 97

Antoine Audoyer

May 28, 1763

Audoyer wrote to Rousseau asking for his explanation of a passage in the Letter to Beaumont *in which he argues against attempting to introduce a new religion to a community without permission of the sovereign. Audoyer said that he could not reconcile this with the introduction of Christianity by the Apostles.*

Here, sir, is the short answer you ask from me regarding the little difficulties that torment you in my *Letter to M. de Beaumont.*

1. Christianity is only Judaism explained and fulfilled. Thus, the Apostles were not transgressing the laws of the Jews when they taught them the Gospel; but the Jews persecuted them, because they did not understand them, or because they feigned not to understand them. That is not the only time such a case has occurred.
2. In my *Letter to M. de Beaumont* I distinguished the forms of worship in which the essential religion is found, and those in which it is not found. The first are good, the others bad; I said that. One is not obliged to conform to the particular religion of the State, and is not even allowed to follow it, except when the essential religion is found in it, as it is found, for example, in the various Christian communions, in Islam, in Judaism. But in paganism, that

was something different. Since very obviously the essential religion was not found in it, it was allowed for the Apostles to preach
against paganism, even among the pagans, and even despite them.

3. Were all that not true, what would follow? Even though it is not
   allowed for members of the State to attack the laws of the country
   on their own initiative, it does not follow that this is not allowed
   to those whom God expressly orders to do so. The catechism
   teaches you that this is the case for the preaching of the Gospel.
   Speaking humanly, I stated the common duty of men, but I have
   not said that they ought not to obey when God has spoken. His
   law can dispense from obeying human laws. This is a principle of
   your faith, which I did not combat. Thus, by introducing a foreign
   religion without the permission of the sovereign, the Apostles
   were not guilty.

This short response, I think, is within your grasp, and I think it suffices. Please calm yourself therefore, sir, and remember that a simple
and ignorant good Christian, such as you assure me you are, ought to
limit himself to serving God in the simplicity of his heart, without worrying himself so much over someone else's sentiments.

JJR

CHAPTER 98

Jacques-François Deluc

July 7, 1763

I fear, my dear friend, that your patriotic zeal might go a little too far on this occasion, and that your love of the laws might expose the most important of all, which is the safety of the State, to some attack. I learn that you and your worthy fellow citizens are contemplating new remonstrances, and the certainty of their uselessness makes me fear that in the end they might compromise the bourgeoisie or the magistrates vis-à-vis one another. In this business I do not claim to give myself an importance which, moreover, I would come by only because of my misfortunes. I know that you have grievances to redress that, although relative to simple private individuals, wound public freedom. But whether I consider this step in relation to myself, or in relation to the body of the bourgeoisie, I find it equally useless and dangerous, and I even add that the solidity of your reasons will turn entirely to your common prejudice, in that, having reduced the sophisms of the response to powder, you will put the Council in the position of being able to reply by means of a dry *case dismissed*, and consequently to return by your fault into possession of its so-called negative right,[1] which would reduce to nothing the one you have of making remonstrances. If, after that, you persist in pursuing the redress of grievances, which you very certainly will not obtain, there is nothing left for you but a single legitimate route whose effect is no less certain, and which, by attacking your sovereignty, would be an ill much worse than the one you want to repair.

I know that an intriguing and sly family,[2] basing itself on a great external reputation, is sapping with redoubled blows the foundations of the Republic, and that the members of that family, skillful mountebanks and two-faced persons, are leading the people through hypocrisy and the great through irreligion. But you and your fellow citizens ought to consider that you yourselves installed it; that it is too late to attempt to pull it down; and that, even supposing a success that is not to be presumed, you could harm yourselves even more than it, and destroy yourselves while humbling it. Believe me, my friends, let it go, it is touching its limit, and I predict that its own ambition will ruin it without the bourgeoisie meddling in it. Thus, in relation to the Republic, what you want to do is useless at this moment; success is impossible or would be fatal; and with time, everything will go back to its natural course.

Relative to me, you know the way I think, and M. d'Ivernois, to whom I opened my heart when he passed through here, will tell you, as I have written to you and to all my friends, that far from desiring remonstrances in these circumstances, I would have wished that they would not have been made, and desire even more that they have no sequel. It is certain, as I wrote to M. Chappuis, that before my letter to M. Favre, remonstrances from some members of the bourgeoisie, sufficient to signify that it disapproved of the procedure and therefore protecting my honor, might have prevented a step that I took only by force, with sadness, and when I could no longer dispense myself from it without consenting to my dishonor. But once taken and my decision made, this step leaving me with nothing but a tender remembrance of my former compatriots and a sincere desire to see them living in peace, every subsequent step, relative to that one, appeared to be out of place, useless, and I neither desired nor approved it. I admit that your

---

1. The opponents of the remonstrators argued that the Small Council had the right to refuse to hear remonstrances, a position against which Rousseau was to argue at length in the *Letters Written from the Mountain.*

2. The Tronchins.

remonstrances honored me by showing that the procedure against me was contrary to the laws and disapproved by the healthiest part of the State. According to this point of view, although I did not acquiesce in these remonstrances, I cannot mind them. Everything further that you will do at present, however, is suited only to destroying the good effect and to making my enemies and yours triumph, as they shout that you are doing to revenge me what you are only doing for the maintenance of the laws.

I implore you then, my virtuous friend, by your love for the fatherland and for peace, to let this business drop, or even openly to abandon its pursuit—at least in what concerns me—so that your example might bring along those who honor you with their confidence, and so that the grievances of a private individual who is no longer anything in the State not disturb its repose. Do not be pained by the judgment people will make about this retreat, or about the harm that liberty could suffer from it. The Council's answer, although phrased with all imaginable skill, offers its flank on so many sides and gives you such great holds, that there is no man who is a little in the know who will not sense the motive of your silence, and who will not judge that you are silent because you have too much to say. As for the legion of laws, since it will become all the greater the more keenly their restoration is sought without obtaining it, it is better to close one's eyes when the mantle of hypocrisy covers over the assaults against freedom, than to furnish the usurpers with the means to consummate the work of their tyranny in the name of God.

As for me, my dear friend, however disposed I was to lend myself to everything that could please my former fellow citizens without wounding my honor, and joyfully to take back a title that was so dear to me—if it had been restored to me willingly, of a common accord, and in a manner that could have made it acceptable to me—the steps you took on that occasion, and the ills that can result from it, force me to change my resolution on this point and to make one from which nothing will make me depart, whatever happens. I declare to you, then, and I have taken an oath on it, that I will not set foot within your walls again in my life and that, satisfied with nourishing in my heart the sentiments of a true citizen of Geneva, I will never take back the title of one. Thus, every step that could tend to return it to me is useless and vain. After having sacrificed my dearest rights to honor, I sacrifice my sweetest hope to peace. Nothing remains for me to do. Farewell.

JJRousseau

CHAPTER 99

Leonhard Usteri

July 18, 1763
Môtiers

You ought, my dear friend, to hold me accountable for the visit that I did not make you. For last month I left, not with M. Moultou, too bad a walker for that, but with M. de Sauttern,[1] for this desired pilgrimage. But the vexation of bad weather, which kept us in a tavern for several days, my weakness, and the length of the trip, made me renounce carrying on with it, whatever desire I might have had to, and we retraced our steps after an absence of ten days, which did not take us any farther than Estavayer. I do not despair of being luckier another time, but my traveling companion has left, and I admit to you that in my condition I do not have the courage to undertake alone a journey of forty leagues going, and as much coming back.

As exasperated as I may be by disputes and objections, and however reluctant I may be to use the precious relations of friendship in these petty wars, I continue to respond to your difficulties, since you so require it. I will tell you, then, with my ordinary frankness, that you do

---

1. Rousseau is referring to Ignace Sauttersheim (1738-67). On Rousseau's relations with him, see *Confessions, CW* 5:515–17.

not appear to me to have thoroughly grasped the state of the question. The great society, human society in general, is founded upon humanity, upon universal beneficence; I say, and I have always said, that Christianity is favorable to that.

But particular societies, political and civil societies, have a completely different principle. These are purely human establishments from which, consequently, true Christianity detaches us, as from everything that is only terrestrial. Only men's vices make these establishments necessary, and only human passions preserve them. Take all the vices away from your Christians; they will no longer need magistrates or laws. Take away from them all human passions, the civil bond instantly loses its entire force; no more emulation, no more glory, no more ardor for preferences; particular interest is destroyed, and for lack of a suitable support, the political State falls into languor.

Your assumption of a political and vigorous society of Christians, all perfect in the strictest sense, is then contradictory. It is even exaggerated, if you do not want to admit into it a single unjust man, not a single usurper. Will it be more perfect than that of the apostles? And, nevertheless, a Judas was found there. Will it be more perfect than that of the angels? And the devil, they say, came from it. My dear friend, you are forgetting that your Christians will be men, and that the perfection that I am assuming in them is the one which humanity can abide. My book is not made for gods.

That is not all. You give your citizens an exquisitely subtle moral tact, and why? Because they are good Christians. What! In your account no one can be a good Christian without being a La Rochefoucauld or a La Bruyère? What was our Master thinking about then, when he blessed the poor in spirit? That assertion, first, is not reasonable, since subtlety of moral tact is acquired only by dint of comparisons, and is even exercised infinitely better upon vices, which one hides, than on virtues, which one does not hide. In the second place, this same assertion is contrary to all experience. One constantly sees that it is in the largest cities, among the most corrupt peoples, that one learns to penetrate hearts, to observe men better, to interpret their speeches better by means of their sentiments, better to distinguish reality from appearance. Will you deny that there are infinitely better moral observers in Paris than in Switzerland, or will you conclude from this that they live more virtuously in Paris than in your home?

You say that your citizens would be infinitely shocked by the first injustice. I believe so. When they would see it, however, it would no longer be time to provide for it, and even less so since they would not easily allow themselves to think ill of their neighbor, nor to give a bad interpretation to what could have a good one; that would be too contrary to charity. You are not unaware that skillful ambitious people are very careful not to begin with injustices. On the contrary, they spare nothing at first to win over public confidence and esteem by the exterior practice of virtue. They throw off the mask and strike great blows only when their party is well bound together, and it is impossible to go back. Cromwell was known to be a tyrant only after having passed fifteen years as the avenger of the laws and the defender of religion.

To preserve your Christian Republic, you make its neighbors as just as it is. Very well. I agree that it will always defend itself well enough, provided it is not attacked. As to the courage that you give its soldiers by means of the simple love of self-preservation, no one lacks that. I have given it an even more powerful motive for Christians, namely love of duty. On that point, I believe I can send you back, as my sole response, to my book, where this point is well discussed. How can you not see that only great passions do great things, and that anyone who has no other passion than that of his salvation will never do anything great in the temporal realm? If Mucius Scaevola had only been a saint, do you believe that he would have caused the siege of Rome to be lifted? Perhaps you will cite the magnanimous Judith to me: but I believe that our less barbarously coquettish hypothetical Christians will not go to seduce their enemies, and then sleep with them so as to massacre them in their sleep.[2]

My dear friend, I do not aspire to convince you. I know that no two heads are organized the same way, and that after many disputes, many objections, many clarifications, each always ends up remaining within his sentiment as before. Once again, I am answering you because you want it; but I will not love you any less for not thinking as I do. I have stated my opinion to the public, and I believed that I ought to do so in important things that concern humanity. What is more, I can always have been mistaken, and doubtless I was often mistaken. I have stated my reasons. It is up to the public, it is up to you to weigh them, to judge them, to choose. As for me, I know nothing more about it, and I find it

---

2. After being captured by the Etruscans, Scaevola thrust his hand into a fire to show his contempt for bodily suffering. He was released and the Etruscans offered favorable terms for peace to the Romans. The widow Judith beheaded the Assyrian Holofernes.

very good for those who have other sentiments to keep them, provided that they leave me in peace with mine.

M. L. M. D. A. whose name you ask me for is the late M. the marquis d'Argenson, who had been minister of foreign affairs, and who, although a minister, did not fail to be an honorable and well-intentioned man.[3]

Congratulate M. and Madame Hess on my behalf;[4] the line of such a worthy couple could be multiplied neither too early nor too much. The pleasure of seeing them again was not forgotten in the visit that I wanted to pay you. I would also have had that of making the acquaintance of M. Gessner and chatting a little with him about the obliging proposition that you made me on his behalf.[5] When will the happy time come, when I will be able to embrace you, and see myself in the midst of your worthy compatriots? In the meantime, I am and will be entirely yours until my last breath.

JJRousseau

---

3. See *Social Contract, CW* 4:132.

4. They had just had a son.

5. The proposal was to have Rousseau's collected writings published in Zurich.

CHAPTER 100

Paul-Claude Moultou

August 1, 1763

I thank you, my dear Moultou, for M. Vernes's book which you sent to me.[1] My condition does not allow me to read it, still less to respond to it; and if I could, I would assuredly not do so. I never respond to any but to those by people I esteem.

I am persuaded that M. Vernes forgives me least for having attacked Helvetius's book, although I did it with all imaginable decency, in passing, and without naming or even referring to him, except in rendering honor to his good character. On M. Vernes's pages 71 and 72 which fell under my eyes, he makes it a great crime for me to have used what he calls the jargon of metaphysics, and he assumes that I needed this jargon to establish natural religion, instead of which I did not need it except to attack materialism. The fundamental principle of the book *On the Mind* is that "to judge is to feel," from which it clearly follows that everything is only body. This principle, being established through metaphysical principles, could not be attacked except by similar reasonings.

---

1. *Letters on the Christianity of M. J.J. Rousseau.*

This is what M. Vernes does not forgive me. Metaphysics edifies him only in Helvetius's book; it scandalizes him in mine.

Nevertheless, I do not approve of the public seeing the item in my letter that concerns him. I even insist that you not show it to anyone; to him alone if you want. I have never had an inclination toward hatred, and I believe that in my place the man in the world most full of hatred would become much more lukewarm over vengeance. My friend, let us allow all those people to triumph at their ease. They will not close to me the fatherland of just souls where I soon hope to arrive.

I admit that at certain moments I would have great need of some consolation. Prey to sufferings without respite and without recourse, I am in the case of the exception made by Lord Edouard in responding to St.-Preux, or never was anyone in the world in it.[2] I have patience, however, but it is very cruel not to have the hand of a friend to close my eyes, me to whom this duty has cost so much, and who has rendered it so wholeheartedly. It is very cruel to leave here, far from her country, this poor girl without friends, without protection, and not even to be able to assure her of the possession of my rags as the wages for twenty years of care and attachment. She has faults, dear Moultou; but she is a beautiful soul. I am wrong to complain that I lack consolations. I find them in her; when we have deplored my misfortunes together, they are almost all forgotten. Yet their sentiment comes back and is aggravated by the continuity of the body's ills.

I wanted to write to dear Gauffecourt. Today I have neither the time nor the strength for it. Tell him, I beg you, that I regret extremely not to be able to accompany him. I desired it too much to ought to hope for it. Let him not fail to embrace for me M. de Conzié, comte des Charmettes, and to testify to him how much I was disposed to accept his invitation, but

> *me anteit saeva necessitas*
> *Clavos trabales et cuneos manu*
> *Gestans aena*[3]

Mlle. Levasseur persists in begging you to send her back her dress if you have not sold it. Good day.

---

2. This refers to the arguments about suicide in *Julie*. See *CW* 6:317–23.

3. "Cruel necessity walks in front of you, carrying in its rough hand the nails and wedges for the beams." Horace, *Odes* 1.35.

CHAPTER 101

Sidoine-Charles-François Séguier, marquis de Saint-Brisson

November 13, 1763
Môtiers

I am very glad, sir, that you have cooled off a little about your work. It will cost me less to tell you the truth that I owe you on this point because you asked me for it, and you will listen to it more peacefully.

Your *Idylls* are an imitation and you have even imitated the style. Now, there are genres in which one imitates with honor but, in the pastoral genre, when the imitator stays beneath his model, he is nothing.

You never reach yours when you philosophize, so be it. But when you depict, when you write, you see less the object you have to depict, or the thing you have to say, than the example you want to follow. You believe you are imitating, and you are copying. One feels that the author is trying hard to depict the morals of a time that is not his own. I prefer the Bible's Ruth to yours. I allow the essences, the aromas, but not the perfume of France. Oh, bah for a Ruth who perfumes herself!

Daphne is not Daphne, she is the Shulamite hopped up and tarted up; what is worse, a précieuse who utters sayings and aphorisms.

"Today when I was in those verdant prairies cut by brooks and, in some places, covered by thick foliage, the weight of the day overwhelmed me. I lay down upon a bed of grass and, closing my eyes to the light, I sought within myself the image of what I love whose features are deeply engraved there through the clouds of a light sleep . . ." Ah, let us breathe! See if you will find anything in the Song of Songs that tires the lungs out like this. See if in it you will find beds of grass, or the image of what one loves, or the clouds of a light sleep. In this long passage there is not a single word that does not betray a French author.

You think you set your pieces off against each other to advantage by contrasting them. Not at all; you only make ill-matched ones. You begin by waxing lyrical to celebrate Lydia: the brilliance of her sublime virtues, the majesty of her charms, her celestial beauty, the miracles that stir you to sing her glory by means of superhuman songs that raise themselves up to the highest heavens . . . and then suddenly the "farmworker Philemon." There is a fall that will break your neck.

Pastoral philosophy ought to be entirely in sentiments or images; yours is in reflections, in maxims; you discuss principles. Shocked yourself by Ariste's metaphysics, you believe that you mend that by means of a note; you are mistaken. A note draws attention to the fault and does not mend it.

You believe that you convey Memnon as well; you are mistaken again. Ariste wants to depict rustic life for his son Daphnis, who is as well acquainted with it as he is. It was necessary to do exactly the opposite of what you have done; that Daphnis, brought up in the city, made a description of it as a young man to his father, that the latter traces out for him in his turn the pastoral life, and that without metaphysics and without maxims, he puts his philosophy in comparison.

Your style is uneven, hardly natural, often stiff. You change it ten times on one page in accordance with the books you are thinking about. You want to be gentle and rhythmical; your anastrophes are harsh; one feels how much it would cost you to take on an easy manner. Your hits are sometimes fortunate, but you often miss. "Cruel Milo, give me back my heart, or give me back your presence!" Presence, what a word! Why not, "give me back my heart or give me back yours?" That was simpler and hit better.

I cannot continue this censure; it displeases me more than it does you. Let us conclude. In your *Idylls* there is more material than is needed for making two good works, and yet it does not make one good one. Why is that? Because your head is not ripe, your pen is not formed. You know how to create, but you do not know how to order. There is much substance in your work, but it is in a state of chaos.

I believe I see a vice in the design. You do not have enough warmth to treat so many little subjects and to make each of them interesting separately from the others. You could, I think, use the same materials more advantageously, but it is necessary to begin by consulting your taste. Here is what I advise you for now. Look for Sannazar's *Arcadia*.[1] I assume that you know Italian well enough to understand it. Read it, and indicate to me what you think, not of the foundation of the work, but of the form and of that manner of linking detached subjects. After that we will talk about it.

I am waiting to send your manuscript back to M. Duchesne for some occasion that is more convenient and as secure as the post. Moreover, it would be necessary to fold the notebooks to make them into a parcel, and that would greatly spoil them. To tell the truth, I do not believe I am rendering you a bad service by delaying a little the occasion for printing it, because I know that you can make something much better of it almost without adding anything to it. But the public will judge you based on what your work will be, and not based on what it could have become. What is more, apply yourself more to actions than to words. That is a piece of advice that I beg you to forgive from the interest I take in your happiness.

I salute you, sir, with all my heart.

---

1. *Arcadia*, by Giacomo Sannazaro (1458–1530).

CHAPTER 102

Prince Louis-Eugène de Wurtemberg

December 15, 1763

You have drawn me out of a state of great uneasiness, Monsieur le duc, by informing me of the resolution you have made to bring up your child yourself. I suggested to you means whose inadequacy I felt myself. Thank heaven, your virtue renders them superfluous. If you persevere, I am no longer troubled about success. All will go well from the sole fact that you will be watching over it yourself. But I admit to you that you thoroughly confound all my ideas. I was very far from believing that there existed a man like you in this century; and had I suspected his existence, I would have been very far from seeking him in your rank. I could not read your last letter without emotion. Is it then true that I have been able to contribute to the virtuous resolutions you have made? I need to believe it to put a counterweight to my afflictions. To have done some good on earth is a consolation that my heart missed. I congratulate you for having given it to me and I honor myself for receiving it from you.

You see your child as precocious. That does not surprise me; you are a father. It is true that a father whom philosophy has preserved as one has eyes that are far from commonplace. Moreover, M. Tissot's testimony certifies yours, and then, you cite facts. Among these facts, there are some that I conceive, others not. Children distinguish very early smells as different, as faint or strong, but not as good or bad. Sensation comes from nature; preference or aversion does not come from it. This observation, which I made particularly about smell, is not applicable to the other senses. Thus, the judgment that the little one brings to bear on this point is already an acquired thing.

She has changed tone to bear witness to her desires; that must be. At first her complaints, indicating nothing but the anxiety of uneasiness, resembled crying. Now, experience teaches her that they are heard and soothed. Her complaining has thus become a language; instead of crying, she is speaking in her way.

From the fact that she sees newcomers and old acquaintances with the same pleasure, you conclude that she will have a loving character. Do not trust this observation too much. Others perhaps would draw from this a sign of coquettishness, rather than of sensitivity. As for me, I take it as a sign different from both of these, and one that does not augur badly. It is that she will have character, for the most certain sign of a weak heart is the empire that habit has upon it.

If your child really is precocious, she will give you much more trouble, but she will compensate you for it much earlier. Thus, take care nevertheless not to anticipate to the point of prematurely applying a method that will not be suitable for her. Observe, examine, verify, and do not spoil anything; when in doubt, it is always better to wait.

What is more, whatever you might do, I have the greatest confidence in your work, and I am persuaded that all will go well. When you are mistaken, which I do not assume, it would never be in a serious matter, and fathers' errors always harm less than tutors' negligence. I have only one uneasiness left, which is that you have undertaken this great task without foreseeing all of its difficulties, and that in presenting themselves from day to day, they might discourage you. At first, when one is in a fervor, nothing has a price. In the end, though, a continuous effort is overwhelming, and the best resolutions that depend on perseverance are rarely proof against time. I beg you, Monsieur le duc, to forgive my frankness; it comes from the admiration you inspire in me. Your undertaking is too fine not to experience obstacles, and it is better to prepare you for them in advance, than [that you] encounter unforeseen ones.

What you tell me about the way you want to acquire friends teaches me how much you deserve to make some. But where will be the men worthy of your being their friend?

I beg Your Supreme Highness to accept my profound respect.

Rousseau

CHAPTER 103

Abbé Alexandre-Louis Benoît de Carondelet

January 6, 1764
Môtiers
Carondelet wrote to Rousseau that he had renounced all of his possessions because of his belief in natural equality. He planned to live the rustic life of a virtuous gentleman.

What, sir, you sent back your family portraits and your titles! You have gotten rid of your seal! These are many more exploits than I would have done in your place. I would have left the portraits where they were, I would have kept my seal because I had it. I would have let my titles go moldy in their corner without even imagining that all of that was worth the trouble of sacrificing. But you are all for great actions. I congratulate you on this with all my heart.

By dint of speaking to me about your doubts, you give me some disquieting ones on your account. You make me doubt whether there is anything you do not doubt. These very doubts, to the extent that they increase, calm you. You rest on them as on a pillow of laziness! All of that would frighten me very much for you, if your great scruples did not reassure me. These scruples are certainly respectable, as founded on virtue; but upon what do you base the obligation to have virtue? It would be good to know whether you are thoroughly settled on this point. If you are, I am reassured. I do not find you as skeptical as you affect to be, and when one is thoroughly settled on the principles of one's duties, the rest is not such a great affair. But if you are not, your anxieties seem hardly reasoned to me. When one is so tranquil while in doubt about one's duties, why be so affected by the decision they impose on us?

Your delicacy about the ecclesiastical station is sublime or puerile, according to the degree of virtue you have attained. Without a doubt this delicacy is a duty for anyone who fulfills all the others. He who is neither false nor a liar about anything in the world, ought not to be so even in that. But I know only Socrates and you for whom reason could pass such a scruple. Because for us other, common men, it would be impertinent and vain to dare to have such a scruple. There is not one of us who does not diverge from the truth a hundred times a day in relations with men regarding things that are clear, important, and often prejudicial. And on a point of pure speculation in which no one sees what is true or false, and which matters neither to God nor men, we would make it into a crime to condescend to our brothers' prejudices, and to say yes where no one has the right to say no? I admit to you that a man, not a saint moreover, who would take into his head in earnest to have a scruple that the abbé de St-Pierre and Fénelon did not have, would from that alone become very suspect to me. What! I would say to myself, this man refuses to embrace the noble station of officer of morality, a station in which he can be the guide and benefactor of men, in which he can instruct them, soothe them, console them, protect them, serve them as an example; and that on account of some enigmas about which neither he nor we understand anything, and which he had only to take and to give for what they are worth, by returning Christianity to its genuine object without any commotion? No, I would conclude, this man is lying, he is deceiving us, his false virtue is not active, it is nothing but pure ostentation. One has to be a hypocrite oneself to dare to accuse of detestable hypocrisy what is at bottom only a formulary that is indifferent in itself, but consecrated by the laws. Sound your heart well, sir, I beseech you. If you find in it that reason as you give it to me, it must determine you, and I admire you. But remember well then that unless you are the worthiest of men, you will have been the maddest.

From the way you ask me for precepts of virtue, one would say that you look upon it as a profession. No, sir. Virtue is only the strength to do one's duty on difficult occasions, and wisdom, on the contrary, is to remove difficulty from our duties. Happy is he who, satisfied with being a good man, has put himself in a position of never needing to be virtuous. If you go to the country only to bring the pomp of virtue there, stay in the city. If you want to practice great virtues at all costs, the station of priest will often make them necessary for you. But if you feel that your passions are moderate enough, your spirit gentle enough, your heart healthy enough to accommodate yourself to an even, simple, and laborious life, go to your estate, turn it to account, labor yourself, be the father of your domestic servants, the friend of your neighbors, just and good toward everyone. Leave behind your metaphysical reveries and serve God in the simplicity of your heart. You will be virtuous enough.

I salute you, sir, with all my heart.

JJRousseau

Moreover, I dispense you, sir, from the secrecy you are pleased to offer me, I know not why. It does not seem to me that I have the air of a very mysterious man in my conduct.

CHAPTER 104

Julie von Bondeli

January 28, 1764

You know well, miss, that correspondents of your order always bring pleasure and are never a bother. I am not unjust enough, however, to require from you an exactitude of which I do not feel myself capable, and the stakes are so unequal between us that if you answered ten of my letters with only one of yours, you would at the very least be square with me.

I find M. Schulthess well paid for his taste for virtue by the interest he inspires in you, and if this taste degenerates into a passion near you, this could very well be somewhat the teacher's fault. However that may be, I wish him too much good to take him away from under your direction by taking him under my own, and neither for happiness nor for virtue will he regret his youth, if he dedicates it to receiving your instruction. Moreover, if, as you think, passions are the smallpox of the soul, happy is he who can still catch it who goes to Köniz to be inoculated. The harm of such a sweet operation would be the danger of not being cured of it. Do not get angry with my sweet talk, please. I do not lavish it on all women and, moreover, one can be somewhat vain.

I cannot, miss, answer your question without the letters of a citizen of Geneva,[1] for this work is perfectly unknown to me, and it is only from you that I know it exists. It is true that in general I am hardly curious about these sorts of writings, and even if they were as obliging as they usually are insulting, I would not go chasing praises any more than insults. What is more, as soon as it is a question of me, all prejudices are in favor of the work being in effect a satire, but are prejudices made to win out over your judgments? Furthermore, I do not see that this book is announced in the *Gazette of Bern*; great proof that it does not insult me.

I do not dare to speak to you about my condition; it would grieve your good heart. I will tell you only that I can provide myself with bearable nights only by chopping wood all day, despite my weakness, to keep myself in a continuous sweat, the slightest suspension of which makes me suffer cruelly. You are right, however, to take some interest in my existence. Despite all my ills, it is still dear to me from the sentiments of esteem and affection that attach me to true merit; and that, miss, is what must not be indifferent to you.

JJRousseau

Accept a scribbling that is not worth the trouble of speaking about and the reading of which I propose to you only under the auspices of the friend Plato.[2]

---

1. A parody of *Julie*.
2. Rousseau enclosed a copy of *On Theatrical Imitation*. See CW 7:337–50.

CHAPTER 105

Abbé de Carondelet

March 4, 1764
Môtiers

I have skimmed through your long letter, sir, in which you set out your sentiments regarding the nature of the soul and the existence of God. Although I had resolved to read nothing more on these matters, I believed I owed you an exception for the trouble you have taken, the goal of which is not easy for me to disentangle. If it is to establish between us an interchange of debate, I cannot gratify you in that. For I never debate, persuaded that each man has his own manner of reasoning which is proper to him regarding something, and which is good for everything to no one else but him. If it is to cure me of the errors you judge me to be making, I thank you for your good intentions; but I can make no use of this, having long since made up my mind regarding these things. Thus, sir, your philosophical zeal is a pure loss with me, and I will not be your proselyte any more than your missionary. I do not condemn your ways of thinking, but deign to leave me mine. For I declare that I do not want to change them.

I also owe you thanks for the care you take in the same letter to remove the uneasiness that your first letters gave me about the principles of the lofty virtue which you profess. As soon as these principles seem solid to you, the duty which derives from them must have for you the same force as if they were so in fact. Hence my doubts regarding their solidity have nothing in them that is insulting to you. But I admit to you that, as for me, such principles would seem frivolous, and as soon as I accepted no others, I feel that in the secret of my heart those would put me very much at my ease regarding the painful virtues that they would appear to impose on me. So much is it true that the same reasons rarely have the same hold in different heads, and that one must never debate about anything!

First, the love of order, to the degree that this order is foreign to me, is not a sentiment that can balance in me that of my own interest. A purely speculative view cannot prevail over the passions in the human heart. It would be to prefer what is alien to me to what is me. This sentiment is not in nature. As to the love of the order of which I am a part, it orders everything in relation to me, and since then I alone am the center of this order, it would be absurd and contradictory if it did not make me relate all things to my particular good. Now, virtue supposes a battle against ourselves, and it is the difficulty of the victory which constitutes its merit. But based on the supposition "Why this battle?" every reason, every motive is lacking. Hence no possible virtue through love of order alone.

The inner sentiment is doubtless a very powerful motive. But the passions and pride adulterate and stifle it early on in nearly all hearts. Of all the sentiments given to us by an upright conscience, the two most powerful, and the only foundations of all the others, are that of the dispensation of a Providence, and that of the immortality of the soul. When these two are destroyed, I do not see what can remain. So long as the inner sentiment would say something to me, it would forbid me, if I had the misfortune of being a skeptic, from alarming my own mother with the doubts that I might have.[1]

Love of oneself is the most powerful and, according to me, the sole motive which makes men act. But how can virtue, taken absolutely and as a metaphysical being, be based on that love? That is what is beyond me. Crime, you say, is contrary to the one who commits it. That is always true, according to my principles, and often very false, according

---

1. Carondelet had written to Rousseau about his quarrels with his mother over his views.

to yours. One must then distinguish the temptations, the positions, the hope—greater or lesser—one has that it will remain unknown or unpunished. Commonly the motive of crime is to avoid a great ill or to acquire a great good. Often it arrives at its goal. If this sentiment is not natural, what sentiment could be? In this life, skillful crime enjoys all the advantages of fortune, and even of glory. Justice and scruples only engender dupes here below. Take away eternal justice and the prolongation of my being after this life, I see nothing more in virtue than a folly to which one gives a beautiful name. For a materialist, the love of oneself is nothing but the love of one's body. Yet when Regulus, so as to keep his word, went to die under torture in Carthage, I do not see what the love of his body had to do with that.

An even greater consideration confirms the preceding ones. It is that in your system the very word "virtue" can have no meaning. It is a sound that beats on the ear, and nothing more. For finally, according to you, everything is necessary; where everything is necessary, there is no liberty; without liberty, no morality in actions; without the morality of actions, where is virtue? As for me, I do not see it. In speaking of the inner sentiment, I should have put in the first place that of free will. But it is enough to refer to it here.

These reasons will seem very feeble to you, I do not doubt it. But they appear strong to me, and that suffices to prove to you that if by chance I became your disciple, your lessons would have made me nothing but a rascal. Now a virtuous man like you would not want to devote his efforts to bringing one more rascal into this world, for I believe that there are certainly as many of those people as hypocrites, and that it is no more suitable to multiply them.

What is more, I must confess that my morality is much less sublime than yours, and I feel that it will even be a great deal if it saves me from your contempt. I cannot deny that your imputations of hypocrisy strike home a bit. It is very true that without having the same sentiment as my brothers in everything, and without disguising mine when the occasion occurs, I accommodate myself very well to theirs. In agreement with them as to the principles of our duties, I do not argue about the rest, which seems not very important to me. While waiting to know with certainty which one of us is right, so long as they allow me into their communion, I will continue to live within it with a genuine attachment. For us, the truth is covered with a veil, but peace and unity are certain goods.

The result of all these reflections is that our ways of thinking are too different for us to be able to agree, and that consequently a longer exchange between us can only be fruitless. Time is so short, and we need it for so many things, that one must not employ it uselessly. I wish you, sir, a solid happiness, the peace of soul which it seems to me that you do not have, and I salute you with all my heart.

JJRousseau

CHAPTER 106

Prince de Wurtemberg

March 11, 1764
The prince had written to Rousseau saying that he had heard that Rousseau might be about to publish a story. He may have heard a rumor about the fairy tale "Queen Whimsical" (CW 12:215–27), which had been published without Rousseau's permission in 1758.

Who, me? Tales! At my age and in my condition? No, Prince, I am no longer in childhood, or rather I am not there yet and, unfortunately, I am not as gay in my illnesses as Scarron was in his.[1] I waste away every day. I have accounts to render and not tales to write.[2] To me this has very much the air of a preliminary rumor spread about by someone who wants to honor me with nice turns in his own fashion. Not satisfied with attacking my foolishness, various authors have begun to impute their own to me. Paris is inundated with works that bear my name, and on which care is taken to make masterpieces of stupidity, doubtless better to fool readers. You would never imagine what underhanded tricks are played on my reputation, my morals, my principles. Here is one that will help you judge the others.

---

1. Paul Scarron (1610–60) is best known for his *Roman comique.*
2. The French plays on the differences between *comptes* (accounts) and *contes* (tales).

All of M. de Voltaire's friends spread around Paris that he is tenderly interested in my fate (and it is true that he does take an interest in it). They make it understood that he is in the most intimate relation with me. Based on this rumor, a woman who does not know me asks me in writing for several clarifications about religion, and sends her letter to M. de Voltaire, asking him to have it passed on to me. M. de Voltaire keeps the letter that is addressed to me, and sends back to that lady, as if in response, the *Oath of the Fifty*.[3] Surprised by such a missive from me, this woman writes me by another route, and that is how I learn what has happened.

You are surprised that my *Letter on Providence* did not keep Candide from being born? On the contrary, it is what gave birth to it; *Candide* is the response to it. The author wrote me a response of two pages in which he beat around the bush, and *Candide* appeared ten months afterward. I wanted to philosophize with him; in response, he mocked me. I wrote to him once that I hated him, and I told him the reasons why. He did not write me the same thing, but he has made me feel it keenly. I avenge myself by profiting from the excellent lessons that are in his works, and force him to continue to do me good despite himself.

Forgive me, prince, that was too many jeremiads; but it is somewhat your fault if I take so much pleasure in pouring my heart out to you. What is Madame la princesse doing? Deign to speak to me sometimes about her condition. When will we have this precious child of love who will be the student of virtue? What will he not become under such auspices, with what charming flowers, what delightful fruits will he not crown the bonds of his worthy parents? Nevertheless, what new cares have been imposed on you; your labors are going to be redoubled; will you be enough for it? Will you have the strength to persevere until the end? Forgive me, M. le duc, your known sentiments are to me the guarantee of your success. Thus, my uneasiness does not come from lack of trust, but from the lively interest that I take in it.

---

3. This work was an attack on religion written by Voltaire but published anonymously.

CHAPTER 107

Lord Marshal Keith

March 31, 1764

Keith wrote to Rousseau that he had been able to repurchase his estate in Scotland. He also offered to give Thérèse a legacy or gift of one hundred louis.

Concerning the acquisition, My Lord, that you have made, and the notice of it you have given me, the best answer I have to make is to transcribe here what I am writing on this subject to the person whom I am asking to forward this letter, in speaking to her about the acclamations of your good compatriots.[1]

"All pleasures may well be for the wicked; yet here is one that I challenge them to taste. He had nothing more urgent to do than to notify me of the change in his fortune; you easily guess why. Congratulate me for all my misfortunes, Madame; they have given me My Lord Marshal for a friend."

In regard to your offers concerning Mlle. Levasseur and me, I will begin, My Lord, by telling you that, far from putting amour-propre into refusing your gifts, I would put a very noble one into receiving them. Thus, no dispute about this. The proofs that you take an interest in me,

-----

1. This is probably Mme. de Verdelin.

of whatever sort they may be, are more suited to make me proud than to humiliate me, and I will never refuse them, let it be said once and for all.

But I have bread at present, and by means of arrangements that I am meditating, I will have it for the rest of my days. What use would the surplus be to me? I lack nothing that I desire, and that one can have with money. My Lord, one must prefer those who need to those who do not need, and I am in the latter case. Moreover, I do not like anyone to speak to me about testaments. I would not want to be—I knowing it—in that of someone indifferent to me; judge whether I would like to know that I was in yours?[2]

You know, My Lord, that Mlle. Levasseur has a small annuity from my publisher on which she can live when she no longer has me. Nevertheless, I admit that the good that you want to do for her is more precious to me than if it concerned me directly, and I am extremely touched by this way found by your heart to satisfy the benevolence with which you honor me. But if it were possible for you to assign her the income of the sum, rather than the sum itself, that would spare me the trouble of seeking to invest it, a sort of business about which I understand nothing.

It appears clear to me that the baron misled us about his name.[3] Regarding me, prudence might have required it, but regarding you the lie is more serious. I assuredly do not intend to excuse it, but I am nevertheless still persuaded that his situation forced him to keep silent and that, if he is an adventurer, at least he is not a scoundrel. I spent enough time with him to be certain about his morals. He did nothing but what was decent here, and did not want my money when he left. I have two of his trunks at home. It is not true that he wanted to betray me, since I went to Pontarlier with him.[4] Who to believe? I do not know. My heart is sickened, but not detached. Since I have not lost all esteem for him, I have preserved some friendship.

I hope, My Lord, that you will have received my preceding letter. Will you grant me some memoranda, could I write the history of your house, and could I give some praises to those good Scots to whom you are so dear and who, for that reason, are also dear to me?

---

2. See *Confessions, CW* 5:47.

3. Sauttersheim.

4. *Confessions, CW* 5:515–17.

CHAPTER 108

Madeleine-Élizabeth Roguin

April 6, 1764
Môtiers

Assuredly, madam, you will be a good mother, and with the zeal that you show for the duties attached to that title, it would have been a great shame if Monsieur Roguin had not put you in a position to fulfill them. You are already anxious about the position in which to place your child, about when you will be able to begin to bathe it in cold water, about the manner of arriving gradually at covering its head, and it is not yet born! This, madam, is a maternal solicitude that is very well placed in certain respects, in others a little premature, but very praiseworthy in every sense, and indeed deserves that I respond to it as well as I can.

In the first place it matters little whether the child is in a willow basket or in something else, so long as it is lying on a bed that is not too soft, a little sideways, and often in the open air. If it is left free, it will not delay in acquiring the strength necessary to put itself in the position that suits it, and moreover it will not always be lying down, since such a good nurse as you want to be will certainly deign to hold it in her arms sometimes.

You ask me at what age one can begin to bathe it in cold water: from birth, madam. A quarter of Christendom, namely all Russians and most of the Greeks, baptize their newborn children by plunging them three times in a row into completely cold, even icy, water. Do the same; baptize your child by immersion twice a day, and do not be afraid of colds.

You are considering from afar when to cover its head; but why cover its head? I never see the necessity for it if it is a boy: if it is a girl, it will be time to consider it at her first communion, and that, less to obey reason than St. Paul, who wants women to have their head covered in Church. Very well, then, since St. Paul wants it so. But the rest of the time, let her wear her hair loose up to the age of thirty, [when] such a hairstyle becomes indecent and ridiculous in a woman.

Since one example says more about all this than a hundred pages of explanation, I enclose here the extract from a memorandum in which you will be able to see the solutions to your difficulties in facts.[1] Although Sophies and Emiles are rare, as you say very well, madam, a few of them are nevertheless being brought up in Europe, even in Switzerland, and what is even more surprising, even in your neighborhood. Success already promises to worthy fathers and mothers the reward for the tenderness that makes them put up with the cares of such a troublesome education, and for the courage that makes them brave the backbiting of the fools, the clergy, and the even more foolish sniggering of the fine wits.

If you want, madam, to make the necessary observations by yourself, take the trouble to go near Lausanne to see M. le prince de Wurtemberg. It is his only daughter who is in question in the memorandum, and if you need more detailed explanations about it, consult the illustrious M. Tissot. To refer you to his advice is the best advice I can give you. Accept, Madame, I beg you, my salutations, and my respect.

JJRousseau

Extracts/ from a memorandum on the condition of a child, received in October 1763.

In fourteen days, my daughter will be four whole months of age. She is well put together etc.

---

1. The attached memorandum is from the Prince de Wurttemberg.

Every day we bathe the little one in the coldest fountain water, and after having wiped her off lightly we leave her naked for a part of the morning. We take her for a walk in the same way outdoors whatever the weather might be, and she is already so used to it, that even the north wind is no longer a trial for her.

We never cover her head, and she wears neither gloves nor stockings. A little very ample shirt, open at the chest, serves as her clothes.

Her bed is made up of a straw filled mattress and a pad, and she never lies down more comfortably than when we spread out her little bed on the grass, for she loves the outdoors prodigiously. So, we are surprised every day by the progress of her strength; she already turns herself very easily on her side and has even already succeeded in sitting up.

After all I have just said you will easily understand that her health is very good . . . she never cries; on the contrary, she laughs at everything that happens.

The hot and the cold, rain, wind, thunder, nothing of all that surprises her, or scares her. Etc.

CHAPTER 109

Prince de Wurtemberg

April 15, 1764
The prince had written to Rousseau, comparing to Rousseau's troubles his own fall into disfavor with the Empress Maria Theresa.

Do not complain about your disfavor, Prince. Since it is the product of your courage and your virtues, it is also the instrument of your glory and your happiness. Doubtless, to vanquish Frederick would have been a lot, but to vanquish in one's own heart the prejudices and passions that subjugate conquerors, like other men, is even more heroic. And tell the truth: how many battles won would have given you in the opinion of men what an hour of enjoyment of the pleasures of conjugal and paternal love gives you at the bottom of your heart? Had your successes done some true good for men, which appears extremely doubtful to me—for what does it matter to peoples who loses or who wins—you would have failed to understand the true goods for yourself and, seduced by public acclamations, you would no longer have put your happiness in anything other than other people's judgments. You have learned to find it in yourself, to be its master, to enjoy it in spite of the queen and in spite of the jealous, and you have conquered it, so to speak. This was the better conquest to make.

The fumes of glory are intoxicating in my profession, as in yours. I do not know whether these fumes got to my head, but they often made my heart ache. In the midst of triumphs, it is very hard for a warrior not to feel the same attack sometimes, for, if the laurels of heroes are more brilliant than ours, they pass through many more hands before crowning their heads, their cultivation is also more difficult, more dependent, and often they are made to pay more dearly for them.

The isolated and unpretentious manner of living that I have chosen, and which makes me more or less nothing on earth, has put me within reach of observing and comparing all conditions, from peasants to grandees. I have easily been able to set aside appearance, for everywhere I have been admitted into association and even familiarity. I incorporated myself, so to speak, into every station, to study them well. I have seen their sentiments, their pleasures, their desires, their internal manner of being. I have always seen that those who knew how to make their situation, not the most dazzling, but the most independent, were closest to all the felicity permitted to man; that the free sentiments which they cultivated, such as love, friendship, were delightful in an entirely different way than those born from the forced relations that station and rank give; finally, that the affections that depended on persons and that were the choices of the heart were infinitely sweeter than those that depended on things and that fortune determined.

Based on this principle, from the first letters with which you honored me, and all the following ones, it seemed to me that you had taken the biggest step to arrive at happiness: that, from prince and general, to make oneself into father, husband, genuine man was not to go toward privations, but toward enjoyments; that your present occupations marked the state of your soul in the least equivocal fashion; that your respect for the sublime Kleinjogg showed how much you deserve respect yourself;[1] finally, that you might have sorrows because every man has some, but that if anyone in the world came close to true happiness through his situation and his sentiments, this ought to be you, and that regarding the disfavor which had led you to that simple and desirable state, you could say, like Themistocles: "We would perish had we not perished."[2] There, Prince, is my manner of thinking about your present and past situation. If I am mistaken, do not correct me.

---

1. Kleinjogg was Jakob Gujer (1716–1785), much admired by Lavater, Mirabeau, and Goethe for his rustic life. He was known as "The Rustic Socrates."

2. Plutarch, *Life of Pericles*. Julie makes the same remark to Saint-Preux (*CW* 6:310).

A woman of the Pays de Vaud who claims she is pregnant wrote to me to ask me for advice about her child's education.[3] Her letter appears to me to be a perpetual mockery of my chimerical ideas. I have taken the liberty of citing to her in response your little Sophie and the way you have the courage to bring her up. I hope I have not committed an indiscretion in doing so; if I have done so, I would ask you to tell me so that I might be more reserved another time.

If you approve that our letters conclude henceforth without formula and without signature, it seems to me that would be more convenient. When sentiments are known, when the handwriting is known, on that point only efforts that seem superfluous to me remain to be taken. While waiting for your example to authorize this usage between us, accept, Monsieur le duc, I beg you, the assurances of my profound respect.

---

3. See letter 108, to Madeleine-Élizabeth Roguin.

CHAPTER 110

"Henriette"

May 7, 1764

The identity of "Henriette" is not known. She wrote to Rousseau using this pseudonym, describing her anguish and arguing that she was an exception to Rousseau's condemnation of learning. As Rousseau indicates in his second letter to her, he had mistakenly thought he knew her identity; he had suspected that "Henriette's" letter had been written by Suzanne Curchod, who later married the financier Jacques Necker.

I am not put off the scent, Henriette, regarding your letter's object, or by your dating it from Paris either. You are seeking less my opinion about the decision you have to make, than my approval of the one that you have made. On every one of your lines, I read these words written in larger characters: *Let us see whether you will have the effrontery to condemn to neither thinking nor reading any longer someone who thinks and writes like this.* This interpretation is certainly not a reproach, and I cannot hold it against you that you put me in the number of those whose judgments matter to you. But in flattering me you do not, I believe, require me to flatter you; and, when your life's happiness is at stake, to disguise my sentiment from you would be to respond badly to the honor you have done me.

Let us begin by setting aside useless deliberations. It is no longer a question of reducing you to sewing and embroidering. Henriette, one does not take off one's head like one's bonnet, and one does not return to simplicity any more than to childhood. The mind, once in effervescence, always remains there, and anyone who has thought will think for her entire life. That is the greatest misfortune of the condition of reflection: the more one feels its ills, the more one increases them, and all our efforts for leaving it only bog us down more deeply in it.

Let us speak, then, not about changing condition, but about the advantage you can draw from yours. This condition is unfortunate; it must always be so. Your ills are great and without remedy. You feel it, you murmur at it, and, to make them bearable, you are looking for at least a palliative. Is that not the object you are proposing for yourself in your plans of studies and occupations?

Your means might be good from another perspective, but it is your end that deceives you, because, not seeing the genuine source of your ills, you are seeking their softening in the source that gave birth to them. You seek them in your situation, while they are your own work. How many persons of merit, born in well-being and fallen into indigence, have borne it less successfully and happily than you have, and yet do not have those sad and cruel awakenings whose horror you describe with so much energy? Why is that? You will say that doubtless they do not have such a sensitive soul. I have not seen anyone in my life who does not say as much. But, in the end, what is this much vaunted sensitivity? Do you want to know, Henriette? In the final analysis it is an amour-propre that compares itself. I have put my finger on the seat of the illness.

All your miseries come, and will come, from having put yourself on display. With this way of looking for happiness, it is impossible for one to find it, for it is impossible ever to obtain in other people's opinions the place to which one lays claim there. If they grant it to us in some respect, they refuse it to us in a thousand others, and a single exclusion torments more than a hundred preferences flatter. It is far worse in a woman who, wanting to make herself into a man, first puts her entire sex against her and is never taken at her word by ours, so that her pride is often as mortified by the honors rendered her as by those she is refused. She never has precisely what she wants because she wants contradictory things and, usurping the rights of one sex without wanting to renounce those of the other, she does not fully possess any.

But the great misfortune of a woman who puts herself on display is to attract, to see, only people who do as she does, and to set aside the solid and modest merit that does not put itself on display and which does not run to where the crowd is assembled. No one judges men so badly and so falsely as pretentious people, for they judge them only after themselves and what resembles them, and that is certainly not seeing humankind by its beautiful side. You are dissatisfied with all your societies; I can well believe it. Those in which you have lived were the least suited to making you happy. In them you found no one in whom you could take that confidence that soothes. How would you have found it among people completely occupied with themselves alone, from whom you were asking for first place in their heart, and who do not even have a second place in it to give? You wanted to shine, you wanted to take precedence, and you wanted to be loved. These are incompatible things. It is necessary to choose. There is no friendship without equality, and equality is never acknowledged among pretentious people. Needing a friend is not enough. To find one, it is necessary to have something to provide for someone else's needs. Among the provisions you have made, you have forgotten that one.

The proceeding by which you acquired knowledge justifies neither its object nor its use. You wanted to appear as a philosopher; that was to renounce being one. It would have been much better to have the air of a girl who is waiting for a husband than of a wise man waiting for incense. Far from finding happiness in the effect of the cares you gave to appearance alone, you have found in them only apparent goods and genuine ills. The condition of reflection into which you threw yourself caused you incessantly, painfully to return to yourself, and nevertheless you want to banish these ideas by the same sort of occupation that gave them to you.

You see the error of the path you have taken and, believing that you are changing it by means of your plan, you are going to the same goal again by means of a detour. It is not for yourself that you would like to return to study; it is still for others. You want to make provisions of knowledge to take the place of looks at another age: you want to substitute the empire of knowledge for that of charms.

You do not want to become the sycophant of another woman, but you want to have sycophants. You want to have friends, that is, a court. For the friends of a young or old woman are always her courtiers. They serve her or leave her; and you are taking measures from afar to keep them so as always to be the center of a sphere, small or large. Without that I believe that the provisions you want to make would be the most useless thing for the object that you really believe you are proposing for yourself. You want, you say, to put yourself in a condition to understand others. Do you need a new acquisition for that? In truth, I do not know what opinion you have of your actual intelligence, but even were you to have Oedipuses for friends, I hardly believe that you are very curious to understand people whom you cannot understand today. Why, then, so many efforts to obtain what you already have? No, Henriette, it is not that. But when you will be a sybil, you will want to proclaim oracles; your true plan is not so much to listen to others as to have auditors yourself. Under the pretext of laboring for independence, you are still laboring for domination. It is thus that, far from lightening the weight of the opinion that is making you unhappy, you want to aggravate its yoke. This is not the way to procure more serene awakenings for yourself.

You believe that the only relief from the painful sentiment that torments you is to distance yourself from yourself. I, on the contrary, believe that it is to bring yourself closer to yourself.

Your entire letter is full of proofs that, until now, the unique goal of all your behavior has been to set yourself off advantageously in other people's eyes. How, having succeeded in public as much as anyone, and bringing back so little inner satisfaction from it, did you not feel that there was not the happiness necessary for you, and that it was time to change plans? Yours might be good for glory, but it is bad for felicity. One must not seek to distance oneself from oneself because that is not possible, and because everything brings us back there no matter what we do. You agree that you passed very sweet hours while writing to me and speaking to me about yourself. It is astonishing that this experience does not set you on the path and does not teach you where you ought to look for, if not happiness, at least peace.

Nevertheless, although my ideas about this differ very much from yours, we nearly agree on what you ought to do. Henceforth, for you, study is Achilles's spear which must cure you of the wound it has made. But you want only to quell the pain, and I would like to remove the cause of the illness. You want to distract yourself from yourself by means of philosophy. As for me, I would like it to separate you from everything, and return you to yourself. Be assured that you will not be satisfied with others until you no longer need them, and that society cannot become pleasant for you except by ceasing to be necessary to you. Never having anything to complain about with regard to those from whom you require nothing, it will then be you who will be necessary to them; and, feeling that you suffice to yourself, they will be grateful to you for the merit that you are willing to put in common. They will no longer believe they are doing you a favor; they will always be receiving it. The pleasures of life will seek you out from the very fact that you are not seeking them out, and that is when, satisfied with yourself without being able to be dissatisfied with others, you will have a peaceful sleep and a delightful awakening.

It is true that studies undertaken with such contrary objects must not resemble each other very much, and there is a great deal of difference between the culture that adorns the mind and that which nourishes the soul. If you had the courage to savor a project whose execution will be very painful for you at first, you would have to change direction a great deal. That would require thinking about it well before setting oneself to work. I am sick, occupied, despondent, I have a slow mind, I need to make painful efforts to leave the little circle of ideas that are familiar to me, and nothing is further removed from your situation. It is not just for me to tire myself out at a pure loss, for I hardly believe that you want to undertake to recast, so to speak, your entire moral constitution. You have too much philosophy not to see this undertaking with fright. I would despair of you if you set yourself to it easily. Let us not go any further, then, for the present. It is enough that your principal question is resolved. Follow the career of letters. There is no longer any other one left for you to choose.

These lines, which I am writing to you hastily, distracted and suffering, perhaps say nothing of what must be said. But the errors that my precipitation may have caused me to make are not irreparable. What was needed above all was to make you feel how much you interest me, and I believe that you will not doubt it upon reading this letter. Until now I looked upon you only as a fine thinker who, if she had received a character from nature, had been careful to stifle it, to annihilate it beneath the exterior, as one of those masterpieces cast in bronze that one admires from the outside and whose inside is empty. But, if you can still weep over your condition, it is not without recourse. So long as a little substance is left in the heart, one must not despair of anything.

CHAPTER 111

Marquis de Saint-Brisson

July 22, 1764
Môtiers
Saint-Brisson had written to Rousseau to say that he had abandoned his military career and quarreled with his mother over his desire to lead a simple country life.

I fear, sir, that you are going a little fast with your plans and, when nothing is pressing, it would be necessary to proportion maturity of deliberations to the importance of the resolutions. Why so brusquely leave the position that you embraced, when you could make arrangements for another at leisure (if one can call a position the way of life that you chose for yourself), by which you will perhaps be as soon put off as by the first? What would you be risking by proceeding a little less impetuously, and by taking advantage of this delay to confirm yourself in your resolutions by a more mature study of yourself? Here you are alone on earth, at the age in which man must depend on everything. I pity you, and it is for that reason that I cannot approve, since you wanted to isolate yourself when that suited you the least. If you believe you followed my principles, you are mistaken: you have followed the impetuosity of your age. Such a dazzling proceeding certainly was worth the trouble of being well weighed before carrying it out. It is done, I know it. I only want to make you understand that the way of maintaining it, or of coming back from it, requires a little more examination than you put into doing it.

This is what is worse. The natural effect of this behavior has been to estrange you from madam your mother. Without you showing it to me, I see the thread of all that. And were there only what you tell me, what good is it to go alarm a mother's tranquil conscience by unnecessarily showing her principles different from her own? As the rule of your behavior, it was necessary, sir, to keep those sentiments inside of you, and their first effect should have been to make you patiently endure the annoyances of your priests, and not to change these annoyances into persecutions, by wanting loudly to shake off the yoke of the religion in which you were born. On this point, I think so little as you do that, although the Protestant clergy is waging an open war on me, and I am very far from thinking as it does on all points, I do not remain any less sincerely united to the communion of our Church, very resolved to live and die in it, if it depends on me. For it is very consoling for an afflicted believer to remain in community of worship with his brothers, and to serve God jointly with them. I will say more: I declare to you that if I had been born Catholic, I would remain a good Catholic, knowing well that your Church puts a very salutary brake on deviations of human reason, which finds neither bottom nor bank when it wants to sound the abyss of things. And I am so convinced of the utility of this brake that I have imposed a similar one on myself, by prescribing myself rules of faith for the rest of my life from which I do not allow myself to depart. Consequently, I swear to you that I have been tranquil only since that time, convinced indeed that without that precaution, I would not have been so in my life. I am speaking to you, sir, with an overflowing heart and as a father speaks to his child. Your estrangement from madam your mother distresses me. In my misfortunes I had the consolation of believing that my writings could do only good. Do you want to take that consolation away from me too? I know that if they do harm it is only for lack of being understood, but I will always have the regret of not having been able to make myself understood. Dear Saint-Brisson, a son estranged from his mother is always in the wrong. Of all the natural sentiments the least altered among us is maternal affection. The right of mothers is the most sacred that I know; in no case can one violate it without crime. Reconcile yourself, then, with yours: whatever the cost might be, pacify her; be sure that her heart will be opened again if yours brings you back to her. Cannot you, without falsehood, sacrifice some useless opinions for her, or at least dissimulate them?

You will never be called upon to persecute anyone; what does the rest matter to you? There are not two moralities. That of Christianity and that of philosophy are the same; both impose on you the same duty here. You can fulfill it. You ought to do so. Reason, honor, your interest, everything wants it, and I require it to respond to the sentiments with which you honor me. If you do it, count upon my friendship, upon all my esteem, upon my efforts if ever they are good for anything to you. If you do not do it, you have only a bad head or, what is worse, your heart is leading you badly, and I want to preserve relations only with people whose head and heart are healthy.

JJRousseau

I was absent when your letter arrived, which made me unable to respond sooner. And I am going to go away again for a tour which my health and the crowd of idle people render necessary. It is well confirmed that the air of this place, although good for others, is unhealthy for me.

CHAPTER 112

Mathieu Buttafoco

September 22, 1764
Môtiers-Travers via Pontarlier

It is superfluous, sir, to seek to arouse my zeal for the undertaking that you propose. The idea alone raises up my soul and transports me. I would believe the remnant of my days very nobly, very virtuously, very happily employed; I would even believe that I had well redeemed the uselessness of the others, if I could make this sad remnant good for something for your brave compatriots, if by means of some useful counsel I could cooperate with the aim of their worthy leader and yours. From that side be certain of me: my life and my heart are yours.

But sir, zeal does not give means, and desire is not power. I do not want foolishly to play the modest person here. I sense well what I have, but I sense even better what I lack.

First, in relation to the thing, I lack a multitude of knowledge relative to the nation and the country, indispensable knowledge whose acquisition will demand much information, clarifications, memoranda, etc. on your part, and on mine, much study and reflection.

In relation to me, I lack more youth, a more tranquil mind, a heart less exhausted with troubles, a certain vigor of genius which, even if one has it, is not proof against years and sorrows. I lack health, time.

Overwhelmed by an incurable and cruel malady, I lack the hope of seeing the end of a long labor, which only the expectation of success can give the courage to pursue. I lack, finally, experience in business, which alone clarifies more about the art of leading men than all the meditations in the world.

If I were feeling passably well, I would say to myself: I will go to Corsica. Six months passed on the spot would instruct me more than a hundred volumes. But how to undertake such a difficult, such a long trip in my condition? Would I bear it? Would I be allowed to pass? A thousand obstacles would stop me going, the sea air would finish destroying me before my return. I admit to you that I want to die among my own people.

You may be pressed for time. A work of this importance can only be a long drawn-out business, even for a man who was feeling well. Before submitting my work to the examination of the nation and its leaders, I want to begin by being satisfied with it myself. I do not want to give anything piecemeal; the work must be unified; one could not judge it separately. It is already no small thing to put myself in a condition to begin; to finish, that is going a long way.

Reflections about the precarious position in which your island remains also present themselves. I know that under a leader such as they have today, the Corsicans have nothing to fear from Genoa. I believe that they also have nothing to fear from the troops that, it is said, France is dispatching there. What confirms me in this sentiment is to see such a good patriot as you appear to me to be remain, despite the dispatch of these troops, in the service of the power that is providing them. But sir, your country's independence is not assured so long as no power recognizes it. And you will admit that it is not encouraging to undertake such a great work, without knowing whether it can be used, even assuming it is good.

It is not to refuse your invitations, sir, that I am making these objections to you, but to subject them to your examination and that of M. Paoli. I believe you are both too good to want my affection for your fatherland to make me consume the little time I have left in efforts that would not be good for anything.

Examine, then, Gentlemen; judge yourselves, and be assured that the undertaking of which you have found me worthy will not fail by my will.

Receive, I beg you, my very humble salutations.

JJRousseau

P.S. I ought to warn you that, if you write to me directly, one must pay postage to Pontarlier, without which letters will not pass through.

Upon rereading your letter, I see, sir, that on the first reading I misunderstood your object. I believed that you were asking for a complete body of legislation, and I see that you are asking only for a political institution, which makes me judge that you already have a body of civil laws, aside from written law, based on which it is a question of tracing a form of government that relates to it. The task is less great, without being small, and it is not certain that as perfect a whole will result from it. This can be judged only based on the complete collection of your laws.

CHAPTER 113

Philibert Cramer

October 13, 1764
Môtiers

I come, sir, to draw upon you, in accordance with the permission you have given me, a letter of 1,300 French livres payable in ten days from receipt to the order of Messieurs Borel, Bosset, and Guyenet. Accept my excuses and my thanks for the efforts you have bestowed on this small business.

My writings can please only those who read them with the same heart that dictated them. What I honor myself for, within myself, with some pride, is that they make me love the good and hate the wicked. My faults must be censured, and my errors corrected; I have made a lot of them: but my sentiments must be loved, because they are good and honorable. I am very glad, sir, for both of us, that the justice you render me puts you in the number of those I ought to love in turn. This is, I hope, a duty that I will fulfill without difficulty.

You say very well that it is impossible to make an Emile. But I cannot believe that you are taking the book that bears that name for a true treatise on education. It is a rather philosophic work on this principle set forth by the author in other writings *that man is naturally good*. To accord this principle with this other truth, no less certain, that men are wicked, it was necessary to show the origin of all the vices in the history of the human heart. That is what I have done in this book, often with precision and sometimes with sagacity. In that sea of passions that submerges us, before seeking to block the way, it was necessary to begin by finding it. I salute you, sir, with all my heart.

JJRousseau

I just noticed, sir, that you pay the postage for your letters. The multitude of those written to me forcing me to have an account with the post office might have concealed that observation from me. Since I do not like to nitpick, I will not pay the postage on mine. I will only have you note that this proceeding is not an ordinary one, and that a man who spends fifty crowns every year on postage for other people's business, can very well spend several sous for his own.

Everyone is complimenting me on an alleged poem in prose that, it is said, I am having published, a folly about which I am assuredly not thinking.[1] I ought to be cured of the whim of the press; but if it ever takes me again, rest assured, sir, that you will not be forgotten.

---

1. This is *The Levite of Ephraim* (see *CW* 7:351–65), which Rousseau had been reading to visitors.

Mathieu Buttafoco

October 15, 1764
Môtiers

I do not know, sir, why your letter of the 3rd reached me only yesterday. This delay forces me to take advantage of the courier to answer you in haste, without which my letter would not arrive in Aix early enough to find you there.

I can hardly hope to be in a condition to go to Corsica. If I could undertake that trip, it would be only during the summer. From now until then, time is precious. It must be saved as much as possible, and it will be lost until I have received your instructions. I am including here a quick note on the first instructions I need; in this undertaking I will always need yours. You must not speak on that point to me, sir, about your inadequacy. To judge you from your letters, I ought to trust your eyes more than my own. To judge your people from you, it is wrong to look for guides outside of itself.

It is a question of such a great object that my temerity makes me tremble; at least let us not add stupidity to it. I have a very slow mind; age and illnesses slow it further. A provisional government has its inconveniences. However attentive one is to making only necessary changes, an establishment like the one we are looking for is not done without a little upheaval, and one should at least try not to have more than one of them. One could begin by casting the foundations, then erect the building more at leisure. That assumes a plan already made, however, and one must meditate the most to trace out this very plan. Moreover, it is to be feared that an imperfect establishment might make its difficulties felt more than its advantages, and that this might give the people a distaste for finishing it. But let us nevertheless see what can be done. Once I have received the memoranda I need, six good months are necessary for me to instruct myself, and at least as much to digest my instructions, so that a year from next spring, I would be able to propose my first ideas about a provisional form, and at the end of three additional years, my complete plan of institution. Since one ought to promise only what depends on oneself, I am not certain of having my work in condition in so little time, but I am so certain of not being able to abridge it that, if it is necessary to draw one of these two limits closer, it would be better for me not to undertake anything.

I am charmed by the trip you are making to Corsica in these circumstances. It can only be very useful to us if, as I do not doubt, you are occupied with our object there. You will see what you must tell me better than I can see what I ought to ask you. But allow me some curiosity that esteem and admiration inspire in me. I would like to know everything that concerns M. Paoli: how old is he? is he married? does he have children? Where did he learn the military art? How did the good fortune of his nation put him in charge of its troops? What functions does he exercise in the political and civic administration? Would this great man resolve to be only a citizen in his fatherland, after having been its savior? Above all speak to me in every respect without disguise: the glory, the repose, the happiness of your people depend here more on you than on me. I salute you, sir, with all my heart.

JJRousseau

I cannot indicate to you the means for having your dispatches reach me. The arrangements for that are not easy to make in my retreat or in my condition, but here are addresses for sending your packages, according to the cities which will be within your reach. You understand that the farther they are from me, the more time will be necessary for the packets to reach me.

> in Paris, in care of M. Duchesne, bookseller, rue St. Jacques
> In Lyon, in care of M. Boy de la Tour and co.

In Geneva, in care of M. d'Ivernois, merchant

In Pontarlier, in care of M. Junet, director of post offices

Memorandum.

A good map of Corsica, in which the various districts are noted and distinguished by their names, even, if possible, by colors.

An exact description of the island, its natural history, its products, its agriculture, its divisions, its districts; the number, size, location of the cities, towns, parishes; the population count of the people as exactly as possible; the state of the fortresses, the ports; industry, arts, the navy; the commerce that is done; the one that could be done, etc.

What is the number, the influence of the clergy; what are its maxims, what is its behavior relative to the fatherland? Are there ancient houses, privileged bodies, nobility? Do the cities have municipal rights?

What are the morals of the people, its tastes, its occupations, its amusements, military order and divisions, discipline, the manner of conducting war, etc.?

The history of the nation up to this moment, the laws, the statutes; everything that concerns the present administration, the inconveniences that are found there, the conduct of justice, public revenues, the economic order, the manner of setting and collecting taxes, what the people can pay annually, more or less.

This contains in general the necessary instructions, but some need to be detailed; it is enough to give a summary of the others. In general, everything that makes the national genius better known could not be explained too much. Often one line, one word, one action says more than a whole book, but it is better to have too much than not enough.

CHAPTER 115

Jean Foulquier

October 18, 1764
Môtiers
Foulquier had sent Rousseau a memorandum about the condition of Protestants in France.

Here, sir, is the memorandum you had the kindness to send me. It appeared to me to be very well done; it says enough and says nothing excessive. There would only be some small errors of language to correct, if one wanted to give it to the public. But that is nothing. The work is good and does not smell too much of its theologian.

It seems to me that for some time the government of France, enlightened by some good writings, is moving rather closer to a tacit tolerance in favor of Protestants. But I also think that the moment of the expulsion of the Jesuits is forcing it to more circumspection than at another time, out of fear that these fathers and their friends might take advantage of this indulgence to combine their cause with that of religion. That being so, this moment would not be the most favorable one for acting at court. While waiting for it to arrive, however, one could continue to instruct and interest the public by means of wise and moderate writings, with the force of clear and precise raisons d'état, and uncluttered by all those bitter and puerile declamations too usual for the Clergy. I even believe that one ought to avoid irritating the Catholic clergy too much; one must state the facts without burdening them with offensive reflections. Conceive, on the contrary, a memorandum addressed to the bishops of France in decent and respectful terms and in which, based upon principles they would not dare to disavow, one would call upon their equity, their charity, their commiseration, their patriotism, and even their Christianity. This memorandum, I know very well, would not take away their ill will, but it would make them ashamed to show it, and would perhaps keep them from persecuting our unfortunate brothers so openly and so harshly. I might be wrong. That is what I think. As for me, I will not write. That is not possible for me. But anywhere that my efforts and my counsel can be useful to the oppressed, in their misfortunes they will always find in me the interest and the zeal that, in the midst of mine, I have found in no one.

Receive, sir, my very humble salutations.

JJRousseau

CHAPTER 116

Pierre-Alexandre DuPeyrou

November 4, 1764
Môtiers
DuPeyrou had sent Rousseau a copy of Voltaire's Philosophic Dictionary.

Many thanks, sir, for the *Philosophical Dictionary*. It is pleasant to read. A good morality reigns in it; one would wish that it was in the heart of the author and of all men. But this same author is almost always in bad faith in the extracts from Scripture. He often reasons very badly, and the air of ridicule and disdain that he casts on sentiments respected by men, spilling over onto the men themselves, appears to me an insult to society and punishable before human tribunals. That is my sentiment, and perhaps my error, which I believe I am allowed to state, but which I do not mean to have adopted by anyone at all.

I am very touched by what you tell me on behalf of M. and Mme. de Buffon.[1] I am very glad to have told you what I thought about this illustrious man before his remembrance rewarmed my sentiments for him, so as to have all the honor of the justice that I like to do him,

---

1. DuPeyrou had heard from Buffon's colleague, Daubenton, that Buffon and his wife had asked DuPeyrou to inform Rousseau of their lively interest in his position, and of their desire to hear good news about him.

without my amour-propre having been mixed up in it. His writings will instruct me and please me my whole life. I believe him to have equals among his contemporaries as thinker and philosopher, but as a writer I am unacquainted with any. His is the finest pen of his age; I do not doubt that this will be posterity's judgment. One of my regrets is not to have been within reach of seeing him more and of profiting from his obliging invitations. I feel how much my head and my writings would have gained by relations with him. I left Paris at the time of his marriage. Thus, I have not had the good fortune to be acquainted with Mme. de Buffon, but I know that he has found in her person and in her merit the lovable and worthy reward for his own. May God bless each of them for being willing to take an interest in this poor outlaw. Their kindnesses are one of the consolations of my life. Let them know, I beg you, that I honor them and love them with all my heart.

I am very far, sir, from renouncing the projected pilgrimages. If the fervor for botany still endures in you, and you do not put off a gray-beard student, I count more than ever on going to follow you in collecting plants this summer. My poor Corsicans now have plenty of other matters to deal with than to go establish utopia in their midst. You know the progress of the French troops; it is necessary to see what results from it. Yet still I have difficulty believing that France wants to become the execration of the universe by delivering this unfortunate people to its butchers. Moreover, if this fine exploit flatters it so much, it will have to decide entirely to destroy the Corsican nation, for that is the only means of subjecting the island to the Genoese. While waiting for what will happen, one must groan softly, and go collect plants.

You make me proud by telling me that Mlle. Bondeli does not dare to come see me because of the proprieties of her sex, and that she is as afraid of me as of a circumcised man. It is more than fifteen years since pretty women in France affronted me by treating me as a poor fellow without consequence, to the point of coming to dine with me tête-à-tête in the most insulting familiarity, to the point of kissing me disdainfully in front of everyone like their nurse's grandfather. Thank heaven, my dignity is well reestablished now that damsels are doing me the honor of not daring to come to see me.[2]

---

2. When she was urged to go see Rousseau, Julie von Bondeli said that out of propriety she would not go uninvited even if it were a question of seeing Plato or the Antichrist.

During my stay at Cressier, a letter from M. d'Escherny came to me here. Upon my return, I did not believe I was in time to answer it, based on the short stay he indicated he was to make in Paris. I see, sir, from your letter that I would have been in time, but that I no longer am, and since I have neither letter nor time to lose, I await the pleasure of seeing him in this country. *Vale*.

CHAPTER 117

"Henriette"

November 4, 1764
Môtiers

If your situation, miss, hardly leaves you time for writing to me, you must conceive that mine leaves me even less to answer you. You are subjected only to your business and the people on whom you depend, and I am subjected to every matter and everyone because each, judging me to be free, wants to dispose of me by right of the first occupant. Moreover, always harassed, always suffering, overwhelmed by troubles and in a condition worse than yours, I use the few moments they leave me to catch my breath. I am too occupied not to be lazy. For a month I have been looking for a moment to write to you at my ease. That moment does not come. I must then write to you on the sly, for you interest me too much to leave you without an answer. I am acquainted with few people to whom I am more attached, and no one who surprises me as much as you do.

If you have found in my letter many things that do not square with yours, that is because it was written for someone other than you. There are in your situation such striking similarities to that of a different person who was precisely at Neuchâtel when I received your letter, that I did not doubt that that letter came from her, and I took up the wrong scent with the idea that someone was trying to put me on it. Thus, I spoke to you less about what you said to me concerning your character, than about what I knew concerning hers. I believed that I found in her mania for putting herself on display (for she is a credentialed savant and a fine wit) the reason for the inner malaise whose detailed account you gave me. I began by attacking that mania as if it had been yours, and I did not doubt that by bringing you back to yourself, I would bring you closer to the repose from which nothing is further away, according to me, than the condition of a woman who puts herself on display.

A letter written based on such a misunderstanding must contain many blunders. Nevertheless, my error contained this good thing, that it gave me the key to the moral condition of the person to whom I thought I was writing, and based on that assumed condition, I believed I caught sight of a plan to follow to draw you out of the anguish that you described to me, without recurring to the distractions which, according to you, are the only remedy for it, and which, according to me, are not even a palliative. You inform me that I am mistaken, and that I have not seen anything of what I believed I saw. How would I find a remedy for your condition, since this condition is inconceivable to me. You are a distressing and humiliating enigma to me. I believed I knew the human heart, and I know nothing about yours. You are suffering, and I cannot relieve you.

What, because nothing foreign to you contents you, you want to flee yourself, and because you have cause to complain of others, because you disdain them, because they have given you the right to do so, because you feel in yourself a soul worthy of esteem, you do not want to console yourself along with it for the disdain inspired in you by those who do not resemble it? No, I understand nothing about this oddity, it is beyond me.

Must this sensitivity that makes you dissatisfied with everything not have folded back on itself; must it not have nourished your heart with a sublime and delightful sentiment of amour-propre; does not one always have in it a resource against injustice and the compensation for insensitivity. It is so rare, you say, to meet a soul. That is true, but how can one have a soul, and not delight in it? If, upon sounding them, one feels others to be constricted and narrow, one loses enthusiasm for them, one detaches oneself from them; but after having found oneself so badly off with others, what a pleasure one has in one's own home. I know how distressing for sensitive hearts the need for attachment makes the impossibility of forming any. I know how sad this condition

is, but I know that, even so, it has some pleasures. It causes streams of
tears to be shed; it gives one melancholy that bears witness to oneself,
and which one would not want not to have. It makes solitude sought
out as the only refuge where one encounters oneself again, along with
everything one has reason to love. I cannot repeat it to you too often:
I know neither happiness nor repose in distance from oneself and, on
the contrary, I feel more from day to day that one can be happy on earth
only in proportion to how much one distances oneself from things
and how much one draws nearer to oneself. If there is some sentiment
sweeter than esteem for oneself, if there is some occupation more lovable than that of increasing this sentiment, I may be wrong. But that is
how I think. Judge, based on that, whether it is possible for me to enter
into your perspective, and even to conceive of your condition.

I cannot keep myself from still hoping that you are mistaken about
the principle of your malaise, and that instead of coming from the sentiment that reflects on yourself, on the contrary it comes from the one
that still links you, unbeknown to you, to the things from which you
believe you are detached, and which perhaps you only despair of enjoying. I would like that to be so; I would see some footing upon which
to act. But if you are accurate, I do not see one. If I had your first letter under my eyes at present, and more leisure to reflect on it, perhaps
I would succeed in understanding you, and I would not spare my effort
to do so, because you genuinely make me uneasy. But that letter is lost
in heaps of papers, it would take more time than I have left to find it
again; I am forced to put off this search to another time. If the lack of
utility of our correspondence did not deter you from writing to me, this
would genuinely be a way of understanding you in the end. But I cannot promise more exactitude in my responses than I am in a condition
to put into them. What I do promise you, and what I will keep well, is
to occupy myself very much with you, and not to forget you in my life.
Your last letter, full of flashes of enlightenment and profound sentiments, affects me even more than the preceding one. Whatever you may
say about it, I will always believe that it depends only on the person who
wrote it to delight in herself and to compensate herself that way for the
rigors of her fate.

CHAPTER 118

Abbé de Carondelet

November 11, 1764
Môtiers-Travers

There you are then, sir, suddenly having become a believer. I congratulate you on this miracle, for it is doubtless one from grace, and reason ordinarily does not operate so suddenly. But please do not honor me for your conversion; I feel that this honor does not belong to me. A man who hardly believes in miracles is not well suited to performing one. A man who neither dogmatizes nor disputes is not a very good converter. I sometimes state my opinion when I am asked, and I believe that it is well intentioned, but I do not have the folly of wanting to make it a law for others, and when they want to make theirs one for me, I defend myself as best I can without seeking to convince them. I have not done anything more with you. Thus, sir, you alone have all the merit of your resipiscence; I surely did not dream of catechizing you.

But now here scruples arise. Yours inspire me with respect for your sublime sentiments, and I admit to you ingenuously that, as for me, who proceeds a little more mundanely, I would be much less tormented by them. I would tell myself first that to confess my faults is useful for correcting myself of them because, making it a law for myself to say everything and to speak truly, I would often be held back from committing them by the shame of revealing them.

It is true that there might be some perplexity over the robust faith that is required in your Church, and which each is not master of having as he pleases. But at bottom, what is at issue in this business? The sincere desire to believe, a submission of the heart more than of reason: for in the end, reason does not depend on us, but the will does so depend, and it is by the will alone that one can be submissive to, or rebellious against, the Church. I would begin, then, by choosing a good priest as my confessor, a wise and sensible man, such as one finds everywhere when one looks for them. I would say to him: I see the ocean of difficulties in which the human mind swims in these matters; mine is not seeking to drown in it. I seek what is true and good. I seek it sincerely. I feel that the docility that the Church requires is a desirable state to be at peace with oneself. I love this state, I want to live in it. My mind murmurs, it is true, but my heart imposes silence on it, and my sentiments are all against my reasons. I do not believe, but I want to believe, and I want it with all my heart. Submissive to faith despite my enlightenment, what argument can I have to fear? I am more faithful than if I were convinced.

If my confessor is not a fool, what do you want him to say to me? Do you want him stupidly to require the impossible of me, that he order me to see red where I see blue? He will say, submit. I will answer: that is what I am doing. He will pray for me and give me absolution without hesitating, for he owes it to he who believes with all his strength and who follows the law with all his heart.

But let us suppose that a poorly understood scruple holds him back. He will be satisfied with exhorting me in secret and pitying me; he will even love me; I am certain that my good faith will win over his heart. You assume that he will go to denounce me to the ecclesiastical judge. And why? What does he have to reproach me for? Of what do you want him to accuse me? Of having fulfilled my duty too faithfully? You are assuming an unreasonable, a frenzied person; that is not the man I chose. In addition, you are assuming an abominable scoundrel against whom I can institute proceedings, give the lie to, perhaps have hanged for having undermined the sacrament at its base, for having caused the most dangerous scandal, for having unnecessarily, uselessly violated the most sacred of all duties, when I was so well within mine that I deserved nothing but praise. This assumption, I admit it, once allowed, appears to have its difficulties.

I find in general that you press them as a man who is not sorry to give birth to them. If everything unites against you, if the priests initiate proceedings against you, if the people curse you, if sorrow makes your parents descend to the tomb, these are, I admit, very terrible inconveniences for not having wanted to take a piece of bread in a ceremony. But what to do, in sum, you ask me? On that score, sir, this is what I have to say to you.

As long as one can be just and true within the society of men, there are difficult duties about which a disinterested friend can be usefully consulted.

But once human institutions are at such a point of depravity that it is no longer possible to live there and to decide without doing harm, then one should no longer consult anyone. One must listen only to one's own heart, because it is unjust and dishonorable to force an honorable man to counsel evil to us. Such is my opinion.

I salute you, sir, with all my heart.

JJRousseau

CHAPTER 119

Pierre-Alexandre DuPeyrou

December 8, 1764
Môtiers
DuPeyrou had agreed to guarantee the financing of a collected edition of Rousseau's works. He had also asked Rousseau to explain the meaning of two Bs that he had written in the margins of the article "Matter" in a copy of Voltaire's Philosophic Dictionary *that Rousseau had returned to him.*

Although the business and the visits with which I am overburdened leave me almost no moment to myself and although, moreover, the one that occupies me now makes it necessary for me to deliberate with you, sir, since you consented to it, nevertheless, not being able to spare enough time for everything, I am giving the preference to the care of calming you about that terrible *B* which worries you, and which appeared to you sufficient to erase or counterbalance the testimony of all my writings and my entire life about the sentiments that I have constantly professed, and that I will profess until my final breath. Since a single letter of the alphabet has so much power, from now on one must believe in the virtues of talismans. This *B* signifies *Bon*, that is certain: but since you are asking me for an explanation for it without transcribing the passages to which it relates and about which I do not have the slightest memory, I cannot satisfy you, unless beforehand you will have kindly sent me those passages, adding to them the meaning that you give to the *B* that worries you. For it is to be presumed that this meaning is not mine. Perhaps, then, by developing my thinking for you, I will come to the end of edifying you on this point. All I can tell you in advance is that, not only am I not a materialist, but I do not even remember having been tempted for a single moment in my life to become one. True it is that I agree with the materialists on a great number of propositions, and those at which you have seen the *B*s are apparently of that number; but it in no way follows that my method of deduction and theirs are the same and leads me to the same conclusions. I cannot for the present tell you anything further, and it is necessary to know what your difficulties are centered on before thinking of resolving them. In the meantime, I have excuses to make to you about the worry my indiscretion has caused you, and I promise you that if I am ever tempted to scribble in the margins of books, I will remember this lesson.

My people have not yet come to seek their answer; but I forewarn you that since you do not disdain to watch over my interests, they will have to deal with you. The service you are rendering me is the greatest that I can receive in my present situation, given my inaptitude for all efforts of this sort and the necessity for me, nevertheless, that they be fulfilled. We will speak about it. Good day, sir.

Chapter 120

Lord Marshal Keith

December 8, 1764

Based on the last letter that you should have received from me, My Lord, you will have been able to judge the pleasure given me by the one with which you honored me on October 24. You have made me feel, and even a little cruelly, to what point I am attached to you, and three months of silence on your part have affected and distressed me more than the Council of Geneva's writ. So many misfortunes have made my heart uneasy, and I always fear to lose what I desire so ardently to preserve. You are my only protector, the only man to whom I have genuine obligations, the only friend upon whom I count, the last to whom I am attached, and to whom others will never succeed. Judge from this whether your kindnesses are dear to me, and whether your forgetfulness is easy to bear.

I am sorry that you are not able to live in your house until a year from now. As long as we are still at castles in Spain, every house is good for us in the meantime. But when finally experience and reason have taught us that there is no genuine enjoyment except in oneself, a commodious lodging and a healthy body become the sole goods in life whose worth makes itself felt from day to day, in measure as one is detached from the rest. Since it has not taken so long to make your garden, I hope that from now on it amuses you, and that you are already drawing from it something to provide those very savory soups which, without being very greedy, I miss every day.

Why cannot I learn from you a more useful, if more thankless, cultivation? Why cannot my good and unfortunate Corsicans be able, through me, to profit from your long and profound observations about men and governments? But I am far from you, and the Gavachos are swarming over them.[1] My Lord, what a servile and tyrannical nation at the same time! Which seems to want to destroy freedom on the earth down to its root, and for whom the greatest of crimes is to resist oppression? No matter. Without considering the impossibility of success, I will occupy myself with these poor people as if my reveries could be useful to them. Since I am devoted to chimeras, I want at least to forge agreeable ones for myself. In considering what men could be, I will seek to forget what they are. The Corsicans are, as you say very well, much closer to that desirable state than any other people. For example, I do not believe that the dissolubility of marriages, very useful in Brandenburg, would be so for a long time in Corsica, where the simplicity of morals and general poverty still make great passions inactive, and marriages peaceful and happy. The women are laborious and chaste; men do not have any pleasures except at home. In that state, it is not good to make them envisage as possible a separation that they have no occasion to desire.

I have not yet received the letter with the translation of Fletcher about which you told me.[2] I was waiting for it to write to you, but seeing that the packet does not come, I cannot defer any longer. My Lord, my heart is ceaselessly full of you. Think sometimes about your younger son.

---

1. The Gavachos were Corsican mountaineers.
2. This is a work on militias.

CHAPTER 121

Alexandre Deleyre

December 20, 1764
Môtiers

I am taking advantage of the departure of Mr. Boswell,[1] a Scottish gentleman who is going to make his tour of Italy, to give you a little hello and to tell you how much your last letter touched and delighted my heart. Although I have never sought out anyone, I have responded with such alacrity to the advances of a thousand people who have sought me out that I threw myself at their heads, so to speak. All of them disappeared at the first setback, and now there you are, almost the only one with whom I have been difficult,[2] remaining, consoling me in my misfortunes, and pardoning me my wrongs. Dear Deleyre, doubtless I have been very slow, but if my sincere friendship still pleases you, do not regard these delays as a loss. I will certainly pay you interest.

I am very glad that Mr. Boswell and you are to become acquainted. I believe that you will both thank me for it. In the first letter he wrote me, he informed me that he was a man *of a peculiar merit*. I was curious to see someone who spoke that way about himself, and I found that

---

1. Boswell had come to Môtiers to introduce himself to Rousseau. They met several times.
2. This reference concerns his lack of warmth toward Deleyre's fiancée.

he had spoken the truth. In his youth his head was muzzy with harsh Calvinist theology, and from it he still has an uneasy soul and dark ideas. I advised him to dedicate his trip to Italy to the study of the fine arts. If you philosophize with him, I beg you to restrain yourself about your own inclinations, and not to present moral objects to him except through what is consoling and tender. He is a convalescent whom the slightest relapse would infallibly kill. I would take an interest in him, even if he had not been recommended to me by My Lord Maréchal. I need say no more to you about it.

I am on the point of concluding some business that would give me repose and bread for the remainder of my days. I need both, for in my exhaustion of body and mind, I can no longer either think or act.

It is a question of a general edition of my writings, which a society wants to undertake here under my eyes, and with which I will take my last leave of the public.

One thing perplexes me: it is the preface, which I am in no condition to write. Would you have the time, would you be in the mood, to burden yourself with that task? I cannot express to you what good you would be doing for me. Of course, however, you would be the one speaking, and you would allow it to bear your name. I would like to think that it would share with mine the fate that awaits it, and that I believe could only be honorable, because posterity is always just. Consider, and answer me when you can; your answer can decide me on the choice I have to make.

I am not entirely of your opinion about the impossibility of giving a good founding to the Corsicans, and I do not believe that it is necessary to employ fanaticism for it. Far from thinking that one must not get mixed up in human affairs so as not to have any reproach to make to oneself, I think on the contrary that one is preparing a very great one for oneself when one neglects to do the good, or at least to attempt it with some hope of succeeding. But now is not the moment for speaking about all that, and today the Corsicans have other things to do than to establish utopia in their midst. It must be admitted that your French are a very servile people, completely sold out to tyranny, very cruel, and very relentless toward the unfortunate. If they knew that a man was free at the other end of the world, I believe they would go for the sole pleasure of exterminating him. Good day.

In the 24th volume of Muratori's collection *Scriptorum rerum Italicarum* there is a little work by P. Cirneo titled *De rebus Corsicis*. This work is not printed separately. Would there be any way to unearth it?

CHAPTER 122

Frédéric-Guillaume de Montmollin

December 23, 1764
Môtiers
Rousseau sent this letter along with a copy of the Letters Written from the
Mountain.

Pity me, sir, for loving peace so much, and always having war. I could
not refuse to take up the defense of my former compatriots, as they
had taken up mine. This is what I could not do without repulsing the
insults with which, out of the blackest ingratitude, the ministers of
Geneva were base enough to overwhelm me in my misfortunes, and
which they have dared to bring even into the sacred pulpit, into which
they are unworthy of ascending. Since they love war so greatly, they will
have it. After a thousand aggressions on their part, here is my first act
of hostility, in which nevertheless I defend one of their greatest prerogatives, that they are spinelessly letting be taken from them; for to insult
the unfortunate at their ease, they willingly crawl under tyranny. Moreover, the quarrel between them and me is entirely personal, or if I make
the Protestant religion enter into it in some way, it is as its defender
against those who want to overturn it. Consider my reasons, sir, and be

persuaded that the more I am placed under the necessity of explaining my sentiments, the more honor will result for your behavior toward me, and for the justice you have rendered me.

Receive, sir, I beg you, my greetings and my respect.

JJRousseau

CHAPTER 123

Pierre-Alexandre DuPeyrou

December 31, 1764
DuPeyrou had written to Rousseau the day before to express his enthusiastic approval of the Letters Written from the Mountain.

Your letter touched me to the point of tears. I see that I did not deceive myself, and that you have an honorable soul. You will be a man precious to my heart. Read the enclosed booklet.[1] Behold, sir, what enemies I have to deal with; behold the weapons with which they attack me. Return this piece to me when you have read it; it will enter into the monuments of my life's history. O, when the veil is drawn back some-day, how posterity will love me! how it will bless my memory! You, love me now, and believe that I am not unworthy of it. I embrace you.

---

1. Rousseau enclosed the pamphlet *Sentiments of the Citizens*, which had been written by Voltaire and published anonymously. Rousseau mistakenly believed that it had been written by Vernes. He republished a version of the pamphlet with his own remarks as marginal notes (*CW* 12:45–49).

CHAPTER 124

Pierre-Alexandre DuPeyrou

January 24, 1765
Môtiers

You may well think, sir, that after having agreed with you that I would write to M. Panckoucke,[1] it is a matter that I have not forgotten. As he is excessively overburdened with business, he has perhaps not found the time to write to you, and he writes to me very rarely. But since he has begun to send you something, that is a sign that he will willingly attend to your errands. He is a man of letters, superior to the condition of publisher, who will do them faithfully and with discernment.

I admit to you that I see only with trepidation the agreement I will make with the company in question if the affair is consummated; so, if it were to fail, I would hardly be punished. Nevertheless, as I will find in it solid advantages, and a very great convenience for the execution of a plan that is dear to my heart, and as moreover I do not want to respond uncivilly to the advances made by these Gentlemen, I wish, if the enterprise fails, that it not be by my fault. Besides, while I find the demands you made in my name a little extreme, I am strongly of the

---

1. Charles-Joseph Panckoucke (1736–98), influential publisher, including of the *Mercure de France.*

opinion that since they have been made, nothing in them be reduced. I have so thoroughly mislaid the model power of attorney that you sent me that I have not been able to find it up to now. Until I find it, I am sending you a note of the pieces, both manuscript and printed, which must make up the collection in the order of the quarto edition. I have added to these some articles in the form of explanations which it would be useful to add to the treatise to prevent any trouble, for that above all is what I fear.

I recognize you well, sir, in the arrangement you propose me should that one fail.[2] But while I am filled with gratitude, I would hardly recognize myself if I could accept it on that footing. Nevertheless, I see in it an opening to get free with your help of a dire predicament in which I find myself. For in the precarious state of my health and my life, I would die cruelly perplexed thinking that my papers, my effects, and my housekeeper are at the mercy of Master Martinet.[3] It will be a great misfortune if the interest which you so kindly take in me, and the confidence I have in you, does not lead us to some arrangement which pleases your heart without making mine suffer. Once you become the trustee of all my affairs, I will be at peace, and it seems to me that the repose of my days will be sweeter when I will be indebted to you for it. I only wish that, beforehand, we could become even more intimately acquainted. I have plans for voyages this summer. Could we not make one together? Will your construction so occupy you that you cannot leave it for a few weeks, even for a few months, should that possibility occur? My dear sir, one has to begin by being well acquainted to know well what one is doing when one binds oneself. I am touched when I think that, after such an unhappy life, perhaps I will still find serene days near you, and that perhaps a chain of reverses has guided me to the man whom Providence calls upon to close my eyes. Besides, I speak to you of my voyages, because by dint of habit, moving has become a need for me. During the whole summer, it is impossible for me to stay more than two or three days in the same place without compelling myself and without suffering.

---

2. The arrangement was an annuity to be paid to Rousseau, and then to Thérèse in the event of his death.

3. This refers to Jacques-Frédéric Martinet, whom the duc de Luxembourg had recommended for handling Rousseau's affairs after his flight.

I believe that I will not need the Venetian *chandellettes*,[4] because we wrote to Naples to have some of Daran's finest catheters, whose effect is proven. Good day, sir.

Note on the pieces which will compose the collection.

First Volume in quarto
Discourse on Inequality
Discourse on Political Economy
On the Social Contract
Extract from Perpetual Peace
Extract from the Polysynody
* Judgment on Perpetual Peace
* Judgment on the Polysynody
* Translation of the first book of Tacitus's History
Volume 2
The New Heloise
Volume 3
Emile, until the end of the Profession of Faith
Volume 4
The continuation of Emile
Letter to the Archbishop of Paris
Letters Written from the Mountain
Volume 5
Letter to M. d'Alembert
Of Theatrical Imitation
* Discourse on the first virtue of the hero
Discourse which won the Dijon prize
Response to an anonymous writing in the *Mercure de France*
Letter on a response by M. Gautier
Reply to the king of Poland
Last reply of J. J. Rousseau
Preface to Narcissus
Narcissus Comedy
* The Foolhardy Engagement. Comedy.
* The Gallant Muses. Opera.
The Village Soothsayer. Intermission.
* Pygmalion, lyrical scene
* Emile and Sophie, or the Solitaries. Fragment.

---

4. Bougie, a catheter in the shape of a slender candle.

* The Levite of Ephraim
* Letters to Sara
* Queen Whimsical Tale
* Translation of Apocolokintosis by Seneca
  Volume 6
On music, Dictionary Article
On Opera, Dictionary Article
* Memorandum read to the Academy of Sciences, 1742
Letter on French music
* Reply to M. Rameau
* Essay on the origin of languages
* Letters and Memoranda on various subjects
General table of contents
N.B. The items preceded by an asterisk are still in manuscript form.

The author reserves the right to suppress those among these pieces that, after mature reflection, he will not find worthy to be part of this collection. He waives publication rights for all of them, however, and cedes this right to the present society in perpetuity. He intends when printing ends to place a preface at the beginning of the first volume, but since he is not yet completely decided on this point, he does not engage to do so.

CHAPTER 125

Marquis de Saint-Brisson

February 3, 1765

I received, sir, your letter of December 27. I also read *Ariste* and *Philo-penes*.[1] Despite the pleasure they both gave me, I do not repent of having spoken ill about the first, and do not doubt that I would have spoken ill about the second, had you consulted me. My dear Saint-Brisson, I will never tell you enough how it pains me to see you entering into a career covered with flowers and strewn with chasms, in which one cannot avoid being corrupted or being ruined, in which one becomes unhappy or bad in measure as one advances, and very often both before one arrives. The occupation of author is good only for he who wants to serve the passions of the people who lead the others; but for he who sincerely wants humanity's good, it is a dire occupation. Will you have more zeal than I for justice, for truth, for all that is decent and good; will you have more disinterested sentiments, a religion that is gentler, more tolerant, purer, more sensible; will you aspire to fewer things; will you follow a more solitary road; will you follow the path taken by fewer people; will you shock fewer rivals and competitors; will you avoid with

---

1. Séguier de Saint-Brisson, *Ariste, ou Les charmes de l'honnêteté* and *Philopenes, ou Du régime des pauvres.*

greater care to cross anyone's interests? And nevertheless, you see, I do not know how there exists in the world a single decent man whose pen my example does not make fall from his hands. Do good, my dear Saint-Brisson, but not through books; far from correcting bad people, they only embitter them. The best book does very little good for men, and much ill to its author. I have already seen you climbing the walls for a brochure which was not even very uncivil. What must you expect if these things already wound you?

How can you believe that I want to go to Corsica when I know that French troops are there? Do you consider that I do not have enough of my misfortunes without seeking others? No, sir, in my despondency I need to catch my breath, I need to go farther away from Geneva to seek a few moments of repose. For on this earth, a long one will be left me nowhere; I can no longer hope for any except in its bosom. I do not know yet in which direction I will go; there are hardly any left me to choose. I would like along the way to find some fixed retreat to which I could altogether transplant myself, where one would have the humanity to receive me and let me die in peace. But where to find it among Christians? Turkey is too far from here.

Do not doubt, dear Saint-Brisson, that it would have been very sweet for me to have you as a travel companion, as consoler, as nurse, but against this same voyage I have great objections related to you. First, remove from your mind the thought of consulting me about anything, and of having the least resource against boredom in conversation with me. The disorientation into which I am thrown by ceaseless agitations has made me stupid; my head is in a lethargy; even my heart is dead. I no longer feel or think. A sole pleasure remains to me in life: I still like to walk, but while walking, I do not even dream. I have the sensations of the objects that strike me, and nothing more. I wanted to try to botanize a little, to amuse myself at least by recognizing a few plants along the way, but my memory is entirely extinguished; it cannot achieve even that. Imagine the pleasure of traveling with such an automaton.

That is not all. I feel the bad effect that travel here would have on you. You are already not in good odor with the devout; do you want to complete your own destruction? Even your compatriots in general do not forgive you for knowing me; how could they forgive you for loving me; I am very annoyed that you named me at the beginning of your *Ariste*. Do not engage in such foolishness again, or I will quarrel with you for good. Tell me, above all, how you think your family will see such a voyage. It will make madam your mother tremble. I tremble myself when I think of the dire effect that it could produce on your relations, and you want me to let you do this; it is to want me to be the worst of men. No, sir, obtain madam your mother's approval and come. I embrace you with the greatest joy, but without that agreement, let us not speak of this anymore. I embrace you with all my heart.

CHAPTER 126

Marquise de Verdelin

February 3, 1765
Môtiers

Amid the cares that the zeal you have for your family gives you, madam, and in the first moment of your convalescence, you busy yourself with me. You foresee the new dangers into which the furor of my enemies, indignant that I have dared to bring to light their injustice, will again plunge me. You are not mistaken, madam. One cannot imagine anything like the rage excited by the *Letters from the Mountain*. The Gentlemen of Bern have just prohibited this work in insulting terms, and I would not be surprised if some harm were done to me on their lands once I again set foot there. In this very country all the king's protection is required to keep me safe. The Council of Geneva, which is breathing fire as much here as in Holland, is waiting for the moment to act openly in its turn and to finish crushing me if possible. Whichever way I turn, I see claws to tear at me and open maws to devour me. I at least hoped for more humanity from France, but I was wrong. Guilty of the irremissible crime of being unjustly oppressed, I must await from it only my coup de grâce. My decision is taken, madam. I will let everything be done, everything said, and I will be quiet: not, however, for lack of something to talk about.

I feel that it is impossible that I am left alone here to breathe in peace. I am safe under the protection of the king, but I am too close to Geneva and Bern to be left tranquil. The passion for this happy tranquility agitates and troubles me more every day. If I did not hope to find it in the end, I feel that my constancy would end by abandoning me. I have some desire to try Italy, whose climate and inquisition are gentler than in France and here. I will try this summer to drag myself that way to seek a quiet lodging there, and if I can find it, I certainly promise that no one will hear speak of me again. Repose, repose, dear idol of my heart, where will I find you? Is it possible that no one wants to let a man who never troubled anyone's repose enjoy some?

You are told then, madam, that M. de Voltaire wrote to me under the name of General Paoli, and that I have fallen into the trap? Those who say this, it seems to me, are hardly doing more honor to M. de Voltaire's probity than to my discernment. Since I have received your letter, this is what happened to me. A knight of Malta who comes from Geneva and who says that he also comes from Italy, came to see me on General Paoli's behalf, making a great show of being assiduous about commissions for me with which he said he was charged, but at bottom saying very little and spreading out for me with an important air some rather paltry documents. With each piece he showed me, he was utterly astonished to see me take out of a drawer the very same piece and show it to him in turn. I saw that this mortified him even more in that, having made every effort to know what connections I could have in Corsica, he was not able to wrest a single word from me on that subject. Since he brought no letters, and since he did not want either to name himself or give me the least notion of who he was, I thanked him for the visits he wanted to continue making me. He did not give up staying here ten or twelve days more without coming back to see me. I do not know what he did. I am told he left again yesterday.

You can well imagine, madam, that Corsica is no longer in question for me for a thousand reasons that it is easy for you to imagine. Those Gentlemen about whom you speak have health, bread, and repose; their heads are free and their hearts blooming with well-being. They can work at their ease. I would very much like to see legislation done in their manner: but upon what would they be able to found it in Corsica? Where the women are very ugly; and very chaste, which is worse.

M. Junet, taking advantage of your kindness, will send you, madam, a memorandum on the subject of a position which would be extremely suitable for him, and which seems to me easy to obtain in the circumstances. He showed me his original accounts, according to which, instead of adding up to only two thousand five hundred pounds as you were told, they annually add up to six thousand francs; from which it follows that, according to these Gentlemen's own calculations, his salary should be 600 francs instead of 250. But it must not be said that I have seen this item, for fear that this will bring him some reproach.

May my projected voyage, madam, not make you renounce yours. I have more need of it than ever, and everything could work out well if you came at the beginning or at the end of the summer. I would rather break off mine than miss seeing you; but if you could come in May or in September, that is enough. I am not the only one here who rejoices at such a sweet hope. The approach to our vale is awful, but the stay here is not so ugly as you may perhaps imagine.

I hope that you will have received the *Letters from the Mountain*, which were brought for you to the Aubeterre Hotel more than fifteen days ago.

Pierre-Alexandre DuPeyrou

February 7, 1765
Môtiers

I do not doubt, sir, that yesterday, day of the Two Hundred, my book was burned in Geneva; at least, all the measures were taken to that end. You will have learned that it was burned on the 22nd at The Hague. Rey informs me that the inquisitor wrote many letters in that country, and that Minister Chais of Geneva has agitated himself greatly.[1] What is more, Rey is left very much in peace. Is not all that amusing? This business was plotted with much secrecy and diligence, for Count Bentinck, who wrote to me just a few days beforehand, knew nothing about it. You will say to me: why did he not stop it at the time of its execution? Sir, everywhere I have powerful, illustrious friends who, I am very sure, love me with all their hearts; but they are all upright, good, gentle, peaceful people who disdain any oblique means. My enemies, on the contrary, are ardent, skillful, scheming, crafty, indefatigable in seeking to ruin, and always maneuver underground like moles. You sense that

---

1. "The inquisitor" refers to Voltaire.

the match is not an equal one. The inquisitor is the most active man that earth has produced; he governs in a way all of Europe.

You must reign, this world is made for the bad people.[2]

I am very sure that, unless I survive him, I will be persecuted until death.

I cannot at all swallow M. de Buffon's supposing that I am bringing his hatred upon myself. Eh, what have I done for that? If I am talked about too much, that is not my fault. I could do without celebrity acquired at such a price. Inform M. de Buffon of whatever your friendship for me will inspire you to, and until I am in a condition to write him, tell him, I pray you, about all the sentiments for him with which you know me to be filled. I am very pleased by the gift that he is willing to give me, but I like his work too much to have been satisfied with the more delayed progress of the in-12. You saw the in quarto at my house, and you even saw that I had been more diligent than you to get in the know.

M. Vernes disavows, loudly and with horror, the libel to which I put his name. He wrote me a decent letter about this, to which I responded in the same tone, offering to contribute as much as I could to disseminate his disavowal. Despite the certainty I thought I had that the work came from him, certain recent facts make me suspect that it could very well be from someone who is hiding under his cloak, and who even seems to have accomplices in the magistracy. What is nevertheless certain, is that the moment my book appeared, Vernes could not control himself, and in his furor said everywhere the same things which are in the piece. He has changed his tone, but he saw that he did not have the laughers on his side. Until more light is shed on this, I will disseminate, as is just, M. Vernes's disavowal, while abstaining from adding any declaration on my part.

Furthermore, the printed version from Paris was very promptly and very peculiarly spread about in Geneva. A number of individuals received copies under wraps by the post, with only these words written in a woman's hand: "Read, good people!" I would give everything in the world to know who this kind woman is who is so profoundly interested in a poor oppressed man, and who knows how to indicate her indignation in terms so brief and so full of energy.

---

2. The line is from Voltaire, *Fanaticism, or Mohammed the Prophet* (1741), act 5, scene 4. In the original it ends with "tyrants" rather than "bad people."

I had foreseen very well, sir, that your calculations would not be acceptable, and that regarding a man you love, your heart would derange your head in matters of interest. We will chat about that more comfortably while we botanize this summer. For, far from renouncing our caravans, even supposing that the voyage to Italy takes place, I very much want to try that the latter not spoil it. Moreover, I will tell you that I feel within me during the last few days a revolution which astonishes me. These last events, which ought to have finished overwhelming me have, I do not know how, made me tranquil, and even rather gay. It seems to me that I was granting too much importance to children's games. There is in all these burnings something so silly and so stupid, that one has to be even more of a child than they to be moved by it. My moral life is finished. Is it worth it to take so much trouble to choose the earth in which I will leave my body? The most precious part of myself is already dead. Men can do nothing more against it, and I no longer see this whole heap of magistrates—such liars, so barbarous, so vile—as anything but so many worms who amuse themselves by gnawing on my corpse.

The traveling machine will therefore assemble itself this summer to go botanizing, and if friendship can still warm it, you will be the Prometheus who will bring me back Heaven's fire. Good day, sir.

CHAPTER 128

Jacques Vieusseux

February 7, 1765

I am sure, s[ir], that my work is currently being burned in Geneva, in imitation of The Hague where, Rey informs me, it has been through the ardent machinations of the minister Chais and the inquisitor Voltaire. The situation in which I find myself is too violent to leave me the freedom to reason well, either about your affairs or about mine. Nevertheless, it seems to me that your project of remonstrance is not only excellent, but needs to be executed in the present circumstance, to prove to all of Europe that you are neither troublemakers nor hotheads, and that you have spared neither cares nor proceedings to arrive at a reconciliation. You have the most noble subject that it is possible to treat. Without departing from the gravity suitable to it, you could with this writing cause the greatest sensation among equitable and disinterested people, and it is toward this that you should always tend. For it appears to me certain that you will obtain nothing from the Council, and that you must from afar dispose all of your batteries for the future, such that if the mediators want to crush you, at least they will be ashamed of doing so.

Forcefully summarize your reasons. Show yourselves unshakable and firm but, at the same time, pierced with pain by their unjust inflexibility. Complain about the dangers to the fatherland, about the blindness of a magistrate who, for the sake of a false point of honor, does not want to listen to anything that is just. Show the most tender respect for them, the most ardent desire to give them your trust again; be touched, regretful, and move them to their depths while speaking from your own; show with dread the perils of a State which they ought to make happy; how much you want to sacrifice for peace as soon as it is not a question of your liberty. Skillfully make them feel the consequences of the steps to which they will reduce you, not only for the sake of liberty, but for their own authority which, depending upon the good will of a minister, may escape them when they are least thinking of it. In a word, be tender, pathetic. Consider that your remonstrance will be your manifesto and that, this piece in your hand, you need to justify yourself before all of Europe of the accusation that you are seditious. It is a very fine piece, sirs, that you could produce, if you penetrate yourself thoroughly with your subject. I would very much like it if someone about whom I am thinking lend you his pen a little. It is the man with whom our friend has reconciled me but, unfortunately, he is leaving for Languedoc.

I would dare think that it is suitable for both of us, if you are not averse, to touch upon me in these circumstances, not to ask for anything in my favor, but only to be aggrieved at my disgraces. It is what I did for you that brought on all my misfortunes. The whole of Europe is not unaware of this; it must not believe that you are abandoning me to their affronts. As it is easy to say too much or too little, however, permit me to note for you here the phrasing that, in my view, you can use without compromising yourself. You will easily understand in what follows at what it must arrive:

> And although all the steps they have taken, superior to all particular interests, have as their goal nothing but the exact observation of the laws, they would think themselves inexcusable if they did not take an interest in the fate of an unfortunate man, full of zeal for his fatherland, who may have committed errors, but who surely, neither for his sentiments nor for his conduct, merits the treatments he has received in his country.

It is I, sir, who had the piece titled *Sentiments of the Citizens* printed in Paris. You did not believe that the notes were from me, no doubt because of my moderation. That proves to me that you still do not know me. If this libel had been undertaken against another, you can be sure that I would not have taken that tone. I have played no part in the envoys for Geneva, and I cannot even imagine by whom they were written.

The work is certainly either from M. Vernes or from an extremely adroit hand who wanted that it be thought his, and I admit to you that the refusal made him, of which you informed me, strengthens the latter suspicion a little at the same time that it explains the decent letter he wrote me and to which I answered even more decently. Until now, I was as sure that he was the author of this piece as if I had seen him write it. Were it ever proved that I was mistaken, I will frankly confess my fault, for when one has made mistakes, one should not blush at fixing them. Is it then so impossible to verify the matter? What is sure is that all of Geneva was witness to M. Vernes's rages, and these same rages are present in this writing. You would oblige me by gathering some precise facts about all this. You could send them, signed, to me here without compromising yourself, and you must be sure that if ever I make use of them, no one will know from whom I had them.

An extract of a supposed letter by the Abbé de Mably was sent to me in an anonymous letter, which I am very sure is not by him. I think that this extract was fabricated to be read before the Two Hundred. I know of nothing so easy to dupe on such matters as the Genevans. In fifteen days, I count on having proof of this falsity. I suspect by whom it has been fabricated, for I know that in Paris the Abbé de Mably often saw Madame Saladin.

P.S. I do not have the time at present, to say the least, to read the *General Solution*.[1] I quickly skimmed a few pages of it. I do not clearly see the real goal of the author, which he is perhaps hiding. It seems to me that in general this goal is more advantageous to you than the contrary. I will dare decide only one thing. It is that it is quite difficult to have more wit than the author. He writes badly, perhaps because he writes with too much wit; one needs a great deal of it to follow him.

---

1. A pamphlet by Théodore Rilliet.

CHAPTER 129

Paul-Claude Moultou

February 18, 1765
Môtiers
Moultou had written to Rousseau about the condemnation of the Letters Written from the Mountain *in Geneva.*

What is happening does not surprise me. I have always predicted it and have always said that in such a case one had to limit oneself to that. Instead of doing everything one can, it is enough to do all one must, and it is done. One could not go further without risking the fatherland and the public peace, which a wise man should never do. When there is no more communal liberty, there remains one resource: to cultivate individual liberty, that is, virtue. The virtuous man is always free: for in always doing his duty he never does anything but what he wills. If the Genevan bourgeoisie knew how to restore its principles, purify its tastes, adopt stricter morals, while leaving these Gentlemen to the degradation of theirs, it would again become so respectable to them that even with their apparent arrogance they would tremble before it; and since mountebanks of every kind and their friends will not always be alive, some change in foreign circumstances could put them within reach of finally getting the courts to examine what force alone decides today.

Please warmly salute the Mr. Ds for me and tell them that I cannot write.[1] Since that is no longer necessary or useful, it is not reasonable to demand it of me. One must not envy the repose that I ask for, and I think I have paid enough for it.

Try to send me before you leave what you spoke to me about, not to make use of it at present, but to make in advance all the necessary arrangements to make use of it one day. I will even have something else, and of a more amusing genre, to propose to you. But we will speak about it at leisure. I embrace you.

---

1. "The Mr. Ds" are the Delucs, father and son.

CHAPTER 130

Pierre-Alexandre DuPeyrou

March 7, 1765
Môtiers

For God's sake, do not get angry, and know how to forgive your friends a few wrongs amid their miseries. I have only one tone, sir, and it is sometimes somewhat harsh. One must not judge me on the basis of my expressions but on that of my behavior; it honors you when my words offend you. In need as I am of the consolations of friendship, I feel the lack of yours, and I complain of it. Is that so disagreeable?

If I wrote to others, how did you not feel the absolute necessity of responding—especially in the circumstances—to people with whom I do not at all correspond habitually, and who come at the height of my misfortune to take the most generous interest in it. I believed that about these very letters you would say to yourself, he does not have the time to write, and that you would remember our conventions. Did I, at such a critical moment, then have to abandon all my interests, all my affairs, even my duties, for fear of failing you in the punctuality of an answer from which you had excused me? You would have been offended by my fear, and you would have been right. Was not the very idea—definitely quite false—which you had that you had saddened me with your letter not a motive for your good heart to make up for the ill you supposed you had done me? God preserve you from afflictions; but in the same case, you can be sure that I would not count your answers. In any other case, never count my letters, or let us break everything off, especially since it will not be long before we break with one another. My character is known to you; I cannot change it.

All your other reasons are only too good. I pity you in your troubles, and your advancing gout grieves me especially deeply, and even more so since, in my extreme need to distract myself, I was promising myself charming walks with you. I still feel that what I am going to say to you may be out of place among your affairs, but I must show you whether I believe that you have a hard heart, and whether I lack confidence in your friendship. I am not making compliments; I prove.

I must leave this country, I feel it. It is too close to Geneva; I will never be left in peace there. There is hardly any but a Catholic country that suits me, and it is from there, since your ministers so badly want war, that one can give them that pleasure until they are glutted with it. You sense, sir, that this move entails some awkwardness. Would you be custodian of my personal effects, until I am settled? Would you like to buy my books, or help me to sell them? Would you be willing to make some arrangement as to my works, which would liberate me from the horror of having to think about them and busy myself with them for the rest of my life? All these rumors are too lively and too crazed to last. At the end of two or three years, all the difficulties about publication will be lifted, especially when I will be no longer. In any case, other places, even in the neighborhood, will not be lacking. Regarding all this, there are details which would take too long to write, and based on which, without your being a merchant and without your giving me alms, this arrangement could be useful to me and not onerous for you. This requires that we confer. We only need to see if your present affairs permit you to think of that one.

You know, then, the sad condition of poor Mad[am]e Guyenet, a pleasant woman, of real merit, with a mind as astute as accurate, and for whom virtue was not a vain word. Her family is greatly afflicted, her husband despondent, and I am torn apart. There, sir, is the object I have under my eyes to console me for a web of misfortunes without example.

I have bouts of dejection. That is rather natural in a state of illness, and these bouts are very perceptible, because they are the moments when I try most to unburden myself. But they are short, and do not affect my behavior. My habitual state is courage, and you will perhaps see it in this business if I am pushed to the limit. For I make it a law to be patient, up to the moment when one can no longer be so without cowardice. I do not know what devil of a bee got into your Gentlemen's bonnets,[1] but there is a great deal of bizarreness to all this din. They will blush at it once they calm down.

But what have you to say, sir, of the carelessness of your ministers, who, given their morals, their gross ignorance, should tremble for fear that one might notice they exist, and who will stupidly pay for the others in an affair which does not concern them. I am persuaded that they imagine that I will remain on the defensive and act the penitent and the supplicant. The Council of Geneva thought so too; I disabused it. I will take care of disabusing them in the same way. Be my witness, sir, of my love of peace, and of the pleasure with which I laid down my arms. If they force me to take them up again, I will take them up again, for I will not let myself be beaten to the ground; that is a point on which I am wholly resolute. What hold do they not give me? Except for around three or four whom I honor and whom I exempt, what are the others? What memories will I not have on their account? I am tempted to make my peace with all the other clergy at the expense of yours, to make of them the goat of atonement for the sins of Israel. The invention is good, and its success certain. Would it not be to serve the State well to cut down their arrogance so far, to degrade them to such a point, that they could never again rouse the peoples? I hope not to yield to revenge, but if I touch them, they are dead; count on it. As for the rest, I must first of all wait for excommunication. For until that moment, they have a hold on me; they are my pastors, and I owe them respect. I have on that point maxims that I will never renounce, and that is the very reason why I find them very unwise to like me better as a wolf than as a ewe.

On a separate sheet

If you deem it advisable to spread the second sheet of this letter, you can do so without fear of compromising me, for my decision is made.

---

1. Or, more literally, "what devil of a fly has stung your Gentlemen."

CHAPTER 131

Marquise de Verdelin

March 8, 1765
Môtiers

At last, madam, no refuge remains for me on earth; there is no longer any to seek save in its bosom. Despite the Lord Marshal, despite the king himself, the ministers are chasing me from here. You know that I have always lived well with your priests; you have seen my ties with the priests of the Oratory, with the austere parish priest of Montmorency, with the venerable priest of Groslay. I have found only friends among your clergy. Among ours I have found only furies; the inquisitors of Goa are lambs compared to them. Ah, madam, if they would let me die in a Catholic country! . . . But there is no longer commiseration or mercy for me to hope for. What to do; what to become? The greatest criminals find refuges; only I can find none. I would still willingly consider England, but which route? How to make it, and especially in my condition! The journey through Germany and Holland is immense, very costly, very arduous; I cannot think of it without dread. Could I not at least obtain a passport to pass through France? I would stop only two days in Paris; I will not pass through there if that is what is wanted. Ah, you know everything that will make this privation painful. If I obtained this passport, could I take advantage of it? It has been five months since I have been able to leave my room . . . Still, if I were alone . . . I would be happier for it; I would no longer live. How will I drag myself along with my poor nurse? Let me at least end my unfortunate days in the most wretched corner of Franche-Comté. Let them shut me up, let them do whatever they want with me, I consent to it all. See to it, dear friend, speak, try, if there remains by any chance any humanity in any man's heart. Either the passport or the refuge, procure something for me, and above all write me a word. One word alone from your hand will revive me. I feel my courage giving way; I have the greatest need of consolations.

As I was finishing my letter in the greatest dejection I have ever been in in my life, I saw my pastor enter my house. I found again during this interview all the vigor I thought I had lost. You may judge of it by the account that I am sending to the king's man. The assembly of the clergy regarding my affair is fixed for next week; I will inform you, madam, of the result. They know my distress and think of exploiting it. Let them. One thing is certain: they will not degrade me. While waiting for the end of this affair, ask for nothing.

CHAPTER 132

Samuel Meuron

March 9, 1765
Môtiers

Yesterday, sir, M. de Montmollin honored me with a visit, during which we had a rather lively meeting. After announcing formal excommunication as inevitable, he proposed, so as to forestall scandal, a mitigation which I refused outright. I told him that I did not want an intermediate situation; that I wanted to be inside or outside, at peace or at war, ewe or wolf. Regarding all this business, he made several objections which I smashed to powder for, since there is neither reason nor justice in everything that is done against me, as soon as discussion begins, I am strong. To show him that my firmness was not obstinacy, much less insolence, I offered, if the Classis were willing to remain at rest, to promise him never again in my life to write on any religious subject. He answered that there were complaints, that I had already made this agreement, and that I had failed to keep it. I answered that this was mistaken; that I may have resolved to do so for myself, but that I had promised this to no one. He protested that he was not the master and feared that the Classis had already made its determination. I answered that I was sorry, but that I had also made mine. As he left, he told me he would do what he could. I told him he would do what he would, and we parted. So, sir, next Thursday or Friday at the latest I will throw sword or scabbard into the river.

As you are my kind defender and patron, I thought I owed you an account of this interview. Receive, I beg of you, my salutations and my respect.

JJRousseau

CHAPTER 133

Frédéric-Guillaume de Montmollin

March 10, 1765

From deference to Monsieur the professor de Montmollin, my pastor, and from respect for the Venerable Classis, I offer, if this is accepted, to undertake in a written document signed by my hand not to publish during my life any new work on any religious matter, and even not to treat any in passing in any new work that I might publish on any other subject and, in addition, I will continue to show by my sentiments and by my conduct the value I place on the happiness of being united with the Church. I beg Monsieur the professor to be willing to communicate this declaration to the Venerable Classis. Drawn up in Môtiers, the 10th of March 1765.

JJRousseau

Chapter 134

Mathieu Buttafoco

March 24, 1765
Môtiers-Travers

I see, sir, that you do not know in what abyss of new misfortunes I find myself engulfed. Since your penultimate letter, I have not been allowed to catch my breath for an instant. I received your first delivery almost without being able to glance at it. As to the one from Perpignan, I have not heard speak of it. I wanted to write to you a hundred times, but continual agitation, all the sufferings of body and mind, the depression of my own affairs, have not allowed me to think of yours. I was waiting for a moment's hiatus. It does not arrive, it will not arrive, and, at the very moment that I am answering you I am, despite my condition, at risk of not being able to finish my letter here.

It is, sir, useless for you to count on the work that I had undertaken. It would have been too pleasant for me to busy myself with such a glorious task. This consolation has been taken from me. My soul, exhausted by worries, is no longer in a condition to think; my heart is still the same, but I no longer have a head; I no longer see anything before me but a stagnant pond; my intelligent faculty is already dead; I am no longer able to follow an object with any attention. And besides, what would you want an unfortunate fugitive—who, despite the protection of the king of Prussia, sovereign of the country, despite the protection of the Lord Marshal who is its governor, both unfortunately too far away, drinks insults like water and, no longer being able to live in this refuge, is forced to go wandering, looking for another without any longer knowing where to find it—to do?

Yet certainly, sir, I know of one worthy of me, and of which I do not believe myself unworthy: it is among you, brave Corsicans, who know how to be free, who know how to be just, and who have been too unfortunate not to be compassionate. See to it, sir, what can be done; speak of it to M. Paoli. I ask to be able to rent a little house in some solitary canton in which to finish my days in peace. I have my housekeeper who, for twenty years, nurses me in my continual infirmities; she is a girl of 45 years, French, Catholic, decent, and well behaved, and who is resolved to come, if it must be done, to the end of the universe to share my miseries and to close my eyes. I will run my little household with her, and I will try not to make the cares of hospitality inconvenient to my neighbors.

But sir, I must say everything to you. This hospitality must be free, not as to the subsistence—I will not be a burden to anyone regarding that—but as to the right of asylum that must be granted to me without interest. For as soon as I am among you, do not expect anything from me regarding the project which occupies you. I repeat, I am no longer in a condition to think about it; and were I not, I would abstain from it from the very fact that I would be living among you. For I had, and will always have, as an inviolable maxim to bear the most profound respect for the government under which I live, without getting mixed up in censuring and critiquing, or reforming in any way. I even have here a further reason, which is of great force for me. From the little I glanced at in your memoranda, I see that my ideas differ prodigiously from those of your nation. It would be impossible for the plan I would propose not to produce many malcontents, and perhaps you first of all. Now, sir, I am filled to the brim with disputes and quarrels. I no longer want to see or to make malcontents around me, whatever the cost may be. I yearn for the fullest tranquility, and my last wishes are to be loved by all that surrounds me, and to die in peace. My resolution on this point is unshakable. What is more, my continual ills absorb me and increase my languidness. My own affairs require more of my time than I am able to give them. My worn mind is no longer equal to any other application. If perhaps the sweetness of a calm life prolongs my days enough to afford me some leisure, and if you consider me able to write your history, I would willingly undertake this honorable work, which would satisfy my heart without fatiguing my head too much, and I would be very pleased to leave to posterity this memorial of my stay among you; but do not ask me for anything more. As I do not want to mislead you, I would reproach myself for acquiring your protection at the cost of a vain expectation.

In this idea which came to me, I consulted my heart more than my strength, for in my condition it is not evident that I can sustain such a long voyage, which is moreover very cumbersome, especially with my housekeeper and my small luggage. Should you encourage me, however, I will attempt it, that is certain, were I to remain and perish along the way. I need, however, at least a moral assurance of being in repose for the remainder of my life; for it is done, sir, I can no longer run. Despite my critical and precarious position, I will wait for your answer in this country before making any decision; but please defer as little as possible, for despite all my patience, I may not be master of events. I embrace and salute you, sir, with all my heart.

P.S. I forgot to tell you that, as to your priests, they will be very demanding if they are not satisfied with me. I never quarrel about anything. I never speak about religion. I naturally even love your clergy as much as I hate ours. I have many friends among the clergy in France, and I have always gotten along very well with them. I do not even scruple to go to mass. But whatever may happen, I do not want to change religion, and I wish no one ever speaks to me of doing so, all the more so since it would be useless.

Letters must be addressed thus:

To Môtiers-Travers, via Pontarlier.

So as not to lose time, in case of confirmation, someone in Livourne would have to be indicated to me to whom I could ask for instructions about the passage.

CHAPTER 135

Consistory of Môtiers

March 29, 1765
Môtiers

Sirs,

Upon your summons, I had resolved yesterday, despite my condition, to appear today before you. But feeling that it would be impossible for me, despite my willingness, to sustain a long session and, on the matter of faith which is the sole object of the summons, reflecting that I could equally explain myself in writing, I did not doubt, sirs, that the gentleness of charity is allied in you to the zeal of faith, and that you would accept in this letter the same answer I could have made orally to Monsieur de Montmollin's questions, whatever they might be.

It seems to me, then, that unless the severity that the Venerable Classis judges appropriate toward me is founded upon a positive law, which I am assured does not exist in this State, nothing is more novel, more irregular, more prejudicial to civil liberty and, above all, more contrary to the spirit of religion than such a procedure in a pure matter of faith.

For, sirs, I beg you to consider that, living as I have for a long time in the bosom of the Church, and being neither a pastor nor a professor, nor charged with any portion of public instruction, I must not be subject—I, a simple individual, a simple member of the faith—to any interrogation or inquisition regarding faith. Such inquisitions, unheard of in this country, sap all the foundations of the Reformation, and wound at the same time evangelical liberty, Christian charity, the authority of the prince, and the rights of subjects, either as members of the Church, or as citizens of the State. I always owe an account of my actions and of my conduct to the laws and to men, but since among us an infallible Church, which would have the right to prescribe to its members what they must believe, is not admitted, once I was received into the Church, I owe only to God alone an account of my faith.

I add to this that, when after the publication of *Emile* I was admitted to the communion of this parish, almost three years ago, by M. de Montmollin, I made a declaration in writing to him, with which he was so fully satisfied that not only did he require no other explanation as to dogma, but he even promised not to require one. I hold myself strictly to his promise, and above all to my declaration. And what an inconsistency, what an absurdity, what a scandal would it not be to have been satisfied with it after the publication of a book in which Christianity seemed to be so violently attacked,[1] and not to be satisfied with it now, after the publication of another book in which the author may err,[2] no doubt, since he is a man, but in which, at least, he errs as a Christian, since he does not cease to support himself, step by step, on the authority of the Gospel? It was then that communion could have been taken from me, but it is at present that it ought to be returned. If you do the contrary, sirs, think of your consciences. As for me, whatever may happen, mine is at peace.

I owe you, sirs, and I want to offer you every kind of deference, and I wish with all my heart that the protection with which the king honors me not be forgotten enough to force me to implore that of the government.

Receive sirs, I pray you, the affirmation of my respect.

JJRousseau

I append here the copy of the declaration based on which I was admitted to the communion in 1762, and which I confirm today.

---

1. *Emile.*
2. *Letters Written from the Mountain.*

CHAPTER 136

Pierre-Alexandre DuPeyrou

April 22, 1765

Friendship is so sacred a thing that the word must not even be employed in ordinary usage. Hence we will be friends, and we will not say "my friend." I formerly had an epithet that I believe I deserve more than ever. In Paris I was only called "The Citizen." Give me back this title which is so dear to me and which I have paid for so dearly; even make it such that it spreads, and that all those who love me never call me sir, but in speaking of me, "the citizen," and in writing to me, "my dear citizen." I charge you with making known what I desire, and I think that all your friends and mine will willingly do me this pleasure. In the meantime, begin by setting the example. As for you, adopt an appellation which pleases you and that I can give you. I like to think that you must one day be my dear host,[1] and I would like to give you that title ahead of time. Be it that one or another, adopt one to your taste, and which will abolish between us that gloomy word "sir" that friendship and its intimacy must banish.

Your little note is very good.[2] Based on what I hear it seems to me important that you take your measures so precisely and so surely that

---

1. Or guest.
2. DuPeyrou's note concerned Theodore de Bèze, reformer of Neufchatel prior to Calvin.

the writing appears before the general in May.[3] I had the pleasure of seeing M. de Pury. He is a worthy man whose help I will never forget. I still suffer a great deal. I embrace you.

Continue to examine the seal on my letters to see if they have not been opened, and for good reason. I will continue to make use of the lyre.[4]

---

3. The Venerable Classis of pastors were to meet on May 1 and 2.
4. A seal with a lyre on it, to replace the very recognizable one with his motto, "Vitam impendere vero."

CHAPTER 137

Marc-Michel Rey

April 27, 1765
Môtiers

Everything is changed in this country regarding me, my dear companion,[1] and the ministers have done so many silly things that they have finally forced the government to open its eyes. In addition, the king's protection, and the constant kindness of My Lord Marshal, put me in the position to live in this country, despite the saintly furor of the clergy, as tranquilly as in any other. Yet I am still resolved not to remain here, and I would already have left it if my condition allowed me to undertake a voyage. But either due to the prolongation of the winter season, or to the continual annoyances of our priestly riffraff, my exacerbated ills do not allow me to consider any voyage at present, and it will soon be the eighth month that I am passing shut up in my room, and without being able to set foot in the street more than two or three times. If it pleased Providence to dispose of a life that no longer has anything but pains for me, I would willingly go and seek in the other the peace that no one wants to leave me in this one.

------

1. The French word is *compère*, which can mean either companion or godfather. Rey had asked Rousseau to be godfather of his child.

I would like with all my heart to be in a condition to benefit from Madame Rey's arrangements regarding her stay and that of my godchild near me. But this whole year is for me so stormy, my fate is so uncertain, I have so many errands to run, so many people must come see me, that I cannot absolutely with certainty dispose of a single moment of my time. Even were I to stay in this country, it is absolutely necessary that I leave Môtiers, and the search for a lodging that would suit me, and the difficulties of a move, would alone occupy me entirely even if I had nothing else to do. As to this winter, it is the season of my sufferings. Obliged almost continuously to wear catheters, I am not in a condition to see anyone during this whole season, especially women. These are obstacles which grieve me, but which do not depend on me to surmount. It is to be hoped that I will be more fortunate another year; but I cannot dispose of myself this year.

I recognize in your offers your friendship and your usual generosity. I am so sure of the kind heart with which you make them, that I would confidently take advantage of them if need arises. The printing of my works in this country has encountered obstacles which probably will not be raised, but if it occurred, it would not depend on me to gain you admittance to the society which formed the enterprise. This company is already too large and, when it was formed, I already had all the trouble in the world to gain admittance for M. d'Ivernois of Geneva, who is my friend. They do not lack capital, and they do not want to waste their efforts due to dividing their profits. But that would not prevent it being very beneficial and agreeable to them if you were willing to interest yourself in their success and they would very willingly negotiate with you alone for sales in England and in Holland.

As to the history of my life, the more I meditate on this enterprise, the more I see that I cannot execute it as I propose to do without postponing publication to a very distant time. If I want to show the truth as it is, I have so many things to say, which are of interest to so many people, and even people in power, that only the course of years could permit me to speak without disguise. Without that, my enterprise fails, and I will only produce an ordinary life, masked and plastered in makeup; whereas in my project I will do something unique and, I dare say, a truly beautiful thing. It is to me such an important object that I consecrate the rest of my life to it. It is absolutely not, however, suitable for your interests or those of your family that you begin with continual advances which will perhaps only pay a return to your children. All I can do to reconcile the good of the thing itself with the desire

I have that the work be executed only by you, is to take such measures in my arrangements that when it will be time to send this work to press, you will have the first offer, that the offer will first be made to you or your son, and that it pass to another publisher only if you cannot, or do not want to, execute it. Even that still has its difficulties, for it matters to me that the manuscript cannot be read by anyone in the world until its execution; but we will see.

Here is Mlle. Levasseur's receipt; please receive her thanks and her respects. You would oblige me in your deliveries to this country not to forget Volumes 8 and 9 of *Modern Universal History*, and to inform me to whom I should give back the two volumes of the ancient one. A thousand greetings to your ladies. I will certainly go see Mademoiselle Dumoulin in Vevey if she goes there and I am still here. You did not inform me if you received the ornaments entrusted to M. Vernède by Madame Boy de la Tour from Lyon. I embrace the dear child and her daddy.

CHAPTER 138

Mathieu Buttafoco

May 26, 1765
Môtiers

The stormy crisis I have just sustained, sir, and the uncertainty as to the decision it would lead me to make, made me postpone answering and thanking you until I had decided. I have now, due to a series of events which, giving me in this country if not tranquility, at least safety, made me decide to stay under the declared and confirmed protection of the king and of the government. It is not that I have lost the more genuine desire to live in yours; but the total exhaustion of my strength, the pains that would have to be taken, the toils that would have to be borne, still other obstacles which arise from my situation, make me at least for the time being abandon my undertaking which, despite these difficulties, my heart cannot yet resolve to abandon altogether. But my dear sir, I am aging, I am withering, strength is abandoning me; desire is inflamed, and hope is being extinguished. However this may be, receive and give to M. Paoli my most lively, my most affectionate thanks for the refuge he was so kind as to grant me. Brave and hospitable people! . . . No, I will never for a moment in my life forget that your hearts, your arms, and your hearths were open the instant there remained almost no other refuge for me in Europe. If I do not have the happiness of leaving my ashes on your island, I will endeavor at least to leave some monument of my gratitude there, and I will honor myself before the whole earth by calling you my hosts and my protectors.

I certainly received M. Paoli's letter from M. le ch[evali]er Rancurel, but in order to have you understand why I answered it in so few words, and in such a vague tone, I have to tell you, sir, that the rumor of the proposition you had made me, having spread I know not how, M. de Voltaire gave everyone to understand that this proposition was a fabrication of his. He claimed that he had written me in the name of the Corsicans a counterfeit letter of which I had been the dupe. As I was very confident in you, I let him go on; I kept on my way, and I did not even speak to you about it. But he did more. He boasted last winter that, despite the Lord Marshal and the king himself, he would have me chased out of this country. He had emissaries, some known, others secret. At the height of the ferment for which my last writing served as a pretext, M. de Rancurel arrives here. He comes to see me on M. Paoli's behalf, without bringing me any letter of his, or yours, or anyone's; he refuses to name himself; he came from Geneva; he had seen my most ardent enemies, as someone wrote to me. His long stay in this country, without any business here, had the most mysterious air in the world. His stay was precisely during the time that the uproar was excited against me. Let me add that he had made every effort to know what connections I might have in Corsica. As he had not named you, I did not want to name you either. Finally, he brought me M. Paoli's letter, whose handwriting I did not know. Consider whether that must not have seemed suspicious to me? What should I have done in such a case?—Entrust him with an answer from which, no matter what might happen, no explanation could be drawn; that is what I did.

I would like at present to speak to you about our business and projects, but this is hardly the time. Overwhelmed by cares, difficulties, forced to seek another lodging five or six leagues from here, the worries of a very inconvenient move would alone absorb me even if I had no others, and these are the least of mine. Taking a bird's-eye view, were my head to recover—which I consider to be impossible—more than a year from now, it would not be in me to busy myself with anything else but myself. What I promise you, upon which you can count from now on, is that for the rest of my life I will no longer occupy myself with anything else but me or Corsica; every other business is banished from my mind. In the meantime, do not forget to gather materials, either for the history, or for the institution, they are the same. Your government seems to be on a footing to be able to wait. I have among your papers a memorandum dated from Vescovado, 1764, which I believe to be yours, and which I consider excellent. The soul and head of the excellent M. Paoli will do more than everything else. With all that, can you lack a good provisional government? Especially since, so long as foreign powers meddle with you, you will hardly be able to establish anything else.

I would very much like it, sir, if we could see one another; two or three days of discussion would clarify many things. I can hardly be tranquil enough this year to propose anything to you. But would it be possible, next year, for you to manage to pass through this country? I have it in mind that we would see one another with pleasure, and that we would leave happy with one another. See, since hospitality has now been established between us, come make use of your right. I embrace you.

JJRousseau

CHAPTER 139

Pierre-Alexandre DuPeyrou

August 8, 1765
Môtiers-Travers

No, sir, never, whatever one may say, will I repent having praised M. de Montmollin. I praised what I knew of him, I praised his truly pastoral conduct toward me. I did not praise his character, which I did not know; I did not praise his veracity, or his rectitude. I will even admit that his exterior, which does not favor him, his manner, his expression, repulsed me despite myself. I was astonished to see so much gentleness, humanity, and so many virtues hide themselves under such a glum physiognomy. But I stifled this unjust inclination: was a man to be judged based on deceptive signs to which his conduct so clearly gave the lie? Was the secret principle of a hardly expected toleration to be malignantly spied upon? I hate this cruel art of poisoning the good actions of others, and my heart does not know how to find bad motives for what is good. The more I felt distance within me toward M. de M., the more I sought to combat it with the gratitude I owed him. Let us suppose this same case to be possible again, and everything I did, I would do again a thousand times.

Today, M. de M. takes off his mask, and shows himself as he truly is. His present conduct explains the preceding one. Clearly his supposed toleration, which leaves him when it would have been most just, comes from the same source as that cruel zeal which has suddenly taken hold of him. What was his object; what is it at present? I do not know. I know only that it could not be good. Not only does he admit me eagerly, honorably to the communion, but he seeks me out, he extols me, he celebrates me when I seem to have lightheartedly attacked Christianity. And when I prove that it is false that I attacked it, or that it is at least false that I had that plan, there he is himself abruptly attacking my safety, my faith, my person. He wants to excommunicate me, to proscribe me; he rouses the parish against me; he pursues me with a relentlessness akin to rage. Are these disparities within his duty? No, charity is not at all inconstant, virtue does not contradict itself, and conscience does not have two voices. After having shown himself to be so little tolerant, he made up his mind too late to be so. This affectation did not suit him, and as it did not deceive anyone, he did well to return to his natural state. By destroying his own work, by doing me more ill than he did me good, he acquits me of all gratitude toward him. I no longer owe him anything but the truth; I owe it to myself; and since he forces me to tell it, I will.

You want to know what in truth happened between us in this business. M. de M. has given his account to the public as a Clergyman, and dipping his pen into that poisoned honey which kills, he managed all the advantages of his position for himself. As for me, sir, I will give you mine in the simple way that honorable people talk among themselves. I will not extend myself in protestations of sincerity. I leave it to your healthy mind, to your heart, which is a friend of the truth, the task of disentangling it between him and me.

Thank Heaven, I am not one of those people who are celebrated and despised. I have the honor of being one of those who are esteemed and driven out. When I took refuge in this country, I brought recommendations for no one, not even for the Lord Marshal. I only have one recommendation which I take with me everywhere, and with the Lord Marshal one needs no other. Two hours after my arrival, writing to H. E. to inform him and to put myself under his protection,[1] I saw an unknown man enter who, calling himself the pastor of the place, made me advances of every kind and, seeing that I was writing to the Lord Marshal, offered to add a few lines in his hand to recommend me.

---

1. H. E. is His Excellence.

I did not accept this offer. My letter was dispatched, and I received the welcome that oppressed innocence can hope for everywhere virtue will reign.

Since, in the circumstance, I did not expect to find such an affable pastor, I told the story from that very day to everyone, and among others to Colonel Roguin who, full of the most affectionate kindnesses for me, had been kindly willing to accompany me all the way here.

M. de M.'s attentions continued. I thought I ought to take advantage of them, and seeing that the September communion was approaching, I decided to write to him to find out if, despite the public rumor, I could present myself there. I preferred a letter to a visit, to avoid the verbal explanations that he might have wanted to take too far. That is even the point on which I was trying to forestall him, for to declare that I wanted neither to disavow nor to defend my book was to say sufficiently that I did not want to address this point in any discussion. And in effect, forced to defend my honor and person regarding this book,[2] I always accepted condemnation on the errors that might be in it, limiting myself to showing that they did not prove that the author wanted to attack Christianity, and that it was wrong to pursue him criminally for that.

M. de M. wrote that I would know his answer the next day; that is what I would have done had he not brought it to me. My memory can deceive me as to trifles, but he anticipated me, it seems to me, and I at least remember that through displays of the liveliest joy he showed me how much the course of action I had taken pleased him. He literally told me that he and his flock considered themselves honored, and that this unhoped-for initiative would edify all the faithful. That moment, I admit, was one of the sweetest of my life. One has to know all my misfortunes, one has to have experienced the pains of a sensitive heart which loses everything that had been dear to it, to judge how consoling it was for me to be attached to a society of brothers who would recompense me for my losses, and for the friends I could no longer cultivate. It seemed to me that, unified in heart with this little flock in affectionate and reasonable worship, I would more easily forget all my enemies. At first, I was moved to tears in church. Never having lived among Protestants, I had made angelic images of them and their clergy. This worship, so simple and so pure, was exactly what my heart needed; it seemed to

---

2. *Emile.*

me made expressly to support the courage and hope of unfortunates. All those who participated in it seemed to me so many genuine Christians, unified by the gentlest charity. Did they ever cure me of such a sweet error! But in any event, I was in error; and it was based on my ideas that I judged the value of being admitted among them.

Seeing as, during this visit, M. de M. said nothing to me regarding my sentiments in matters of faith, I thought that he was saving this discussion for another time. Knowing how these Gentlemen are inclined to arrogate to themselves the right which they do not have of judging the faith of Christians, I declared to him that I did not intend to submit to any interrogation or to any clarification, whatever it might be. He answered that he would never require one, and on that point he has kept his word so well, I always found him so careful to avoid any discussion of doctrine, that until the last affair he has never said a single word to me about it, although I have happened to speak to him about it sometimes myself.

Things went on in this way as much before as after the communion: always the same attentions on the part of M. de M., and always the same silence on theological matters. He even carried the spirit of tolerance so far, and displayed it so openly in his sermons, that I was sometimes worried for him. As I was sincerely attached to him, I did not at all hide my alarms from him, and I remember one day that he was preaching ardently against the intolerance of Protestants, I was very frightened to hear him heatedly maintain that the reformed Church had great need of a new reformation, as much in doctrine as in morals. I hardly imagined then that he would shortly furnish such great proof of this need himself.

His tolerance and the honor he received for it in society excited the jealousy of several of his colleagues, especially in Geneva. They did not cease to harass him with reproaches and to set traps for him, into which he finally fell. I am sorry for it, but it is surely not my fault. If M. de M. had wanted to maintain such a pastoral conduct by means worthy of it, if he had been satisfied to use for his defense, with courage and frankness, the sole weapons of Christianity and truth, what example was he not giving to the Church, to Europe entire, what triumph was he not assuring for himself? He preferred the weapons of his occupation and, feeling them getting soft against the truth for his defense, he wanted to make them offensive by attacking me. He was mistaken. These old weapons, powerful against those who fear them, weak against those who brave them, broke. He had aimed badly for success.

A few months after my admission, one night I saw M. de M. enter my room. He looked embarrassed. He sat down and kept silence for a long time; he finally broke it with one of those long exordiums, the frequent need of which made a talent in him. Then, coming to his subject, he told me that the decision he had made to admit me to the communion had brought him many sorrows and his colleagues' blame; that he was reduced to justifying himself for having done this in a way that could shut their mouths; and that if the good opinion he had of my sentiments made him do away with the explanations that another would have required in his place, he could not without compromising himself let it be believed that there had been none.

With that, quietly pulling a paper from his pocket, he began to read, in a projected letter to a Genevan minister, details of discussions that had never existed, but where in truth he placed very opportunely here and there some words taken on the fly and with an entirely different object. Consider, sir, my astonishment. It was such that I needed the whole length of this reading to recover while listening to him. In the places where the fiction was at its strongest, he interrupted himself, saying: "You see the necessity . . . my situation . . . my position . . . one must lend oneself a little to . . ." This letter, as to that, was written with quite a bit of skill, and he more or less took great care to have me say in it nothing but what I could have said in effect. Having finished, he asked me if I approved of this letter, and if he could send it as it was.

I answered that I was sorry that he was reduced to such resources; that as for me, I could say nothing similar but that, since he took responsibility for saying it, it was his affair and not mine; nor did I see anything in it that I was obliged to deny. Since all of this, he began again, can harm no one and can be useful to you as well as me, I easily pass over a small scruple which would only prevent what is good. But tell me, in addition, whether you are happy with this letter, and if you do not see anything in it to change to make it better. I told him that I thought it was good for the end he was proposing. He pressed me so much that, to please him, I indicated a few slight corrections which did not signify greatly. Now, one must know that the way we were sitting, the writing desk was in front of M. de M. but, during this whole little discussion, he pushed it as if by chance in front of me and, since I was holding his letter so as to reread it, he presented the pen to me to make the indicated changes, which I did with the simplicity I adopt in all things. That done, he put his paper in his pocket, and went away.

Forgive these lengthy details; they were necessary. I will spare you those of my last meeting with M. de M., which is easier to imagine. You understand what one can answer to someone who comes to tell you coolly: sir, I am under orders to bash your head in, but if you would kindly break your leg, perhaps that will be satisfactory. M. de M. must sometimes have had to deal with some nasty business. Yet I have never in my life seen a man as embarrassed as he was when facing me in that one. Nothing is more uncomfortable in such a case than to be grappling with an open and frank man who, not battling you with subtleties and ruses, attacks you frontally at every moment. M. de M. assures us that upon leaving him I said that if he came with good news, I would embrace him; if not, that we would turn our backs on one another. I may have said equivalent things, but in more decent terms, and as to these latter expressions, I am quite sure not to have used them at all. M. de M. may recognize that he is not so easily making me turn my back as he had thought.

As to the devout pathos of which he makes use to prove the necessity of taking severe measures, one senses for what sort of people he does this, and neither you nor I have anything to say to them. Leaving aside this inquisitor's jargon, I am going to examine his reasons related to me, without entering into the reasons he may have had regarding others.

Bored with the sad occupation of author for which I was so ill-made, I had for a long time resolved to renounce it. When *Emile* appeared, I had declared to all my friends in Paris, Geneva, and elsewhere that it was my last work, and that in completing it I was laying down my pen, never to take it up again. I still have many letters seeking to dissuade me from this plan. Upon arriving here, I said the same thing to everyone, to you as well as to M. de M. He is the only one who took it into his head to transform this remark into a promise, and to claim that I had agreed with him not to write anymore, because I had shown him the intention of not doing so. If I told him today that I meant to go tomorrow to Neuchâtel, would he act on this statement, and if I failed to do so, put me on trial? It is absolutely the same thing, and I no more thought of making a promise to M. de M. than to you of a resolution of which I was simply informing both of you.

Would M. de M. dare to say that he understood the thing otherwise? Would he dare affirm, as he dares to make it understood, that it is based on this supposed agreement that he admitted me to the communion? The proof to the contrary is that, upon the publication of the *Letter to the Archbishop of Paris*, M. de M., far from accusing me of having broken my word to him, was very pleased with this work, and praised it to me and everyone, without saying a word then about that fabulous promise that he accuses me today of having made him before. Note, however, that this writing is much more forceful about mysteries and even miracles than the one about which he is now making so much noise.[3] Note, again, that I also speak in it in my own name, and no longer in the Vicar's name. Can one look for subjects of excommunication in the latter, which were not even subjects of complaint in the former?

Had I made this promise, of which I never thought in my life, to M. de M., would he maintain that it was so absolute that not the least exception could be borne, not even to have a memorandum printed for my defense when I would be put on trial? And what exception was more permitted me than one in which, justifying myself, I also justified him, where I showed that it was false that he had admitted into his Church an aggressor against religion? What promise could acquit me of what I owed to others and to myself? How could I suppress a defensive writing for the sake of my honor, for that of my old compatriots, a writing that so many great motives made necessary, and in which I had to fulfill such sacred duties? Who will M. de M. convince that I promised him to endure ignominy in silence? Even at the present time, when I made a formal agreement with a respectable body, who in this body would accuse me of breaking it if, forced by M. de M.'s affronts, I decided to repel them as publicly as he dares utter them?[4] Whatever promise a decent man may make, it will never be required of him, and presumed still less, that it extends to letting himself be dishonored.

In publishing the *Letters Written from the Mountain*, I did my duty and did not fail M. de M. He judged it so himself since, after the publication of the work, of which I had sent him a copy, he did not change his way of behaving with me. He read it with pleasure, spoke of it to me with praise: not a word which smelled of objection. Since then, he still saw me for a long time, always with the greatest friendliness. Never the least complaint about my book. At that time, a general edition of my works was being spoken of. Not only did he approve of this enterprise; he even wanted to invest in it. He informed me of this desire, which I did not encourage, knowing that the company which had been formed

---

3. *Letters Written from the Mountain.*

4. Rousseau had just agreed not to publish anything while he lived in the jurisdiction of Neuchâtel.

was already too numerous and did not want any other associate. Upon seeing my slight enthusiasm, which he noticed too much, he reflected, a while after, that the proprieties of his position did not permit him to enter such an enterprise. That is when the Classis decided to oppose it and made representations to the court.

Besides, we were still on such perfectly good terms, and my last work presented so little obstacle to it that long after its publication, M. de M., chatting with me, told me that he wanted to ask the court for an increase in emolument, and suggested that I put a few lines in a letter he was writing for that purpose to the Lord Marshal. This kind of recommendation seeming too familiar to me, I asked him for fifteen days to write about it beforehand to the Lord Marshal. He fell silent, and no longer spoke to me about this business. From then on, he began to see the *Letters from the Mountain* in a different light, without nevertheless disapproving of a single word of it in my presence. Only once he said to me: "As for me, I believe in miracles." I could have answered him: "I believe in them quite as much as you."

Since I am on the subject of my wrongs with M. de M., I must admit to you, sir, that I recognize that I have others as well. Filled with gratitude toward him, I sought every occasion to mark it, as much in public as in private. But I did not turn this sentiment, which is so noble, into a traffic in interests. Example has not won me over; I do not know how to buy sacred things. M. de M. wanted to know about all my affairs, to become acquainted with all my correspondents, direct, hear my will and testament, govern my little household—that I did not suffer. M. de M. likes to stay at table for a long time; for me, it is a real torment. He has rarely had a meal at my house; I have never had one at his. Finally, I have always rejected with every regard and all respect possible the intimacy which he wanted to establish between us. It is never a duty as soon as it does not suit both.

These are my wrongs. I confess them, without being able to repent them. They are great, if one wishes, but they are the only ones, and I call on anyone who knows this region a little to attest whether I have not often made myself disagreeable to decent people by my zeal in praising in M. de M. what I found praiseworthy in him. The part he had played previously made him odious, and they did not like to see me erase by means of my own history that of the ills of which he was the author.

Even so, whatever secret discontents he had against me, he would never have selected such a badly chosen moment for them to erupt, if other motives had not brought him again to seize the momentary opportunity that he had at first allowed to escape. He saw too clearly how his conduct would be shocking and contradictory. What battles must he not have felt within himself before daring to display such a clear transgression? For, pass whatever condemnation one wants on the *Letters from the Mountain*: will they, in the end, say more than *Emile*, after which I was, not passed over, but admitted to the holy altar; more than the *Letter to M. de Beaumont*, about which not a single word was said? Let them, if one wishes, be only a tissue of errors. What will follow from this? That they did not at all justify me, and that the author of *Emile* remains inexcusable; but never that the author of the *Letters Written from the Mountain* in particular must be condemned. After having pardoned a man for the crime of which he is accused, does one punish him for having defended himself badly? That is, however, what M. de M. is doing here, and I defy him, him and all his colleagues, to cite from this last work any of the sentiments that they censure which I cannot prove were more forcefully established in the preceding ones.

But incited in an underhanded way by other people, he seizes the pretext presented to him. Sure that in crying impiety without rhyme or reason, one always puts the people in a rage, after the fact, he rings the tocsin in Môtiers against a poor man for having dared to defend himself among the Genevans and, feeling very well that only success could save him from blame, he spares nothing to secure it. I live in Môtiers; I do not want to speak of what goes on there. You know it as well as I do. No one in Neuchâtel is unaware of it; strangers who come see it, groan, and I keep quiet.

M. de M. excuses himself on the grounds of orders from the Classis. But let us suppose them to be executed by legitimate means. If these orders were just, how did he wait so long to sense it? How did he not anticipate them himself, he whom they especially concerned? How, after having read and reread the *Letters from the Mountain*, did he not find a word in it to correct, or why did he say nothing to me about it, to me his parishioner, during several visits he made me? What had become of his pastoral zeal? Would he want to be considered an imbecile, who does not know how to see what is in a book—in his field—except when it is shown to him? If these orders were unjust, why did he submit to them? Ought a minister of the Gospel, a pastor, persecute a man he knows to be innocent, from obedience? Was he unaware that even to appear before the consistory is an ignominious penalty, a cruel affront for a man my age, especially in a village, where no other consistorial matters are known save admonitions about morals? It is now ten years since I was dispensed in Geneva from appearing before the consistory on a much more legitimate occasion and—for which I almost reproach myself—contrary to the clear text of the law. But it is not surprising that in Geneva proprieties are known that are unknown in Môtiers.

I do not know what M. de M. takes his readers for when he tells them that there was no inquisition in this business. It is as if he were saying that there was no consistory, for on this occasion it is the same thing. He makes it understood, he even assures, that there was not to be any temporal consequence. The contrary is known to all the people in the know about the project. And who does not know that by fraudulently influencing the religion of the State Council, it had already been incited to take steps which tended to take away the king's protection from me? The necessary step to finish things off was excommunication. After which, new remonstrations to the State Council would have done the rest; one had committed to them, hence the pain of not having been able to succeed. For in any event, what does it matter to M. de M.? Does he fear that I will present myself to take communion from his hand? Let him be reassured; I am not inured to communions, as I see so many people are. I admire these devout stomachs, always so ready to digest the sacred wafer: mine is not so robust.

He said that he only had one very simple question to ask me on the part of the Classis. Why then, in citing me, did he not have me notified of this question? What is this ruse, to make use of surprise, and to force people to answer at that very instant, without giving them a moment to think? It is that along with this question from the Classis, of which M. de M. speaks, he was on his own accord keeping in reserve others about which he does not speak at all, and for which he did not want me to have the time to prepare. It is known that his plan was absolutely to find me at fault, and to disconcert me by so many deceptive interrogations that he would succeed. He knew how languishing and feeble I was. I do not want to accuse him of having the aim of exhausting my strength; but when I was cited, I was ill, unable to go out, and had been staying in my room for six months. It was winter, it was cold, and, for a poor invalid, that is a strange specific, a session in which one stands for several hours, interrogated without any pause on theological matters, before old men the best educated of whom declare that they do not understand them. No matter. I was not even asked if I was able to leave my bed, if I had the strength to go, if I had to be carried; they did not bother with that. Pastoral charity, occupied with matters of faith, does not lower itself to the terrestrial cares of this life.

You know, sir, what happened in the consistory in my absence, how my letter was read, and the remarks made there to prevent it having an effect. Your records on that come from a good source. Can you conceive that after this, M. de M. suddenly changes position and title, and that having himself made commissioner of the Classis in order to solicit the affair, he immediately again becomes pastor in order to judge it? "I acted," he says, "as pastor, as chief of consistory, and not as a representative of the Venerable Classis." It was very late to change roles, after having adopted such a different one until then. Let us fear, sir, people who so willingly act as two persons in the same affair. It is rare that these two make one good one.

He supports the necessity of taking severe measures regarding the scandal caused by my book. Here are altogether new scruples that he did not at all have at the time of *Emile*. The scandal was at the very least just as great; the Clergy and the journalists made no less noise. There was burning, and bawling, and I was insulted throughout Europe. M. de M. finds reasons today for excommunicating me in the ones which did not prevent him then from admitting me. Following the precept, his zeal takes every form to act according to time and place. But who is it, tell me, who aroused the scandal in his parish over my last book, about which he complains? Who affected to make a horrendous noise about it, both himself and through people positioned for the purpose? Who, among this entire people of such saintly maniacs, would have known that I had committed the enormous crime of proving that the Council of Geneva had wrongly condemned me, if care had not been taken to tell them by painting this singular crime in the colors that everyone knows? Who among them is even able to read my book and to understand what is at issue in it? Let us except if you will M. de M.'s ardent satellite, that grand Marshal whom he cites so proudly, that great Clerc,[5] the Boirude of his Church,[6] so knowledgeable in horse-shoes and in books on theology. I want to believe that he is able to read on an empty stomach, and without spelling out a whole line. Who else in the horde can do as much? In glimpsing on my pages the words "Gospel" and "miracles," they would have believed they were reading a book of devotion, and knowing me to be a good man, they would have

---

5. This refers to Jean-Henry Clerc. Rousseau goes on to play on the fact that the term *clerc* can mean either cleric or ironmonger.

6. Boirude, a character from Boileau's *Lutrin*, is a sacristan who is the staunch supporter of his curate.

said, "May God bless him, he edifies us." But they have been so often assured that I am an abominable man, an impious man, who said that there is no God and that women do not have souls that, without thinking of the very contrary language used with them before, they repeated in turn: he is impious, a villain, he is the Antichrist, he must be excommunicated, burned. They were charitably answered, no doubt: but cry out and let us act; everything will be well.

The ordinary way the Gentlemen of the Clergy proceed seems to me to be admirable for reaching their goal. After having in principle established their jurisdiction over every scandal, they stimulate scandal about whatever object pleases them and then, as a result of the scandal that is their work, they take hold of the affair in order to judge it. There is the wherewithal to become masters of all peoples, of all the laws, of all the kings, and of the whole earth without one having the least word to say to them. Do you remember the story of that surgeon whose shop looked out onto two streets and who, leaving by one door, maimed the passersby, then, craftily slipping back in, went out again from the other to bandage them? That is the story of all the clergy in the world, except that the surgeon at least cured his wounded, and that these Gentlemen in treating theirs finish them off.

Let us not enter, sir, into the secret intrigues which should not see the light of day. But if M. de M. had only wanted to execute the Classis's order or to acquit his conscience, why the relentlessness which he put into this business? Why this tumult stirred up in the country? Why these violent sermons? Why these confabulations? Why so many silly rumors spread about, in an attempt to frighten me with the cries of the populace? Is this not well known to the public? M. de M. denies it, and why not, since he certainly denied having laid claim to two votes in the consistory? As for me, I see three, if I am not mistaken. First, that of his deacon, who was there only as his representative; then his own, which produced equality; and finally, the one he wanted to have to break the tie in the votes. Three votes for him alone; that would have been many, even to absolve. He wanted them to condemn and could not obtain them. Where was the harm? M. de M. would have been too happy had his consistory, wiser than he, gotten him out of trouble with the Classis, with his colleagues, with his correspondents, with himself. I did my duty, he would have said; I pursued the matter vigorously; my consistory did not judge as I did; it absolved Rousseau against my advice. It is not my fault. I withdraw; I cannot do more without injuring the laws, disobeying the prince, and troubling public peace. I am too good a Christian, too good a citizen, too good a pastor to attempt anything like that. After having failed, he could still, with a little skill, preserve his dignity and recover his reputation. But irritated amour-propre is not so wise. We forgive others even less for the ill we wanted to do to them than for the one we really did them. Furious to see that great credit about which he likes to boast come to nothing before Europe, he cannot quit the game He says in an assembly of the Classis that he is not without hope of renewing it. He attempts to do so in another consistory, but to be less out in the open, he does not propose it himself; he has it proposed by his Marshal, by this instrument of his machinations, whom he calls as a witness that he did not engage in any. Is this not a subtle discovery? It is not that M. de M. is not subtle; but a man blinded by anger no longer engages in anything but silliness when he gives himself over to his passion.

He also lacks this resource. You would think that at least, then, his efforts would stop there. Not at all. In the subsequent assembly of the Classis, he proposes another expedient, founded on the impossibility of eluding the activity of the prince's officer in his parish. That is to wait until I have passed into another, and there to start proceedings again from scratch. Due to this fine expedient, the choleric sermons start again; the people are set to murmur again, counting on forcing me finally to leave the parish by dint of unpleasantness. That is too much, in truth, for a man as tolerant as M. de M. claims he is, who is only following the orders of his corps.

My letter is lengthening a great deal, sir, but it must. And why would I cut it short? Would multiplying the formulas it contains shorten it? Let us leave to M. de M. the pleasure of saying ten times in a row, "Dunyazad, my sister, are you asleep?"[7]

I have not at all begun to address the question of right: I have forbidden myself this subject. I limited myself in the second part of this letter to proving to you that M. de M., despite the beatific tone that he affects, was not guided in this affair by the zeal of faith or by his duty, but that he has, according to practice, made God serve as an instrument of his passions. Now, consider whether for such ends, honest means are used, and dispense me from entering into details that would make virtue groan.

----

7. A formula used by Scheherazade at the end of each of the tales of the *One Thousand and One Nights*.

In the first part of my letter, I relate facts contrary to those advanced by M. de M. He had the cunning to arrange pieces of evidence to which I could not answer except by the faithful account of what happened. From these contrary assertions by him and by me, you will conclude that one of the two is a liar, and I admit that this conclusion seems correct to me.

Wanting to finish my letter and put down his pamphlet, I am leafing through it again. Numberless observations present themselves, and one must not always begin again. Nevertheless, how am I to pass over what I have at this moment under my eyes, p. 128: "What will our ministers do, was being said publicly? Will they defend the Gospel, so openly attacked by its enemies?" It is therefore I who am the enemy of the Gospel because I am indignant that it is disfigured and debased. Eh! Would that these so-called defenders imitated the use I would like to make of it! If only they took from it what would make them good and just; if only they left in it what is useless for anyone, and which they understand no more than I do!

"If a citizen of this country had dared say or write something approaching what M. R. advances, would we not take severe measures against him?" Assuredly not. I dare to believe this for the honor of this State. Peoples of Neuchâtel, what then would be your rights, if on some point that would furnish the ministers matter for chicanery, they could pursue in your midst the author of a factum printed at the other end of Europe for his defense in a foreign country? M. de M. chose me to impose, through me, this new yoke upon you. But would I be worthy of having been received among you, if I left through my example a servitude that I did not find there?

"Does M. Rousseau, new citizen, then have more privileges than all the ancient citizens?" I do not even demand theirs here; I demand only those that I have as a man, and as a simple stranger. The correspondent whom M. de M. has speak, this marvelous correspondent whom he does not name and who praises him so highly, is a singular reasoner, it seems to me. I want, according to him, to have more privileges than all the citizens because I resist vexations that no other citizen ever endured. To take away from me the right to defend my purse against a thief who would want to take it from me, he would then only have to say to me: "You are amusing not to want me to rob you! I would willingly rob a local man if he passed by instead of you."

Note that here Monsieur the professor de Montmollin is the sole sovereign, the despot who condemns me, and that the law, the consistory, the magistrate, the government, the governor, even the king who protect me are so many rebels against the supreme authority of Monsieur the professor de Montmollin.

The anonymous [pamphlet] asks "if I did not submit as citizen to the laws of the State and to the customs," and from the affirmative which assuredly will not be contested, concludes that I have submitted myself to a law which does not exist and to a custom which has never taken place.

To this, M. de M. responds that this law exists in Geneva and that I myself complained that it was violated to my detriment. Hence the law which exists in Geneva, and which does not exist in Môtiers, is violated in Geneva to issue a decree against me and is followed in Môtiers to excommunicate me. Grant that this puts me in a pleasant position! It was no doubt during one of his moments of playfulness that M. de M. reasoned that way.

He jokes in nearly the same tone in a note on the offer that I was willing to make to the Classis on condition that I was left in repose. He says that it is mockery, and that one does not dictate in this way to one's superiors.

First, he is engaging in mockery himself when he claims that offering very obsequious and very reasonable satisfaction to people who are complaining, though they are in the wrong, is to dictate to them.

But the joke is to have called the Gentlemen of the Classis my superiors, as if I were a clergyman. For who does not know that the Classis, having jurisdiction only over the clergy, and having in addition nothing to command to anyone, its members are, as such, no one's superiors? Now, to call me a clergyman is, in my view, quite a misplaced joke. M. de M. knows very well that I am not a clergyman, and that, thank Heaven, I have very little calling to become one.

Another few words on the letter that I wrote to the consistory, and I am done. M. de M. promises few commentaries on this letter. I think that he does very well, and that he would have done even better not to have made any at all. Permit me to review those that concern me. The examination will not take long.

"How to answer," he says on p. 163, "to questions of which one is unaware?" As I did: by proving in advance that one does not have the right to question.

"A faith, of which one owes an account only to God, is not published throughout Europe."

And why would a faith of which one owes an account only to God not be published throughout Europe?

Note the strange pretension of preventing a man from telling his sentiment when one attributes others to him; of shutting his mouth and of making him speak.

"He who errs as a Christian willingly corrects his errors." Amusing sophism!

He who errs as a Christian does not know that he errs. If he corrected his errors without knowing them, he would err no less, and what is more he would lie. That would no longer be to err as a Christian.

"Is it to rely on the Gospel's authority to make miracles doubtful?" Yes, when it is through the Gospel's very authority that one renders miracles doubtful.

"And to ridicule it." Why not, when by relying on the Gospel one proves that what is ridiculous lies only in the interpretations of theologians?

I am sure that M. de M. was very pleased with himself for his laconism. It is always easy to respond to good reasonings by inept sayings.

"As to Theodore of Beza's note on p. 40, he did not want to say anything else except that a Christian's faith does not rely uniquely on miracles."

Take care, Monsieur the professor: either you do not understand Latin, or you are a man of bad faith.

This passage, *non satis tuta fides eorum qui miraculis nituntur*, does not at all mean, as you claim, that "the Christian's faith does not rely uniquely on miracles."

On the contrary, it means, very precisely, that "the faith of whoever relies on miracles is not very solid." This meaning relates very well to S[aint] John's passage, upon which it is a commentary, and which says of Jesus that some believed in him upon seeing his miracles, but that he did not for all that entrust his person to them, "because he knew them well." Do you think that he would have greater confidence today in those who make so much noise about the same faith?

"Would one not believe that one hears M. Rousseau say in his *Letter to the Archbishop of Paris* that one ought to erect statues to him for his *Emile*?" Note that this is said when, pressed by the comparison between *Emile* and the *Letters from the Mountain* M. de M. does not know how to escape. He gets himself out of trouble with a frolic.

If one had to follow his digressions inch by inch, if one had to examine the weightiness of his affirmations, analyze the singular reasonings he gives us, we would never finish; and one must finish. At the end of all that, proud of having named himself, he boasts about it. I do not see there much of anything to boast about. Once one has decided regarding certain things, there is little merit in naming oneself.

As for you, sir, who out of consideration for him maintain the anonymity for which he reproaches you, name yourself, since he wants it. Accept from decent people the praise due you. Show them the worthy advocate of the just cause, the historian of truth, the defender of the rights of the oppressed, of those of the prince, the State, and the peoples, all attacked by him in my person. My defenders, my protectors are known; let him show in his turn his own anonymous man and his partisans in this affair.[8] He has already named two; let him finish. He has done me much harm; he wanted to do me much more. Let everyone know his friends and mine. I want no other revenge.

Receive, sir, my tender salutations.

JJRousseau

---

8. "His own anonymous man" refers to Durey de Morsan.

CHAPTER 140

David Hume

December 4, 1765
Strasbourg

Your kindness, sir, moves me as much as it honors me. The worthiest
response I can make to your offers is to accept them, and I accept them.
I will leave in five or six days to go throw myself into your arms. This is
the advice of My Lord Marshal, my protector, my friend, my father; it
is that of Madame de Verdelin, whose enlightened benevolence guides
me as much as consoles me; finally, I dare say that it is that of my heart,
which takes pleasure in owing much to the most illustrious of my contemporaries, whose goodness surpasses his glory. I long for a solitary
and free retreat where I can finish my days in peace. If your beneficent
attentions procure it for me, I will enjoy at the same time both the sole
good that my heart desires, and the pleasure of receiving it from you.
I salute you, sir, with all my heart.

JJRousseau

CHAPTER 141

François-Henri d'Ivernois

December 30, 1765
Paris

My good friend, I have received your letter of the 23rd. I am very cross that you have not been to see M. de Voltaire. Could you have thought that this course of action would pain me? How little you know my heart! Eh, please God that a happy reconciliation between you, produced by this illustrious man's attentions, making me forget all his wrongs, would deliver me without admixture to my admiration for him. During those times when he treated me most cruelly, I always had much less aversion for him than love for my country. Whoever may be the man who gives you back peace and liberty, he will always be dear and respectable to me. If it is Voltaire, he can moreover do me as much harm as he wants; my constant wishes until my last breath will be for his happiness and glory.

Let the mountebanks threaten; *tel fiert qui ne tue pas*.[1] Your fate is almost in M. de Voltaire's hands: if he is for you, the mountebanks will do you very little harm. I advise and exhort you, after you have

---

1. "Some strike who do not kill." The device of the house of Solaris in Turin, where Rousseau served for a time as a lackey. *Confessions*, CW 5:80.

sufficiently sounded him out, to have confidence in him. It is not believable that, able to be the admiration of the universe, he would want to become its horror. He senses the advantage of his position too well not to put it to use for his glory. I cannot think that he would want, by betraying you, to cover himself in infamy. In a word, he is your sole resource; do not deprive yourself of it. If he betrays you, you are lost, I admit; but you are equally so if he does not involve himself with you. Give yourself over to him, therefore, fully and frankly; gain his heart by this trust. Lend yourself to every reasonable compromise. Secure the laws and freedom, but sacrifice amour-propre to peace. Above all, no mention of me, so as not to embitter those who hate me. And if M. de Voltaire is useful to you, as he must be if he understands his glory, lavish honors upon him and consecrate to Phoebus Apollo peacemaker, *Phoebo pacatori*, the medallion that you had destined for me.

As to the rest, whatever turn events take, do not be anxious for yourself personally. You will not be troubled by the mediation should it take place; I believe I can answer for that. I thought, so as better to serve you, that I ought not to make use of my friends who are recognized and declared as such. I made use of means that our enemies will not be able to bring to light, because they are known to no one. Thank you for the parcel you sent me by M. Dominicé. I do not yet have news of it, but I count on having some before my departure, which is fixed for the 5th of the month, unless my ill health opposes it. So do not write to me here again until further notice. I embrace you tenderly.

CHAPTER 142

David Hume

March 22, 1766
Wootton

You see already, my dear patron, by the date of my letter, that I have arrived at my destination. But you cannot see all the charms that I find there; one would have to know the place and read into my heart. You must at least read the sentiments which concern you and that you have so thoroughly deserved. If I live in this pleasant refuge as happy as I hope to be, one of the sweet aspects of my life will be to think that I owe them to you. To make someone happy is to deserve to be so. May you find within yourself the prize of all that you have done for me. Alone, I might perhaps have found hospitality, but I would never have relished it so much if I had not received it from your friendship. Preserve it for me always, my dear patron; love me for myself who owes you so much; for yourself; love me for the good you have done me. I feel all the worth of your sincere friendship, and I ardently desire it. I want to respond to it by all of mine, and I feel in my heart that by which to convince even you one day that it too is not without some worth. Since, for the reasons we spoke about, I do not want to receive anything by post, please, when you do the good work of writing to me, give your letter to M. Davenport. The matter of my vehicle is not yet arranged, because

I know that I have been deceived.[1] This is a small fault, which may only be the work of an obliging vanity if it does not recur. If you put a hand to this, I advise you to abandon once and for all these little ruses whose principle cannot be good when they turn into traps for simplicity. I embrace you, my dear patron, with the same heart that I hope and desire to find in you.

JJRousseau

---

1. Hume and Davenport had agreed to tell Rousseau that the cost of transportation from London to Wootton was lower than it actually was.

CHAPTER 143

François Coindet

March 29, 1766
Wootton

I received your letters, dear Coindet, and those of Madame de Chenonceaux. I put off answering until I arrived at a place of rest where I could breathe. I had great need of it, I swear to you. The vicinity of London was as importunate as London itself, because of the immense crowd of curious people. I responded on the spot to Mme. de Chenonceaux's last letter; the subject absolutely required it. It is extremely important to me to know if my letter reached her and if it has not suffered some delay, so that I can judge the fidelity of the people to whom I confided it. I have also indirectly received news of M. Watelet, and new proofs of his charitable pains, by his recommendations in my favor. Writing to him sometimes will be one of the sweetest uses of my leisure. I wish that he were tempted to come and see my solitude. In some respects, it would not be unworthy of taking up his gaze and his talents. I am annoyed that I can make no use of the address that you gave me, but I am fifty leagues from London and thoroughly determined not to return there unless I cannot do otherwise. Here am I, as if regenerated by a new baptism, having been thoroughly soaked while crossing the sea. I have cast off the old man, and apart from a few friends, among whom I count you,

I am forgetting everything that is related to that foreign land which is called the continent. The authors, the decrees, the books, those acrid fumes of glory which make one weep; all of these are follies from the other world in which I no longer take part and that I am going to hasten to forget. I cannot yet enjoy the charms of the countryside, as this country is still buried under snow; but in the meantime, I take a rest from my long excursions, I catch my breath, I enjoy myself. I can testify that during fifteen years that I have had the misfortune of practicing the sad trade of man of letters, I have contracted none of the vices of that condition: envy, jealousy, the spirit of intrigue and of charlatanry have not for an instant come near my heart. I do not even feel soured by the persecutions, the misfortunes, and I leave the career as healthy of heart as I entered it. That, dear Coindet, is the source of the happiness I will taste in my retreat, if they would be willing to leave me in peace there. People in society do not conceive that one can live happily and content face to face with oneself, and I cannot conceive that one can be happy in any other way. With what will one be contented in life, if one is not contented with the only man that one does not leave. That is a great deal of moral teaching for a man of the world, but not too much for a hermit. Instead of speaking to you about you, I am speaking to you about me. That is not very polite, no doubt, but it is very natural. Do the same with me, speak to me about yourself in turn, and be sure that you will please me greatly. The difficulty is to have your letters reach me, as for several good reasons, I do not receive any by the post, which does not even come to the village neighboring this house. While waiting for more convenient arrangements, have your letter to London given to "M. Davenport next door Lord Egremont's; Piccadilly."[1] By this means it will reach me. I embrace you with all my heart.

JJRousseau

---

1. In English in the original.

CHAPTER 144

David Hume

March 29, 1766
Wootton

You will have seen, dear patron, from the letter that Mr. Davenport must have given you, how greatly to my taste I find myself situated here. I would perhaps be more at ease if fewer attentions were paid to me. But the cares of such a gallant man are too obliging to make one cross, and since everything is mixed with inconveniences in life, that of doing too well is one of those one can most easily tolerate. I find a greater one in not being able to make myself understood by the servants, or especially in not being able to understand a word they say to me. Luckily, Mlle. Levasseur serves me as interpreter, and her fingers speak better than my tongue. I even find in my ignorance an advantage which can compensate me, which is to drive away the idlers by boring them. Yesterday, I received a visit from the Minister who, seeing that I was only speaking French to him, did not want to speak to me in English, such that the interview passed almost without a word. I acquired a taste for this expedient; I will make use of it with all my neighbors if I have any, and should I learn English, I will never speak to them save in French, especially if I have the good luck that they do not know a word of it. That is nearly the ruse of monkeys who, say the blacks, do not want to speak, even though they can, for fear that they will be made to work.

I am obliged to you for being willing to settle Mr. Stewart's account. I find in it two items which I do not know about. One of 1 pound 14 shillings for some coffee, and the other of 5 shillings for a grinder. It is true that Mr. Stewart was willing to see to these errands, but I did not receive them, neither in my luggage nor otherwise, and have no notice of them except through his account.

It is not at all true that I agreed with Mr. Gosset to receive a model as a present. On the contrary, I asked him the price, which he told me is a guinea and a half, adding that he wanted to do me the courtesy, which I did not accept. Please, then, would you be willing to pay him for the model in question; Mr. Davenport will be so kind as to reimburse you. If he does not consent to it, it must be returned to him and bought from him by someone else. It is intended for M. DuPeyrou, who has wanted for a long time to have my portrait, and had one made in miniature which does not at all resemble me. You are better provided than he is,[1] but I am sorry that, through such flattering diligence, you have taken from me the pleasure of fulfilling the same duty toward you. Have the goodness, my dear patron, to have this model delivered to Messrs. Guinand and Hankey, little S'Hellens, Bishopsgate Street, to send to M. DuPeyrou on the first sure occasion.

It has been freezing since I have been here; it has snowed every day; the wind cuts one's face; despite that, I would rather live in the hole of one of the rabbits in this warren than in the most beautiful apartment in London. Good day, my dear patron, I embrace you and love you with all my heart.

JJRousseau

Mlle. Levasseur thanks you for honoring her with your remembrance and asks you to accept her respect.

---

1. This is a reference to the portrait that Hume had commissioned from Allan Ramsay.

CHAPTER 145

Henry Baldwin

April 7, 1766
Wootton
Baldwin was the editor of the Saint James Chronicle, *which had published a satirical letter purporting to be by Frederick the Great. It was actually written by Horace Walpole, who was one of Hume's friends.*

You have failed, sir, in the respect that every individual owes to crowned heads, by publicly attributing to the king of Prussia a letter full of extravagance and of meanness, by which alone you should have known that he was not its author. You even dared to transcribe his signature, as if you had seen it written by his hand. I inform you, sir, that this letter was fabricated in Paris and, which saddens and tears at my heart, that the impostor has accomplices in England.

You owe the king of Prussia, truth, and me to print the letter I am writing you and that I sign, as reparation for a fault for which you would no doubt reproach yourself, if you knew of what darkness you are making yourself the instrument. Sir, my sincere salutations.

JJRousseau

CHAPTER 146

David Hume

June 23, 1766
Wootton

I thought, sir, that my silence, interpreted by your conscience, said enough. But since it is part of your plans not to hear it, I will speak. You hid yourself badly; I know you, and you are not unaware of that. Without prior relations, without quarrels, without disagreements, without knowing each other except through literary reputation, you hastened to offer me your friends and your assistance. Touched by your generosity, I throw myself into your arms. You bring me to England, in appearance to obtain a refuge for me there, and in effect to dishonor me. You applied yourself to this noble task with a zeal worthy of your heart, and with a success worthy of your talents. That was more than enough to succeed. You live in society, and I live in my retreat; the public likes to be deceived, and you are made to deceive them. Yet I know a man that you will not deceive: that is yourself. You know with what horror my heart repulsed the first suspicion of your schemes. I told you while embracing you with my eyes filled with tears that if you were not the best of men, you had to be the blackest. As you think about your secret behavior, you will sometimes say to yourself that you are not the best of men, and I doubt that with this idea you will ever be the happiest.

I give free rein to your friends' maneuvers, to yours, and I abandon to you with little regret my reputation during my life, very sure that one day justice will be done to both of us. As to the good offices in matters of interest with which you conceal yourself, I thank you and dispense you from them. I owe it to myself no longer to have any association with you and not to accept, even to my own advantage, any matter that you would mediate. Goodbye, sir, best wishes for the most genuine happiness. But since we must no longer have anything to say to one another, this is the last letter you will receive from me.

JJRousseau

CHAPTER 147

David Hume

July 10, 1766
Wootton

I am ill, sir, and hardly in a condition to write. But you want an explanation; it must be given to you. It was only up to you to have had it a long time ago. You did not want it then. I was silent. You want it today; I am sending it to you. It will be long. This is vexing, but I have much to say, and I do not want to have to do it again.

I do not live with people; I do not know what goes on among them; I have no party, no associates, no intrigues. I am told nothing. I only know what I feel, but since I am made to feel it well, I know it well. The first care of those who plot nefarious deeds is to protect themselves from juridical proofs; it would not be good to file a suit against them. Inner conviction admits of another kind of proof that regulates the sentiments of a decent man. You will know upon what mine are based.

You ask with a great deal of confidence that your accuser be named. That accuser, sir, is the only man in the world who, deposing against you, could make me listen: you. I will yield without reserve and without fear to my open character, which is an enemy of all artifice. I will speak to you with the same frankness as if you were another, in whom I had the full confidence that I no longer have in you. I will give you the history of the movements of my soul and of what has produced them and, naming Mr. Hume as a third person, I will make you yourself the judge of what I should think of him. Despite the length of my letter, I will not follow any other order in it except that of my ideas, beginning with the signs and finishing with the demonstration.

I left Switzerland, tired of barbarous treatments, but which at least put in peril nothing save my person and left my honor safe. I followed the movements of my heart to go join the Lord Marshal, when I received in Strasbourg from Mr. Hume the most affectionate invitation to go with him to England, where he promised me the most pleasant welcome, and more tranquility than I found there. I was torn between the old friend and the new; I was wrong. I preferred the latter; I was even more wrong: but the desire to know for myself a celebrated nation of whom so much good and so much bad was said, won out. Certain of not losing George Keith, I was flattered to acquire David Hume. His merit, his rare talents, the well-established decency of his character, made me desire to add his friendship to the one with which his illustrious compatriot honored me, and I was in a way glorying at showing a fine example to men of letters of a sincere union between two men whose principles were so different.

Before the invitation from the king of Prussia and the Lord Marshal, uncertain as to the location of my retreat, I had asked for and obtained from my friends a passport from the French court, which I used to go to Paris to join Mr. Hume. He saw, and perhaps saw too much, the welcome I received from a great prince and, I dare say, from the public.[1] I lent myself to this splendor from duty, but with repugnance, considering how much the envy of my enemies would be irritated by it. The perceptible increase in goodwill for Mr. Hume that the good deed he was to do produced in all Paris was a very sweet spectacle for me. He must have been touched by it as I was; I do not know if he was in the same manner.

We left with one of my friends,[2] who was making the trip to England almost solely for me. Upon disembarking at Dover, thrilled to be finally touching this land of freedom and to have been brought there by this illustrious man, I throw myself at his neck, I embrace him tightly without saying anything, but while covering his face with kisses and tears, which said enough. It is not the first, or the most noticeable, time when

---

1. The "great prince" is the prince of Conti.
2. Jean-Jacques de Luze.

he could have seen in me the shock of a stirred heart. I do not know what he does with these memories; if they come to him, I have it in mind that he must sometimes be perturbed by them.

There were celebrations when we arrived in London. People from every order eagerly show me goodwill and esteem. Mr. Hume graciously presents me to everyone. It was natural to attribute to him, as I did, the greater part of this warm welcome. My heart was full of him. I spoke about him to everyone, I wrote about him to all my friends; my attachment to him acquired new force every day. His seemed to me to be of the most affectionate sort, and he sometimes showed signs of it that touched me very much. Having a large portrait made of me was not, however, of that number.[3] This whim seemed to me to make too much of a public display, and I found in it I do not know what air of ostentation which did not please me. That is all I could have passed over regarding Mr. Hume if he had been the kind of man to throw his money away, and if he had in a gallery the portraits of all his friends. Besides, I will freely admit that in this I could have been wrong.

But what seemed to me among one of the genuine and most estimable acts of friendship and generosity, the worthiest in a word of Mr. Hume, was the effort he made on his own to solicit a pension from the king for me, to which I assuredly had no right to aspire. A witness of his zeal in this business, I was deeply stirred. Nothing could please me more than a service of this kind, assuredly not because of interest, for perhaps, too attached to what I own, I do not know how to desire what I do not have; and, having through my friends and by my own work enough bread on which to live, I have ambitions for nothing more. But the honor of receiving testimonies of kindness, I will not say from so great a monarch, but from such a good father, such a good husband, such a good master, such a good friend, and above all such a decent man, affected me markedly. And when I considered further regarding this grace, that the minister who had obtained it was probity incarnate, that probity which is so useful to peoples and so rare in his position, I could not but glory in having as benefactors three of the men in the world that I would most have liked to have as friends. Thus, far from refusing the pension that was offered, I put only one necessary

---

3. The portrait painted by Allan Ramsay.

condition on accepting it, namely, a consent which, without failing in my duty, I could not do without.[4]

Honored by everyone's attentiveness, I tried to respond to it properly. Yet my ill health and the habit of living in the country made me find the stay in the city inconvenient. Straightaway, country houses are presented in droves; they are offered for me to choose in all the provinces. Mr. Hume takes charge of the offers, makes them to me, and even takes me to two or three neighboring places in the country. I hesitate for a long time over the choice; he increased this uncertainty. I finally determine on this province. Beforehand, Mr. Hume arranges everything; difficulties are smoothed over. I leave, I arrive at this solitary, convenient, and pleasant lodging. The master of the house foresees everything, provides for everything; nothing is lacking. I am tranquil, independent. Here is the moment, so longed for, when all my ills must end. No, that is when they begin, more cruelly than I had yet experienced them.

I have spoken to this point without preparation, from the heart, and doing justice with the greatest pleasure to Mr. Hume's good offices. If only what remains for me to say were of the same nature! Nothing that can honor him will ever cost me. One is not permitted to haggle over benefits except when one is accused of ingratitude, and Mr. Hume now accuses me of ingratitude. I will therefore dare to make an observation which he renders necessary. Estimating his efforts in terms of the pains and time that they cost him, their worth is inestimable, even more so because of his goodwill. As to the real good they have done me, they have more appearance than weight. I did not come as a beggar looking for bread in England; I brought mine. I only came to seek refuge, and that is open to any stranger. Moreover, I was not so unknown that, arriving alone, I would have lacked help and services. If a few people sought me out because of Mr. Hume, others also sought me out for my sake; and, for example, when Mr. Davenport was kindly willing to offer me the refuge in which I live, it was not for him, whom he did not know, and whom he saw only to ask him to make and to support his obliging offer. Thus, when Mr. Hume now tries to alienate this decent man from me, he seeks to take away what he did not give me. Everything that was done for good would have been done in about the same way without him, and perhaps better. But the bad would not have been done; for why

---

4. Rousseau had previously refused the help of Frederic II and refused to accept the pension unless Frederic's consent could be obtained.

do I have enemies in England? Why exactly is it that these enemies are Mr. Hume's friends? Who can have drawn their hostility upon me? It is not I, who has never seen them in my life and who does not know them. I would have none if I had come alone.

I have spoken to this point only of facts that are public and well known, which by their character and because of my gratitude have had the greatest éclat. Those which remain for me to say are not only private, but secret, at least as to their causes, and all possible measures have been taken so that they remain hidden from the public. Well known, however, to the person concerned, they no less bring about his own conviction.

Shortly after our arrival in London, I noticed there a muted change of mind with regard to me which soon became very perceptible. Before I came to England, it was one of the countries in Europe in which I had the best reputation—I almost dare say, the most esteem. The newspapers were full of my praise, and there was only a single cry of indignation against my persecutors. This tone was sustained upon my arrival. The newspapers announced it in triumph; England honored itself in being my refuge, and it justly glorified its laws and its government. Suddenly, and without assignable cause, this tone changes, but so forcefully and so quickly that of all the public's caprices one hardly ever sees one so astonishing. The signal was given in a certain magazine, as full of inanities as lies, in which the author, well instructed or feigning to be so, gave out that I was the son of a musician. From that moment, everything in print spoke of me only in an equivocal or dishonest way. All that was related to my misfortunes was disguised, altered, presented in a false light, and always as little to my advantage as possible. Far from speaking of the welcome I had received in Paris, and which had created only too much talk, it was not even supposed that I had dared appear in this city, and one of Mr. Hume's friends was very surprised when I told him that I had been there.

Too accustomed to the public's inconstancy still to be affected by it, I did not cease to be astonished by this very abrupt change, by this accord, so singularly unanimous that not one of those who had praised me so much when I was absent seemed, when I was present, to remember my existence. I found it bizarre that precisely after Mr. Hume's return— he who has so much credit in London, so much influence upon men of letters and booksellers, and such great connections with them—his presence had produced an effect so contrary to that which one could have expected from him; that among so many writers of every kind, not one of his friends showed himself to be one of mine. One could very well see that the people who spoke of me were not his enemies because, while they rang the praises of his public character, they said that I had crossed France under his protection, thanks to a passport that he had obtained for me at court. Little more was needed for them to have it understood that I had made the trip in his train and at his expense.

This signified nothing yet, and was only singular; but what was more so was that his friends' tone with me changed no less than the public's. I take pleasure in saying that their efforts, their good offices were always the same, and very great, in my favor; but, far from showing me the same esteem, the one above all about whom I want to speak and with whom we stayed upon our arrival accompanied all that with such harsh, and sometimes such shocking, remarks, that one would have said that he sought to oblige me only in order to have the right to show me contempt.[5] His brother, at first very welcoming, very decent, soon changed, with so little moderation that he did not even deign in their own house to address me a single word, nor respond to my salutation, nor undertake any of the duties one undertakes at home toward strangers. Yet nothing new had happened save the arrival of J. J. Rousseau and David Hume. Surely the cause of these changes did not come from me, unless too much simplicity, discretion, and modesty is a way of displeasing the English.

As for Mr. Hume, far from adopting a revolting tone with me, he tended to the other extreme. I have always suspected coarse flattery. He engaged in all kinds toward me,[6] to the point of forcing me, when I was not able to keep it in any longer, to tell him how I felt. His conduct certainly excused him from extending himself in words. Since he wanted to say some, however, I would have wished that he had sometimes substituted a friend's voice for his insipid praises. But I never found in his talk anything that felt like true friendship, not even in the way he spoke of me to others in my presence. One would have said that in wanting to obtain patrons for me, he sought to take their benevolence away from me, that he wanted that I be assisted by them, rather than loved, and I have often been surprised by the revolting turn he

---

5. Rousseau is referring here to John Stewart.

6. Rousseau's note: "I will tell you only about one, which made me laugh. This was to make it so that, when I came to see him, I would always find on his table a volume of the *Heloïse*, as if I were not sufficiently acquainted with Mr. Hume's taste not to be assured that, of all the books in existence, the *Heloïse* must be the most boring for him."

gave to my conduct with people who could be offended by it. An example will make this clear. Mr. Penneck, of the Museum, friend of the Lord Marshal, and vicar of a parish where they wanted to settle me, comes to see us. Mr. Hume—I was present—apologizes on my behalf for not having preempted him. "Doctor Maty had invited us to the Museum for Thursday, where Mr. Rousseau was supposed to see you, but he preferred to go with Mrs. Garrick to the Comedy." One cannot do so many things in one day. You will admit, sir, that this was a strange way of contriving to obtain Mr. Penneck's benevolence.

I do not know what Mr. Hume could have said secretly to his acquaintances, but nothing was more bizarre than their way of conducting themselves toward me with his approval, sometimes even with his assistance. Even though my purse was not empty, though I had no need of anyone's and though he knew this very well, one would have said that I was only there to live at public expense, and that the only issue was to give me alms in such a way as to save me a little from the embarrassment. I can say that this continuous and shocking affectation is one of the things which most made me come to dislike the stay in London. It is surely not on this footing that a man toward whom one wants to attract a little respect must be presented. But this charity may be interpreted in a benign way, and I consent to it. Let us proceed.

A false letter addressed to me from the king of Prussia, and full of the cruelest malignity, is disseminated in Paris. I am surprised to learn that it is one Mr. Walpole, a friend of Mr. Hume, who is spreading this letter around. I ask him if this is true; his sole answer is to ask me from whom I have heard this. A moment before, he had given me a card for this same Mr. Walpole, so that he would undertake to take charge of papers that are important to me and that I want to have safely brought from Paris.

I learn that the son of the mountebank Tronchin, my most mortal enemy, is not only Mr. Hume's friend, his protégé, but that they live together, and when Mr. Hume sees that I know this, he confides it to me, assuring me that the son does not resemble the father. I stayed several nights in this house at Mr. Hume's with my housekeeper, and based on the air and the welcome with which his hostesses—who are his friends—honored us, I judged the way either he, or this man whom he says does not resemble his father, may have spoken to them about her and about me.

These combined facts, which have a certain general appearance, imperceptibly induce anxiety in me, which I thrust away with horror.

Yet the letters that I write do not arrive; I receive some which have been opened, and all have passed through Mr. Hume's hands. If one of them escapes him, he cannot hide his ardent avidity to see it. One night, I see again in him a maneuver with a letter which strikes me.[7] After dinner, both of us staying silent by his fire, I notice that he is looking at me fixedly, which often happened with him, and in a manner difficult to convey. This time his cold, intense, mocking, and prolonged gaze became more than disquieting. To rid myself of it, I tried to stare at him in turn. But as I hold my eyes fixed on his, I feel an inexplicable trembling, and I am soon forced to lower them. The physiognomy and tone of the good David are those of a good man; but from where, good God, does this good man borrow the eyes with which he stares at his friends?

The impression made upon me by this look remains with me and agitates me. My distress increases to the point of perturbation. If I had not unburdened myself, I would have suffocated. Soon, a violent remorse takes hold of me, and I become indignant with myself. Finally, in a transport which I still remember with delight, I throw myself on his neck, I hug him tightly. Choked with sobs, soaked with tears, I cry out in a broken voice: "No, no, David Hume is not a traitor. If he were not the best of men, he would have to be the blackest." David Hume returns my embrace politely, and while striking me with little taps on the back, repeats several times in a tranquil tone: "What, my dear sir! Eh, my dear sir! What then, my dear sir!" He says nothing more to me. I feel my heart tightening. We go to bed, and I leave the next day for the province.

Having arrived in this pleasant refuge to which I had come from so far seeking repose, I was to find it in a convenient and charming,

---

7. Rousseau's note: "I have to say what this maneuver is. In his absence, I was writing an answer to a letter that I had just received at Mr. Hume's table. He arrives, very curious to know what I was writing and almost unable to prevent himself from reading it. I fold my letter without showing it to him and, as I was putting it in my pocket, he avidly asks for it, saying that he will send it the next day by post. The letter remains on the table. Lord Nuneham arrives, Mr. Hume leaves for a moment. I pick up the letter again, saying that I will have the time to send it the next day. Lord Nuneham offers to send it with the packet for M. the ambassador of France, and I accept. Mr. Hume returns while Lord Nuneham is making his envelope; he takes out his seal. Mr. Hume offers his own with such alacrity, that it must be preferred. The bell is rung. Lord Nuneham gives the letter to Mr. Hume's lackey to give to [Lord Nuneham's] who is waiting downstairs with his coach, so that he can carry it to the ambassador. Mr. Hume's lackey is hardly out the door when I say to myself: I bet that his master will follow him; he did not fail to do so. Not knowing how I could leave Lord Nuneham alone, I hesitated for a time before following Mr. Hume in turn. I did not see anything, but he saw very well that I was worried. Thus, although I have not received any answer to my letter, I do not doubt that it has arrived; but I doubt, I admit, that it was not read beforehand."

solitary house whose master, an intelligent man of merit, spared nothing of what could make me like my stay there. But what repose can one enjoy in life when the heart is agitated? Troubled by the cruelest uncertainty, and not knowing what to think of a man I ought to love, I sought to free myself from this gloomy doubt by restoring my confidence in my benefactor. For why, by what inconceivable whim, would he have so much zeal on the outside for my well-being, along with secret projects against my honor? Among the observations that had worried me, each fact was small in itself; there was only their astonishing concord. Perhaps, with knowledge of other facts that I did not know, Mr. Hume could, with a clarification, provide me with a satisfying solution. The only inexplicable thing would be if he refused a clarification that his honor, and his friendship for me, made equally necessary. I saw that there was something I did not understand and was dying to understand. Therefore, before making an absolute decision about him, I wanted to make a last effort, and write to him to bring him back, if he were letting himself be seduced by my enemies, or to make him explain one way or the other. I wrote him a letter,[8] which he must have found quite natural if he were guilty but quite extraordinary if he was not. For what could be more extraordinary than a letter at the same time full of gratitude for his services and of anxiety regarding his sentiments, and in which, putting so to speak his actions on one side and his intentions on the other, instead of speaking about the proofs of friendship he had given me, I ask him to love me because of the good he had done me? I did not take my precautions far enough ahead to keep a copy of this letter; but since he did take his, let him show it. Whoever will read it, seeing a man tormented by a hidden pain that he wants to make understood but does not dare say, will be curious, I am sure, to know what explanation this letter will have produced, especially following upon the preceding scene. None, nothing at all. Mr. Hume is satisfied in response to speak to me about the obliging pains Mr. Davenport proposes to take on my behalf. As to the rest, not a word about the principal subject of my letter, or about the state of my heart whose torment he must easily see. I was even more struck by this silence than I had been by his composure during our last conversation. I was wrong. This silence was very natural after the other one, and I should have expected it. For when one has dared to say to someone's face, "I am tempted to believe that you are

---

8. Rousseau's note: "It appears from what he wrote me last that he is very happy with this letter and that he finds it very good."

a traitor," and he does not have the curiosity to ask, "regarding what," one can count on his not having such curiosity in his life, and provided that the indications testify against him, that man is judged.

After the reception of his letter, which was very delayed, I finally decided, and resolved not to write to him again. Everything soon confirmed my resolution to break off all relations with him. Curious to the last degree about the details of the least of my affairs, he did not limit himself to finding out about them in conversation with me, but I learned that after he had begun by making my housekeeper admit that she was informed about them, he had not let a single tête-à-tête with her go by without questioning her, to the point of importunity, about my activities, my resources, my friends, my acquaintances, about their names, their condition, where they lived, and with a Jesuitical skill had asked her and me the same things separately. One must be interested in a friend's affairs, but one must be satisfied with what he wants to tell one, especially when he is as open and trusting as I am. All this gossip's petty nattering could not be less suitable for a philosopher.

At that same time, I receive two more letters that have been opened. One from Mr. Boswell, whose seal was in such a bad state that, when he received it, Mr. Davenport remarked upon it to Mr. Hume's lackey; and the other from M. d'Ivernois in a package for Mr. Hume, which had been resealed with a hot iron that, unskillfully applied, had burned the paper around the imprint. I wrote to Mr. Davenport to ask him to keep in his possession all the letters which would be given to him for me, and not to give any to anyone under any pretext whatever. I do not know if Mr. Davenport, who was far from thinking that this precaution concerned Mr. Hume, showed him my letter, but I know that everything told the latter that he had lost my confidence, and that he did not stop going on his merry way without troubling to regain it.

But what became of me when I saw the alleged letter, which I had not yet seen, from the king of Prussia in the newspapers, this fake letter printed in French and English, given out as real, even with the king's signature, and when I recognized M. d'Alembert's style as surely as if I had seen him write it?

Instantly a ray of light came to illuminate the secret cause of the astonishing and swift change of the English public regarding me, and I saw in Paris the center of the plot which was being executed in London.

M. d'Alembert, another very intimate friend of Mr. Hume's, was for a long time a hidden enemy, and was only spying out occasions to harm me without compromising himself. He was the only one of the men of letters with a certain name and of my old acquaintances who did not come to see me and who did not have a message sent to me the last time I passed through Paris. I knew about his secret dispositions, but I did not worry about them much, being content to inform my friends as the occasion arose. I remember that one day, when I was being questioned about him by Mr. Hume, who then questioned my housekeeper in the same way, I told him that M. d'Alembert was an astute and crafty man. He contradicted me with a warmth that astonished me, as I did not know at the time that they got along so well, and that it was his own cause that he was defending.

Reading this letter alarmed me greatly, and feeling that I had been drawn to England due to a project which was beginning to be executed, but whose goal I did not know, I felt the peril without knowing where it could be or from what I had to protect myself. I then remembered four frightening words by Mr. Hume, that I will recount in what follows. What to think of a piece of writing in which my miseries were made a crime, which tended to take from me everyone's commiseration in my misfortunes and which, to make the effect crueler still, was given out under the name of the very prince who had protected me? What consequence ought I to augur from such a beginning? The English people read the newspapers, and are already not very well inclined toward foreigners. Clothing that is unlike their own is enough to put them in a bad temper. What must a poor foreigner expect from this during his country walks, the sole pleasure of life to which he has limited himself, when these good people will be persuaded that he likes lapidation? They will be highly tempted to provide that amusement. But my pain, my profound and cruel pain, the most bitter that I have ever felt, did not arise from the peril to which I was exposed. I had braved too many others to be very moved by that one. The treachery of a false friend, whose prey I was, was what brought to my too sensitive heart despondency, sadness, and death. In the impetuosity of a first movement, of which I have never been the master, and which my skillful enemies know how to arouse to make use of it, I write letters full of disorder where I disguise neither my turmoil nor my indignation.

Sir, I have so much to say that, along the way, I am forgetting half of it. For example, an account in the form of a letter of my stay at Montmorency was brought by some booksellers to Mr. Hume, who showed it to me. I consented to have it printed. He undertook to take care of it; it never appeared. I had brought a copy of the *Letters from M. DuPeyrou*, which contained the account of Neuchâtel's affairs regarding me.

I gave it to the same booksellers at their request to have them translated and reprinted. Mr. Hume undertook to look after this; they never appeared.[9] As soon as the false letter from the king of Prussia and its translation appeared, I understood why the other writings remained suppressed, and I wrote about it to the booksellers. I wrote other letters which have probably circulated in London. Finally, I made use of the credit of a man of merit whose occupation it was to have a declaration of the imposture put into the newspapers. In this declaration I let all my pain show and did not disguise its cause.

Up to this point, Mr. Hume seems to have operated in the shadows; you will henceforth see him in the light and operating in the open. One has only to proceed on a straight course with crafty people; sooner or later they reveal themselves by their very ruses.

When the alleged letter from the king of Prussia was published in London, Mr. Hume, who certainly knew that it was only purported since I had told him so, says nothing about it, does not write to me, remains silent, and does not even think of making, for the sake of his absent friend, any declaration of the truth. All that was needed to reach the goal was to let people talk and stay quiet; that is what he did.

Mr. Hume, having been my guide to England, was in a way my protector there, my patron. If it were natural that he took up my defense, it was no less so that, having a public protest to make, I address myself to him. Having already ceased writing to him, I was far from starting again. I addressed myself to someone else. First slap on my patron's cheek. He does not feel it.

By saying that the letter was fabricated in Paris, it mattered little to me whether one understood that it was from M. d'Alembert, or from his mouthpiece Mr. Walpole; but in adding that what distressed and tore at my heart was that the impostor had accomplices in England, I explained myself with the greatest clarity to their friend who was in London, and who wanted to pass as mine. He was surely the only one in England whose hatred could tear and distress my heart. Second slap on my patron's cheek. He does not feel it.

On the contrary, he malignantly feigns that my affliction arose only from the publication of this letter, to make me pass for a vain man who is very affected by a satire. Vain or not, I was mortally distressed; he knew it and did not write me a single word. This tender friend who is

____

9. Rousseau's note: "The booksellers have just notified me that this edition is finished and ready to appear. That may be, but it is too late, and what is worse, too appropriate."

so solicitous that my purse is full seems very little concerned whether my heart is torn.

Another writing soon appears in the same papers, from the same hand as the first, even more cruel if that were possible, in which the author cannot disguise his rage about the welcome I had received in Paris. This writing no longer distressed me; it taught me nothing new. Libels could go on without affecting me, and the flighty public itself was getting tired of being so long occupied with the same subject. This is not in the interest of the plotters who, having my reputation as a decent man to destroy, want to be done with it one way or the other. They had to change weapons.

The affair of the pension was not over. It was not difficult for Mr. Hume to obtain from the minister's humanity and the prince's generosity that it be so. He was charged with informing me, and he did so. That moment was, I admit, one of the most critical of my life. How much it cost me to do my duty! My prior commitments, the obligation to correspond with respect for the king's generosity, the honor of being the object of his attentions, that of his minister, the desire to show how mindful I was of them, even the advantage of being a little more at ease as I approach old age burdened with troubles and ills, finally the awkwardness of finding a decent excuse to elude a benefit already almost accepted, everything made the necessity of renouncing it difficult and cruel. For I assuredly had to or make myself the vilest of all men, by becoming willingly obligated to the one who had betrayed me.

I did my duty, not without effort. I wrote directly to General Conway, with as much respect and honesty as was possible for me. Without an absolute refusal, I did not allow myself to accept it for the present. Mr. Hume had been the negotiator in this affair, even the only one who had spoken to me about it. Not only did I not answer him, even though it was he who had written to me, but I said not a word about him in my letter. Third slap on my patron's cheek, and as to that one, if he does not feel it, it is assuredly his fault. He feels nothing.

My letter was not clear, nor could it be for General Conway, who did not know what gave rise to this refusal; but it was very much so for Mr. Hume, who knew it very well. Yet he pretends that he is misled, as much regarding the subject of my pain as that of my refusal, and in a note he writes me, he gives me to understand that the continuation of the king's generosity will be arranged if I change my mind about the pension. In a word, he intends at all costs and whatever happens to remain my patron despite me. You can well imagine, sir, that he did not expect an answer and that he received none.

Roughly around that same time, for I do not know the dates, and this exactitude is not necessary here, a letter from M. de Voltaire appeared, addressed to me, with an English translation which outdid the original. The noble object of this witty work is to draw upon me the disdain and hatred of those among whom I took refuge. I did not doubt that my dear patron had been one of the instruments of this publication, especially when I saw that in attempting to alienate from me those in this country who could make life pleasant for me, the name of the person who brought me there was omitted. It was no doubt known that this was a superfluous attention, and that with respect to this, nothing remained to be done. The name, so unskillfully forgotten in this letter, made me remember what Tacitus says about Brutus's portrait which was omitted at a funeral, that it stood out to everyone precisely because it was not there.

Mr. Hume, then, was not named, but he lives with people who were named. He has as friends all my enemies, that is well known. Elsewhere, the Tronchins, the d'Alemberts, the Voltaires; but there is much worse in London. For I have no one there as enemies except his friends. And why would I have others there? Why do I even have those? What have I done to Lord Littleton whom I do not even know? What have I done to Mr. Walpole, whom I do not know any better? What do they know about me, except that I am unfortunate and the friend of their friend Hume? What then has he said to them, since it is only through him that they know me? I certainly believe that with the role he plays, he does not unmask himself before everyone; that would be no longer to be masked. I certainly believe that he does not speak about me to General Conway or to the Duke of Richmond as he does in his secret conversations with Mr. Walpole and in his secret correspondence with M. d'Alembert. But let the plot being woven in London since my arrival be discovered, and we will see if Mr. Hume does not hold its main threads.

At last, the moment believed to be suitable for striking the final blow arrives. Its effect is prepared for with a new satirical writing which is put in the papers. If I still had the slightest doubt until then, how could it have held firm with this writing, since it contained facts that were known only by Mr. Hume, exaggerated, it is true, to make them odious to the public.

It is said in this writing that I open my door to the great and close it to the little people. Who knows to whom I have opened or closed my door except Mr. Hume, with whom I lived, and by whose agency all those I saw came. Exception must be made for one of the great,[10] whom I received gladly without knowing him, and whom I would have received even more gladly had I known him. It was Mr. Hume who told me his name once he had left. Upon learning it, I was really grieved that, deigning to go up to the second story, he did not enter the first.

As to the little people, I have nothing to say. I would have liked to see fewer people but, not wishing to displease anyone, I let myself be guided by Mr. Hume, and I received as best I could all those he presented to me, without distinction between the little people and the great.

It is said in this same writing that I receive my relatives coldly, "not to say anything more." This generalization consists in my having once received rather coldly the only relative I have outside Geneva, and that in the presence of Mr. Hume. It is necessarily either Mr. Hume, or this relative, who has furnished this point. Now my cousin, whom I have always known to be a good relative and a decent man, is not capable of furnishing items for public satires against me. Besides, limited by his condition to the society of businessmen, he does not live with men of letters or with those who furnish articles in the papers, and even less with those who occupy themselves with satires. Hence this point does not come from him. At most I could think that Mr. Hume would have tried to make him chatter, which is not utterly difficult, and that he would have given a turn to what he said to him in a way most favorable to his aims. It is good to add that after my rupture with Mr. Hume, I had written about my sentiments regarding him to that cousin.

Finally, it is said in this same writing that I am subject to changing my friends. One does not have to be very astute to understand what this prepares.

Let us distinguish. I have very solid friends from 25 and 30 years ago. I have newer ones, no less sure, that I will keep longer if I live. I have not in general found the same reliability with those I have made among men of letters. So, I have sometimes changed them, and I will change them so long as they are suspect, for I am very determined never to keep friends out of propriety. I only want to have some to love them.

If ever I have had a certain and intimate conviction, I have one that Mr. Hume furnished the materials for this writing. Even more: not only do I have this certitude, but it is clear to me that he wanted me to have

---

10. The Duke of Brunswick.

it. For how to suppose such an astute man, unskillful enough to expose himself to this degree, as wanting to hide himself?

What was his goal? Nothing at least is clearer. It was to bring my indignation to its highest pitch, to bring about the blow he was preparing with more flourish. He knows that to make me do many silly things, it is enough to get me angry. We are at the critical moment which will show whether he reasoned well or badly.

One has to be as self-possessed as Mr. Hume, one has to have his phlegm and all his strength of mind, to make the decision he did after all that has happened. In my predicament, writing to General Conway, I could only fill my letter with obscure phrases to which Mr. Hume, as my friend, gave the interpretation he pleased. Supposing, then, even though he knew very well that the opposite was true, that it was the secrecy clause that pained me, he obtains from the general his willingness to use his credit to remove it. Then, this stoical and truly impassive man writes me the friendliest letter, in which he informs me that he used his credit to get the clause lifted but that, above all, they need to know whether I want to accept it without this condition, so as not to expose H. M. to a second refusal from me.

This was the decisive moment, the end, the object of all his work. He needed an answer; he wanted one. So that I could not excuse myself from providing one, he sends Mr. Davenport a duplicate of his letter, and not satisfied with this precaution, he writes to me in another note that he cannot stay any longer in London to serve me. My head was almost spinning as I read that note. In all my days I have found nothing more inconceivable.

He finally has it, this so desired answer, and is already hurrying to exult in it. Already writing to Mr. Davenport, he calls me a ferocious man and a monster of ingratitude. But he needs more. His measures have been well taken, or so he thinks; no proof against him can slip out. He wants an explanation. He will have it and here it is.

Nothing concludes it better than the last remark which gives rise to it. Alone it proves everything, and without rejoinder.

I want to suppose that, by some miracle, not a thing about my complaints against him reached Mr. Hume. He knows nothing about them, he is as perfectly ignorant of them as if he had not slipped into acquaintance with anyone who knew of it, as perfectly as if during that time he had lived in China. But my direct conduct when we were alone; the last words—so striking—that I said to him in London; the letter which followed, full of anxiety and fear; my obstinate silence, more energetic than words; my bitter and public complaint on the subject of d'Alembert's letter; my letter to the minister who did not write to me, in response to the one he had written himself, and in which I do not say a word about him; finally my refusal, without deigning to address myself to him, to acquiesce in the affair that he negotiated in my favor, my knowing it, and without any opposition from me: all that speaks by itself in the strongest tone, I do not say to any man who had some sentiment in his soul, but to any man who is not befuddled.

What! After I have broken off all relations with him for almost three months, after I have not responded to a single one of his letters, however important its subject might be, and surrounded by public and private marks of the affliction which his infidelity causes me, this enlightened man, this fine genius who is naturally so clear-sighted and voluntarily so stupid, sees nothing, hears nothing, feels nothing, is moved by nothing, and without a single word of complaint, of justification, of explanation, continues to give himself the greatest, most assiduous pains—despite me—for me. He affectionately writes to me that he can no longer stay in London to assist me, as if we agreed that he will stay there for that purpose! This obliviousness, this impassiveness, this obstinacy are not natural; this must be explained by other motives. Let us set forth this behavior in broad daylight, for this is a decisive point.

In this affair, Mr. Hume must necessarily be the greatest or the last of men; there is no middle ground. It remains to see which of the two it is.

Despite so many marks of disdain on my part, did Mr. Hume have the astonishing generosity sincerely to want to assist me? He knew that it was impossible for me to accept his good offices so long as I had the sentiments for him that I had conceived. He had himself eluded explanation. Thus, assisting me without justifying himself, he made his efforts useless. He was therefore not generous.

If he supposed that in this state I would accept his cares, he then supposed that I was despicable. It was therefore for the sake of a man whom he judged to be despicable that he solicited a pension from the king with such ardor. Can one think of anything more extravagant?

But that Mr. Hume, always following his plan, had said to himself: here is the moment of execution. For, pressing Rousseau to accept the pension, he will have to accept or refuse. If he accepts it, with the proofs I have in hand, I dishonor him completely. If he refuses it after having accepted it, every pretext has been removed; he will have to say why. That is what I am waiting for; if he accuses me, he is lost.

If, I say, Mr. Hume reasoned like this, he did something very consistent with his plan, and thereby very natural indeed here. There is only this sole way of explaining his behavior in this affair for, based on any other supposition, it is inexplicable. If this is not demonstrated, nothing ever will be.

The critical condition to which he has reduced me reminds me acutely of the four words I spoke about before, that I heard him say and repeat at a time when I hardly penetrated their force. It was the first night that followed our departure from Paris. We were sleeping in the same room, and several times during the night I hear him cry out in French extremely vehemently: "I've got J.-J. Rousseau." I do not know whether he was awake or sleeping. The phrase is remarkable in the mouth of a man who knows French too well to be mistaken as to the force and the choice of words. Nevertheless, I took, and could not fail at that time to take, his words in a favorable sense, even though the tone indicated it even less than the phrase. It is impossible for me to convey any idea of this tone, and which corresponds very well with the looks about which I spoke. Every time he said these words I felt a shudder of fear which I could not control; but I only needed a moment to recover and laugh at my terror. The next day, everything was so perfectly forgotten that I did not even think of it during all of my stay in and around London. I only remembered it here, where so many things have reminded me of these words, and remind me, so to speak, at every instant.

These words, whose tone resounds in my heart as if they had just been said, the long and dreadful looks shot at me so many times; the little taps on the back with the words "my dear sir" in response to the suspicion of being a traitor; all this affects me to such a degree after the rest, that these memories, were they the only ones, would close off any return to confidence. There is not one night during which these words "I've got J.-J. Rousseau" do not ring again in my ear, as if I were hearing them again.

Yes, Mr. Hume, you have got me, I know it, but only through things which are external to me. You have got me through opinion, through men's judgments; you have got me through my reputation, perhaps through my safety. All the prejudices are for you. It is easy for you to have me pass as a monster, as you have started to do, and I already see the barbarous exaltation of my implacable enemies. The public, in general, will not show me greater mercy. Without any other examination, it is always on the side of services rendered, because each is pleased to invite others to render them to him by showing that he knows how to appreciate them. I easily foresee the result of all this, especially in the country to which you have brought me and where, without friends, a stranger to everyone, I am almost at your mercy. Sensible people will understand, however, that far from having been able to seek out this affair, it was the most terrible thing that could have happened to me in my position. They will feel that only my invincible hatred for all falseness, and the impossibility of showing esteem to the one for whom I have lost it, could have prevented me from dissimulating when so many interests made it a law for me. But sensible people are few, and it is not they who make noise.

Yes, Mr. Hume, you have got me through all the bonds of this life; but you have not got me through my virtue, or through my courage, which is independent of you and of men, and which will remain entire in me despite you. Do not think of frightening me through dread of the fate which awaits me. I know men's judgments, I am accustomed to their injustice, and I have learned not to fear them much. If your decision is made, as I have every reason to believe, you can be sure that mine is no less made. My body is enfeebled, but my soul has never been firmer. Men will do and say what they want. No matter. What does matter to me is to finish as I started, to be upright and true until the end whatever may happen, and not to have to reproach myself for an act of cowardice in my miseries any more than for one of insolence in my prosperity. Whatever opprobrium awaits me and whatever misfortune threatens me, I am ready. Although I am to be pitied, I will be less so than you, and I leave you for all vengeance the torment of respecting, despite yourself, the unfortunate that you crush.

As I finish this letter, I am surprised by the strength I had to write it. If one died of pain, I would be dead from it with every line. Everything is equally incomprehensible in what is happening. Conduct such as yours is not in nature; it is contradictory; and yet it is demonstrated for me. An abyss on each side! I perish in one or the other. I am the unhappiest of men if you are guilty; I am the vilest if you are innocent. You make me want to be this despicable object. Yes, the state in which you would see me prostrate, trampled under your feet, crying out for mercy and doing everything to obtain it, loudly making public my indignity, and rendering the most resounding homage to your virtues, would be for my heart a state of flourishing and joy after the state of suffocation and death in which you placed it. I have only one more word to say to you. If you are guilty, do not write to me anymore. It would be useless, and you will surely not fool me. If you are innocent, deign to justify yourself. I know my duty; I love it and will always love it, however harsh it may be. There is no disgrace from which a heart not born for it cannot return. Again, if you are innocent, deign to justify yourself. If you are not, farewell forever.

JJRousseau

CHAPTER 148

Antoine-Jacques Roustan

September 7, 1766
Wootton

You well deserve, sir, the exception I most willingly make for you to the decision I have taken to break off all correspondence of letters, and not to write to anyone except in case of necessity. I do not for a moment want to leave you with the false opinion that I see only a Clergyman in you, and I would add that I am very far from taking the view of ecclesiastics in general that you suppose. The Clergy are much less my enemies in themselves than blind and conspicuous instruments in the hands of my enemies, who are skillful and hidden. The Catholic clergy, which alone had cause to complain of me, never did or wished me any harm, and the Protestant clergy, which only had cause to praise me, did and wished me harm only because it is as stupid as sycophantic, and because it did not see that its enemies and mine made it act so as to ruin me against all its genuine interests.

I return to you, sir, for whom my sentiments have not changed, because I believe yours to be the same, and because men of your substance acquire to a lesser extent the spirit of their station than they bring their own to it. I did not fear that Mr. Hume's clamors would make an impression upon you, or upon M. Abauzit, or upon any of those who know me. As to the public, it is dead to me; its senseless judgments have killed it in my heart. I no longer know any other good than peace of soul and days finished in repose far from the tumult and men. If the bad do not want to forget me, no matter; as for me, I have perfectly forgotten them. Mr. Hume, by loading me publicly with the affronts that you know, has promised to publish the facts and pieces of evidence which authorize them. Perhaps today he would wish not to have made that commitment, but well, it is made. If he fulfills it, you will find in his account the clarification that you ask for. If he does not fulfill it, you will be able to judge it in the same way; such a silence after all the noise he has made would be decisive. Each one must have his turn, sir; at present, it is Mr. Hume's. Mine will come late, but it will come nonetheless; I have faith in Providence. I have a defender whose actions are slow but sure. I await them and stay silent.

I am touched by M. Abauzit's recollection and his obliging worries. Please salute him tenderly and respectfully for me. Emphasize that it is not possible for a man who knows how worthily to honor his virtue to be deprived of it himself. Assure him that whatever Mr. Hume, the journalists, the plenipotentiaries, and all the powers of the earth may do or say, my soul will always remain the same. It has passed through every trial and has withstood them; it is not in the power of men to change it.

I thank you for the offer you make to inform me of what is going on, but I do not accept it. I foresee all too well what will happen, as I predicted everything that is happening. The Genevan bourgeoisie has never given the lie to the high opinion I had of it. Its conduct, always wise, moderate, and firm in such cruel circumstances, presents a perhaps unique example, and one very worthy of being famous. Never did they deserve to enjoy freedom more than in the moment of losing it, and I dare say that theirs eclipses the glory of those who have taken it from them. You should, sir, undertake the noble enterprise of celebrating these magnanimous men by performing the funeral oration for their freedom. Your heart alone, even without your talents, would suffice to make you execute this enterprise in a superior way, and never have Isocrates and Demosthenes treated such a great subject. Do it, sir, with majesty and simplicity; do not permit yourself any satire or invective; not a shocking word against the destroyers of the Republic. The facts, without adding any reflections when they are at their expense. Turn your gaze away from triumphant iniquity and see nothing but virtue in chains. Imitate that ancient priestess of Athens who never wanted to pronounce imprecations against Alcibiades, saying that she was the minister of the gods not to excommunicate and curse, but to praise and bless. I salute and embrace you with all my heart.

JJRousseau

CHAPTER 149

Karoline-Friederike von Salm-Grumbach, Countess of Wartensleben

September 27, 1766
Wootton

The case that you set out for me, madam, is at bottom very common, but mixed with such extraordinary things that your letter seems like a novel. Your young man does not belong to his age: he is either a prodigy or a monster. There are monsters in this age, I know it all too well, but they are more vile than courageous, and more deceitful than ferocious. As to prodigies, one sees so few of them that it is not worth the trouble to believe in them, and if Cassius is one by the strength of his soul, he is assuredly not one by his good sense and his reason.

He boasts of sacrifices which, although they are horrifying, would be great were they painful, and would be heroic were they necessary but in which, for lack of either one of these conditions, I see nothing but an extravagance, which makes me augur very badly of the one who has made them. Admit, madam, that a lover who forgets his love during a voyage, who falls in love again when he sees her again, who marries her and then goes away and forgets her once more, who promises curtly to come back for the birth of her child, and does not do it, who comes back finally to tell her that he is abandoning her, who leaves and writes only to confirm this fine resolution, admit, I say, that if this man felt love he hardly felt it, and that the victory about which he boasts with so much pomp probably costs him much less than he is telling you.

But let us suppose this love to be violent enough to honor itself with the sacrifice; where is the necessity for it? That is what is beyond me. Let him occupy himself with the sublime employment of freeing his fatherland, that is very fine, and I want to believe that it is useful; but not to permit himself any sentiment foreign to this duty, why this? Do not all the virtuous sentiments support one another, and can one destroy one without weakening all of them? "I thought for a long time," he says, "that I could combine my affections with my duties." There is nothing there to combine when these affections themselves are duties. "The illusion ceases, and I see that a genuine citizen must abolish them." What is this illusion, and where did he get this atrocious maxim? If there are sad situations in life, if there are cruel duties which sometimes force us to sacrifice others to them, to rend our heart in order to obey pressing necessity or inflexible virtue, are there any, can there ever be any which force us to stifle sentiments as legitimate as those of filial, conjugal, and paternal love? And does any man who makes it an express law for himself no longer to be a son, or husband, or father, dare to usurp the name of citizen, dare to usurp the name of man?

One would say, madam, upon reading your letter, that it is a question of conspiracy. Conspiracies can be heroic acts of patriotism, and there have been such; but they are almost always only punishable crimes, whose instigators think much less of serving the fatherland than of subjugating it, of freeing it from its tyrants than of being one. As for me, I declare to you that I would not for anything in the world want to have been mixed up in the most legitimate conspiracy because, in the end, these kinds of enterprises cannot be executed without discord, disorders, violent acts, sometimes effusion of blood, and in my view the blood of a single man is worth more than the freedom of the whole human race. Those who sincerely love freedom have no need of so many engines to find it. Without causing either revolutions or disorders, whoever wants to be free, effectively is.

Let us assume, notwithstanding, that this great enterprise is a sacred duty which must reign over all others, must he for all that annihilate them, and are these different duties incompatible to such a degree that one cannot serve the fatherland without renouncing humanity? Is your Cassius then the first who has formed the project of freeing his, and have those who have executed it done it at the cost of the sacrifices about which he boasts? The Pelopidases, Brutuses, the true Cassiuses, and so many others, did they need to abjure the rights of blood and of nature in order to accomplish their noble purposes? Were there ever better sons, better husbands, better fathers than these great men? Most of them, on the contrary, organized their enterprises within the bosom of their families, and Brutus dared, without necessity, to reveal his secret to his wife, solely because he thought that she was worthy of being its keeper. Without going so far to look for examples, I can, madam, cite a more modern one, that of a hero who lacks nothing to stand alongside those of antiquity than to be as well known as they are. This is Count Louis de Fiesque,[1] when he wanted to smash the fetters of his fatherland Genoa and free it from Doria's yoke. This young man, so amiable, so virtuous, so perfect, formed this great purpose almost from his childhood, and brought himself up, so to speak, to execute it. Although he was very prudent, he confided it to his brother, his family, and his wife, who was as young as he. After very great, very slow, very difficult preparations, the secret was so well kept, the enterprise was so well organized and so completely successful that the young Fiesque was the master of Genoa when he died of an accident.

I do not say that it is wise to reveal these kinds of secrets, even to those close to us, without the greatest necessity for doing so; but it is one thing to keep one's secret, and another to break off with those from whom one is hiding it. I will even grant that in meditating upon a great purpose, one is sometimes obliged to give oneself over to it to the point of forgetting for a time duties that are perhaps less pressing, but no less sacred as soon as they can be fulfilled. But that as a deliberate intention, from gaiety of heart, knowing it, wanting it, one has along with the brutality of forever renouncing everything that must be dear, that of burdening someone with this cruel declaration, that, madam, is something that no imaginable situation can either authorize or even suggest to a man in his senses who is not a monster. Thus, I conclude, if regretfully, that your Cassius is at least crazy, and I admit to you that he entirely seems to me to be an ambitious man who is encumbered by his wife, who wants to cover with the mask of heroism his inconstancy and his projects of aggrandizement. Now, those who can at his age make use of such ruses are people whom one does not restore, and who are rarely worth the effort.

---

1. The patrician Giovanni Luigi Fiesco (1523-47), who was at the center of a conspiracy against Andrea Doria (1468-1560).

I can, madam, be mistaken; it is up to you to judge. I wish that I had more pleasant things to say. But you ask me for my sentiment; I either must tell you, or be quiet, or deceive you. Of the three options I chose the most honest, and the one which could most show you, madam, my deference, and my respect.

JJRousseau

CHAPTER 150

Antoine-Jacques Roustan

December 20, 1766
Wootton

Of the two letters, sir, about which you speak in the one you took the trouble to write me on the 13th of this month, I have only received the last one and answered it last Saturday. The one dated October 25th did not arrive.

My poor old friend Lenieps in the Bastille! Eh! My God, that is certainly using a cannon to kill a mosquito. This good man, easygoing and simple, attached in his heart to the laws and to freedom but, besides, without friends, without credit in his fatherland, could not have placed or fired one servant there. Since his daughter's death, his sorrows and years were pushing him with great strides toward the grave. This event will throw him into it. Here is one of those great coups d'état of these Gentlemen the Negatives. They have force on their side, and they succeed, stupid as they are. If things were less desperate, however, one could well say upon seeing the way in which these people behave: *Quos vult perdere Jupiter, dementat.*[1]

---

1. "Those whom Jupiter wants to ruin he first deprives of reason."

Would you happen to know in London someone from Lausanne called M. Deyverdun? Is he a man of letters, a man with a pen? You would oblige me by being willing to do some research on this point, if you are well placed to do it without appearing to do so and without naming me.

You see, sir, how familiarly I speak to you. That is the only kind of compliment that I want to make you, and I believe the one that might please you most. I salute you with all my heart.

CHAPTER 151

Pierre-Alexandre DuPeyrou

January 8, 1767
Wootton

May God lavish his benedictions on my dear host who, by a perfect reconciliation, grants my heart the peace that it needed. In these circumstances I take as a good omen the one you announce for the rest of my days at the end of your no. 38. If I can obtain that the public forgets me, count on my no longer reawakening their memories. Posterity will do me justice; I am very sure of it. This consoles me for my contemporaries' affronts.

A reconciliation is without contradiction a very sweet thing, but it is preceded by such sad moments that we must not purchase any more at such a price. The first source of our little misunderstanding arose from a defect in your memory, and from the confidence that you did not cease to have in it. In your two penultimate letters, for example, speaking about what you said to M. de Luze, you suppose that you wrote to me that he said that I had not at all slept in Calais in the same room as Mr. Hume, a fact which is very true. If, in effect, that is what you had written to me before, I would have been greatly in the wrong to be offended by it, and my answers would be very ridiculous. But, my dear Host, your no. 33 did not at all mention Calais, and distinctly pronounced that I had never slept in the same room as Mr. Hume. Here are your own words: "De Luze doubts that you had in fact written that you slept in the same room where Hume was because, he says, it is he de Luze who always along the way occupied the same room as Hume, and you were alone in yours." This word "always" is decisive, it seems to me, not only for Calais, but for the whole way, and my response, most blamable for its outburst, is very correct as to the reasoning.

In your no. 36 you inform me that I have publicly broken with Mr. Hume. My dear Host, where did you get this? Are you then putting to my account the racket made by the good David, while I did not say a single word, except to him alone, with the greatest secrecy, and only when he forced me to? As I was informed about his project, I feared the outburst of this rupture more than death. I defended myself from it with all my strength, and I did so finally only through well-sealed letters, while he had his make a grand tour, to send them to me opened through Mr. Davenport. These letters, if he had not shown them, would have been seen only by him, and I would not even have spoken about them to anyone in the world, except the Lord Marshal and you. Do you call that breaking off publicly?

In your no. 38, you accuse me of putting some malice into my letter of the 10th of July. What I have just said responds in advance to this accusation. Malice consists in the intent to ruin. Had my letter contained dreadful things, what harm could they do to Mr. Hume, being seen by him alone? There may have been some brutality in this letter, but never malice, since it could not prejudice him to whom it was written unless he wanted it to. But pray, reread this letter with less prejudice. In the position I was in while writing it, it is, I dare say, a prodigy of strength of soul and moderation. Forced to explain myself to an exceptional scoundrel who, under the trappings of aid, works to defame me, I push restraint so far as to speak to him only in the third person, to avoid in what I had to say to him the harshness of addressing him directly. That letter is full of his praises (you see how he has returned them). Everywhere, reason which discusses, not a single insulting or bad-tempered remark, not a movement of indignation, not a harsh word, except when the force of reasoning makes it so necessary that one could not take away the word without weakening the argument; even then, the word is neither direct nor affirmative, but hypothetical and conditional. If you condemn this letter, I am even more upset, as I want the soul of the one who dictated it to be judged by it.

This severity of judgment, which goes so far as injustice, is as far from your heart as it is from your reason, and only comes from a defect in your memory. You receive clarifications that make you change your ideas, and you forget that I am not informed about this change. You see that my rupture with Mr. Hume is public, and you forget that I have played no part in its publicity. You see that I say harsh things to him which are printed, and you equally forget that it is he who forced me to say them to him, and that it is he who had them printed. What you write either escapes you or is modified, and the result of all this is that I always seem to you to be unreasoning, because instead of responding to your present idea at which I could not guess, I respond to the one you communicated to me and that you no longer remember.

There would be two remedies for this that are in your power. The first would be that you would be willing to presume a little less on your memory and a little more on my reason, such that when my answer does not tally well with what you believe you wrote me, you would suppose that it must be that you wrote me something else, rather than conclude that I do not know what I am saying. The other would be to keep copies of the letters you write me, so that you can have recourse to them as needed for my answers. A third means would be that every time I respond to some point in your letters, I begin by transcribing in mine the point to which I am responding; but this way of arming oneself to the teeth with one's friends seems so cruel to me, that I would rather a hundred times present myself naked and be distressed.

In addition to the very condemnable outbursts for which I reproach myself on my side, I will try also to cure myself of a defective pride which makes me neglect useful advice to warn you regarding what is being said against me. For example, when you began to speak to me about M. de Brühl with great praise, I did not want to respond in any way about that; and in effect I have nothing to say against this praise, because I do not at all know M. de Brühl's character. But what I should nevertheless have said to you is that he came to see me at Chiswick, and that his approach, his air, his tone, his manners repulsed me to such a point that it was not in me to welcome him.

I will finish with this disagreeable subject so as never to speak of it again. Regarding certain questions you raise in your letter, I would have many things to say that I do not dare confide to paper. I do not know yet whether the friend who was to come this autumn will be able to come this spring;[1] I fear that he is wrapped up in the misfortunes of the fatherland. If he does not come, I see only a single resource for speaking

---

1. D'Ivernois.

to you safely: that is a code upon which I am working, and which I will have to risk sending to you by post for lack of a safer means. Examine very carefully the condition of the seal of letter that will contain it to know if it has been opened. I tell you in advance that it will be sealed with the arabesque talisman with which you are familiar, and whose imprint cannot be lifted and reapplied without it showing. I have just received from M. de Cerjat an invitation that is too obliging for me not to recognize its source. When you have my code, we will say more about it. Farewell, my dear Host. I feel all your friendship, and you must know my heart enough to be able to judge mine. A thousand tender respects for the good mama. The Lord Marshal used to tell me that the winters are mild in England. We have a foot of ice and three feet of snow here. I have never felt such a biting cold in my life.

I have just been informed that the newspapers say that the Lord M[arshal]'s health is very poor. Eh, what! My God! Always misfortunes, and always of the worst kind! What reassures me a little is that when I compare the date of his last letter with that of this news, I believe it to be false; but I cannot prevent myself from feeling extremely anxious. He will perhaps not write to me for a long while. If you have recent news of him, I beseech you to give it to me. I embrace you.

Please receive the thanks and respect of Mlle. Levasseur.

I intend in a few days to draw upon your bankers a bill of exchange for eight hundred francs.

CHAPTER 152

Victor de Riqueti, marquis de Mirabeau

January 31, 1767
Wootton

To console the unhappy is worthy of the friend of men. The letter, sir, that you honored me by writing, the circumstances in which it was written, the noble sentiment which dictated it, the respectable hand from which it comes, the unfortunate to whom it is addressed, everything concurs to give it in my heart the reward it receives from yours. While reading you, and consequently loving you, I have often desired to be known and loved by you. I did not expect that you would be the one to make the overtures, and precisely when I was universally abandoned. But generosity does not know how to do anything by halves, and your letter contains its plenitude. How beautiful it would be for the friend of men to give a retreat to the friend of equality! Your offer penetrated me so deeply, I find its object so honorable for both, that by another quite contrary effect, you will perhaps make me unhappy by the regret of not making the most of it. For, however sweet it would have been for me to be your guest, I see little hope of becoming so. My age, more advanced than yours, the great distance, my ills which make travel very painful, the love of repose, of solitude, the desire to be forgotten so as to die in peace, make me dread to come nearer to the great cities where my vicinity might awaken the kind of attention which is my torment. Besides, to speak only of what would keep me closer to you, without being uncertain about my safety from the Parlement of Paris, I owe it that respect of not going to defy it in its jurisdiction, as if to make it tacitly admit its injustice. I owe it to your minister, whom too many afflicting signs make me feel I have had the misfortune of displeasing, and that without my being able to imagine any other cause than a misunderstanding all the crueler in that, without it, what drew disgrace upon me ought to have merited favors.[1] Ten words of explanation would prove this. But it is one of the misfortunes attached to human power and to those who depend on it that, once the great are in error, nothing will make them change their minds. Thus, sir, so as not to expose myself to new storms, I persist in the sole choice which can assure me the repose of my final days. I love France, I will regret it all my life; if my fate depended on me, I would go there to finish my days, and you would be my host, since you do not like my having a patron. But to all appearances, my wishes and my heart will alone make the voyage; my bones will remain here.

I have not had Mr. Hume's indifference, sir, toward your writings, and I could speak about them to you so well since they are, along with two treatises on botany, the only books which I brought with me in my trunk. But apart from the fact that I believe your sublime amour-propre to be too far above the petty vanity of authors not to disdain these formulas of praise, I am already too far from these kinds of subjects to be able to speak about them with precision and even with pleasure. Everything that is related in some way to literature and to an occupation for which I was certainly not born, has become so perfectly unbearable to me, and memory of it recalls so many sad ideas, that in order not to think about it anymore I made the decision to rid myself of all my books, which were very inopportunely sent me from Switzerland. Yours and mine departed along with all the rest. I have become so disgusted with all reading that it is impossible for me to reread any one of my own writings. Even the fatigue of thinking becomes more painful for me every day. I like to dream, but freely, by letting my head wander, and without subjecting myself to any topic. Now that I am writing to you, I leave my pen at every moment to tell you a thousand charming things as I walk, which disappear as soon as I return to my paper. This idle

---

1. He is referring to a note in the *Social Contract* about Choiseul. See *Confessions*, CW 5:463–64.

and contemplative life, of which you do not approve, and for which I do not make excuses, becomes more delightful to me every day. To wander alone aimlessly and ceaselessly among the trees and rocks which surround my dwelling, dreaming or rather raving at my ease and, as you say, gaping at crows. When my brain heats up too much, calming it by analyzing some moss or some grass; finally, giving myself over without servitude, without hindrance, to my fantasies which, thank Heaven, are all in my power. That, sir, is for me the supreme happiness, to which I imagine nothing superior in this life, and even in the other.

If I went to one of your estates, you can count on my not taking the slightest pain in favor of the proprietor. I will see you stolen from, pillaged, robbed, without ever saying a single word about it to you or anyone. All my misfortunes come to me from this ardent hatred of injustice that I have never been able to tame. I accept it as a given. It is time to be wise, or at least tranquil. I am weary of wars and quarrels. I am very sure never to have any with decent people, and I no longer want any with rascals, for only those are dangerous. See then, sir, please, what a useful man you would put in your house. God forbid that I would want to degrade your offer with this objection, but it is one according to your maxims, and one must be consistent.

In censuring this nonchalance, you will repeat that to be good only for oneself is to be good for nothing; but I believe that whoever is truly good for himself is, in some respect, good for others. Besides, consider that it does not belong to every friend of men to be, as you are, benefactors in reality. Consider that I have neither position nor fortune, that I am getting old, that I am infirm, abandoned, persecuted, detested, and that in wanting to do good I would do harm, especially to myself. I have received my notice from nature and men; I have taken it and want to profit from it. I no longer deliberate whether it is well or badly done, because the decision has been made, and nothing will make me depart from it. May the public forget me as I forget it. If it does not want to forget me, no matter; let it admire me or tear me apart, I am indifferent to all of that. I try to know nothing about it, and when I learn about it, it hardly worries me. If the example of an innocent and simple life is useful to men, I can still do them that good; but it is the only one, and I am thoroughly determined to live only for myself and my friends—a very small number, but proven, and sufficient for me. Still, I could have done without them, even though I have a loving and tender heart for which attachments are a real need; but these needs have often cost me so dearly that I have learned to suffice to myself, and I have preserved the health of my soul enough to be able to do so. Never has a hateful, envious, vindictive sentiment approached my heart. The memory of my friends gives a charm to my reverie that the memory of my enemies does not at all trouble. I am entirely where I am, and not at all where those who persecute me are. Their hatred, when it does not act, troubles them only, and I leave it to them as sole revenge. I am not perfectly happy, because there is nothing perfect here below, especially happiness: but I am as close to it as I can be in this exile. Very little more would fulfill my wishes. Fewer physical ills, a milder climate, a clearer sky, calmer air, and especially hearts that are more open so that, when my heart feels the need to unburden itself, it felt that it did so in another's. I have this happiness at the moment, and I profit from it, but not entirely with impunity. Your letter will leave me with memories that will not fade, and that will sometimes make me less tranquil. I do not like arid countries, and Provence does not attract me much. But this estate in Angoumois, which is not yet under full production, and where one can sometimes encounter nature, will often cost me regrets that will not all be for it. Good day, Monsieur le marquis. I hate formulas, and I ask you please to exempt me from them. I salute you very humbly, and with all my heart.

JJRousseau

François-Henri d'Ivernois

January 31, 1767
Wootton

Never, sir, have I written, said, or thought anything like the extravagances which you are told have been found written in my hand among M. Lenieps's papers, or anything that M. de Voltaire publishes, with his ordinary impudence, as written or signed by me in minister Montmollin's hands. Your inexhaustible credulity no longer angers me, but it still astonishes me, and all the more so on this occasion that you have been able to see in our association that I am not a visionary, and in the *Social Contract* that I have never approved of democratic government. Do you then have such a great opinion of my enemies' probity as to believe them incapable of inventing lies, and can they obtain your esteem at the expense of the one you owe me?

While the ease with which you believe everything reveals so little of it to me, mine for you and your magnanimous compatriots increases from day to day. Courage and firmness are not what strikes me in them; I expected it. But I admit that I did not expect to see so much wisdom at the same time amid the greatest dangers. This is the first time that a people presented such a grand and beautiful spectacle; it deserves to be inscribed in the splendors of history. Your magistrates, sir, conduct themselves in this whole affair like a people of madmen, and you conduct yourselves, amid the terrible perils that threaten you, with all the dignity of the most respectable magistrates. I believe that I see the Roman senate seated gravely in the public square, waiting for death at the hands of the Gauls. This is the first and the last time, since our meeting in Thonon,[1] that I will have permitted myself to speak about your affairs, but I could not refuse this note of admiration for the one you inspire in me. You know what my constant advice was during this meeting, and since I willingly do you the justice that is due to you, I hope that you will not refuse me the one you owe me on this occasion either. I have nothing more to say to you. Such men assuredly do not need counsel, and it is not up to me to give it. My service is done for the rest of my life; all that remains is to die in peace if I can.

You do not doubt, my friend, the affectionate eagerness I would have to see you. Nevertheless, it is best for my repose and for your benefit that we give ourselves over to this pleasure only when all will be ended, one way or the other, in your city.[2] The public, which knows me so little and judges me so badly, does not doubt that I always go about sowing discord among you, and it is claimed that I was myself seen last month hidden in Switzerland for that purpose. Every good that you would do would be bad as soon as it was presumed that I am the one who counseled it. Only come crowned with an olive branch, then, so that we can taste the pleasure of seeing one another in all its purity. May this happy moment soon arrive; no one in the world will feel it more than your friend's heart.

JJRousseau

Mlle. Levasseur is always touched by your remembrance, and aspires with no less ardor than I to the pleasure of seeing you again. I do not repeat this to you in every letter, because you must never doubt it. She lost her mother this past summer. The air in England suits her only poorly; she bears it, however, and at this moment she is doing better than I.

---

1. Rousseau met with Genevan representatives, d'Ivernois, the Delucs, Jacques and Pierre Vieussieux, and J.-P. Voullaire, August 5–12, 1764, in Thonon-les-Bains on the French shore of Lake Geneva.
2. Geneva.

CHAPTER 154

Richard Davenport

February 5, 1767
Wootton

One good turn brings another, and this, sir, is the honorable function you must fulfill. I have learned that the interdiction of commerce with France is reducing the poor people in Geneva to doing without bread, that those who are well-off are making common contributions to help them, and that a collection is being made for this purpose among the Genevans who are in London. You have put me in a position to contribute to it without inconveniencing myself by the restoration of the rights paid for my books. I pray you to make the proceeds over entirely to charity, by giving this little sum to those responsible for the monies for the collection. I do not know who it is, but I do not doubt that M. Dutens knows it, or, if he does not, M. Roustan, pastor of the Swiss Church "Meard's Court Dean Street Soho Square," knows it without fail. I do have a cousin of mine in London who is familiar with this, but I do not like him to meddle in my affairs, as he wants to meddle in them too much. I cannot tell you how moved I am by the fate of this unfortunate people, which sees its bread and its freedom taken away at the same time.

I am impatiently waiting for news of your recovery. As for me, I continue to be so ill in body and soul that I have not been able until now to write the letter to the Duke of Grafton. It will be, I hope, for Saturday next. I received the second packet, and I thank you for both. I wanted to joke about your deliveries and the provisions they contain, but I have never in my life felt less like laughing. A thousand greetings, as much from Mlle. Levasseur as from me to your dear children and to the ladies of your house. Permit me also to assure you of her respect. You know, sir, how devoted I am to you.

JJRousseau

CHAPTER 155

Pierre-Alexandre DuPeyrou

March 2, 1767

My dear host, the day before yesterday I was sending you my No. 9 containing what you know. I have learned since then that it was made to pass through a depot which was kept secret from me, and I will bet that this number will not arrive in your hands as it left mine. So I will wait for news from you before I make use of it.[1] Besides, it is absolutely impossible to open and close the package without it showing.

Having no news of M. de C[erjat], I guess that he has not received my letter. You tell me to address myself to him in case of need. The advice is admirable, but less easy to follow than to give. If it were as easy as you figure to address myself to M., I would have no need of him. Letters, far from aiding me, ruin me. The only thing that could be useful to me would be to see someone in whom I have confidence, someone upon whom I can count, to whom I can give something in safekeeping, were it only a servant. That is the only essential service I can receive. But so long as I am told from far away: address yourself to me or to so-and-so, it is as if I am being told nothing, for it is impossible for me. You judge

---

1. The code mentioned in a previous letter.

my situation by yours; you are very much mistaken. Mine is becoming more critical every day and is approaching a point that frightens me. Until now our correspondence has remained free. What happened to me the day before yesterday made me see that it can cease to be so, without it being in my power to reopen it. And then, what will become of me in the heart of this island, where I cannot take a step without someone else's assistance? What troubles me more than myself are my papers. If no one comes to my aid and I must die here, my decision is made. I will burn them, as I am very determined not to let them fall into my enemies' hands if I can. I cannot avoid having the way by which I risk this letter known, and so I cannot count on the same happiness a second time if it passes through without obstacle. I will therefore not write anything which requires secrecy anymore until we have a code by which to understand one another. For, not letting myself be rebuffed by the trouble, I am going to start another entirely different one; but how to hope that it will reach you. One must admit that I am an unfortunate mortal. I embrace you.

I have lost the Lord M[arshal], that is certain, without my being able to know why or how. I predicted that they would erect batteries near him, I warned him. He had made me the most beautiful promises in the world. If he let himself be taken by surprise, how will you resist, you whom one "it is said" rattles, and whom a wagoner persuades of the most inconceivable absurdities. For it is now down to you, that is certain, and I even foresee the way. But of what use is foresight to me, but to make me feel in advance the ills that I cannot avoid? As much as I can judge the project, it is to make me die of sorrow, as soon as can be done on this island; it is the surest way that has been imagined to stifle my complaints. Yet I am not a man who complains very much. I must know how to groan and be quiet; that is an occupation I have been learning for a long time. Necessity, fatal necessity, how terrible are your blows; neither reason nor truth nor wisdom can shield us from them.

CHAPTER 156

Marquis de Mirabeau

March 25, 1767

Your letter, s[ir], of Feb[ruary] 20 reached me promptly enough, and I can assure you that the very agreeable things I read in it are nevertheless not what pleased me most. Do not, however, expect a well-ordered correspondence from me; that is an agreement I do not want to make because I feel that I am not in a fit state to keep it, even with you. Every task one must fulfill costs me and weighs on me for the sole reason that one must do it. But I particularly have such an aversion for writing letters, that I yield to the pleasure of receiving them from people I love only after having assured myself that they do not require an answer. For such a great enemy of injustice, I will perhaps not appear to you to be very consistent. Yet I believe that I am, for according to me, it is an injustice to others to impose upon myself—even for my own benefit— a law that I cannot bear, and it is not one to me, to refuse this law by renouncing, if with regret, its advantages. It is certain that your letters please me and do me good, but writing harms me extremely, writing is a duty that kills me. I cannot submit myself to this duty except for the strongest necessity. In all my projects of temporal beatitude, to have neither watch nor writing desk has always been my favorite article. Nothing fatigues me more than writing, if not thinking; and I would have to fatigue myself for a month to respond to one of your pages. Do not require of me in proportion to the worth of what you are writing, but in proportion to what it costs you, and with one page I would have paid for ten of your letters; in place of which, on the basis of the other calculation, it would be entirely the contrary, and all my time would not suffice for it. If you want to see the generosity which you have shown me through to the end, do me good for free, do not require from my answers more precision than I can put in them. When it is not to be found there, accuse me of negligence, not of indifference, for you would assuredly be very wrong. Finally, since I must always be in debt to you, do not haggle over more or less, and overlook, I pray you, the same inequality in the number and the amount of our letters as we must very well overlook, despite you and me, in the value of their content.

You want to offer me, you say, another philosophy. Philosophy, to me. Eh! Monsieur le marquis, you do me an honor that I hardly deserve. Systems of all kinds are too far above me. I put none in my life or in my conduct. To reflect, compare, quibble, persist, combat is no longer my affair. I let myself go to the impression of the moment without resistance and even without scruple, for I am perfectly sure that my heart only loves what is good. All the evil that I have done in my life, I did by reflection; and the little good that I may have done, I did by impulsion. This means that I yield to my inclinations with confidence; they are so simple, so easy to follow; to content them it costs others and me so little that, in truth, to harden oneself against them is to want to struggle at any cost. You suppose that I flee society because of aversion for it; you are mistaken on these two points. I do not hate it and I do not flee it. I hate the bother that I find in it, and I mortally hate this bother. Without it, society would be pleasant for me, but the bother poisons it, and I renounce a good that I can do without so as to avoid an ill which is unbearable to me. Others tell me they do not find this bother in it; good for them, but I do find it there. Do you want to argue over a fact of sentiment? I have to talk when I have nothing to say, stay in place when I would want to walk, sit when I would want to stand, shut up in a room when I yearn for the open air, that I go here when I want to go elsewhere, that I eat at the hour others prefer, that I walk with their gait, that I answer their compliments or their sarcasms, that I answer red or green notes not a word of which I understand, that I reason with the reasoners, that I follow the floridness of the witty, that I say insipid things to women; in short, that I do all day what I know the least and displeases me most, and that I do nothing, I do not say only of what

I would want to do, but of what nature and the most pressing needs demand, beginning with pissing, a nexed more frequent and more tormenting for me than for any other. I still shudder when I imagine myself among a circle of women, forced to wait for a high-flown talker to finish his sentence, not daring to go out without being asked if I am leaving, finding on a well-lit staircase other fine ladies who delay me, a courtyard full of coaches always in motion ready to crush me, housemaids who look at me, those Gentlemen the lackeys who line the walls and make fun of me, finding not a street, an arch, a miserable little corner that suits me, not being able, in a word, to piss without an extravaganza and on some noble leg in white stockings. Sir, were this the only point at issue, it would be enough to make me loathe living in a city. I who even hates plains and always seeks dark places thick with undergrowth to be able two hundred times a day to stop at my ease, upon the instant of need, without being seen even by the countryfolk. I get up at the hour that one goes to bed in Paris, I go to bed before they have supper there; my day is almost ended before it is started there. My first care is to go wandering in the countryside in my nightcap: I come and go, enter, and leave again every quarter of an hour. I can only live *sub dio*,[1] I can breathe only amid prairies and woods. I suffocate in a room, in a hall, in a house, in a street, in the Place Vendôme. The cobblestones, the gray of the walls and the roofs give me nightmares, and you would like me to pass my life, say, or rather to end it, amid all that. I will have to pass the three best quarters of it cloistered in this sad or rather in this horrible prison, not knowing what to do, what to become, having only the dreadful resource of books, or of the dire writing desk or else, at sixty, I will have to renounce my old habits to make myself entirely new ones, as if I were healthy enough to bear such a change. For with the habits I have acquired and the invincible tastes by which I feel that I am subjugated at my age, if harsh necessity ever calls me back to stay in cities, it will be only to get myself buried there.

I greatly consent to your not approving of my way of life, so long as you do not undertake to make me change it. There is no kind of reasoning which could make me commit to take on another, so long as I feel that mine suits me. I promise you to seek out society as soon as it is necessary for me; until then, permit me to remain as I am. And I permit you with all my heart in exchange to find that I am terribly wrong.

---

1. "Under the sky"; literally, "under god."

Until now, I have only spoken about the physical; let us start anyway by examining this point, and we will pass on to others.

I need neither your purse, nor your friends, nor your credit, nor your knowledge, nor almost your time, and in two days, in 24 h[ours] you can be rid of me. I need your virtuous soul, your good sense, a few easy and simple attentions, and the most profound secrecy, that is all. And with that, you can assure the peace of an unfortunate man's last days who places all his hopes in you alone.

I am not one to importune you with my lamentations. I do not have to speak to you of my misfortunes, or of my enemies, or of their plots, or of anyone in the world save myself alone. All I have to say to you is a matter of one minute.

But I am no longer at trials; I have made them. I am now at the result, and I hold to it.

PART V

The Final Years

June 1767–1778

Rousseau arrived back in France in May 1767. He was advised by friends to live under an assumed name to avoid arrest, and he adopted the name "Renou." He began to use his own name again at the beginning of 1770. Finally, in June of that year he moved to Paris, where he lived quietly for the rest of his life. In addition to his *Considerations on the Government of Poland*, he worked on his three great autobiographical works: the *Confessions, Rousseau: Judge of Jean-Jacques*, and the *Reveries*.

For the first year and a half after his return from England, Rousseau kept up a steady correspondence. After that, because he wrote fewer letters and, perhaps, because he was less careful about keeping copies, there remain relatively few extant letters. Indeed, for the last five and a half years of Rousseau's life, there remain only sixty-eight, under 3 percent of his total correspondence. A very large percentage of these letters, particularly the ones from 1773–75, discuss botanizing.[1] For the entire period covered in this section there are just under six hundred letters. We are presenting twenty-five of them.

---

1. These and Rousseau's other letters on botany can be found in *CW* 8:130–249.

CHAPTER 157

Marquis de Mirabeau

July 26, 1767
Trie

I ought, sir, to have written to you when I received your last note, but I preferred to delay for a few more days to repair my negligence, and to be able to speak to you at the same time about the book you sent me. Being unable to read it entirely, I chose the chapters in which the author makes waves, and which seemed to me the most important. This reading satisfied me less than I had expected, and I feel that the traces of my old ideas, shriveled up in my brain, no longer allow such new ideas to make strong impressions. I have never been able to understand very well what was this manifest evidence which serves as a basis for legal despotism, and nothing appeared to me less self-evident than the chapter which treats all these pieces of evidence. This quite resembles the system of the abbé de St-Pierre, who maintained that human reason always proceeded by perfecting itself, given that each century adds its enlightenment to that of the preceding centuries. He did not see that human understanding has always one and the same measure, and a very narrow one; that it loses on one side quite as much as it gains on the other; and that prejudices, always being reborn, take away from us as much acquired enlightenment as cultivated reason can replace. It seems to me that the natural and political laws can never constitute evidence, except by considering them in the abstract. In a particular government, which is composed of so many different elements, this evidence necessarily disappears. For the science of government is only a science of combinations, of applications and exceptions, according to times, places, and circumstances. Never will the public see as evident the relations and the interplay of all that. And for goodness' sake, what will happen, what will become of your sacred rights of property during great dangers, during extraordinary calamities, when your disposable values will no longer suffice, and when the *salus populi suprema lex esto* will be pronounced by the despot?[1]

But let us suppose all this theory of natural laws is always perfectly evident, even in its applications, and of a clarity that is proportional to all eyes. How can philosophers who know the human heart give to this evidence so much authority over men's actions, as if they were unaware that each very rarely conducts himself by his enlightenment, and very frequently by his passions? It is proved that the despot's most genuine interest is to govern legally; that is always recognized. But who conducts himself by his truest interests? Solely the wise man, if he exists. You, therefore, sirs, make of your despots so many wise men. Nearly all men know their true interests, and do not follow them any better for all that. The spendthrift who eats his capital knows perfectly that he is ruining himself and goes along on his way just the same. Of what use is it that reason enlightens us, when passion conducts us?

Video meliora proboque, deteriora sequor.[2]

That is what your despot—ambitious, spendthrift, avaricious, in love, vengeful, jealous, feeble—will do. For that is what they all do, and what we all do. Sirs, permit me to tell you: you give too much force to your calculations, and not enough to the inclinations of the human heart, and to the play of passions. Your system is very good for the people of utopia. It is worth nothing for the children of Adam.

This, according to my old ideas, is the great problem of politics, which I compare to the squaring of the circle in geometry, and to that

---

1. *Salus populi suprema lex esto*: "Public safety is the supreme law." This is one of Cicero's maxims in *De legibus*. A version of this phrase is used as an epigraph by Locke in *The Second Treatise of Government*.

2. "I see the good, I love it, and I do evil." Ovid, *Metamorphoses* 7.20–21.

of longitudes in astronomy: *Find a form of government which puts the law above man.*

If this form can be found, let us seek it and try to establish it. You claim, sirs, to find this dominant law in the distinctness of the other laws. You prove too much: for this distinctness must have been present in all governments, or will never be in any.

If unhappily this form is not to be found, and I confess naively that I do not believe that it can be, my advice is that one must pass to the other extreme and put man all at once as much above the law as he can be, consequently establish arbitrary despotism, and the most arbitrary possible. I would wish that the despot could be God. In a word, I do not see a tolerable mean between the most austere democracy and the most perfect Hobbism, for the conflict between men and the laws, which gives rise in the State to a continuous intestinal war, is the worst of all political conditions.

But the Caligulas, the Neros, the Tiberiuses! . . . My God! . . . I throw myself on the ground and groan for being a man.

I did not understand everything you say about laws in your book, and what the new author says about them in his.[3] I find that he treats the different forms of government a little lightly, and elections above all very lightly. What he said about the vices of elective despotism is very true: its vices are terrible. Those of hereditary despotism, about which he did not speak, are even worse.

Here is a second problem which for a long time has been turning over in my mind:

Find within arbitrary despotism a form of succession which is neither elective nor hereditary, or rather which is both at the same time, and by which we are assured, as much as is possible, to have neither Tiberiuses nor Neros.

If I ever have the misfortune of occupying myself once more with this insane idea, I will reproach you all my life for having taken me out of my tool rack. I hope that will not happen; but sir, whatever happens, do not talk to me anymore about your *legal despotism.* I would not know how to savor it nor even understand it; and I see in this nothing but two contradictory words, which united signify nothing to me.

I know even less about your principle of population. It seems to me inexplicable in itself, contradictory to the facts, and impossible to

---

3. Rousseau is referring to Pierre-Paul Lemercier de La Rivière, whose *Natural and Essential Order of Political Societies* had just been published.

reconcile with the origin of nations. According to you, sir, the multiplying of population should have started only when it had really ceased. According to my old ideas, as soon as there was a penny's worth of what you call wealth, or disposable value, as soon as the first exchange was made, the multiplying of the population had to cease. That is also what happened.

Your economic system is admirable. Nothing is more profound, truer, better discerned, more useful. It is full of great and sublime truths which carry one away. It extends itself to everything; the field is large. But I fear that it will end with countries very different from those toward which you are claiming to go.

I wanted to mark my obedience by showing you that I had at least glanced over you. Now, illustrious friend of men and mine, I prostrate myself at your feet to conjure you to have pity on my condition and my misfortunes, to leave my dying head in peace, no longer to awaken ideas which are nearly extinguished, and which cannot be reborn without sinking me into new chasms of ills. Love me always, but send me no more books; do not require me to read anymore; do not even try to enlighten me if I am led astray: it is no longer time. One does not convert sincerely at my age. I may be mistaken, and you can convince me, but not persuade me. In any event, I never debate. I would rather give in and be quiet. Find it acceptable that I keep this resolution. I embrace you with the most tender friendship and with the most genuine respect.

CHAPTER 158

Claude-Henri Watelet

December 1767–January 1768
Watelet had written to Rousseau to compliment him on the Dictionary of
Music.

You treat me as an author, sir; you compliment me on my book. I have
nothing to say to that; it is the custom. This same custom requires
that in modestly swallowing your incense, I return a great part of it to
you. That, however, I will not do. For while you have very genuine, very
pleasing talents, the qualities I honor in you erase them in my eyes; it is
through them that I am attached to you, it is through them that I have
always sought your goodwill. One has never seen me seek out people
with talents who had only talents, yet I applaud myself for those to
which you assure me I owe your esteem, since they procure me a good of
which I make so much. Mine, such as they are, have however depended
so little upon my will, they have brought me so many ills, they abandoned me so quickly, that I would have liked to hold this friendship for
which you permit me to flatter myself from something which had been
less dire for me, and which I could say was more truly mine.

It will be for your glory, sir, at least so I desire and hope, that I will
have blamed the magical in opera. If I was wrong, as may very well be,
you will have refuted me through fact, and if I am right, success in a bad

genre will make your triumph even more dazzling. You see, sir, based on constant experience of the theater, that it is never the choice of genre, good or bad, which decides the fate of a piece. If yours is interesting despite the machines, it must succeed if it is supported by good music, and you will have had, like Quinault, the merit of a difficulty conquered. If one supposes that it is not, your taste, your pleasant poetry will at least have adorned it with charming details which will make it agreeable, and that is enough to please in French opera. Sir, I swear to you that I cling much more to your success than to my opinion, not only for you, but also for your young musician. For the long voyage that the love of the art has made him undertake and that you have encouraged guarantees for me that his talent is not mediocre. One must, in this genre, as well as in many others, already have much within oneself to feel how much one needs to acquire. Sirs, present your piece soon, and were I to be hanged, I will go see it, if I can.

I beg you, sir, to be willing to share with Mme. Le Comte how much her memory has left an impression on me.

CHAPTER 159

Marquis de Mirabeau

January 13, 1768

To write to you, my illustrious friend, I have let the time pass for silly compliments dictated not by the heart, but by the day and the hour, and which strike in their moment like the spring of a clock. My sentiments for you are too genuine to have need of being told, and you deserve them too much to fail to know them. I pity you from the bottom of my heart for the troubles in which you find yourself. For whatever you may say of it, I see you embarked, if not on literary quarrels, at least on economic and political quarrels, which may perhaps be even worse if it were possible. I am ready to faint at the sole memory of all that. Permit me not to speak of it anymore, not to think of it anymore, except for the tender interest I take in your repose and your glory. I can very well keep my hands high during the battle,[1] but I cannot resolve to look at it.

Let us talk of songs; that will be better all around. Could it be possible that you are thinking in earnest of composing an opera? O, how lovable you would be, and how much more I would like to see you sing at the opera than cry in the wilderness. Not that you are not listened

---

1. Exod. 17:11–13.

to nor read; but you are not followed, nor does anyone want to understand you. By my faith, sir, let us do as the wet nurses do who, when the children are quarrelsome, sing to them and make them dance. Your sole proposition has already put me, me the old babbler, among those children, and little is lacking for my hoary muse to be ready to reawaken upon hearing the accents of yours, or even the sole sign of those accents. I will not say more about it today, for your proposition has all the earmarks of a hollow bait, to see if the old madman would still bite the hook. Now that you almost have the pleasure, tell me promptly what is going on, and I will tell you frankly, I, what I think of it, and what I think I can do. After that, if you are so moved, we can chat about it with my agreeable countrywoman,[2] who will give you very good advice regarding all that. Goodbye, my illustrious friend; I embrace you with respect but with all my heart.

---

2. Mme. de Pailly, Mirabeau's mistress.

CHAPTER 160

François-Henri d'Ivernois

January 29, 1768
Trie

I have, my worthy friend, received your parcel of the 22nd, and it would have equally reached me at the address I gave you if you had not taken the useless precaution of the double envelope, under which it is not even appropriate that the name of your friend appears in any way. It is with the greatest pleasure that I finally had news of you. I was deeply moved, however, that you sent your family to Lausanne; that sufficiently informs me to what extremity your poor city, and so many good people of which it is full, are on the eve of being reduced. As persuaded as I am that nothing here below is worth being bought at the price of human blood, and that there is no more freedom on earth except in the heart of the just man, I nevertheless do feel that it is natural to courageous people who have lived free to prefer an honorable death to the harshest servitude. Even so, even in the clearest case of just defense of yourselves, my certitude that had you for a moment the advantage, your misfortunes would then be only greater and surer, proves to me that, whatever the case may be, acts of violence can never get you out of the critical situation in which you find yourselves except by aggravating your misfortunes. Since then you are lost in any event, supposing that one dares to push the thing to the extreme, you are ready to bury yourselves under the ruins of the fatherland. Do more: dare to live for its glory when it no longer exists. Yes, sirs, in the case I am supposing, there remains one last option to choose, and it is, I dare say, the only one worthy of you: that is, instead of soiling your hands with your compatriots' blood, to abandon to them these walls which ought to have been the refuge of freedom and which will no longer be anything but a den of tyrants. It is for all of you to leave it, all together, in broad daylight, your women and your children in the middle, and since you must wear chains, at least to go wear those of a great prince, and not the unbearable and odious yoke of your equals. Do not imagine that, in such a case, you will remain without refuge: you do not know what esteem and what respect your courage, your moderation, your wisdom have inspired toward you throughout Europe. I do not imagine that any sovereign is to be found in it, I except none, who would not receive with honor, I dare say with respect, this immigrating colony of men too virtuous not to know how to be as loyal subjects as they were zealous citizens. I do understand that in such a case several among you would be ruined, but I think that people who know how to sacrifice their lives to duty would know how to sacrifice their goods to honor and congratulate themselves on this sacrifice and that, after all, this is only a final expedient for preserving one's virtue and innocence when all the rest is lost. With my heart full of this idea, I would not forgive myself for not having dared to communicate it to you. Besides, you are enlightened and wise. I am very sure that you will make the best choice in everything, and I cannot believe that things will be left to proceed to the point when it is good to have foreseen in advance so as to be ready for any event.

If your affairs leave you a few moments to give to other things which are no less than urgent, here is one which is dear to my heart, and regarding which I would like to ask you please to obtain some clarification during one of the trips that I suppose you will make to Lausanne as long as your family is there. You know that in Nyon I have an aunt who brought me up and whom I have always loved tenderly, although once, as you may remember, I sacrificed the pleasure of seeing her to my haste in going to join our friends.[1] She is very old, and nurses a very old husband. I am afraid that she has more trouble than her age brings with it, and I would like to help her pay for a servant to relieve her.

---

1. In August 1764, Rousseau passed through Nyon on his way to Thonon to meet some Genevan representatives and a number of his acquaintances.

Unfortunately, although I have increased neither my manner of living nor my outlays for food, do not have a domestic in my pay, and am lodged and warmed here without charge, my position makes my life here so costly that my pension barely suffices for the inevitable expenses that weigh me down. Please see, dear friend, [if] one hundred French francs could soften the life of my poor old aunt a little, and if you could make her accept them. In that case the first year would run from the beginning of this one, and you could draw [the sum] on me in advance as soon as you would have arranged that little affair. But I conjure you to see that this money is used according to its purpose, and not for the benefit of covetous relatives or neighbors, who often harass old people. Forgive me, dear friend, I am choosing my time very badly; but it may be that there is none to lose.

I will always receive news of you with pleasure, and I presume that it will reach me safely. Yet out of prudence it is advisable that we write to each other only when it will be necessary, so that our correspondence, innocent as it is, does not arouse anyone's attention. When the situation of your voyage to Normandy arises, remember everything I recommended to you regarding the one to England; it is the same situation, and without exception, for greater safety. I embrace you with all my heart. Mlle. Renou is very touched by your memory and salutes you a thousand times.

CHAPTER 161

Étienne-François de Choiseul, duc de Choiseul

March 27, 1768
Trie

My Lord,

You deign to listen to me. Of what a weight do I feel myself relieved! If you had been willing to see me, it seems to me that I would have had no need to say anything to you, and that you would instantly have read into my heart.

A word told me by M. de Luxembourg upon my departure for Switzerland authorizes the detail into which I am going to enter, and which would be superfluous if he had given you my answer. But the best and most lovable of men has not always been the most courageous.

You have been given interpretations of some passages in my writings which are not only so false, but so little natural, that the public has never even suspected them, but also so contrary to my views that the only one of these passages that has been cited to me contains the truest, greatest, dare I say, worthiest eulogy that you will perhaps ever receive, and whose application only too much modesty could have prevented you from perceiving. Monsieur le duc, I have no protestations to make. I will tell you the facts, and you will judge.

All the ministers who preceded you for a long time appeared to me to be greatly below their positions; all the persons, no matter the sex,[1] who have meddled with administration have had, according to me, only small views, half talents, base passions, and avarice rather than ambition. Well, I had for them all a disdain which was perhaps unjust, but which went so far as hatred, and which I have never disguised very much. All my inclinations, on the contrary, were on your behalf from the first moment. I anticipated that you were going to give back to the ministry the brilliance which had been obscured by those people. And when it was rumored that, between you and one of the persons about whom I just spoke, one of the two would displace the other, I made on your behalf wishes which were not always as secret as they should have been. A little after, M. de Luxembourg, by chance, spoke to you about me and, based on the trial I had made in Venice,[2] you offered to employ me. I was all the more appreciative of this offer in that people in positions of power have never spoiled me with their kindness. At about the same time the celebrated family pact was brought to light.[3] What did I not augur of an administration which began in this way! I was then polishing the *Social Contract*, my heart full of you; I brought to bear my judgment and my prognostication with a confidence that time has confirmed, and that the future will not belie.

You whom truth honors, recognize its language. The passage whose explanation I have just given you is the only one in which I wanted to speak of you. If sinister interpretations have been sought for some other, I call upon common sense to refute them, and I am prepared to show everywhere what I wanted to say. Would I have thus stupidly contradicted myself, by making the eulogy and the satire of the same at the same time? Is that then in my character? Have I been seen waxing hot and cold like this from the same mouth? Let one imagine a stranger in my place, in France's bosom, where he likes to be, liking to publish bold but general truths, whose writings have never been sullied either by satire or by any personal and malign application, who never repulsed the envenomed phrases of his adversaries save with decency and dignity, and who always founded his proud security upon principles and irreproachable maxims. Can one ever conceive that such a

---

1. An allusion to Mme. de Pompadour.
2. Rousseau had been secretary to the French ambassador to Venice in 1743–44.
3. A pact between France and Spain, dated August 15, 1761.

man, animated until then by great and noble sentiments, would shift all of a sudden, without object, without motive, to the extremes of the most brutal, the most extravagant ferocity; freely proceed to provoke the indignation of a minister who is the hope of a nation and who has just shown goodwill toward him; and seek so late, in his misfortunes, to take away from himself the esteem and sympathy of the public which, while loving satire, says with reason about punished satirists, "He only got what he deserved"? I know men and their inconsistencies. I know too well that I am not exempt from them. But I resolutely declare that this one is not in nature. Besides, if I had been capable of thinking and writing such follies, would I have abstained from saying them, I who am so confident, so open, so given to showing my thoughts about everything? The earth is covered with my implacable enemies, all of whom were my friends or feigned to be, and this remark adds to the weight of what I will affirm. My Lord, I defy any soul alive to have ever heard me speak of you and of your administration except with the greatest honor. Finally, deign to consider how I came back to this country. To go to London, I crossed France with a passport, which I was told was necessary. Under my own direction, I came back alone to deliver myself entirely to you, to throw myself into your arms, if I dare speak this way, with eagerness, without precaution, without fear, without any other guarantee than your humanity and my innocence, and knowing full well that you would not have been at a loss for pretexts to oppress me if you had wanted to. Although I felt that I had fallen into disfavor with you, I counted on your generosity, and I did well. But this conduct proves the truth of my esteem and what I thought of you at all times. A man who in the depth of his heart would have felt guilty could have found the same safety in the same refuge, but never would he have dared to seek it.

That, Monsieur le duc, is what I had to tell you, and what I would ardently have wished to tell you directly, although I do not at all know how to talk. But my heart would have spoken for me, and you would have heard its language. Without being free of anxiety about the route of my letter, I assuredly do not fear that once it has reached your hands, it could ever ruin me; but a natural inclination made me hope, I admit, that in presenting myself to you, this inclination would not act on me alone. Certain that I had fallen into disfavor with you only through the effect of an error, I always hoped that this error would be destroyed, and that I would finally have some part of your kindness. I count on it now, I have rights to it, I dare say, and I will claim them without blushing.

For of all the graces that you could disperse, I aspire only to that of enjoying under your protection the repose and freedom that I did not deserve to lose, and which I will never abuse.

Please accept, My Lord, I beg you, my sincere and profound respect.

JJRousseau

If you honor me with an answer under the name of Renou, three words suffice—"I believe you"—and I am happy.

CHAPTER 162

Pierre-Alexandre DuPeyrou

November 21, 1768
Bourgoin
Rousseau had been falsely accused of borrowing a small sum from a stranger in a tavern and then refusing to pay it back.

I hope, my dear Host, concerning your last letter, that as I write this one, the dear mama is already walking about her room with the aid of a good support. I bless Heaven for this happy treatment, and I find that she and you also ought to consider yourselves lucky. After such a terrible accident, there is certainly good fortune, especially at her age, in coming out of it like this; and to be truly equitable, in this life one must know how to take account of the good as well as the bad. As for me, one of the scales of the balance remains for me to fill entirely from the other, for I see nothing to put in it.

Thank you for the judicial decision regarding Thévenin. I sent it to M. de Tonnerre, with the express condition (which moreover was not very necessary to stipulate) not to make any use of it which could ruin the wretch. Your supposition, that he was the dupe of another impostor, is absolutely incompatible with his own statements, with that of the tavern keeper Jeannet, and with everything that has happened. But if you absolutely want to stick to it, so be it. You say that my enemies have too much intelligence to choose such an absurd calumny. Take care that in granting them so much intelligence, you do not yet grant them enough. For their object being only to see what my demeanor was vis-à-vis a false witness, clearly the more absurd and ridiculous the accusation was, the more it reached the goal. If this goal had been to persuade the public, you would be right; but it was something else. They knew very well that I would get out of this affair, but they wanted to see how I would get out of it. That is all. They know that Thévenin did not lend me nine francs. No matter. But they know that an impostor can embarrass me; that is something.

Your maxims, my very dear Host, are very stoic and very beautiful, although somewhat exaggerated, as are Seneca's, and as generally are those of all who philosophize tranquilly in their study on the misfortunes from which they are far away, and on the opinions of men who honor them. I have assuredly learned to value the opinion of others only for what it is worth, and I think I know at least as well as you for how many things peace of soul compensates. That it alone takes the place of everything and alone makes the unfortunate happy; that, I admit, I cannot accept, not being able, so long as I am a man, totally to count as nothing the voice of suffering nature and the cry of demeaned innocence. As it is always important for us, however, and especially in adversity, to extend ourselves toward this sublime impassivity which you say you have reached, I will try to benefit from your sayings, and to respond to it as did the Athenian architect to another's harangue: "What he says, I will do."

Certain discoveries, perhaps amplified by my imagination, have thrown me for a few days into a feverish agitation which has done me a great deal of harm and which, as long as it lasted, prevented me from writing to you. All is calm, I am content with myself, and I hope not to cease being so, since nothing more can happen to me from men which I have not learned to expect and for which I did not prepare myself. Good day, my dear Host. I embrace you with all my heart, for my wife and for me. Give me the good news soon that the dear mama is entirely back on her feet. Amen.

Laurent Aymon de Franquières

January 15, 1769
Bourgoin

I feel, sir, the uselessness of the duty that I fulfill in answering your last letter. But well, it is a duty that you impose upon me, and I fulfill it willingly—if badly—given the distractions of my condition.

My design, in telling you here my opinion regarding the principal points of your letter, is to tell it to you simply and without seeking to make you adopt it. That would be against my principles, and even against my taste. For I am just; and as I do not at all like for anyone to seek to subjugate me, I do not seek to subjugate anyone either. I know that common reason is very blinkered, that as soon as one leaves its narrow limits, each has his own which is proper only to him, that opinions propagate themselves through opinions, not through reason, and that whoever yields to another's reasoning—already a very rare thing—yields through prejudice, through authority, through affection, through laziness; rarely, perhaps never, through his own judgment.

You inform me, sir, that the result of your research regarding the author of things is a state of doubt. I cannot judge such a state because it has never been mine. I believed in my childhood through authority, in my youth through sentiment, in my maturity through reason; now

I believe because I have always believed. While my extinguished memory no longer sets me again on the track of my reasonings, while my enfeebled judgment no longer allows me to begin them again, the opinions that followed from them remain in all their force. Without having the will or the courage to put them into deliberation again, I hold to them with confidence and in good conscience, certain of having brought to their discussion, in the vigor of my judgment, all the attention and good faith of which I was able. If I am mistaken, it is not my fault; it is that of nature which did not give my head a greater measure of intelligence and reason. I have no more today; I have much less. Upon what foundation would I begin again to deliberate? The moment is pressing; departure is approaching. I will never have the time or the strength to finish the great work of a recasting. Permit that in any event I take with me the consistency and the firmness of a man, not the discouraging and timid doubts of an old babbler.

From what I can remember of my ancient ideas, from what I perceive of the march of yours, I see that, not having followed the same road in our searches, it is hardly astonishing that we did not arrive at the same conclusion. Balancing the proofs for the existence of God with the difficulties, you have not found either side weighty enough to decide, and you have remained in doubt. I did not proceed that way. I examined all the systems on the formation of the universe that I could have known; I meditated on those that I could imagine; I compared them all as best I could. I decided, not for the one which presented no difficulties, for they all presented some, but for the one which seemed to me to have the fewest. I told myself that these difficulties were in the nature of the thing, that the contemplation of the infinite would always exceed the bounds of my understanding, that, since I must never hope fully to conceive the system of nature, all that I could do was to consider it from the perspectives that I could grasp, and that one must know how to ignore the rest in peace. I admit that in this research I thought like those people about whom you speak, who do not reject a clear and sufficiently proved truth because of the difficulties that accompany it and that one cannot remove. I had then, I admit, such an audacious confidence, or at least such a strong persuasion, that I would have defied all philosophers to propose any other intelligible system about nature to which I would not have opposed stronger, more invincible objections than those they could oppose to mine. And so, I had to resolve to stay without believing anything, as you do, which did not depend on me; or reason badly; or believe as I did.

An idea which came to me 30 years ago has contributed perhaps more than any other to make me unshakable. Let us suppose, I said to myself, the human species having aged until today in the most complete materialism, without any idea of divinity or soul having ever entered the human mind. Let us suppose that philosophical atheism had exhausted all its systems to explain the formation and march of the universe by the sole action of matter and necessary movement—a phrase which, moreover, I have never been able to conceive. In this condition, sir, excuse my frankness, I still supposed what I had always seen and what I felt must be, that instead of resting quietly in their systems as in the bosom of truth, their anxious partisans sought ceaselessly to speak about their doctrine, to clarify it, extend it, explain it, palliate it, correct it, and, like one who feels the house he inhabits trembling under his feet, to prop it up with new arguments. Let us finally terminate these suppositions by that of a Plato, of a Clarke who, standing up suddenly in their midst,[1] would have said to them: My friends, if you had started the analysis of this universe by that of yourselves, you would have found in the nature of your being the key to the constitution of this same universe, which you seek in vain without that. Then, explaining to them the distinction between the two substances, he would have proved to them by the very properties of matter that, whatever Locke may say, the supposition of thinking matter is a genuine absurdity. He would have shown them what is the nature of a truly active and thinking being, and from the establishment of this being that judges, he would finally have ascended to the confused but sure notions of the supreme being. Who can doubt that, struck by the brilliance, the simplicity, the truth, the beauty of this ravishing idea, mortals, blind until then, enlightened by the first rays of the divinity, would have offered to it by acclamation their first homages, and that above all thinkers and philosophers would have blushed to have contemplated for so long the outside of this immense machine without finding, without even suspecting, the key of its constitution and, always crudely blinkered by their senses, without ever knowing how to see anything but matter where everything showed them that another substance gave life to the universe and intelligence to man? It is then, sir, that the fashion would have been this new philosophy, and that the young and the wise would have found themselves in agreement; that a doctrine so beautiful, so

---

1. Samuel Clarke (1675–1729) was the author of *A Demonstration of the Being and Attributes of God: More Particularly in Answer to Mr. Hobbes, Spinoza, and Their Followers.*

sublime, so sweet and so consoling for every just man, would have really encouraged all men toward virtue; and that this beautiful word "humanity," hackneyed now to the point of insipidity, to the point of ridicule, by the least humane people on earth, would have been more deeply imprinted in hearts than in books. A simple transposition of time would then have sufficed to make the philosophical fashion take the entirely opposite course, with this difference that today's, despite its tinsel of words, does not promise us a very estimable generation, or very virtuous philosophers.

You object, sir, that if God had wanted to oblige men to know him, he would have made his existence evident to all eyes. It is up to those who make faith in God a dogma that is necessary for salvation to respond to this objection, and they respond to it with revelation. As for me, who believes in God without believing this faith to be necessary, I do not see why God would have obligated himself to give it to us. I think that everyone will be judged not according to what he believed, but according to what he did, and I do not believe at all that a system of doctrines is necessary for works, because conscience takes its place.

I certainly believe, it is true, that one must be in good faith in one's belief, and not make it into a system that favors our passions. As we are not wholly intelligence, we could not know how to philosophize with such disinterest that our will does not influence our opinions a little: one can often judge a man's secret inclinations by his purely speculative sentiments. And that being established, I think that it might well be that he who did not want to believe would be punished for not having believed.

Yet I believe that God has sufficiently revealed himself to men both by his works and in our hearts, and if there are some who do not know him, that is according to me because they do not want to know him, or because they do not need him.

In the latter case is savage man without culture,[2] who has not yet made any use of his reason, who, governed only by his appetites, does not need any other guide, and who, following only nature's instinct, works through movements that are always right. This man does not know God, but he does not offend him. In the former case, on the contrary, is the philosopher who, by dint of wanting to exalt his intelligence, to refine, to subtilize what has been thought until him, finally shakes all

---

2. *Sauvage,* translated here as "savage," means wild, unsociable, or undomesticated. It has no necessary implication of savagery.

the axioms of simple and primitive reason, and by dint of always wanting to know more and better than others, succeeds in knowing nothing at all. The man who is both reasonable and modest, whose understanding, exercised but limited, feels its limitations and closes itself up within them, finds within these limits the notion of his soul and that of the author of his being, without being able to go beyond this to make these notions clear and to contemplate either one as closely as if he were himself a pure mind. Then, seized with respect, he stops, and does not touch the veil, content to know that the immense being is underneath. That is the point to which philosophy is useful for practice. The rest is nothing more than idle speculation, for which man was not made, from which the moderate reasoner abstains, and into which the vulgar man does not enter. This man, who is neither a brute nor a prodigy, is man properly speaking, the mean between the two extremes, and constitutes 19/20ths of humankind. It is for this numerous class to sing the psalm *Cæli enarrant*,[3] and it is this one which in effect sings it. All the peoples of the earth know and adore God, and although each clothes him in its fashion, under all this diverse clothing one always nevertheless finds God. The small number of elite which has higher pretensions to doctrine, and whose genius does not limit itself to common sense, wants a more transcendent one. That is not what I blame it for. But that it starts from this point to put itself in place of humankind and to say that God has hidden himself from men because the smaller number no longer sees him, in that I find it to be wrong. It can happen, I agree, that the torrent of fashion and the play of intrigue extend the philosophical sect and persuade the multitude for a moment that it does not believe in God. But this passing fashion cannot last, and however one goes about it, there will always in the end have to be a God for man. Finally, were the divinity, by forcing the nature of things, to become more evident to us, I do not doubt that in the new College one would for the same reason increase in subtility to deny it. In the end, reason takes the direction that the heart gives it; and when one wants to think differently from the people in everything, one gets there sooner or later.

All of this, sir, does not appear very philosophical to you. Nor does it to me but, always in good faith with myself, I feel joining itself to my reasonings, although they are simple, the weight of inner assent. You want us to mistrust it. I could not think as you do on this point, and

---

3. *Cæli enarrant gloriam dei*: "The heavens declare the glory of God."

on the contrary, I find in this internal judgment a natural safeguard against the sophisms of my reason. I even fear that on this occasion you are confusing the secret inclinations of our hearts which lead us astray, with the more secret, even more internal dictamen, which cries out and murmurs against these interested decisions, and brings us back despite ourselves onto the road to the truth. This inner sentiment is that of nature itself. It is a call from nature against reason's sophisms, and what proves this is that it never speaks more loudly than when our will yields with the greatest indulgence to the judgments that it persists in rejecting. Far from believing that he who judges according to it is subject to being mistaken, I believe that it does not deceive us, and that it is the light of our feeble understanding, when we want to go further than we can conceive.

And after all, how often does philosophy itself, with all its pride, have recourse to this internal judgment which it affects to despise. Was it not it alone which made Diogenes walk, as his sole answer, before Zeno who denied motion? Was it not by it that the whole of philosophical antiquity responded to the Pyrrhonians? Let us not go so far away: while the whole of modern philosophy rejects minds, suddenly bishop Berkeley arises, and maintains that there is no body. How has one managed to respond to this terrifying logician? Remove the inner sentiment, and I defy all the modern philosophers together to prove to Berkeley that there are bodies. Good young man, who seem to me so well-born: in good faith I conjure you; and permit me to cite here an author who will not be suspect for you, that of the *Philosophical Thoughts*.[4] Let a man come tell you that, casting by chance a multitude of printer's characters, he saw the *Aeneid* all arranged result from this throw.[5] Admit that, instead of going to verify this miracle, you will answer him coldly: sir, that is not impossible, but you are lying. By virtue of what, I ask you, will you answer him in this way?

Eh, who does not know that, without the internal sentiment, there would soon remain no trace of truth on earth, that we would all successively be the plaything of the most monstrous opinions in measure as those who maintained them would have more genius, skill, and wit and that, finally, reduced to blushing for our reason itself, we would soon not know what to believe or what to think.

---

4. Diderot.

5. Diderot refers to Voltaire's *Henriade*, rather than to the *Aeneid*.

But the objections . . . doubtless there are insoluble ones for us, and many, I know. But once more, give me a system in which there are none, or tell me how I ought to make up my mind. Even further, according to the nature of my system, so long as my direct proofs are well established, the difficulties ought not to stop me, given the impossibility for me, mixed being as I am, to reason precisely regarding pure minds and sufficiently to observe their nature. But you materialists who speak to me about a unique, tangible substance subject by nature to the inspection of the senses, you are obligated not only to tell me nothing but what is clear and well-proven, but to resolve all my difficulties in a manner that is fully satisfactory, because you and I possess all the instruments necessary for this solution. And, for example, when you make thought arise from combinations of matter, you must show me these combinations and their result in a perceptible manner, according to the sole laws of physics and mechanics, since you admit no others. You, Epicurean, you compose the soul from subtle atoms. But what are you calling "subtle," I ask you? You know that we do not at all know any absolute dimensions, and that nothing is small or large except relatively to the eye which looks at it. As a supposition, I take an adequate microscope and I look at one of your atoms. I see a big boulder of hooked rock. From the dance and hooking together of such boulders, I wait to see thought result. You, modernist,[6] you show me an organic molecule. I take my microscope, and I see a dragon as big as half my room. I wait to see such dragons mold and wind themselves around one another until I see result from the whole a being which is not only organized but intelligent; that is, a being that is not an aggregate and which is rigorously one, etc. You inform me, sir, that the world fortuitously arranged itself like the Roman Republic. For the parity to be precise, the Roman Republic would have had to be composed not of men, but of pieces of wood. Show me clearly and perceptibly the purely material generation of the first intelligent being, and I ask you for nothing more.

But if everything is the work of an intelligent, powerful, benevolent being, whence the evil on earth? I admit to you that this oh-so-terrible difficulty has never struck me much, whether because I have not conceived it well, or because in fact it does not have all the solidity that it seems to have. Our philosophers have revolted against metaphysical entities, and I know of no one who makes as many. What do they

---

6. Rousseau's is the first noted use of this term in French.

understand by "evil"? What is "evil" in itself? Where is the "evil" relative to nature and to its author? The universe subsists, order reigns in it and preserves itself. Everything in it perishes successively, because such is the law of material and moved beings; but everything in it is renewed and nothing degenerates in it, for such is its author's order, and this order does not belie itself. I see no evil in all that. But when I suffer, is that not an evil? When I die, is that not an evil? Gently: I am subject to death because I received life. There was for me only one means of not dying at all; that was never to be born. Life is a positive good, but finite, whose limit is called death. The limit of what is positive is not negative, it is zero. Death is terrible to us, and we call this terror an evil. Pain is also an evil for he who suffers it, I agree. But pain and pleasure were the only means to attach a sensitive and perishable being to its own preservation, and these means are managed with a goodness worthy of the supreme Being. As I write this, I have just again experienced how much the sudden cessation of an acute pain is a vivid and delicious pleasure. Will one dare say to me that the cessation of the most vivid pleasure is an acute pain? The sweet enjoyment of life is permanent; to taste it, it suffices not to suffer. Pain is only a warning, importunate but necessary, that this good which is so dear to us is in peril. When I looked closely at all this, I found, I proved perhaps, that the sentiment of death and that of pain are almost null according to the order of nature. It is men who have sharpened it. Without their insane refinements, without their barbarous institutions, physical ills would not strike us, would hardly affect us, and we would not feel death.

But moral evil! Another work of man, in which God has no other part than to have made him free and, in that, like him. Will one then have to rail at God for men's crimes and for the ills these bring upon them? Will one then, upon seeing a battlefield, have to reproach him for having created so many broken legs and arms?

Why, you will say, have made man free, since he was going to abuse his freedom? Ah! M. de Franquières, if ever there existed a mortal who did not abuse it, this mortal alone honors humanity more that all the villains who cover the earth degrade it. My God! Give me virtues, and place me one day beside the Fénélons, the Catos, the Socrateses. What will the rest of the human species matter to me? I will not blush at having been a man.

I told you, sir, that it is a question here of my sentiment, not of my proofs, and you see this all too well. I remember once having met along my way this question of the origin of evil and of having touched upon it; but you have not read these tiresome repetitions, and I have forgotten them. We both did very well. All I know is that the facility I found in resolving it came from the opinion that I have always had of the eternal coexistence of two principles: one active, that is God; the other passive, that is matter, which the active being combines and modifies with full power, but yet without having created it or being able to annihilate it. This opinion got me jeered at by the philosophers to whom I told it: they decided that it was absurd and contradictory. That may be, but it did not seem to me to be such, and I found in it the advantage of explaining without difficulty, and clearly as I wanted, so many questions in which they get themselves tangled; among others the one you proposed to me here as insoluble.

Moreover, I dare to believe that my sentiment, hardly decisive regarding any other matter, must be a little regarding this one, and when you will know my destiny better, perhaps one day you will say as you think of me: Who else has the right to increase the measure he has found to the ills that man suffers here below?

You attribute to the difficulty of this same question, of which fanaticism and superstition have taken advantage, the ills that religions have caused on this earth. That may be, and I even admit to you that all formulas in matters of faith seem to me so many chains of iniquity, falseness, hypocrisy, and tyranny. But let us never be unjust, and to aggravate evil, let us not take away the good. To tear all belief in God out of the hearts of men is to destroy all virtue in them. That is my opinion, sir. Perhaps it is false; but so long as it is mine, I will not be so cowardly as to hide it from you.

To do good is the sweetest occupation of a well-born man: his probity, his benefaction, are not the work of his principles, but that of his good natural disposition. He yields to his inclinations while practicing justice, as the bad man yields to his while practicing iniquity. To satisfy the taste which carries us to do good is goodness, but not virtue.

This word virtue means "strength." There is no virtue without combat; there is none without victory. Virtue does not only consist in being just, but in being so by triumphing over one's passions, by reigning over one's own heart. Titus, making the Roman people happy, pouring out everywhere mercies and benefits, could not lose a single day and not be virtuous; he certainly was in sending back Berenice.[7] Brutus making his

---

7. Titus Caesar Vespasianus (39–81 CE) lived openly for a time with his lover, Berenice (28–?), a queen of the Herodian dynasty, but then sent her away.

children die could only be just. But Brutus was a tender father; to do his duty he tore at his entrails, and Brutus was virtuous.

You see here in advance the question brought back to its point. This divine simulacrum about which you speak offers itself to me through an image which is not ignoble, and I believe I feel, with the impression this image makes on my heart, the heat which it can produce. But in the end, this simulacrum is again nothing but one of those metaphysical entities that you do not want men to make into gods for themselves. It is a pure object of contemplation. To what point do you extend the effect of this sublime contemplation? If you want only to draw from it a new encouragement to do good, I agree with you; but that is not what is at issue. Let us suppose your decent heart prey to the most terrible passions, from which you are not protected since, in the end, you are a man. Will this image, which in calm times paints itself so ravishingly there, lose none of its charms and not become tarnished at all amid the waves? Let us set aside the discouraging and terrible supposition of the perils which can tempt virtue when it despairs. Let us only suppose that a too sensitive heart burns with an involuntary love for the daughter or wife of his friend, and that he is master of enjoying her between heaven, which sees nothing of this, and himself, who does not want to say anything about it to anyone; that her charming figure, adorned by all the attractions of beauty and voluptuousness, attracts him. In the moment when his inebriated senses are ready to yield to their delights, will this abstract image of virtue come to dispute his heart with this real object which strikes him? Will it appear to him most beautiful at that moment? Will it tear him from the arms of her whom he loves to yield himself to the fruitless contemplation of a phantom that he knows to be without reality? Will he end like Joseph, and will he leave his coat?[8] No sir, he will shut his eyes and succumb. The believer, you will say, will succumb in the same way. Yes, the weak man; he, for example, who writes to you. But give them both the same degree of strength and see the difference in the fulcrum.

The means, sir, of resisting violent temptations when one can yield to them without fear by saying to oneself: what is the point of resisting? To be virtuous, the philosopher needs to be so in men's eyes; but under God's eyes, the just person is very strong. He counts this life, its goods and ills, and all of its vainglory, as so little! He perceives so much

---

8. Joseph fled his master Potiphar's wife, leaving his coat behind, when she tried to seduce him. Gen. 39:12–20.

beyond it! Invincible force of virtue, no one knows you except the one who feels all his being and who knows that it is not in men's power to dispose of it. Do you sometimes read Plato's *Republic*? See in the second dialogue with what energy Socrates's friend,[9] whose name I have forgotten, paints the just man overwhelmed with the affronts of fortune and men's injustice, defamed, persecuted, tormented, prey to the opprobrium of crime and deserving all the prizes for virtue, already seeing death approach, and sure that the hatred of the bad will not spare his memory when they will no longer be able to do anything to his person. What a discouraging picture, if anything could discourage virtue. Socrates himself, frightened, cries out and believes he must invoke the Gods before answering; but without the hope of another life, he would have answered badly for this one. Yet should everything end for us with death, which cannot be if God is just, and consequently if he exists, the sole idea of this existence would still be for man an encouragement to virtue and a consolation in his miseries, which he lacks who, believing himself alone in this universe, feels at the bottom of his heart no confidant for his thoughts. It is always a sweetness in adversity to have a witness that one did not deserve it. It is a pride truly worthy of virtue to be able to say to God: You who read in my heart, you see that I make use, as a strong soul and as a just man, of the freedom that you gave me. The real believer, who everywhere feels himself to be under the eternal eye, likes to honor himself before heaven for having fulfilled his duties on earth.

You see that I did not dispute with you about this simulacrum which you presented to me as the sole object of the wise man's virtues. But my dear sir, return now to yourself, and see how this object cannot be allied—is incompatible—with your principles. How do you not feel that this same law of necessity which, according to you, alone regulates the march of the world and all events, also regulates all men's actions, all the thoughts in their heads, all the sentiments in their hearts; that nothing is free, that everything is forced, necessary, inevitable, that all the movements of men dictated by blind matter, depend on his will only because his will itself depends on necessity; that there are consequently neither virtues, nor vices, nor merit, nor demerit, nor morality in human actions, and that the words "decent man" and "villain" must be for you completely empty of meaning? They are not, however; I am

---

9. Glaucon.

quite sure. Despite your arguments, your decent heart protests against your sad philosophy. The sentiment of freedom, the charm of virtue, make themselves felt in you despite yourself, and that is how from every side the strong and salutary voice of the inner sentiment recalls to the bosom of truth and virtue every man whose badly conducted reason leads astray. Bless, sir, this holy and beneficent voice which brings you back to man's duties, that the philosophy in fashion would end by making you forget. Abandon yourself to your arguments only when you feel them to be in accord with the dictamen of your conscience, and every time that you will feel a contradiction between them, be sure that it is they who deceive you.

Although I do not want to quibble with you, nor follow your two letters blow by blow, I can nevertheless not deny myself a word on the parallel between the wise Hebrew and the wise Greek. As an admirer of both, I can hardly be suspected of prejudices in speaking about them. I do not believe that is also your case. I am hardly surprised that you give to the [second] all the advantage.[10] You have not become acquainted enough with the other one, and you have not taken enough care to disengage what is truly his from what is foreign to him and disfigures him in your eyes, as in those of many other people who, according to me, have not looked at him more closely than you. Had Jesus been born in Athens, and Socrates in Jerusalem; had Plato and Xenophon written the life of the first, Luke and Matthew that of the other, you would speak very differently. What does him wrong in your mind is precisely what makes the elevation of his soul more astonishing and more admirable, namely his birth in Judea among the vilest people who perhaps existed then; whereas Socrates, born among the most educated and amiable, found all the help he needed to rise easily to the tone he adopted. He arose against the sophists as Jesus did against the priests, with this difference, that Socrates often imitated his antagonists, and that if his beautiful and gentle death had not honored his life, he would have passed for a sophist like them. As for Jesus, the sublime flight of his great soul always elevated him above all mortals, and from the age of twelve until the moment that he perished of the cruelest as well as the most infamous of all deaths, he did not belie himself for a moment. His noble project was to raise his people, to make them again a free people, and worthy of being so; for it was there that one had to begin. The profound study

---

10. Rousseau had written "first," but the letter to which he is responding makes it clear that the reference was given to the second, not the first.

he made of the law of Moses, his efforts to reawaken enthusiasm and love for it in hearts, showed his goal as much as was possible so as not to frighten the Romans. But his vile and cowardly compatriots, instead of listening to him, took to hating him for his genius and his virtue, which reproached them for their unworthiness. Finally, it was only after he saw the impossibility of executing his project that he extended it in his head, and that, not being able to carry out a revolution among his people by himself, he wanted to carry one out in the universe through his disciples. What prevented him from succeeding with his first plan, in addition to the baseness of his people, incapable of all virtue, was the too great gentleness of his own character, a gentleness which pertains more to the angel and to God than man, which never abandoned him for a moment, even on the cross, and which makes one who knows how to read his life as one must through the hodgepodge with which these poor people disfigured it, shed torrents of tears. Happily, they respected and faithfully transcribed his speeches, which they did not understand. Remove a few oriental or badly rendered turns of phrase, one sees not a word that is not worthy of him, and that is where one recognizes the divine man who, from such paltry disciples, nevertheless made, in their crude but proud enthusiasm, eloquent and courageous men.

You object to me that he performed miracles. This objection would be terrible were it accurate. But you know, sir, or at least you may know that, according to me, far from Jesus having performed miracles, he declared very positively that he would not perform any and showed a very great disdain for those who asked for them.

How many things would remain for me to say! But this is an enormous letter. I must end it. This is the last time that I will return to these matters. I wanted to gratify you, sir; I do not repent it. On the contrary, I thank you for making me take up again a thread of ideas which is almost erased, but the remains of which can have their use for me in my condition.

Farewell, sir; remember from time to time a man that you would have loved, I flatter myself, had you known him better, and who occupied his thoughts with you in moments when one hardly thinks of anyone but oneself.

Renou

CHAPTER 164

Paul-Claude Moultou

February 14, 1769
Monquin

I have been turned out, dear Moultou. I have left the marshy air of Bourgoin to come occupy on the height an empty and solitary house that the lady to whom it belongs has been offering me for a while, and where I was received with a hospitality which was noble, but too good to make me forget that I am not at home. Having made this decision, my condition no longer allows me to think of another dwelling; decency itself would not permit me to leave this one so promptly after having consented to have it arranged for me. My situation, necessity, my taste, all lead me to limit my desires and my pains to finishing in this solitude days whose end, thank God and despite anything you could say, I do not believe to be very far off. Burdened by the ills that come from life and men's injustice, I joyfully approach a sojourn in which all of this does not penetrate at all, and meanwhile, if I can, I do not want to occupy myself with anything except coming closer to myself, and tasting here, among the companion of my misfortunes, my heart, and God which sees it, a few hours of sweetness and peace while I wait for the last one. So, my good friend, speak to me of your friendship for me, it will always be dear to me. But no longer speak to me of projects. There is no longer any other for me in this world than that of leaving it with the same innocence with which I lived in it.

I saw, my friend, in a few of your letters, notably in the last one, that the torrent of fashion is overtaking you, and that you are beginning to vacillate in sentiments that I believed to be unshakable in you. Ah! Dear friend, how did you do this? You, in whom I always believed I saw such a healthy heart, such a strong soul, are you then ceasing to be content with yourself, and is the secret witness of your sentiments beginning to become importunate? I know that faith is not indispensable, that sincere incredulity is not a crime, and that one will be judged on what one will have done and not on what one will have believed. But take care, I conjure you, to be fully in good faith with yourself. For not having believed and not having wanted to believe are very different things, and I can conceive how someone who has never believed will never believe, but not how someone who believed can cease to believe. Again, what I ask of you is not so much faith, as good faith. Do you want to reject universal intelligence? Final causes are blindingly obvious. Do you want to stifle the moral instinct? The internal voice rises in your heart, strikes down the petty arguments in fashion, and cries out to you that it is not true that the decent man and the villain, that vice and virtue, are nothing. For you are too good a reasoner not to see in an instant that in rejecting the first cause and forming everything from matter and motion, one takes away all morality from human life. Eh what, my God, the unfortunate just man prey to all the ills of this life, without even excepting opprobrium and dishonor, would have no compensation to expect after it, and would die as an animal after having lived as a God.[1] No, no, Moultou, Jesus whom this age has disavowed because it is unworthy of knowing him, Jesus, who died for having wanted to make an illustrious and virtuous people of his vile compatriots, the sublime Jesus, did not at all die entirely on the cross; and I who am only a puny man full of weaknesses, but who feels in myself a heart which a culpable sentiment has never approached, it is enough that in feeling the dissolution of my body approach, I feel at the same time the certitude of living. The whole of nature is guarantor of this for me. It is not in contradiction with itself; I see in it an admirable physical order, and which never belies itself. The moral order must correspond to it. It was nevertheless turned upside down for me during my life; it will therefore

---

1. This formulation could also mean "in God."

begin upon my death. Forgive me, my friend, I feel that I am being repetitive; but my heart, full for me of hope and confidence, and for you of interest and attachment, could not refuse itself this brief effusion.

[I no] longer think of L.[2] and probably my voyages are over. Even so, I lately received a letter from the patron of the hut,[3] as full of generosities and friendship as any he has ever written to me, which gives his approval for another proposition which had been made to me; but always making projects no longer suits me. I want to enjoy, between nature and myself, the few days that I have left without being led up the garden path anymore, if I can, among men who have treated me so badly and known me even more badly. Although I can no longer bend down to botanize, I cannot renounce plants, and I observe them with more pleasure than ever. I am not at all telling you to send me yours, because I hope that you will bring them. That moment, dear Moultou, will be very sweet for me. Farewell, I embrace you. Share all the sentiments of my heart with your worthy other half, and both receive the respects of mine. She will remain to be pitied. It is certainly despite her, it is certainly despite us, that she and I have not been able to fulfill great duties. But she has fulfilled some very respectable ones. How many things which ought to be known will be buried with me, and how much my cruel enemies will take advantage of the impossibility of speaking in which they have placed me.

You can continue to write me quite simply at "Bourgoin."

P.S. I forgot to tell you about the letter to M. de Mirabeau. I wrote to him out of pure willingness to oblige, for him alone and not at all to be printed, after some strong and frequent urging on his part to read *The Essential Order of Political Societies* which he sent me,[4] and to tell him what I thought of it. I did so with the letter in question, written impetuously, in haste, and confided in the secrecy of friendship. He answered it with another long letter for which he asked, a long time after, with entreaties, permission to print. I could not refuse him my consent for his letter, with which he also had mine printed, without having informed me beforehand in any way. I have not seen this printed version, nor have I even been able to reread my letter, whose draft I have been unable to find and of which I recall nothing, except that I gave him

---

2. Lavagnac.

3. The Dombes, offered to Rousseau by Conti.

4. *L'ordre naturel et essentiel des sociétés politiques* (1767), a major work of the Physiocratic movement, by Lemercier de la Rivière.

my opinion directly, as he had wanted it, but that as for the rest it was very careless and not at all in a condition to see the light of day. That, dear Moultou, is the exact truth. So you see that I am not able to send you this letter, since I do not have it, and since I have not even seen it again. Do not take this as an excuse; and be sure that I will never seek any regarding you.

CHAPTER 165

Laurent Aymon de Franquières

March 25, 1769
This letter accompanied the earlier one to Franquières when Rousseau finally sent it.

Here it is, sir, this miserable drivel for which my humiliated amour-propre has for so long made you wait, for lack of feeling that a much more noble amour-propre ought to have shown me how to overcome that one. What does it matter that my verbiage seems miserable to you, so long as I am content with the sentiment that dictated it to me. As soon as my improved condition restored my strength a little, I made the most of it by rereading it and sending it to you. If you have the courage to go to the end, I ask you please after that to have the goodness to send it back to me, without telling me anything about what you will have thought of it, and which moreover I understand. I salute you, sir, and embrace you with all my heart.

Renou

CHAPTER 166

Louise-Rose de la Chaussade, comtesse de Berthier

January 17, 1770
Monquin

Your letter, madam, would require a long answer, but I fear that the passing turmoil in which I find myself does not permit me to do it as it should be done. It is difficult to accustom myself enough to affronts and imposture, even to the most comical, so as not to feel, each time they are renewed, the turbulence of a proud heart becoming indignant arise before the mocking laugh that ought to be my sole response to all that. I believe, though, that I have gained much; I hope to gain more. I see as fairly near the moment when I will make it an amusement to follow in their subterranean maneuvers these hordes of black moles who tire themselves out throwing dirt on my feet. In the meantime, nature still suffers a little, I admit; but the ill is short lived; soon it will be nothing. I turn to you.

I have always had a somewhat romantic heart, and while writing to you I fear that I have not fully recovered from this inclination. Excuse me then, madam, if a few visions mingle with my ideas; and if a little reason mingles in as well, do not disdain it in whatever form and with whatever retinue it presents itself. Our correspondence has begun in such a way as to make it forever interesting to me: an act of virtue whose cost I know well; a need for nourishment for your soul, which makes me presume vigor for digesting it and the health which is its source. That internal void of which you complain makes itself felt only by hearts made to be filled. Narrow hearts never feel a void, because they are always full of nothing. There are some, on the contrary, whose voracious capacity is so great that the puny beings which surround us cannot fill it. If nature has given you the rare and dire present of a heart too sensitive to the need to be happy, do not seek anything external which could suffice for it: it must nourish itself only from its own substance. Madam, all the happiness that we want to derive from what is foreign to us is a false happiness. People who are not prone to any other do well to be contented by it; but if you are as I suppose, you will never be happy except by yourself; do not expect anything for that but from yourself. This moral sense, which is so rare among men, this exquisite sentiment of the beautiful, the true, the just, which always reflects on us, holds the soul of whoever is endowed with it in a continual rapture which is the most delicious of enjoyments. The harshness of fate, the nastiness of men, unforeseen ills, calamities of all kinds can numb it for a few moments but never extinguish it, and almost smothered under the crushing burden of human miseries, at times a sudden explosion can restore its first brilliance. It is believed that it is not to a woman of your age that one must say such things, and I believe, on the contrary, that it is only at your age that they are useful and that the heart can open to them. Sooner, it would not be able to understand them; later, its habit is already formed; it can no longer appreciate them.

How to go about doing this, you will say to me? What to do to cultivate and develop one's moral sense? That, madam, is where I wanted to arrive. The taste for virtue is not acquired through precepts; it is the effect of a simple and healthy life. One soon succeeds in loving what one does when one does only what is good. But to acquire this habit that one begins to appreciate only after having acquired it, one needs a motive. I offer you one which your condition suggests. Nurse your child. I hear the clamors, the objections. Out loud, the embarrassment, no milk, a husband whom one disturbs . . . under one's breath, a woman who inconveniences herself, the boredom of domestic life, the ignoble cares, abstinence from pleasures . . . Pleasures? I promise you some, and which will truly fill your soul. It is not through heaped-up pleasures that one is happy, but through a permanent state which is not made up of distinct acts. If happiness does not dissolve, so to speak, into our soul, if it only touches it, skims it in a few places, it is only apparent, it is nothing for it. The sweetest habit that can exist is that of domestic life, which keeps us closer to ourselves than any other; nothing identifies itself more strongly, more constantly with us, than our family and our children. The sentiments that we acquire or that we reinforce through these intimate relations are the truest, most durable, most solid which can attach us to perishable beings, because death alone can extinguish them, whereas love and friendship rarely live as long as we do. They are also the purest, since they derive more closely from nature, from order, and, by their force alone, distance us from vice and depraved tastes. No matter how hard I search for where one can find true happiness if there is any on this earth, my reason shows it to me only there . . . Countesses do not ordinarily go there to look for it, I know. They do not make themselves wet nurses and governesses; but they must also know how to do without being happy. They must, substituting their noisy pleasures for genuine happiness, use up their lives in a convict's labor to escape boredom, which suffocates them as soon as they breathe; and those whom nature endowed with this divine moral sense, which charms when one yields to it and which weighs on us when one eludes it, must resolve to feel their heart incessantly groan and sigh while their senses amuse themselves.

But I who speak of family, children . . . madam, pity those whom a fate of iron deprives of such a happiness. Pity them if they are only unhappy; pity them much more if they are culpable. As for me, one will never see me, prevaricator of the truth, in my straying bend my maxims to my conduct. One will never see me falsify the holy laws of nature and of duty so as to extenuate my faults. I would rather expiate than excuse them, and when my reason tells me that I did in my situation what I had to do, I believe it less than I do my heart which complains, and which contradicts it. Condemn me then, madam, but listen to me. You will find a man who is a friend of the truth even onto his faults, and who does not himself fear to recall the memory of them when some good can result from it. Nevertheless, I give thanks to Heaven for having watered only me with the bitterness of my life and for having safeguarded my children from them. I prefer that they live in an obscure condition without knowing me, than to see them in my misfortunes basely fed by the treacherous generosity of my enemies, fervent to teach them to hate and perhaps to betray their father. And I would a hundred times prefer to be this unfortunate father who neglected his duty from weakness and who weeps over his fault, than to be the perfidious friend who betrays his friend's confidence and who, to defame him, divulges the secret which he poured into his bosom.

Young woman, do you want to work to make yourself happy? Begin first by nursing your child. Do not place your daughter in a convent. Rear her yourself. Your husband is young; he has a good natural disposition. That is what we need. You do not tell me how he lives with you. No matter: were he given over to all the tastes of his age and his time, you would tear him from them through yours without telling him anything. Your children will help to restrain him by bonds as strong, and more constant, than those of love. You will pass the simplest life, that is true, but also the sweetest and the happiest of which I have any idea. But once more, if that of a bourgeois household disgusts you and if opinion subjugates you, cure yourself of the thirst for happiness which torments you, for you will never staunch it. Those are my ideas; if they are false or ridiculous, forgive the error for the intention. I am perhaps deceiving myself, but it is sure that I do not want to deceive you. Good day, madam. The interest you take in me touches me, and I swear to you that I return it fully.

All your letters have been opened; the last has been, this one will be, nothing is more certain. I would be willing to tell you why, but my letter would not reach you. Since you are not the one they are after, and it is not your secrets that are being sought in them, I do not think that what you might have to say to me would be exposed to much indiscretion; but still, you should be warned.

CHAPTER 167

Abbé Jean Maydieu

February 9, 1770
Monquin via Bourgoin
The abbé had written Rousseau for advice, but his letter does not survive.

> Poor blind men that we are!
> Heaven! Unmask these impostors,
> And force their barbarous hearts
> To open to the eyes of men.[1]

In truth, sir, your letter is not from a young man who needs advice; it is from a wise man very capable of giving it. I cannot tell you how much your letter struck me. If you really are made of the stuff which it announces, it is to be desired for the good of your pupil that his parents are aware of the worth of the man they have placed near him.

I am, and for so long, so far from the ideas to which you seek to restore me, that they have become entirely foreign to me. Nevertheless, I will, to the degree that it is within my reach, fulfill the duty you impose upon me. I am thoroughly persuaded, however, that you had

---

1. For almost the whole of 1770, Rousseau generally began his letters with this quatrain.

better refer to yourself rather than to me regarding the best way to proceed in the difficult situation in which you find yourself.

As soon as one has gone astray from the straight road of nature, nothing is more difficult than to return to it. Your child has acquired a habit, all the less easy to correct in that everything that surrounds him necessarily must prevent the effect of the pains you take to succeed in doing so. It is ordinarily the first habit contracted by children of quality, and it is the last that one can make them lose, because what is needed for that is the concurrence of reason, which comes to them later than to all other children. Do not be too afraid, therefore, that the effect of your efforts does not respond at first to the warmth of your zeal. You must expect little success until you have the hold which can bring it about, but that is not a reason to slacken off in the meantime. You are in a boat which a very rapid current is dragging backward; it takes a great deal of work not to lose ground.

The way you have taken, and that you fear is not the best, will doubtless not always be so, but it seems to me to be the best in the meantime. There are only three instruments for acting on human souls: reason, sentiment, and necessity. You have uselessly employed the first; it is not likely that the second would have had more effect; the third remains. My advice is that, for a while, you must stick with it, all the more so since the first and most important philosophy for man in every condition and every age is to learn to bend under the hard yoke of necessity, *clavos trabales et cuneos manu gestans ahœna.*[2]

Clearly opinion, that monster which devours humankind, has already stuffed the little fellow's head with its prejudices. He looks upon you as a man he has employed, a kind of domestic servant, made to obey him, to gratify his whims and, in his little judgment, it seems to him extremely strange that it is you who claim to subject him to yours, for that is how he sees everything you prescribe him. All his behavior with you is only a consequence of that maxim, which is not unjust but which he applies badly, that "it is up to him who pays to command." According to that view, what does it matter if he is wrong or right; he is the one who pays.

Try along the way to erase this opinion with more accurate opinions, to correct his errors with more sensible judgments. Try to make him understand that there are more estimable things than birth and riches;

---

2. "Carrying in his rough hand nails and wedges for the beams" (Horace, *Odes*, 1.35.18–19).

and to make him understand this, one must not say it to him, one must make him feel it. Force his vain little soul to respect justice and courage, to get down on its knees before virtue; and for that, do not go looking for books for him; for him, the men in books will never be anything but men from another world. I know of only one model which can be real in his eyes, and that model is you, sir. The post which you hold is in my eyes the noblest and greatest one on earth. May the vile people think what they want of it; as for me, I see you in the place of God: you are making a man. If you see things with the same eye as I do, how this idea must elevate you inside yourself! How it can make you great in effect, and that is what is needed, for if you were so only in appearance, and if you only played at virtue, the little fellow would inevitably see through you and all would be lost. But if this sublime image of the great and beautiful in you strikes him once, if your disinterestedness teaches him that riches cannot do everything, if he sees in you how much greater it is to command oneself than valets, if in a word you force him to respect you, from that instant you will have subjugated him; and I vouch that however much he may pretend, he will no longer find it all the same whether you agree with him or not, especially if, in forcing him to honor you at the bottom of his little heart, you show him at the same time that you set little store on what he thinks himself, and no longer want to tire yourself making him admit his wrongs. It seems to me that with a certain serious and formal way of exerting your authority, you will in the end succeed in asking him coldly in turn: what does it matter if we agree or not? And he will find, he, that it does matter. It will only be necessary not to join harshness to this coolness, which will make you hateful. Without entering into explanations with him, you will be able to say to others in his presence: I would have made it my delight to make his childhood happy, but he did not want it, and I would rather that he be unhappy as a child than despicable as a man. As to punishments, I think as you do, that one must never come to blows except in the sole case that he would have begun to do so himself. His chastisements must never be anything but abstinences, drawn as much as possible from the nature of the offense. I would even want you always to submit to them along with him if that were possible, without affectation, without it seeming that it costs you, and in a way that he can somehow read in your heart, without your telling him, that you feel so fully the privation that you are imposing on him that you are submitting to it yourself without thinking of it. In a word, to succeed, you would need to make yourself almost impassive and feel only through your student or for him. That, I admit, is an enormous task, but I see no other means of success. And this success seems to me to be assured on one side or the other, for even though, with so many cares, you were not to have the good fortune of having made a man, is it nothing to have become one?

All of this presumes that the disdainful haughtiness of the child is only the little vanity of the little grandeur with which his maids will have swelled up his little soul. But it could also happen that it is the effect of the harshness of an indomitable and proud character who does not want to yield except to himself. This hardness, proper only to the natural dispositions which have a lot of substance and which are scarcely found in the country where you live,[3] is probably not that of your student. If, however, it turned out to be so (and that is easy to discern) then you would have to take good care not to follow the method I have just talked about, and to strike hardness with hardness. Woodworkers never make use of iron on iron. This is what one must do with inflexible spirits who always resist force; there is only one hold on them, but an amiable and certain one; that is attachment and goodwill. One must tame them like lions, with caresses. One risks little in spoiling such children. Everything consists in making them love you once; after that you could make them walk on red hot irons.

Excuse, sir, my poor head—which digresses, rambles, and loses itself following the least idea—for all this dotard's drivel. I do not have the courage to reread my letter for fear of being forced to start over. I wanted to show you the genuine desire I would have to gratify you and to applaud your respectable pains. But I am very persuaded that with the talents that you appear to me to have, and the zeal which animates them, you need only yourself to guide as wisely as possible the subject that Providence has placed in your hands. I honor you, sir, and salute you with all my heart.

---

3. Versailles and Paris.

CHAPTER 168

Marie-Jean-Antoine-Nicolas de Caritat, marquis de Condorcet

February 16, 1770
Monquin

> Poor blind men that we are!
> Heaven! Unmask these impostors,
> And force their barbarous hearts
> To open to the eyes of men.

I am deeply touched, sir, by the honor you do me in sending me your essays on analysis.[1] I feel that I am worthy of them because of my sensibility, even though I am hardly so because of my intelligence, which is too limited to put me in a condition to read this work. My enfeebled head would no longer permit me to follow even if I had the necessary knowledge to do that. How I envy you the pleasure of cultivating profound studies which lead to truths that an isolated man can tell his fellows with impunity, without having to be attached to parties and provide himself with supporters! If I were to be reborn, I would try to be your disciple, to be worthy of the honor of being one day your emulator

---

1. *Principes de physique.*

and your friend. But not being able in my ignorance to be anything but your stupid admirer, I thank you at least for the moment of genuine sweetness that your obliging attention casts over my sad existence. I salute you, sir, and honor you with all my heart.

JJRousseau

CHAPTER 169

Abbé Maydieu

March 14, 1770
Monquin
The letter to which this is a reply has not been found.

> Poor blind men that we are!
> Heaven! Unmask these impostors,
> And force their barbarous hearts
> To open to the eyes of men.

I would like, sir, for love of you, that the application which it pleases you to make of your quatrain were natural enough to be believable. But since you prefer to excuse than to accuse yourself of a promptness that I could myself have had in your place, so be it. I will not hold forth on that.

Since the printing of *Emile* I have reread it only once, six years ago, in order to correct a copy, and the continual turmoil in which they love to make me live has so fully overcome my poor head, that I have lost the little memory that was left me, and barely retain a general idea of the content of my writings. Yet I remember very well that there must be in *Emile* a passage related to the one you cite; but I am perfectly sure that it is not the same one, because it presents, thus disfigured, a meaning too different from the one of which I was full in writing it. I may very well not have thought of avoiding in this passage the meaning that could have been given to it if it had been written by Cartouche or by Raffiat,[1] but I could never have expressed myself so incorrectly according to the meaning I gave it myself. You may perhaps be pleased to learn the anecdote which brought me to this idea.

The late king of Prussia, already a great connoisseur of military discipline, passing one of his regiments in review, was so displeased by the maneuver that, instead of imitating the noble use that Louis XIV in anger made of his cane, he forgot himself to the point of striking with his the major who was in command. The outraged officer steps back two paces, lays his hand on one of his pistols, shoots it at the feet of the king's horse, and with the other blows his own brains out. This remarkable action, about which I never think without a surge of admiration, came back to me forcefully while writing *Emile*, and I applied it within myself to the case of an individual who dishonors another, although I modified the act by the difference of the persons [involved]. You feel, sir, that as great and sublime as the battered major is when, ready to take his own life, and as a consequence master of that of the offender and proving it to him, he nevertheless respects it as a virtuous subject, and elevates himself by that very act above his sovereign and dies while sparing him, the same clemency would be foolish vis-à-vis an obscure brute. The major making use of his first shot would have been nothing but a madman; the private individual losing his would only be a fool.

But a virtuous man, a believer, can have scruples about disposing of his own life, without however being able to resolve to survive his honor, the loss of which, even unjustly, carries with it civil hardships a hundred times worse than death. On this matter of honor, the insufficiency of the laws still leaves us in the state of nature; I believe this is proved in my *Letter to d'Alembert on the Theater*. A man's honor can have no real defender or real avenger save himself; far from it being the case here that clemency, which virtue prescribes in every other case, is permitted, it is forbidden, and to leave one's dishonor unpunished is to consent to it. One owes it one's vengeance, one owes it to oneself, one even owes it to society and to the other honorable people who compose it. This is one of the important reasons which make dueling extravagant, less because it exposes the innocent to perishing, than because

---

1. Leader of a band of young thieves.

it exposes him to perishing without vengeance and leaving the guilty triumphant. And you will note that what makes the major's remarkable action truly heroic is less the death he gives himself than the proud and noble revenge which he knows how to take on his king. It is his first pistol shot which gives the second its force; what a subject he takes from him, and with what remorse does he leave him! Again, the case between individuals is completely different. Yet if honor prescribes vengeance, it prescribes a courageous one: he who revenges himself as a coward, instead of erasing his infamy, brings it to its height; but he who revenges himself, and dies, is indeed rehabilitated. If therefore a man disgracefully, unjustly degraded by another, goes to look for him, pistol in hand, in the amphitheater of the Opera, blows his brains out in front of everyone, and then letting himself tranquilly be brought before judges, says to them: "I just committed an act of justice that I owed to myself and which belonged only to me; have me hanged if you dare," it may well be that in effect they will have him hanged because, in the end, whoever causes a death deserves it, and he must even have counted on it. But I answer that he will go to the ordeal with the esteem of every equitable and sensible man, as he would with mine. If this example intimidates the testers of men a little and makes honorable people who do not seek out sword fights walk with their heads a little higher, I say that the death of this courageous man will not be useless to society. The conclusion, as much of this detail as of what I said on this subject in *Emile*, and which I often repeated when this book appeared to those who spoke to me on this point, is that "one does not at all dishonor a man who knows how to die." I will not say here if I am wrong; that could be discussed at leisure in what follows. But wrong or not, whether this doctrine deceives me, you will permit, nevertheless, despite your illustrious pronouncer of oracles, that I do not consider myself to be dishonored.

I come, sir, to the question you propose regarding your pupil. My sentiment is that one must not force a child to eat anything. There are sorts of repugnance which have their cause in the particular constitution of the individual, and those are invincible; the others, which are only whims, are not durable, unless one makes them so by dint of attention to them. There could be some truth in the instance of foresight alleged to you, if (a thing which is almost unheard of) it were a matter of foods of prime necessity, such as bread, milk, and fruits. One would at least have to try to conquer this repugnance without the child perceiving it and without thwarting him, which could, for

example, be done by subjecting him to great hunger, and only finding, as if by chance, the food he finds repugnant. But if this attempt
does not succeed, my advice would not be to persist. If it is a matter of
mixed dishes such as are served at table among the great, the precaution seems at first rather superfluous. For it is not obvious that the little fellow will find himself in the woods or elsewhere reduced to truffle
stews or chocolate profiteroles for all nourishment. But perhaps there
is another object that you are not being told, and which is not without
foundation. Your student is made one day to take his place at the little
suppers of kings and princes. He must like everything they will like; he
must prefer everything they will prefer; he must in everything have the
tastes they will have. It does not belong to a good courtier to have exclu-
sive ones. You must understand from this and many other things that
it is not an Emile that you must rear; so be sure thoroughly to refrain
from being a J. J. For as you see, that does not succeed in bringing happiness in this life.

Ready to leave this abode, I no longer have an address to give you
that is established enough to receive letters; hence you will accept that
our correspondence ends here. Farewell, Monsieur Maydieu.

JJRousseau

CHAPTER 170

Marc-Antoine-Louis Claret de La Tourette

June 2, 1770
Lyon

> Poor blind men that we are!
> Heaven! Unmask these impostors,
> And force their barbarous hearts
> To open to the eyes of men.

I have learned, sir, that the project has been formed of raising a statue to M. de Voltaire,[1] and that all who are known by some printed work are permitted to take part in this enterprise. I have paid dearly enough for the right to be admitted to this honor to dare to claim it, and I beg you to be willing to interpose your good offices so as to have me enrolled among the subscribers. I hope, sir, that the generosity with which you honor me, and the occasion for which I take advantage of it here, will make it easy for you to pardon the liberty I am taking. I salute you, sir, very humbly and with all my heart.

JJRousseau

---

1. The nude statue of Voltaire by Jean-Baptiste Pigalle.

CHAPTER 171

Marc-Antoine-Louis Claret de La Tourette

July 4, 1770
Paris

> Poor blind men that we are!
> Heaven! Unmask these impostors,
> And force their barbarous hearts
> To open to the eyes of men.

I wanted, sir, to give you an account of my voyage when I arrived in Paris, but I needed a few days to organize myself and to get back in touch with my old acquaintances. Fatigued by a voyage of two days, I spent three or four days in Dijon from which, for the same reason, I went to make a similar stay in Auxerre, after having had the pleasure as I was passing through of seeing M. de Buffon, who welcomed me most kindly. In Montbard I also saw M. Daubenton the subdelegate, who after an hour or two of walking together in the garden told me that I already had the first beginnings, and that by continuing to work, I could become something of a botanist. But the next day, having gone to see him before my departure, I roamed with him through his nursery, despite the rain which inconvenienced us greatly, and recognizing almost nothing, I belied so well the good opinion he had had of me the day before that he retracted his praise and said nothing more to me at all. Despite this failure, I did not leave off botanizing a little along my way, finding myself in familiar territory in the country and in the woods. In almost all of Bourgogne I saw the earth covered to the right and left with that same tall yellow gentian that I could not find in Pilat. The fields between Montbard and Chablis are full of *Bulbocastanum*,[1] but its bulb is much more acrid than those in England, and almost inedible; *Oenanthe fistulosa*[2] and pasque flower (*pulsatilla*) are there also in great quantities; but having traversed Fontainebleau forest very much in haste, I saw nothing that was at all remarkable, save *Geranium grandiflorum* that I once found by chance under my feet.[3]

I went yesterday to see M. Daubenton at the king's Garden.[4] While I was walking there, I met M. Richard, gardener at the Trianon, whose acquaintance, as you may well consider, I hastened to make. He promised to show me his garden, which is much more fertile than that of the king in Paris. Hence here I am in both, within reach of acquiring some knowledge of exotic plants, about which, as you may have seen, I am perfectly ignorant. To see Trianon more at my ease, I will choose a time when the Court will not be at Versailles, and I will try to supply myself with double of everything I will be permitted to take, to be able to send you what you might not have. I also saw M. Cochin's garden, which seemed very beautiful to me; but in the absence of the master, I did not dare touch anything.[5] Since my arrival, I am so burdened with visits and dinners, that if this continues it is impossible that I will be able to last and, unfortunately, I lack the strength to protect myself. If, however, I do not very soon adopt another pace, my stomach and my botany are in great peril. All of this is not the way to take up copying music again in a very lucrative fashion, and I am afraid that by dint of dining in town I will end up dying of hunger at home. My distressed soul needed some recreation, I feel it, but I fear that here I am unable to regulate its measure, and I would rather be entirely within myself than entirely outside of myself. I have not found, sir, any society that is more

---

1. An umbellifer with an edible tuber that is commonly called "earth chestnut" or "pig nut."

2. Water dropwort, another umbellifer, with angular stems and small pinkish-white flowers.

3. *Geranium grandiflorum* is a kind of pelargonium, commonly called "geranium."

4. Louis-Jean-Marie Daubenton (1716–1800), who collaborated frequently with Buffon.

5. Claude-Denis Cochin (1698–1786), doyen of Parisian magistrates and a renowned collector of rare plants.

temperate and which suits me more than yours, no welcome more in accord with my heart than the one I received under your auspices from the adorable Mélanie. If it were given me to choose an even and sweet life, I would want every day of mine to pass the morning in work, either on copying or on my herbarium; lunch with you and Mélanie; feed my ear and my heart for one or two hours on the sound of her voice and her harp; then walk tête-à-tête with you for the rest of the day, botanizing and philosophizing according to our whim. Lyon has left me with regrets which will perhaps one day bring me nearer to it. If that happens you will not be forgotten, sir, in my projects; may you take part in their execution. I am vexed that I do not know the address of Monsieur your brother here. If he is still here, I would not have delayed so long in going to see him, giving him my regards, and asking him to be so good as to sometimes give you and [Mme. de Fleurieu] my regards.

If my paper were not ending, if the post were not about to go, I would not myself know how to finish. My chatting is not better organized on paper than it is in conversation. Please bear the one as you have borne the other. *Vale, et me ama.*[6]

JJRousseau

---

6. "Goodbye, and love me."

CHAPTER 172

"Henriette"

October 25, 1770
Paris

The storms which have buffeted me for so many years have erased a multitude of recollections from my memory. I confusedly remember the name Henriette and her letters, but that is not enough for me to want to see her until she has fully explained to me who she is, what she wants from me, why she has remained for so long without giving any sign of life, and why she suddenly takes it into her head to reappear with such urgency.

She must know that dire experiences have taught me to know the people I have to deal with, and the means—so worthy of them—which they use to encircle me.

If Henriette is decent, virtuous, if she loathes trickery and duplicity, if she is worthy of my listening to her, and I take an interest in her, let her give me all the information about herself that my experience and my misfortunes make necessary, and let her then wait until I have acquired at my leisure the information that she ought not to dread.

Its effect, if I am happy with it, will be to return to her of my own accord, and to do with respect to her what she does with respect to me today. She must be sure in such a case that I will not forget her.

I need friends more than she does, but I do not want them to choose me; I want to choose them. If, regardless of this letter, Henriette persists in coming to see me because it suits her, without troubling herself as to whether it also suits me, she is judged, and I will refuse her. She can now decide what suits her.

JJRousseau

CHAPTER 173

Unknown correspondent

November 24, 1770
Paris

> Poor blind men that we are!
> Heaven! Unmask these impostors,
> And force their barbarous hearts
> To open to the eyes of men.

Be satisfied, sir, you and those who direct you. You absolutely had to have a letter from me. You wanted to force me to write, and you have succeeded, for it is well known that when someone tells you that he wants to kill himself, one is obliged in conscience to exhort him not to do so.

I do not know you, sir, and have no desire to know you; but I find you very much to be pitied, and even more so than you think. Nevertheless, in all the detailing of your misfortunes, I do not see on what to ground the terrible resolution that you assure me you have taken. I know indigence and its weight at least as well as you; but never has it alone sufficed to cause a man of good sense to take away his life. For anyway, the worst that can happen is to die of hunger, and one does not gain a good deal by killing oneself to avoid death. There are, however, cases when misery is terrible, unbearable; but there are some in which it is less harsh to suffer it: that is yours. How, sir, at twenty, alone, without family, with health, intellect, arms, and a good friend, do you see no other refuge against misery than the tomb? Surely you have not considered it well.

But opprobrium . . . Death is to be preferred. I agree. But still, one must begin by assuring oneself that the opprobrium is very real. An unjust and harsh man persecutes you; he threatens to take away your freedom. Well, sir, supposing he executes his barbaric threat, will you be dishonored because of it? Do chains dishonor the innocent who bears them? Did Socrates die in ignominy? And where then, sir, is this superb morality that you spread out so pompously in your letters, and how with such sublime maxims does one make oneself opinion's slave like this? That is not all; one would say upon hearing you that you have no other alternative but to die or to live in captivity. But not at all, you have the quite simple expedient of leaving Paris; that is even better than leaving life. The more I reread your letter, the more I find anger and animosity in it. You take pleasure in the image of your blood gushing out on your cruel relative; you kill yourself rather from vengefulness than despair, and you think less of getting yourself out of trouble than of punishing your enemy. When I read the more than severe reprimands which you are pleased to heap on poor Saint-Preux, I cannot help believing that if he were here to answer you, he could with a little more justice in turn make some to you.

I agree nevertheless, sir, that your letter is very well written, and I find you very loquacious for a desperate man. I would like to be able to congratulate you on your good faith as on your eloquence, but the manner in which you narrate our interview does not really permit me to. It is certain that ten years ago I would have thrown myself at your head and would have heatedly taken up your affair; and it is probable that, as in so many similar affairs in which I have had the misfortune to meddle, the impetuosity of my zeal would have ruined me more than it would have served you. The most terrible experiences have made me more reserved. I have learned to welcome new faces only with circumspection, and because of the impossibility of fulfilling all the many duties imposed upon me at the same time, to mingle only with people that I know. Yet I have not refused you the advice you asked me for. I did not approve of the tone of your letter to M. de Moras; I told you what I found to correct in it, and the proof that you understood well what I was telling you is that you responded to it several times. Yet you come and tell me today that the sadness that I showed you did not allow you to understand what I say to you, and you add that after mature deliberation you seemed to perceive that I was blaming you for having abandoned yourself a little too much to your hatred. But really, no very mature deliberation was needed to perceive that, for I had articulated it clearly, and I had assured myself that you understood me very well. You asked me for advice, I did not refuse it. I did more: I offered you, I offer you again in what depends on me, to lighten the harshness of your situation. I do not see, I admit to you, what you can complain about regarding my welcome. If I did not grant you trust, it is because you did not inspire me with any.

You do not want, sir, to tell your benefactor, your consoler, about the state of your soul and of your last resolution, afraid that, wanting to take up your defense, he would compromise himself uselessly with a powerful enemy who would never forgive him for it. You address your-self to me for that, no doubt because of my great credit and the means I have to serve you, and because one more enemy does not seem to you to be a great matter for someone in my situation. I am obliged to you for the preference; I would make use of it if I were sure of being able to serve you. Sure, however, that the interest that I would be seen to take in you would only ruin you, I remain within the limits of what you have asked of me.

With regard to the judgment I would bring to bear on the resolution that you inform me you have taken, when I learn of its execution, it will surely not be to think that "this was the goal, the end, the moral object of life," but on the contrary that "this was the height of confusion, delirium, and furor." If there were some situation in which man had the right to deliver himself from his own life, it would be for ills that are intolerable and without remedy, but not for a harsh but temporary situation, or for ills that a better fortune can end as soon as tomorrow. Misery is a condition that is never without resources, especially at your age. It always leaves a well-founded hope of seeing it end when one works at it with courage and has the means to do so. If you fear that your enemy will execute his threat, and you do not feel in yourself the constancy to bear this misfortune, yield to the storm and leave Paris. Who is stopping you? If you prefer to brave it, you can do so, not with-out danger but without opprobrium. Do you think you are the only one who has powerful enemies, who is in peril in Paris, and yet who lives there tranquilly daring men to do their worst, content to say to himself: I remain within the power of my enemies whose cunning and power I know, but I managed such that they could never harm me justly. Sir, he who speaks to himself in this way can live tranquilly in their midst, and is not tempted to kill himself.

CHAPTER 174

Marie-Jeanne Girardot Thellusson de Vermenoux

April 6, 1771

A violent cold, madam, which leaves me in no fit state to speak without becoming extremely tired, makes me decide to write you my sentiment regarding your child, so as not to leave him any longer in the state of suspension in which I sense that you keep him with difficulty, even though according to me it has no drawback. I will admit to you, to begin with, that the more I think about your luminous exposition, the less I can persuade myself that the inflexibility of character that he is manifesting at such a tender age is the work of nature. This rebelliousness, or if you wish, madam, this firmness, is not as rare as you believe among children reared as he is in opulence, and I know at this very moment in Paris of another very similar example, the similarity of which struck me very much. Whereas, among other children reared with less apparent solicitude and who have thereby been made to feel their importance less, I have never in my life seen such an example. But let us at present leave this observation, which would lead us too far away, and whatever may be the cause of the ill, let us speak about the remedy.

In my view, you find yourself, madam, in a favorable circumstance which you can put to good use. The child is beginning to lose patience at his boarding school; he ardently desires to come back; but his pride, which never permits him to lower himself to entreaties, prevents him from fully manifesting his desire. Follow this indication to acquire over him an ascendancy whose effect in what follows will not be easy for him to elude. If there were not a little cruelty in increasing his alarms, I would want that one begin by frightening him completely and, without anyone telling him precisely whether he will stay or whether he will return, he saw some kind of preparations as if in order to make him leave the paternal house completely, and that one avoided giving him an explanation of these preparations. When you see him at his most anxious, you will then choose your moment to speak to him and do so with such a serious and firm air, that he will be thoroughly persuaded that it is for good.

"My son, it costs me so much to keep you far away from me that if I listened only to my inclination, I would keep you here from this moment. But it is my too great tenderness for you which prevents me from yielding to it. While you were here, I saw with the deepest pain that instead of responding to your mother's attachment and giving back to her in everything the readiness to oblige that she liked to have for you, you only applied yourself to making her endure opposition which, coming from you, tears her apart too much for her to be able to endure it any longer, etc.

"I have therefore resolved to place you far from me to spare myself the affliction of being at every moment the object and the witness of your disobedience. Since you do not want to respond to the tender care that I wanted to take of your education, I prefer that you go become a bad lot far from my sight than to see my dear son fail at every instant in what he owes to his mother. Besides, I do not despair that firm and sensible people, who will not have for you the same fondness as I do, will make a success of taming your rebelliousness through necessary treatments that your mother would never have the courage to make you endure, etc.

"These, my son, are the reasons for the decision I took regarding you, and the only one you allow me to make so as not to deliver you to your defects and make me totally unhappy. I do not leave you in Paris so as not to have to combat ceaselessly, by seeing you too often, the desire to bring you closer to me. But neither will I keep you so far away that, if one is satisfied with you, I cannot have you come here sometimes, etc."

I am much mistaken, madam, if all his haughtiness holds fast against this unexpected blow, whose full effect he will feel, especially given the tender attachment that you know him to have for you, and which in that moment will silence all his other inclinations. He will cry, he will groan, he will emit cries to which you will not be, nor will appear, impervious; but always speaking to him of his departure as a settled thing, you will show him regret that he has let this arrangement come about to the point that it can no longer be revoked. That, according to me, is the path by which you will bring him without trouble to a capitulation which he will accept with transports of joy, all the articles of which you will settle without his balking at any. Even with all this, you will not appear to count very much on the solidity of this treaty. You will receive him in your house rather as a test than as a constant reunion, and his voyage will seem to be deferred rather than broken off, assuring him, however, that if he really keeps his engagements he will make the happiness of your life by dispensing you from distancing him from you.

It seems to me that this is the way to make with him the most solid agreement that is possible with a child, and he will have reasons for keeping this agreement that are so powerful and so much within his reach that, to all appearances, he will become supple and docile for a long time.

That, madam, is what appeared to me to be the best thing to do in the circumstances. There is a continuity of regimen that must be observed which cannot be detailed in a letter, and which can only be determined by examining the subject. Besides, it is not a mother as gentle as you, it is not a mind as clear-sighted as yours that must be guided through all these details. I told you so, madam, and I imbibed it thoroughly during our only conversation: you need no one's advice for the great and respectable task which you have taken on and which you fulfill so well. I nevertheless had to carry out the one your modesty imposed on me. I did it from obedience and from duty, thoroughly persuaded, however, that to know what is best to do, it was enough to observe what you would do.

CHAPTER 175

Carl Linnaeus

September 21, 1771
Paris

Accept with kindness, sir, the homage of a very ignorant, but very zealous disciple of your disciples, who owes in great part to meditation on
your writings the tranquility which he enjoys, in the midst of a persecution all the crueler as it is more hidden and covers with a mask of
benevolence and friendship the most terrible hatred that hell has ever
aroused. Alone with nature and you, I pass delightful hours during my
walks in the countryside, and I derive a more genuine benefit from your
Philosophia botanica than from all the books on morality. I learned with
joy that I am not entirely unknown to you, and that you are even willing
to reserve a few of your productions for me. Be persuaded, sir, that they
will become my cherished reading, and that this pleasure will become
even livelier because I have it from you. I amuse my old childhood by
making a little collection of fruits and grains. If among your treasures
of this kind there were to be found a few scraps with which you wanted
to make a happy man, deign to think of me; I would receive them, sir,
with gratitude, the only return that I can offer, but that the heart from
which it comes does not make unworthy of you. Farewell, sir, continue

to open and to interpret the book of nature for men. As for me, satisfied with deciphering a few words as I follow you on the page of the vegetable kingdom, I read you, I study you, I meditate on you, I honor you, and love you with all my heart.

JJRousseau

CHAPTER 176

Isabelle Guyenet

September 1772

How my heart bleeds for your situation, my dear Isabelle. Despite the consolations that Heaven has arranged for you, I sense all its harshness, I lament it, and this sentiment increases my regret at not being near you. My presence would not cure your ills; it is a misfortune for which perhaps all human wisdom could not find a remedy. But at least we would weep together, and it seems to me that there are no tears which do not become less bitter as they mingle with those of a friend. Alas, why did you not listen to me while it was still time! But a fatal tendency dragged you along. Every other door to happiness, you said to me, was closed to you. What else was left to do than to help you open the only one which could lead you to it. It has not led you to it, nonetheless. Would you have found it by another road? I do not know. There are destinies that a harsh fatality ordains, that neither prudence nor virtue can allow us to avoid, and to which all that remains is to submit, by taking refuge, so to speak, within oneself, by seeking all one's resources in one's innocence and in one's duty. Such is yours, dear Isabelle. The hopes that you could base on your husband's return seem to me, I admit, very uncertain. If he were a vicious man to whose passions one could give a different tendency, the ill would perhaps not be without remedy. But, my dear child, let us admit it; he is a nullity. He has neither vice nor virtue in his soul; he has no kind of resilience; he gives way to every impetus, and the one toward disorder is always ascendant, because the tendency to it is most habitual and the easiest. So his life will pass by in gross debauchery without his liking it, because he lacks the strength to get out of it; and when by long habit of letting himself be carried away, the little activity left him will be destroyed, he will be left to you, not because he will detach himself from the rest of it, but because he will no longer be [attached to] anything.

My dear Isabelle, dare I give you a harsh, but necessary, piece of advice, and the only one that can lighten your pains. Forget your husband, and devote yourself entirely to your children, to your dear children in whom Heaven has placed all the hope of your life and all the compensation for your ills. Give them virtues, talents, well-chosen and directed knowledge. All the misfortune of their father came from the idle, erring, and nonchalant life in which he passed his youth. Draw from this very misfortune the utility of the example for his children. Teach them not only to occupy themselves, but what is still more important, to love occupation, and try by the continual habit of work to make idleness boring for them. This advice in summary form says everything and suffices. Minds like yours are not those that must be made to dwell on details.

I must tell you about an idea which came to me as I was meditating on your situation and on your husband's profound negligence. I do not believe that he is absolutely without entrails, but habit at length stifles nature, and I doubt that he can be powerfully moved that way. There is another sentiment to which I believe he is even more susceptible: that is vanity. Petty vanity is the dominant illness of your country, and I have seen on more than one occasion that your husband was not exempt from this illness. I think that if there is some way to bring him back, it is by uniting these two sentiments against him in all their force. The inconvenience of the attempt that I am imagining is that it can only be carried out when your children are older. In any event, however, better late than never, and this delay can also have its advantages. I would therefore, when his eldest son is ten or eleven, speak to him roughly like this.

"Although I feel with the bitterest suffering the wrong that your behavior does to your children, I am determined never to use the resources that the laws offer unfortunate mothers to shield them and their children from the misery into which they are brought by the disorders of a senseless father. In whatever way you make use of it, you will continue to be the master of the remainder of their fortune and mine. But I do not believe you to be denatured enough to oppose the means that my tenderness wishes to employ to secure them at least from being reduced to dying of hunger or begging for their bread. Permit that, for lack of their patrimony that you have dissipated, I have your two sons learn trades so they can live. It is a duty from which nothing can excuse me, or you either. Besides, good workers do nothing to dishonor their father, whereas beggars or thieves will very much do so. Etc."

I can hardly believe that such a speech would have no effect on him. But to put the thing in its worst light, I do not at all mean that this would be only a comminatory proposition, and I frankly declare to you that were you to place them in apprenticeships even without necessity, as long as it is with decent people where their morals will run no risk, I would look upon this conduct as a very judicious care on your part, without letting myself be hampered by the clamor of a few relatives who are more vain than sensible. Moreover, I could be wrong. That, however, is my sentiment, and whether you adopt it or not, I ask you please at least that it be received by your heart as mine offers it to you.

CHAPTER 177

Philippe-Louis-Maximilien-Ernest-Ghislaine, comte de Sainte-Aldegonde

February 13, 1774
Paris

My poor Monsieur de Sainte-Aldegonde! How you make me groan over human misery! How I pity you, and how I pity even more everything that has the misfortune of belonging to you or approaching you! What a sad and miserable philosophy is the one which, for the sake of the feigned search for I know not what metaphysical truth no less foreign than useless to man, makes you renounce reason, humanity, all your duties and, served by twenty valets, in the bosom of opulence and the comforts of life, makes you for all assistance reproach the indigent for not going to gnaw on the bark of trees. I would have only pity for your confusion if I believed that it came only from your head; but what frightens me is the too well-founded fear that its source lies elsewhere. Nothing is more suited for nourishing this fear and for increasing it than your last letter. Enjoying a large fortune, you have been deceived by a false friend who coveted it, knew your weaknesses, subjugated you through them, and tried to profit from them. That is altogether simple and in the very natural order of things in this life. Yet here is your amour-propre in convulsion, and because you have been duped by a cajoler, you are ready to yield to despair, while your heart, blinded by philosophical pride and deaf to the sweetest sentiments of nature, shuts itself off to the most genuine attachments, which are clothed in a simpler form. You dress your follies in the name of virtue, and to enjoy this virtue within an intimate relationship, trampling underfoot, along with the oaths that bind you, the pleasures and the duties that surround you to make you the happiest of mortals, you go gravely seeking the model of another even more sublime virtue in a theater actress who could not care less about you, who, in order to draw from your fortune, honors you with some part of the fruit she carries, or feigns to carry, and who, in my view, you are nevertheless treating today more harshly than is suitable for a gallant man in the situation in which you have placed yourself with her. In the excess of your pains, you ask me for advice regarding these terrible catastrophes, quaking, what is more, lest you be frustrated of the glory that you find in giving existence to your fellow through this heroine's canal. Finally (and this is what confuses me) a sudden reminiscence makes you end this pathetic letter with a short and cold marginal note on the imminent childbirth of your wife, of this adorable and respectable woman, as full of wisdom, good sense, and gentleness as of charms, without appearing to be aware of the happiness she lavishes upon you, without saying a word about the one your only child will have in having such a worthy mother and in being shaped by her during the first years. I admit, Monsieur de Sainte-Aldegonde, that it was while I was finishing reading this singular letter that I no longer knew what to think of you. Ah! You would arrange your sentences less artfully with a guiding line if the mind which dictates them were better regulated.

You call yourself a fanatic of virtue. As to fanatic, I will grant you that. The idea of virtue that you have, however, must indeed be a very singular one for you to have gone looking for it among actresses, and in the way you went about it.

There you are, Monsieur de Sainte-Aldegonde; I would not know how to continue this letter, which is already too long, without getting angry, and I would not be crazy enough to try to reason with you. But let us conclude something. You ask me for advice. Here is the advice I have to give you, and for which you now have the most pressing need. I exhort and conjure you to consent, from this moment on, to be the happiest of husbands and fathers, since that depends on you alone; to mistrust the aberrations of your head; entirely to leave to your excellent companion the governance of your child during its first years, without involving yourself in contradicting in any way nature's wish, which makes the mother alone necessary to the child until the age when it is appropriate for the father to get involved. If you undertake this commitment, and if you remain faithful to it, I will not refuse to confer with you on the means to give it the best education possible afterward, and I am disposed to take an interest in it with all my heart. But if, without listening to either nature or reason, you persist in wanting to follow this extravagant experiment which it is said you are planning, and to make a beast of your child, his tender mother will die of pain, the child will finish by being locked up, the father will give decent people the horrors and, as for me, it would be in vain that he would persist in writing to me; I am determined no longer to answer him and never to receive him again. Farewell, Monsieur de Sainte-Aldegonde, that is my advice and my resolution. My wife thanks you for the honor of your remembrance, and we both salute you very humbly.

JJRousseau

Fatigue and repugnance at writing a letter prevents me from rewriting this one. In asking you to please pass over this liberty, I do not imagine that its scribbling will be what you will excuse with the greatest difficulty. As there is a risk that it will be opened, I am not joining to it the letters you sent me. I will give them to be sent back to you to the same person who brought them, and I put this one in the post only because it is pressing.

CHAPTER 178

Christoph Willibald Glück

April 17, 1774
Monsieur le Chevalier,

I am going home, delighted by the rehearsal of your opera *Iphigenia*.[1]

You have carried out what I thought was impossible until today.[2] Please accept my sincere congratulations and my very devoted salutations.

JJRousseau

---

1. *Iphigenia in Tauris* (1774). Rousseau wrote a detailed letter to Burney on Glück's *Alceste* (CW 7:486–505).

2. The impossible task to which Rousseau refers is writing good music to French lyrics.

CHAPTER 179

Élizabeth-Jeanne-Pierrette de Corancez

January 9, 1778
Paris

I read, madam, in the number 5 of the pages that you had the kindness to send me, that one of the Gentlemen among your correspondents, who calls himself "The Gardener of Auteuil," had reared swallows. I would very much like to know how he went about it, and how the swallows that he reared acted in his home during the winter. After infinite pains, I had succeeded in Monquin in getting some to nest in my room. I even often had the pleasure of seeing them, with the windows closed, remain tranquil enough to chirp, play, and frolic together at their ease, while waiting for me to want to open the windows for them, very sure that this would happen soon.[1] Indeed, I even got up to do that every day before four. But it never entered my mind, I admit, to try to rear any of their offspring, persuaded as I was that this was not only useless, but

---

1. Rousseau's note: "The swallow is naturally familiar and confiding, but that is a foolishness for which it is too well punished not to be corrected of it. With patience one even accustoms it to live in closed apartments, as long as it does not perceive the intention of holding it captive there, but as soon as one abuses this confidence, which one never fails to do, it loses it forever. From that moment it no longer eats, it struggles ceaselessly, and it finishes by killing itself."

impossible. I am delighted to learn that it is not and, as for me, I would be very obliged to the "gardener of Auteuil" if he would be willing to communicate his secret to the public.

Please accept, madam, I beg you, my thanks and my respect.

JJRousseau

Jean-Louis Bravard Deyssac, or des Bravards d'Eyssat, comte Duprat

February 3, 1778
Paris

You reignite, sir, the stub of a wick that is almost extinguished; but there is no more oil in the lamp and the least breath of wind can extinguish it without return. As much as I can still desire something in this world, I desire to go finish my days in the pleasant refuge that you are kindly willing to prepare for me. All my heart's wishes are to be there, but the difficulty is that one must transport oneself there. At this moment, I am half-crippled by rheumatism; my wife is in no better condition than I; old, infirm, I feel at every instant discouragement gaining on me; every attention, every effort to make, every fatigue to be sustained frightens my indolence. I would need all the things I need to approach, for I no longer feel enough vigor in myself to go seek them. And it is precisely in this state of annihilation that, deprived of every service and of all assistance in everything that surrounds me, I have nothing more to hope for except from myself. You, Monsieur le comte, the only one who has not abandoned me in my misery, look, I beg you, to what your generosity can do to give me back the activity that I need. You offer me someone you have chosen to watch over my effects and to take pains of which I am incapable. Oh, I accept, and little less is needed to make me strive a little: for if by myself I can gather up two nightcaps and five or six shirts, that will be a lot. There is nothing but my wife and my herbarium in the world which can give me back a bit of activity. If we embark alone under our own guidance, at the first difficulty, at the least obstacle, I will be stopped short and will never arrive. I like to delude myself in my castles in Spain with the idea that you will be here, sir, with M. the commander, that you will deign to needle my laziness a little, that my little arrangements would be done more quickly and better under your eyes; that if you extended your act of mercy to the point of then permitting that we make the journey following one of you, and perhaps both, how then everything would be smoothed over! How well everything would go! But it is a castle in Spain, and of all those that I have built in my life, I have never seen any come to be. May God will that this will not be so for the hope of arriving at yours.

As to the rest, I do not dislike the precautions which seem suitable to you so as to avoid causing too much of a sensation. I do not find going to mass repugnant; on the contrary, whatever religion it may be, I will always believe that I am with my brothers among those who assemble to serve God. But neither is it a duty I wish to impose on myself. Even less to have it believed in the country that I am Catholic. I assuredly very much want not to scandalize men, but I want even more never to deceive them. As to changing my name, after having proudly taken mine again despite everyone so as to come back to Paris, and having used it there for eight years, I can now very well depart from it in order to leave, and I do not refuse to do so; but my experience of the past teaches me that it is a very useless, and even ruinous, precaution, because of the air of mystery which is joined to it and which the people always interpret badly. You will decide about this, since you know the country as you do. On that point, as regarding all the rest, I hand myself over to your prudence and friendship. Please accept, Monsieur le comte, my very humble salutations.

JJRousseau

CHAPTER 181

Comte Duprat

March 15, 1778
Paris

I see, sir, that despite all your generosity, which is dear to me, and of which I would like to take advantage, the only real remedy for my ills which remains within my reach is patience. My wife's condition, worse for some time and which makes mine from day to day more worrisome and sadder, almost takes away the hope of completing, and the courage to attempt, the long voyage that would have to be undertaken to reach the refuge that you have been kindly willing to prepare for us. What is at least already very certain is that it is impossible to make it alone. My wife, cast down by her illness, remembers, what is more, the accommodations into which we have been shoved and the way we have been treated there during our other voyages when, younger and in better health, we had more courage and strength to bear the fatigue and the distress. She would rather die here than expose herself again to all these indignities, and we both believe that the presence of a third party, were it only a servant, would protect us from enough so that we could, armed with gentleness and resignation, bear the rest. This deliberation, sir, about which we have still only had very vague explanations, is the first and the most important, without which all the others are useless.

I know that your generous benevolence will bestow its attentions upon facilitating this transportation for us, but it is also a matter of knowing what it can do to make it practicable for us, and that essentially consists in finding some acquaintance who, having the same voyage to make, would be willing to tolerate us in his following, to procure bearable accommodations for us, and to protect us as much as possible from the obstacles and outrages which, under a false air of attentions and cares, will await us on the way. If this occasion cannot be found, as I have reason to fear, the only option which remains for me is to wait here for your arrival, or that of M. the commander, and to have patience while we wait, as I hope to do until the end unless some unforeseen resource presents itself, on which I would be very wrong to count.

As to the cares here regarding the rags that I may leave, that is a point of too little importance for you to deign to occupy yourself with it thus in advance. We will not lack people eager to receive this little deposit. My silence regarding M. de Neuville seemed to me to be a very clear answer; but you want an express answer; one must obey. With the humor I know myself to have it would, anyway, take him far fewer pains to make me forget his dispositions with regard to me than he took to make them known to me. In the meantime, however, ready to render him with the most genuine zeal all the services which could depend on me, I feel hardly inclined to ask him for some. It seemed, on the basis of your presentation in your preceding letter, that you had someone in mind for this purpose. I can assure you as to this of my entire confidence in whoever would come to me on your behalf.

As to mass and the incognito, you know my principles and sentiments on these points; they will always be the same. Experience has made me learn the uselessness and the inconveniences of those little mysteries which are only a badly played game. You say, sir, that I will not be questioned; it will be known, then, that one must not question me. For, in any event, that is a right that, with little respect for my age, both the little people and the great cavalierly arrogate to themselves. I protest to you that I will make it a great portion of my happiness to please you in everything suitable and reasonable; but on this point I do not want to contract an obligation. Farewell, sir, whatever may be the success of the cares that you deign to take for me, I am touched by them as I should be, and memory of them will never be erased from my heart. My wife shares my gratitude, and we both beg you to accept our humble salutations.

JJRousseau

Correspondents

Alembert, Jean Le Rond d' (1717–83). Mathematician and coeditor (with Diderot) of the *Encyclopédie*.

Alissan de La Tour, Marie-Anne (1730–89). After separating from her husband, she took on the surname Franqueville. In 1761 she began an anonymous correspondence with Rousseau, along with her friend Marie-Madeleine Bernardoni, claiming that she resembled Julie. Their voluminous correspondence continued over the next fifteen years and was published in translation into English in two volumes in 1804. She also wrote pamphlets defending Rousseau during and after his quarrel with Hume.

Audoyer, Antoine (unknown). Stocking manufacturer and teacher who lived in Geneva.

Baldwin, Henry (1734–1813). English publisher who established the *St. James's Chronicle* in 1761. He had published a letter ridiculing Rousseau shortly after Rousseau's arrival in England.

Barillot, Jacques (ca. 1684–1748). Genevan publisher and bookseller. He and his son published the first editions of Montesquieu's *Spirit of the Laws* and of Rousseau's *First Discourse*.

Bernardoni, Marie-Madeleine (unknown). From a noble family, she began an anonymous correspondence with Rousseau, claiming to have a friend (Marie-Anne Alissan de La Tour) who resembled Julie.

Berthier, Louise-Rose de la Chaussade, Comtesse de (ca. 1747–1817). Corresponded with Rousseau when he lived in Monquin in 1769 and met him later in Paris. When her husband was jailed during the Revolution, she appealed for and received his release partially on the grounds of her friendship with Rousseau.

Boissy, Louis de (1694–1758). Dramatist and editor of the gazette and literary magazine *Mercure*, which played a significant role in the "quarrel of the ancients and the moderns."

Bondeli, Julie von (1731–78). Leader of an intellectual circle in Bern, she corresponded with many of the young men who corresponded with and visited Rousseau in his exile from France after 1762. Rousseau admired her critique and defense of *Julie* and said that she combined Voltaire's pen with Leibniz's head.

Borde, Charles (1711–81). A writer whom Rousseau had known in Lyon in the 1730s. He wrote two critiques of the *First Discourse*.

Boufflers, Marie-Charlotte-Hyppolite de Campet de Saujon, Comtesse de (1725–1800). Mistress of the prince de Conti and cousin of the duchesse de Luxembourg. One of the people who urged Rousseau to seek refuge in England under David Hume's auspices. For an account of Rousseau's relations with her, see *Confessions* 10, *CW* 5:434–44.

Buttafoco, Mathieu (1731–1806). Corsican military officer. He corresponded with Rousseau about going to Corsica to assist in drafting a new set of laws after Corsica gained its independence from Genoa.

Carondelet, Alexandre-Louis Benoît, Abbé de (1744–?). From a prominent family. During the Revolution he was a member of the National Assembly.

Choiseul, Étienne-François de Choiseul, Duc de (1719–85). Foreign minister of France. Rousseau praised him in the *Social Contract* but later believed that Choiseul had misunderstood the praise as criticism.

Coindet, François (1734–1809). Genevan who worked in Paris for the bankers Vernet, Thellusson, and Necker. He met Rousseau in Geneva in 1754 and was for a time a regular companion. He helped with arrangements for the engravings for *Julie* and with the distribution of copies of several of Rousseau's works.

Condorcet, Marie-Jean-Antoine-Nicolas de Caritat, Marquis de (1743–94). A prominent mathematician, especially in the history of probability and statistics, enthusiastic exponent of the Enlightenment, and perpetual secretary of the Academy of Sciences. He supported the French Revolution but was ultimately put in prison and died there of unknown causes, perhaps by taking poison.

Conzié, François-Joseph de (1707–89). A cultivated aristocrat and neighbor of Les Charmettes, which was rented by Mme. de Warens. Rousseau discussed music and literature with him and made use of his library.

Corancez, Élizabeth-Jeanne-Pierrette de (née Romilly) (1744?–1814). Daughter of a friend of Rousseau. Her father and husband were editors of the *Journal de Paris*. Her husband, Olivier de Corancez, published anecdotes from his acquaintance with Rousseau in the last twelve years of his life in the *Journal de Paris* and then in a book titled *De J.-J. Rousseau*.

Cordonnier de l'Étang, Antoine (1716–92). French clergyman who shared musical interests with Rousseau.

Cramer, Claire (née Delon) (?–1787). Genevan, married to the publisher Gabriel, who published the complete works of Voltaire and a Genevan edition of the *Encyclopedia*. She was close to Voltaire and acted in many of his plays.

Cramer, Philibert (1727–79). Genevan publisher, brother of Gabriel Cramer.

Créqui, Renée-Caroline de Froullay, Marquise de (1714–1803). Rousseau frequented her salon beginning in 1744. She helped to persuade Rousseau to leave France after the publication of *Emile* in 1762. They corresponded intermittently until 1776.

Davenport, Richard (?–1771). Rented Wootton Hall in Staffordshire to Rousseau during his stay in England. He unsuccessfully attempted to mediate between Rousseau and Hume during their quarrel.

Deleyre, Alexandre (1726–97). A protégé of Montesquieu, he was a contributor to the *Encyclopedia*, secretary to the French ambassador to Vienna, and coeditor of *Histoire générale des voyages*. During the Revolution he was elected to the National Convention and the Committee on Public Instruction.

Deluc, Jacques-François (1698–1780). A watchmaker who was active in Genevan politics. He and Rousseau became close when Rousseau visited Geneva in 1754. He provided information about Geneva when Rousseau was writing the *Letters Written from the Mountain*.

Deschamps, Dom Léger-Marie (1716–74). A Benedictine monk who corresponded with Rousseau about his manuscript *Le vrai système ou le ot de l'énigme métaphysique et morale*.

Diderot, Denis (1713–84). Diderot met Rousseau in 1742. General editor of what became the core manual of the Enlightenment, the *Encyclopedia*, as well as a prolific author in his own right, he recruited Rousseau to contribute articles to the *Encyclopedia* and encouraged him to write the *First Discourse*. Their friendship ended in 1758.

DuPeyrou, Pierre-Alexandre (1729–94). Born in Surinam, he became a wealthy resident of Neuchâtel. He met Rousseau in 1762 and corresponded with him until 1771. He remained a strong supporter of Rousseau and arranged for the publication of his collected writings after his death.

Dupin de Francueil, Suzanne (1718–54). Married to Charles-Louis, with whom Rousseau did research in chemistry in the 1740s. They had a chemistry laboratory at the Chateau of Chenonceau. Charles-Louis was the stepson of the celebrated Mme. Louise-Marie-Madeleine Dupin. Rousseau worked as secretary for both of them from 1743 until the publication of the *First Discourse*.

Duprat, Jean-Louis Bravard Deyssac, or des Bravards d'Eyssat, Comte (1744–94). French military officer and a friend who often visited Rousseau when he was in Paris. He was guillotined during the Revolution.

Égly, Charles-Philippe Monthénault d' (1696–1749). Lawyer, literary man, and director of the *Journal de Verdun*.

Épinay, Louise Florence Pétronille Tardieu d'Esclavelles, Madame d' (1726–83). She had the Hermitage built for Rousseau, and he rented it from 1756 to 1757. She was the mistress of Friedrich Melchior Grimm and previously of Rousseau's employer Dupin de Francueil. Sophie d'Houdetot was her sister-in-law.

Favre, Jacob (1690–1773). First syndic of Geneva, to whom Rousseau wrote to renounce his citizenship.

Foulquier, Jean (?–1790). French Protestant who became a refugee in Switzerland.

Franquières, Laurent Aymon de (1744–90). Son of a prominent family from near Grenoble. In addition to writing two letters to Rousseau, he visited Voltaire.

Frederick II (called the Great), King of Prussia (1712–86). Offered Rousseau refuge in Neuchâtel.

Fréron, Élie-Catherine (1719–76). Important editor and opponent of the Enlightenment.

Glück, Christoph Willibald (1714–87). A composer who became famous in Vienna. He came to Paris in 1773.

Guyenet, Isabelle (née d'Ivernois) (1735–97). A member of the extended Roguin family. She spent much time with Rousseau in Môtiers. He came to refer to her as his daughter.

"Henriette." Pseudonym for one of the more well-known correspondents who wrote to Rousseau to ask for advice. Her identity has never been discovered.

Hess, Caspar (1727–1800). Professor of philosophy at Zurich who visited Rousseau in 1762.

Houdetot, Élisabeth-Sophie-Françoise Lalive de Bellegarde, Comtesse d' (1730–1813). Sister-in-law of Mme. d'Épinay and lover of the marquis de Saint-Lambert. Rousseau fell in love with her in 1757, and the ensuing events led to his rupture with Diderot, Grimm, and Mme. d'Épinay.

Hume, David (1711–76). Scottish philosopher. He invited Rousseau to England. Their subsequent quarrel led to a pamphlet war in which writers from all over Europe chose sides.

Ivernois, François-Henri d' (1722–78). Genevan businessman who was one of Rousseau's strongest supporters.

Keith, George (1686–1778). Exiled Scottish lord who had a long military and diplomatic career. He was governor of Neuchâtel under Frederick the Great. He was considered a dear friend by Rousseau, but he refused to choose sides in the quarrel between Rousseau and Hume.

La Tourette, Marc-Antoine-Louis Claret de (1729–93). Government official in Lyon and significant botanist.

Le Sage, George-Louis I (1676–1759). Huguenot who published scientific and literary works in Geneva.

Lenieps, Toussaint-Pierre (1697–1774). A Genevan banished in 1731 for his participation in critiques of the government. He and Rousseau celebrated the Escalade, a Genevan holiday, in Paris. He provided Rousseau with information about Genevan history and government. He was arrested by the French for his promotion of antigovernment activities in Geneva and spent a year and a half in the Bastille.

Levasseur, Marie-Thérèse (1721–1801). Rousseau's companion from around 1745 until his death in 1778. They were married in a civil ceremony in 1768.

Linnaeus, Carl (1707–78). Swedish botanist and zoologist. He developed the standard taxonomy for plants used by Rousseau.

Luxembourg, Charles-François-Frédéric II de Montmorency-Luxembourg, duc de (1702–64). He became maréchal de France in 1757. He and his wife became close with Rousseau and invited him to stay in a small house near his chateau.

Luxembourg, Madeleine Angélique de Neufville, Duchesse de (1707–87). Wife of the duc de Luxembourg. She took charge of the publication of *Emile*. Rousseau's decision to leave France rather than stand trial for publishing the book was influenced by the fact that she would have been implicated in his offense.

Malesherbes, Chrétien-Guillaume de Lamoignon de (1721–94). Head of the book trade for France during most of Rousseau's career. He corresponded with Rousseau about botany as well as about issues of censorship and was the recipient of some of Rousseau's most celebrated personal letters. The great-grandfather of Alexis de Tocqueville, he was guillotined during the Revolution after having acted (unwillingly) as defense attorney for the king.

Marcet de Mézières, Isaac-Ami (1695–1763). Genevan watchmaker and acquaintance of Rousseau's father.

Martin, Jean-Ami (1736–1807). A Genevan pastor who visited Rousseau in Montmorency in 1759.

Maucourant de Morancourt, André (1694–post-1769). Editor of the *Gazette de Bern*, a journal that was critical of *Emile*.

Maydieu, Jean, Abbé (1742–1800). Jesuit priest who wrote and translated numerous novels and other books.

Meuron, Samuel (1703–77). State counselor at Neuchâtel and staunch defender of Rousseau during his exile.

Mirabeau, Victor de Riqueti, Marquis de (1715–89). Physiocrat economist, known as "the friend of men," from the title of one of his books. He offered Rousseau refuge on one of his estates.

Montmollin, Frédéric-Guillaume de (1709–83). Pastor in Môtiers. Originally he was on very good terms with Rousseau. Under pressure after the publication of the *Letters Written from the Mountain*, however, he became violently opposed to Rousseau and gave sermons referring to him as the Antichrist.

Moultou, Paul-Claude (1731–87). Genevan pastor. Rousseau entrusted various manuscripts to him for publication after his death.

Néaulme, Jean (1697–1780). Publisher in Amsterdam. He was one of the original publishers of *Emile*.

Offreville, Grimprel d' (ca. 1737–?). Member of the Royal Academy of Cherbourg.

Perdriau, Jean (1712–86). Pastor and professor of belles-lettres at the Genevan Academy.

Rey, Marc-Michel (1720–80). Born in Geneva, he became a publisher in Amsterdam. He published several works by Rousseau and gave a pension to Thérèse. Rousseau was the godfather of one of his children.

Ribotte, Jean (1733?–1805). A Protestant merchant in Montauban. He helped to publicize the persecution of Protestants in France.

Roguin, Madeleine-Élizabeth (1727–1806). Married to a nephew of Daniel Roguin (1691–1771). A military officer for the Dutch, and later a banker in Paris, whom Rousseau considered to be his most reliable friend, and part of his circle at Môtiers. Rousseau affectionately referred to the entire extended family as the "Roguinerie."

Rousseau, Isaac (1672–1747). Rousseau's father. Having raised Rousseau until the age of ten, he left Geneva in 1722 after a quarrel, leaving Jean-Jacques in the care of his sister and brother-in-law. He spent several years as a watchmaker in Istanbul.

Roustan, Antoine-Jacques (1734–1808). Genevan pastor. He collaborated with Jacob Vernes on a journal and wrote numerous religious and historical works. Roustan wrote critiques of Rousseau's account of civil religion and of the "Profession of Faith of the Savoyard Vicar." He maintained a friendly correspondence with Rousseau from 1757 to 1767.

Saint-Brisson, Sidoine-Charles-François Séguier, Marquis de (1738–73). After reading *Emile*, he wrote to Rousseau saying that he intended to abandon his military career and become a carpenter and writer. Rousseau wrote a number of letters to persuade him to give up his plans and reconcile with his family.

Saint-Florentin, Louis Phélypeaux, Comte de, Duc de la Vrillière (1705–77). He was a member of the Academy of Sciences when Rousseau presented his system of musical notation there for consideration, and he was subsequently in charge of the French government department that controlled theaters. He later became Duc de la Vrillière.

Sainte-Aldegonde, Philippe-Louis-Maximilien-Ernest-Ghislaine, Comte de (1747–1821). An army colonel who wrote to Rousseau saying that he was going to abandon his fortune. Rousseau attempted to dissuade him.

Scheyb, Franz Christoph (1704–77). Austrian state official.

Thellusson de Vermenoux, Marie-Jeanne Girardot (1736–81). Wife of a wealthy banker. She wrote to Rousseau for advice about bringing up her child.

Tressan, Louis-Élisabeth de La Vergne, Comte de (1705–83). Founder of the Academy of Nancy.

Tronchin, Théodore (1709–81). Celebrated Genevan doctor and member of a leading oligarchic political family. Friendly relations between him and Rousseau from 1755 to 1759 were then broken off. Tronchin had worked to bring Rousseau back to Geneva but ultimately supported burning his works.

Turpin de Crissé, Lancelot, Comte de (1716–95). Soldier and author on military matters.

Usteri, Leonhard (1741–89). Pastor and professor from Zurich who visited Rousseau in Montmorency and Môtiers.

Verdelin, Marie-Madeleine, Marquise de (1728–1810). A neighbor of Rousseau when he lived in Montmorency. She visited him in Môtiers and helped obtain a passport to allow him to pass through France on his way to England with Hume.

Vernes, Jacob (1728–91). Genevan pastor, renowned preacher, and contributor to the *Encyclopedia*. He engaged in friendly correspondence with Rousseau from 1754 to 1762 but then broke with him over the "Profession of Faith" in *Emile*. Rousseau later suspected him of being the anonymous author of the pamphlet *Sentiment des citoyens*, which was actually written by Voltaire.

Vernet, Jacob (1698–1789). Calvinist minister and professor at the Academy of Geneva who had relations with Fontenelle and Montesquieu. He maintained good relations with Rousseau from 1754 until after the publication of *Emile*.

Vieusseux, Jacques (1721–92). One of the leaders of Rousseau's supporters in Geneva.

Voltaire, François-Marie Arouet, called (de) (1694–1778). The young Rousseau was an avid reader of his poetry, plays, and *Lettres anglaises*. Their correspondence began with an exchange over the opera *Les fêtes de Ramirre* in 1745.

Warens, Françoise-Louise de La Tour, Dame de (1699–1762). Rousseau first met her in Annecy after he ran away from Geneva in 1728. After a period in Turin, he returned to live with her in 1729. They lived together (with some short absences by Rousseau) until he left for Paris in late 1741 or early 1742.

Wartensleben, Karoline-Friederike von Salm-Grumbach, Countess of (1733–83). She wrote to Rousseau for his opinion on a young man who sacrificed all of his relationships with friends and family to patriotism.

Watelet, Claude-Henri (1718–86). A wealthy *fermier-général*, he was a respected painter and etcher and an expert on gardens.

Wurtemberg, Louis-Eugène de, Prince (1731–95). He wrote to Rousseau for advice about bringing up his children.

Bibliography

Bernardi, Bruno. "Rousseau Lecteur de ses lecteurs: La controverse de 1758 sur les 'cercles.'" *Annales de la Société Jean-Jacques Rousseau* 47 (2007): 320–50.

Cranston, Maurice. *Jean-Jacques: The Early Life and Work of Jean-Jacques Rousseau, 1712–1754*. Chicago: University of Chicago Press, 1982.

Cranston, Maurice. *The Noble Savage: Jean-Jacques Rousseau, 1754–1762*. Chicago: University of Chicago Press, 1991.

Cranston, Maurice. *The Solitary Self: Jean-Jacques Rousseau in Exile and Adversity*. Chicago: University of Chicago Press, 1997.

Crogiez Labarthe, Michelle. "L'Art poétique de Rousseau dans sa correspondence." *Annales de la Société Jean-Jacques Rousseau* 47 (2007): 429–51.

Damrosch, Leo. *Jean-Jacques Rousseau: Restless Genius*. Boston: Mariner Books, 2007.

Darnton, Robert. "A Police Inspector Sorts His Files: The Anatomy of the Republic of Letters." In *The Great Cat Massacre and Other Episodes in French Cultural History*, 145–90. New York: Basic Books, 1984.

Hendel, Charles W. *Citizen of Geneva: Selections from the Letters of Jean-Jacques Rousseau*. New York: Oxford University Press, 1937.

Malesherbes, Chrétien-Guillaume de Lamoignon de, and Jean-Jacques Rousseau. *Correspondance*. Paris: Flammarion, 1992.

McAlpin, Mary. *Gender, Authenticity, and the Missive Letter in Eighteenth-Century France: Marie-Anne de La Tour, Rousseau's Real-Life Julie*. Lewisburg, PA: Bucknell University Press, 2006.

Pascal, Blaise. *Œuvres complètes*. Edited by Jacques Chevalier. Paris: Gallimard, 1962.

Ray, William. *Story and History: Narrative Authority and Social Identity in the Eighteenth-Century French and English Novel*. Oxford: Blackwell, 1990.

Rousseau, Jean-Jacques. *The Collected Writings of Rousseau*. Edited by Roger D. Masters and Christopher Kelly. 13 vols. Hanover, NH: University Press of New England, 1991–2010.

Rousseau, Jean-Jacques. *Correspondance complète de Jean-Jacques Rousseau: Édition critique*. Edited by R. A. Leigh. 52 vols. Geneva: Institut et Musée Voltaire, 1965–98.

Rousseau, Jean-Jacques. *Lettres*. Edited by Jean-Daniel Candaux, Frédéric S. Eigeldinger, and Raymond Trousson. Geneva: Éditions Slatkine, 2012.

Rousseau, Jean-Jacques. *Lettres philosophiques: Anthologie*. Edited by Jean-François Perrin. Paris: Le Livre de Poche, 2003.

Rousseau, Jean-Jacques, and Marie-Anne Alisson de La Tour. *Jean-Jacques Rousseau/Madame de La Tour: Correspondance*. Edited by Georges May. Arles: Actes Sud, 1998.

Index

www.ingramcontent.com/pod-product-compliance
Lightning Source LLC
Chambersburg PA
CBHW020735020826
48980CB00016B/340